Envisioning God in the Humanities

WESTAR SEMINAR ON GOD AND THE HUMAN FUTURE

The Westar Seminar on God and the Human Future stays true to Westar's dual mission of (1) conducting collaborative, cumulative research in the academic study of religion, and (2) promoting religious literacy in public discourse. The Seminar on God and the Human Future emerges from the academic fields of Philosophy of Religion, Critical Theory, and Radical Theology. The Seminar seeks to reimagine the concept of God and the value of religion in the 21st century. All publications arising from the Seminar that are placed in this series aim to invoke dialogue and participation in the task of addressing critical issues in religion today.

Envisioning God in the Humanities

Essays on Christianity, Judaism, and Ancient
Religion in Honor of Melissa Harl Sellew

EDITED BY
Courtney J. P. Friesen

FOREWORD BY
Calvin J. Roetzel

CASCADE Books • Eugene, Oregon

ENVISIONING GOD IN THE HUMANITIES
Essays on Christianity, Judaism, and Ancient Religion in Honor of Melissa Harl Sellew
Weststar Seminar on God and the Human Future

Copyright © 2018 Courtney J. P. Friesen. All rights reserved. Except for brief quotations in critical publications or reviews, no part of this book may be reproduced in any manner without prior written permission from the publisher. Write: Permissions, Wipf and Stock Publishers, 199 W. 8th Ave., Suite 3, Eugene, OR 97401.

Cascade Books
An Imprint of Wipf and Stock Publishers
199 W. 8th Ave., Suite 3
Eugene, OR 97401

www.wipfandstock.com

PAPERBACK ISBN: 978-1-5326-3716-2
HARDCOVER ISBN: 978-1-5326-3717-9
EBOOK ISBN: 978-1-5326-5613-2

Cataloguing-in-Publication data:

Names: Friesen, Courtney J. P., editor. | Roetzel, Calvin J., foreword.
Title: Envisioning God in the humanities : essays on Christianity, Judaism, and ancient religion in honor of Melissa Harl Sellew / edited by Courtney J. P. Friesen, foreword by Calvin J. Roetzel.
Description: Eugene, OR: Cascade Books, 2018. | Weststar Seminar on God and the Human Future | Includes bibliographical references and index.
Identifiers: ISBN 978-1-5326-3716-2 (paperback). | ISBN 978-1-5326-3717-9 (hardcover). | ISBN 978-1-5326-5613-2 (ebook).
Subjects: LCSH: Sellew, Melissa (Philip) Harl. | Bible. New Testament—Criticism, interpretation, etc. | Gnostic literature—Relation to the New Testament. | Church history—Primitive and early church, ca. 30–600. | Judaism—History—Post-exilic period, 586 B.C.–210 A.D.
Classification: BS2395 E65 2018 (print). | BS2395 (ebook).

Manufactured in the U.S.A.   NOVEMBER 6, 2018

Scripture quotations marked (RSV) are taken from the Revised Standard Version of the Bible, copyright © 1946, 1952, and 1971 National Council of the Churches of Christ in the United States of America. Used by permission. All rights reserved worldwide.

Scripture quotations marked (NRSV) are taken from the New Revised Standard Version Bible, copyright © 1989 National Council of the Churches of Christ in the United States of America. Used by permission. All rights reserved worldwide.

Scripture quotations marked (NASB) are taken from the New American Standard Bible® copyright © 1960, 1962, 1963, 1968, 1971, 1972, 1973, 1975, 1977, 1995 by The Lockman Foundation. Used by permission. www.Lockman.org/.

Scripture quotations marked (ESV) are from the ESV® Bible (The Holy Bible, English Standard Version®), copyright © 2001 by Crossway, a publishing ministry of Good News Publishers. Used by permission. All rights reserved."

Quotations marked (NETS) are taken from *A New English Translation of the Septuagint* © 2007 by the International Organization for Septuagint and Cognate Studies, Inc. Used by permission of Oxford University Press. All rights reserved.

Contents

Foreword / *Calvin J. Roetzel* / ix
Contributors / xiii
Introduction: An Appreciation / *Courtney J. P. Friesen* / xv
Abbreviations / xxiii

PART 1: NEW TESTAMENT GOSPELS AND ACTS: FROM SOURCES AND REDACTION TO NARRATIVE STRATEGIES

1. From Mark to Mark to Mark: Continuity and Discontinuity in the Narrative History of Mark's Gospel / Charles A. Bobertz / 3
2. Figs, Pigs, and Imperial Rome: Jesus and the Barren Fig Tree in Mark 11 / Stephen Potthoff / 16
3. Double Obfuscation of Class Struggle in Luke 13:10–17: Regulation of Labor, Alienation, and Failed Revolutions / Steven J. Friesen / 36
4. "The Thoughts of Many Hearts": Interior Characterization in the Gospel of Luke / Mark Reasoner / 57
5. The Pentecost Narrative of Acts: History, Tradition, and Literature / Glen W. Menzies / 72

PART 2: RECONCEIVING "GNOSTIC" CHRISTIANITY FROM CORINTH TO NAG HAMMADI

6. Contesting the Gift of *Gnosis* in 1 Corinthians / Geoffrey S. Smith / 97

CONTENTS

7. "Why Can't a Woman Be More Like a Man?": Making Mary Male (Thomas 114) in the Gendered World of Antiquity / Stephen J. Patterson / 115
8. The *Gospel of Judas* and the End of Sethian Gnosticism / David Brakke / 133
9. The Persistence of Crafted Memories: The Nag Hammadi Cartonnage, Upper Egyptian Monasticism, and the Literary Sources / James E. Goehring / 153

PART 3: SOUNDINGS FROM JEWISH AND GRECO-ROMAN CULTURE

10. Messianism in Septuagint Amos? / W. Edward Glenny / 175
11. Jewish-Christian Relations in Smyrna: Rhetoric, Reality, and the Limits of Historical Knowledge / Michael W. Holmes / 189
12. Could Luke Read Latin? New Evidence That He Did / Dennis R. MacDonald / 203
13. The House Gathering and the Poor in the Gospel of Mark / Dennis E. Smith / 212
14. Jesus and Sympotic Desire / David H. Sick / 221
15. Gluttony and Drunkenness as Jewish and Christian Virtues: From the Comic Heracles to the Christ of the Gospels / Courtney J. P. Friesen / 243
16. The Drama of Apocalypse: From Tragic Hymns to the Hymns of Revelation / Justin P. Jeffcoat Schedtler / 262
17. Divine Chemistry: Nymphs, Sacrament, and Substance in the Greco-Roman World / Rabun Taylor / 284

Subject Index / 313

Foreword

CALVIN J. ROETZEL

TRACKING ONE'S STUDENTS AND taking pleasure in their development is surely one of the highest joys of teaching. In a sense they become like children. And what pleasure I have taken in following Melissa Sellew's emergence as one of the brightest and most reliable New Testament scholars in this country. While the undergraduate I knew and advised was Philip, the consistent trait spanning all of the years of treasured acquaintance with this person has been her search for and commitment to truth in the inward being. This person is a living incarnation of Polonius' adage in Hamlet: "to thine own self be true, and it must follow, as the night the day, thou canst not then be false to anyone" ["anyone" for any man] (I, iii, 73). My remarks will trace this laudable and consistent trait in this one whom I have the great pleasure of sharing in this effort to honor. My tribute is respectfully offered to Melissa.

Schooled from undergraduate days in the classics, fervently attentive to historical detail, acutely aware of the ferment in first-century religious movements, and willing to make daring but honest judgments about the integrity or lack thereof in New Testament scholarship, Melissa's influence on the scholarly discourse has been more substantial than she, given her characteristic modesty and caution, ever recognized.

One of my greatest teaching pleasures came in the early days of my thirty-five-year tenure at Macalester College when then Philip found his way into the department and into a seminar on Paul's Romans. I was young and green, and my colleague Lloyd Gaston was brilliant and a bit

FOREWORD

crazy, and Philip found his way into the classes of both. I can still clearly remember his presence like it was yesterday in that seminar circle of fifteen. What a gifted and fascinating collection that was. I can still see the faces of the students around the table on the third floor of a crumbling Old Main, can hear some of the remarks, even some of the profanity made in pregnant moments. Out of that group of fifteen, five later earned PhDs in some phase of graduate study, three in New Testament; all secured academic positions across this land, and all have enriched and positively influenced the discipline and the academic world we inhabit. Philip struck me at the time as one of the brightest of the group, and though a bit shy, insecure, and risk averse, he would gently take on more assertive seminar members.

Four members of that onetime seminar collaborated twenty-five years later to edit and present a surprise Festschrift to me at my Macalester retirement. That gesture was surely one of the happiest surprises of my life. I was and still am grateful for their thoughtfulness and intelligence. Trading on my *Letters of Paul: Conversations in Context*, their JSNT Supplement volume was titled *Pauline Conversations in Context*. Edited by four members of the gang of fifteen—Janice Capel Anderson, Philip Sellew, and Claudia Setzer, with a touching testimonial from the pen of the now-late Juanita Garciagodoy—and essays by departmental colleagues Lloyd Gaston (the crazy one) and David Hopper (the solid, esteemed-theologian one). That editorial assembly and presentation left me speechless and still brings tears to my eyes. Those efforts well illustrate generosity as a trait that secures the tie between Philip and Melissa.

Philip's undergraduate honors thesis was spectacular even though it came within a whisker of being late. That scare blossomed on the last night before submissions were due when his dearest friend, college sweetheart, and later lifetime companion, Kathleen, typed all night to rescue him. Even that heroic effort almost fell short. As I recall, in the haste to finish with the help of lots of coffee in the wee hours, an accidental spill tinted some white pages brown. Nevertheless, with and without coffee stain the thesis came in and was brilliant. The sharing of that crisis obviously cemented a partnership that was lifelong, and on the day of graduation with proud parents and relatives in attendance I joined Philip and Kathleen in a union "till death do us part." Not all recommendations are fun to write, but his I did with pleasure and enthusiasm; he was admitted to Harvard, and this young couple left on a life-shaping journey to Harvard where both found fulfilling roles.

FOREWORD

Through my involvement in the Society of Biblical Literature I was able without seeming too intrusive to follow Philip's progress through his degree programs. One conversation deserves recalling. After a meeting at the SBL, Father George MacRae, SJ, Harvard Divinity School faculty member and dean, and president of the SBL and I sat side by side in the bus on our way to the airport. In a casual conversation with Father MacRae, I asked about Philip, and he volunteered a stunning compliment. He said that of all of the preliminary exams he had read at Harvard, Philip's was the best. I was so proud of this stellar, shy student, and I was not surprised.

When Philip was later hired for a temporary teaching position at Harvard, Helmut Koester was in the process of crafting his important *Introduction to the New Testament*. He asked Philip to collaborate on that project, and Philip did so through multiple editions. Any careful reader of that introduction who knows Philip can see his fingerprints throughout the two volumes and can read with appreciation the credit given him in the Preface for his assistance "every step" of the way onto the two volume production. Out of that service ideas came for some of Philip's most seminal works, such as his groundbreaking essay, "*Laodiceans* and the Philippians Fragments Hypothesis," published in the *Harvard Theological Review* (87 [1994] 17–28). There one may see the care, caution, and brilliance bound in a perfect union to produce the totally credible thesis that Paul's Philippians is a composite of several letter fragments later pieced together.

When a position in Classics and New Testament opened at the University of Minnesota, I felt honored to write to then chair, Prof. Tom Kraabel, in support of Philip's candidacy, and another for his later tenure and promotion. Then much later, in one of the highlights of my career, I felt privileged to be offered a position in the Department of Classical and Near Eastern Studies at the same university where I would be a colleague of this onetime amazing student. I could there see up close and personally how effectively he served the department and university, advised students we shared, and taught with skill, passion, and fundamental integrity even as he said goodbye to his beloved companion for life, Kathleen.

Now, this amazing person comes to a new part of the quest for truth in the inward being. The owning of a transgender status, as dramatic, freeing, and difficult as it must have been, elicits nothing but deep admiration and praise for honoring a trait as basic as her life itself and present from the beginning in the breast of this person: "To thine own self be true, and it must follow, as the night the day, thou canst not then be false to anyone."

I am so honored to share in this effort to honor and give thanks for the life, scholarship, teaching, humanity, honesty, and depth of character of Melissa. All who know this great soul are, I trust, enriched, humanized and challenged by their association. Like a doting parent I trust I can be forgiven for saying, "I am so proud."

Contributors

Charles Bobertz, Professor of Theology, Saint John's University

David Brakke, Professor of History and Joe R. Engle Chair in the History of Christianity, The Ohio State University

Courtney J. P. Friesen, Assistant Professor of Religious Studies and Classics, University of Arizona

Steven J. Friesen, Professor, Louise Farmer Boyer Chair in Biblical Studies, University of Texas at Austin

W. Edward Glenny, Professor of New Testament Studies and Greek, University of Northwestern, Saint Paul

James Goehring, Professor of Religion, University of Mary Washington

Michael W. Holmes, University Professor of Biblical Studies and Early Christianity Emeritus, Bethel University

Justin P. Jeffcoat Schedtler, Assistant Professor of Religion, Wartburg College

Dennis R. MacDonald, John Wesley Professor of New Testament and Christian Origins, Claremont School of Theology

Glen W. Menzies, Research Coordinator, Museum of the Bible

CONTRIBUTORS

Stephen J. Patterson, George H. Atkinson Professor of Religious and Ethical Studies, Willamette University

Stephen Potthoff, Associate Professor of Religion and Peace Studies, Wilmington College

Mark Reasoner, Professor of Biblical Theology, Marian University

Calvin J. Roetzel, Sundet Professor of New Testament and Christian Studies (Emeritus), University of Minnesota

David H. Sick, Associate Professor of Greek and Roman Studies, Rhodes College

Dennis E. Smith†, LaDonna Kramer Meinders Professor of New Testament Emeritus, Phillips Theological Seminary

Geoffrey S. Smith, Assistant Professor of Religious Studies, University of Texas at Austin

Rabun Taylor, Professor of Classics, University of Texas at Austin

†Died September 16, 2017.

Introduction: An Appreciation

COURTNEY J. P. FRIESEN

IT IS, PERHAPS, A tautology that the humanities aim at the discovery of what it means to be human. Scholars within the humanistic disciplines, by research and reflection on past and present artifacts of societies and individuals, move us toward a more acute appreciation of the best (and also the worst) capabilities of our own natures. There is, of course, no guarantee that being a lifelong, professional student and scholar in these fields makes one a better human. Therefore, it is especially inspiring to study with and learn from an individual who embodies the ideals of the humanistic enterprise, not merely through the professional achievements that one accumulates on a *curriculum vitae*, but more fundamentally within their inner self. Within such conjunctions, the intellectual and academic enterprise offers glimpses into something transcendent, momentary visions of the human giving way to the divine. Melissa Harl Sellew is just such a person. The collaboration of this volume, *Envisioning God in the Humanities*, is a testament to the range of fellow academics— students, friends, and colleagues—who have found Melissa's intellectual insights, her teaching and mentoring, and her friendship to be enriching and empowering.

The existence of the humanities is increasingly, it seems, in need of justification. In periods of economic downturn, funding cuts, and budgetary constraints, these academic disciplines are often an easy target for elimination. Their monetary payoff is not straightforwardly measured, and that they produce an irreplaceable public good is no longer taken as self-evident. Consequently, the urgency of articulating the relevance of the humanities is more immediate than ever. Our increasingly technocratic world grows ever more impatient with the intellectual attentiveness required to reflect on a poem, a monument, or a noun declension. Yet, it is precisely the de-humanization resulting from the unrelenting digitization of knowledge that calls for the redisciplining of our minds toward humanity. And it is precisely the paradoxical uselessness of art, literature, and philosophy that position them as prophetic champions of human dignity and inspired celebrants of beauty.

This is, above all, what I learned as a student of Melissa Sellew: a deep and rigorous engagement with texts and ideas empowers us to understand difference and diversity; to problematize unquestioned assumptions; and to seek for beauty, even in unexpected places. Participation in this collective exercise *can* render us better people. Toward this end, Melissa invited all of her students to join her in attitudes of empathy and compassion, and to share with her the delight of discovering ancient and foreign worlds, and thereafter to engage with one's own world with enhanced, critical appreciation.

In her own research, Sellew has pioneered lines of inquiry that are both broad and deeply penetrating. Her doctoral studies at Harvard under Helmut Koester established her as an authoritative scholar of the sources and composition of the synoptic gospels. Her dissertation paved the way for this and was followed by several rigorous studies. A particularly acute challenge for scholars has been distinguishing the extent to which the Gospel of Mark deployed existing written sources and where the author composed his own material. Careful attention is needed to patterns of language exhibited across the gospel—nevertheless, with due caution, she advanced fresh insights in this regard for several Markan texts.[1] As a means of extending her scholarly conversations beyond the confines of the academy, Sellew also participated in the Jesus Seminar— she was a fellow in its earliest years and later served as the editor of its journal *Forum* from 1990 to 1994.[2]

---

1. Especially important are "Oral and Written Sources in Mark 4.1–34"; and "Composition of Didactic Scenes in Mark's Gospel."

2. She also published numerous articles in *Forum* ("The Last Supper Discourse in Luke 22"; "Beelzebul in Mark 3: Dialogue, Story, or Sayings Cluster?"; "Aphorisms of Jesus in Mark: A Stratigraphic Analysis"; "Tracking the Tradition: On the Current State of Tradition-Historical Research"; "Pious Practice and Social Formation in the Gospel of Thomas") and contributed to seminal publications of the Seminar, including to sections on the Gospel of Mark and Oxyrhynchus 840 in Miller, ed., *Complete Gospels* (org. 1992) and in Dewey and Miller, eds., *Complete Gospel Parallels* (2012).

INTRODUCTION: AN APPRECIATION

Over time, Melissa's research on the gospels advanced in new directions. In one study, for instance, she draws on theoretical insights from the study of narrative in order to analyze the use of interior monologue by Jesus in Lukan parables. Here, she demonstrates that the evangelist deployed this technique so as to establish the hero's power for discerning the inner workings of the human mind.[3] In the mid-1990s, Melissa's research on the gospels began to center on Thomas in particular. While this text had often figured prominently within her reconstructions of the earliest collections of Jesus' sayings, she now turned her attention toward this gospel as a religious artifact of its own right. In this vein, she began charting a course toward an analysis of the literary composition of the Gospel of Thomas in order to delineate its own distinctive message rather than simply as an atomized compilation of disconnected sayings.[4] In addition, with appropriate care, she has explored the possibilities for reconstructing the particular characteristics of the communities within which this gospel was used as a formative text.[5]

Along with her work on gospels both within and without the canon, Sellew has maintained an ongoing interest in papyrology.[6] In addition to her own published work, together with her colleague Nita Krevans, in 2013, Melissa partnered with Zoouniverse and the University of Oxford to launch the Ancient Lives Project at the University of Minnesota. This citizen science collaboration deploys an online interface enabling volunteer participants to engage in deciphering fragments from among the countless unidentified Oxyrhynchus papyri. In conjunction with this, Melissa secured a grant from the National Endowment for the Humanities to expand this research into the area of early Christianity.

While the contours of Sellew's scholarship are firmly rooted in the disciplines of New Testament and Early Christian studies, her undergraduate majors at Macalester College were in Classics and History, and her research and teaching exemplify a deep engagement with the

---

3. "Interior Monologue as a Narrative Device."

4. See esp. "Death, the Body, and the World in the Gospel of Thomas"; "*Gospel of Thomas*: Prospects for Research," 339–46; "Jesus and the Voice from beyond the Grave"; "James and the Rejection of Apostolic Authority."

5. See, e.g., "Pious Practice and Social Formation in the Gospel of Thomas"; "Thomas Christianity"; "Reading Jesus in the Desert."

6. See "Early Coptic Witness to the *Dormitio Mariae*"; cf. also "Achilles or Christ?," esp. 80–82.

xvii

INTRODUCTION: AN APPRECIATION

Greco-Roman world.[7] The Department of Classical and Near Eastern Studies proved to be an especially congenial atmosphere to maintain such interdisciplinary work. Melissa offered a breadth of courses on classical languages and literatures (along with Coptic, her favorite language to teach), including, for example, advanced graduate seminars on Greek hymns, Asclepius cult, and the interpretation of Homer. Moreover, she directed and examined a remarkable range of master's and doctoral theses, many of which move effectively among fields of Judaic studies, New Testament and early Christianity, and Classics. The fruits of her cross-disciplinary teaching career are on display throughout the pages of this volume.[8]

The organization of *Envisioning God in the Humanities* is meant to reflect the trajectories of Melissa's own research interests. The foreword by her undergraduate professor and later colleague at the University of Minnesota, Calvin Roetzel, attests to the longevity of the profound friendships that have emerged across her career. Next, Part 1 concerns the New Testament gospels and Acts, exploring numerous topics with diverse methodological approaches. Charles Bobertz builds on Sellew's work on the textual history of Mark to shed light on nascent Christian conceptions of ritual. Stephen Potthoff and Steven Friesen examine political and class conflicts in two well-known pericopae, the former in the symbolism of the barren fig tree of Mark 11, the latter through the implications of Jesus healing on the Sabbath in Luke 13 for the regulation of labor. Mark Reasoner develops Sellew's explorations of interior monologue as a narrative strategy in Luke, which is followed by Glen Menzies' inquiry into historical events potentially underlying the Pentecost narrative in Acts.

Moving beyond "canonical" narratives, Part 2 consists of four essays on wider dynamics in ancient Christianity in connection to the vexed problem of "Gnosticism." First, Geoffrey Smith reexamines the place of *gnosis* in first-century Corinth as it pertains to Paul's view of spiritual gifts and his polemic against human wisdom. The remaining essays concern the Nag Hammadi Library, including the gender ideology embodied within the Gospel of Thomas (Stephen Patterson), the place of the *Gospel*

7. See, for example, "Jesus and the Voice from beyond the Grave," esp. 54–71; "Secret Hymn about Rebirth."

8. The contributions of Rabun Taylor and Justin Jeffcoat Schedtler have their origins in Sellew's graduate seminars on Asclepius cult and Greek hymns, respectively. The variety of doctoral dissertations that she supervised is evident also—authors in this volume include Glen Menzies, David Sick, Stephen Potthoff, Ed Glenny, and Courtney Friesen.

of *Judas* within the variety of Gnostic Christianities (David Brakke), and the significance of the materiality of Coptic codices for monastic communities in Egypt (James Goehring).

The third and final section of the volume takes a wider interdisciplinary view of ancient literature and religion in order to explore interconnections with Christian origins. Beginning with Hellenistic Judaism, Ed Glenny considers the role of messianism in the Septuagint's interpretation of key passages in Amos, a phenomenon that becomes especially salient in early Christian appropriations of scripture. Michael Holmes offers a reappraisal of the portrayal of Jews/Judeans in the *Martyrdom of Polycarp*, suggesting that their role in persecutions against Christians more likely arises from intra-Christian conflicts than any genuine Jewish activities. Characteristically incisive and provocative, Dennis MacDonald proposes that Luke knew Latin, which he argues on the basis of the evangelist's dependence on uniquely Latin literary sources. Dennis Smith and David Sick both consider early Christian dining practices in view of Greco-Roman customs, the former focusing on matters of social stratification, the latter on the erotic implications of the Greek *symposium* and Roman *cena*. Courtney Friesen and Justin Jeffcoat Schedtler explore the saliency of ancient drama for Judaism and Christianity; Friesen explores how the actions of the comic Heracles were of interest to moralists, and Jeffcoat Schedtler demonstrates that the chorus of Greek and Roman theater functions analogously to the heavenly choir in the book of Revelation. Finally, Rabun Taylor theorizes regarding the origin and function of nymphs as a distinctive category of devotion in Greek and Roman religion.

This volume would not be possible apart from the generous assistance of numerous individuals. First, I wish to express my enduring gratitude to the contributors who enthusiastically offered these exceptional studies. The editorial staff at the Westar Institute welcomed the proposal wholeheartedly and aided it along the way to completion. Thanks are especially due to David Galston, Cassandra Farrin, and Bill Lehto. Finally, at the University of Minnesota, Melissa's colleagues and my former professors, Nita Krevans and Bernard Levinson, offered timely counsel and encouragement on numerous occasions. To all these individuals I offer my sincerest appreciation, and together we present this volume to you, Melissa, as a small token of our thankfulness and admiration.

Editor's Note: In the preparation of this volume, considerable efforts were taken to include a diverse range of scholars with invitations extended to numerous individuals across genders. Due to various personal and professional circumstances, however, several were, with regret, unable to participate. The resulting gender representation is not what it might have been. While this is regrettable, it does not reflect the remarkable extent to which Professor Sellew has worked throughout her career to include and empower people regardless of identity, background, and status.

Works Cited[9]

Sellew, Melissa (Philip) Harl. "Achilles or Christ? Porphyry and Didymus in Debate over Allegorical Interpretation." *Harvard Theological Review* 82 (1989) 79–100.

———. "Aphorisms of Jesus in Mark: A Stratigraphic Analysis." *Forum* 8 (1992) 141–60.

———. "Beelzebul in Mark 3: Dialogue, Story, or Sayings Cluster?" *Forum* 4 (1988) 93–105.

———. "Composition of Didactic Scenes in Mark's Gospel." *Journal of Biblical Literature* 108 (1989) 613–34.

———. "Death, the Body, and the World in the Gospel of Thomas." *Studia Patristica* 31 (1997) 530–34.

———. "An Early Coptic Witness to the Dormitio Mariae at Yale: P.CtYBR inv. 1788 Revisited." *Bulletin of the American Society of Papyrologists* 37 (2000) 37–70 + pls. 2-4.

———. "The Gospel of Mark." In *The Complete Gospel Parallels*, edited by Arthur J. Dewey and Robert J. Miller. Salem, OR: Polebridge, 2012.

———. "The Gospel of Mark: Introduction, Translation, and Notes." In *The Complete Gospels: Annotated Scholars Version*, edited by Robert J. Miller, 9–52. Sonoma, CA: Polebridge, 1992. Rev. ed. 1994.

———. "The *Gospel of Thomas*: Prospects for Future Research." In *The Fiftieth Anniversary of the Nag Hammadi Library*, edited by John D. Turner and Anne McGuire, 327–56. Nag Hammadi and Manichaean Studies 44. Leiden: Brill, 1997.

———. "Gospel Oxyrhynchus 840: Introduction and Notes." In *The Complete Gospels: Annotated Scholars Version*, edited by Robert J. Miller, 412–15. Sonoma, CA: Polebridge, 1992. Rev. ed. 1994.

———. "Interior Monologue as a Narrative Device in the Parables of Luke." *Journal of Biblical Literature* 111 (1992) 239–53.

———. "James and the Rejection of Apostolic Authority in the Gospel of Thomas." In *Delightful Acts: New Essays on Canonical and Non-canonical Acts*, edited by Harold W. Attridge, et al., 193–207. Wissenschaftliche Untersuchungen zum Neuen Testament 391. Tübingen: Mohr/Siebeck, 2017.

———. "Jesus and the Voice from beyond the Grave: *Gospel of Thomas* 42 in the Context of Funerary Epigraphy." In *Thomasine Traditions in Antiquity*, edited by J. Ma. Asgeirsson, et al., 39–73. Nag Hammadi and Manichaean Studies 59. Leiden: Brill, 2006.

---

9. The publications listed here are illustrative not exhaustive.

INTRODUCTION: AN APPRECIATION

———. "The Last Supper Discourse in Luke 22." *Forum* 3 (1987) 70–95.
———. "Oral and Written Sources in Mark 4.1–34." *New Testament Studies* 36 (1990) 234–67.
———. "Pious Practice and Social Formation in the Gospel of Thomas (Thomas 6, 14, 27, 53, 104)." *Forum* 10 (1994) 47–56.
———. "Reading Jesus in the Desert: The *Gospel of Thomas* Meets the *Apophthegmata Patrum*." In *The Nag Hammadi Codices and Late Antique Egypt*, edited by Hugo Lundhaug and Lance Jenott. Studien und Texte zu Antike und Christentum 110. Tübingen: Mohr/Siebeck, forthcoming.
———. "A Secret Hymn about Rebirth: Corpus Hermeticum XIII.17–20." In *Prayer from Alexander to Constantine: A Critical Anthology*, edited by Mark Kiley, 165–170. London: Routledge, 1997.
———. "Thomas Christianity: Scholars in Quest of a Community." In *The Apocryphal Acts of Thomas*, edited by Jan N. Bremmer, 11–35. Studies on Early Christian Apocrypha 6. Leuven: Peeters, 2001.
———. "Tracking the Tradition: On the Current State of Tradition-Historical Research." *Forum* 9 (1993) 217–36.

Abbreviations

Scripture Abbreviations

Gen	Genesis
Exod	Exodus
Lev	Leviticus
Num	Numbers
Deut	Deuteronomy
Judg	Judges
1, 2 Sam	1, 2 Samuel
1, 2 Kgs	1, 2 Kings
Ps(s)	Psalm(s)
Isa	Isaiah
Jer	Jeremiah
Ezek	Ezekiel
Dan	Daniel
Hos	Hosea
Mic	Micah
Zech	Zechariah
Matt	Matthew
Rom	Romans
1, 2 Cor	1, 2 Corinthians
Gal	Galatians
Eph	Ephesians
Phil	Philippians
Col	Colossians
1 Thess	1 Thessalonians
1 Tim	1 Timothy
1 Peter	1 Peter
Rev	Revelation

ABBREVIATIONS

Additional Abbreviations

1 Apol.	Justin Martyr, *First Apology*
1 Clem.	*First Clement*
1Q	Qumran Cave 1
4Q	Qumran Cave 4
Acts Thom.	*Acts of Thomas*
Aen.	Vergil, *Aeneid*
Ag. Ap.	Josephus, *Against Apion*
Alleg. Interp.	Philo, *Allegorical Interpretation*
Am.	Ovid, *Amores*
Ant.	Josephus, *Jewish Antiquities*
Ap. John	*Secret Book according to John*
Arist.	Plutarch, *Aristides*
b.	Babylonian Talmud
Bacch.	Euripides, *Bacchae*
BCE	Before the Common Era
BDAG	Walter Bauer, Frederick W. Danker, W. F. Arndt, and F. W. Gingrich. *Greek- English Lexicon of the New Testament and Other Early Christian Literature*. 3rd ed. Chicago: University of Chicago Press, 2000
Bell. civ.	Appian, *Bella civilia*
BG	Berolinensis Gnosticus
Cal.	Suetonius, *Gaius Caligula*
Carm.	Horace, *Carmina*
CE	Common Era
Cels.	Origen, *Against Celsus*
Cher.	Philo, *On the Cherubim*
Civ.	Augustine, *The City of God*
Contempl.	Philo, *On the Contemplative Life*

ABBREVIATIONS

Creation	Philo, *On the Creation of the World*
CSEL	Corpus scriptorum ecclesiasticorum latinorum
Def. orac.	Plutarch, *De defectu oraculorum*
Deipn.	Athenaeus, *Deipnosophistae*
Dial.	Justin, *Dialogue with Trypho*
Diatr.	Epictetus, *Diatribai*
Drunkenness	Philo, *On Drunkenness*
Embassy	Philo, *Embassy to Gaius*
Ep.	*Epistulae*
Eph.	Ignatius, *To the Ephesians*
Epig.	Martial, *Epigrams*
ESV	English Standard Version
ET	English Translation
Flight	Philo, *On Flight and Finding*
G^1	Greek *Life of Pachomius*
Gen. Rab.	*Genesis Rabbah*
Good Person	Philo, *That Every Good Person Is Free*
Gos. Eg.	*Egerton Gospel*
Gos. Jud.	*Gospel of Judas*
Gos. Phil.	*Gospel of Philip*
Herc. fur.	*Hercules furens*
IG	*Inscriptiones graecae*. Editio minor. Berlin, 1924–
Il.	Homer, *Iliad*
Inf. Gos. Thom.	*Infancy Gospel of Thomas*
Inst.	Lactantius, *The Divine Institutes*
J.W.	Josephus, *Jewish War*
Joseph	Philo, *On the Life of Joseph*
Jub.	*Jubilees*

ABBREVIATIONS

K.-A.	R. Kassel and C. Austin, eds., *Poetae Comici Graeci*. 8 vols. Berlin: de Gruyter, 1983–
LCL	Loeb Classical Library
LSJ	Henry George Liddell, Robert Scott, and Henry Stuart Jones. *A Greek-English Lexicon*. 9th ed. Oxford: Clarendon, 1996
LXX	Septuagint
m.	Mishnah
Magn.	Ignatius, *To the Magnesians*
Mart. Pol.	*Martyrdom of Polycarp*
Mem.	Xenophon, *Memorabilia*
Metam.	Ovid or Apuleius *Metamorphoses*
MPG	Patrologia graeca
MT	Masoretic Text
Myst.	Iamblichus, *De mysteriis*
NASB	New American Standard Bible
Nat.	Pliny, *Natural History*
NETS	New English Translation of the Septuagint
NRSV	New Revised Standard Version
Od.	Homer, *Odyssey*
Or.	Dio Chrysostom, *Orationes*
Pax	Aristophanes, *Peace*
Pelag.	Jerome, *Adversus Pelagianos*
Phil.	Cicero, *Orationes philippicae*
Phld.	Ignatius, *To the Philadelphians*
Plant.	Philo, *On Planting*
Pol.	Ignatius, *To Polycarp*
Praep. ev.	Eusebius, *Praeparatio evangelica*
Q	Quelle

ABBREVIATIONS

QE	Philo, *Questions and Answers on Exodus*
QG	Philo, *Questions and Answers on Genesis*
Quaest. conv.	Plutarch, *Quaestionum convivialum*
Resp.	Plato, *Republic*
Rewards	Philo, *On Rewards and Punishments*
RSV	Revised Standard Version
Ruth Rab.	Ruth Rabbah
SBo	Coptic Sahidic-Bohairic *Life of Pachomius*
Sib. Or.	*Sibylline Oracles*
Smyrn.	Ignatius, *To the Smyrnaeans*
Spec. Laws	Philo, *On the Special Laws*
SVF	*Stoicorum veterum fragmenta*. H. von Arnim. 4 vols. Leipzig, 1903–1924.
Symp.	*Symposium*
T. Jos.	*Testament of Joseph*
T. Jud.	*Testament of Judah*
T. Levi	*Testament of Levi*
T. Reu.	*Testament of Reuben*
TDNT	*Theological Dictionary of the New Testament*. Edited by Gerhard Kittel and Gerhard Friedrich. Translated by Geoffrey W. Bromiley. 10 vols. Grand Rapids, 1964–1976
Theoph.	Eusebius, *Theophania*
Tim.	Plato, *Timaeus*
Trall.	Ignatius, *To the Trallians*
TrGF	*Tragicorum graecorum fragmenta*. Bruno Snell, et al. 5 vols. Göttingen: Vandenhoeck & Ruprecht, 1971–2004
Vit. Apoll.	Philostratus, *Vita Apollonii*

Part 1

New Testament Gospels and Acts: From Sources and Redaction to Narrative Strategies

1

From Mark to Mark to Mark

Continuity and Discontinuity in the Narrative History of Mark's Gospel

CHARLES A. BOBERTZ

In her own *Festschrift* article for her teacher, the late Helmut Koester, Melissa Sellew offered an appraisal of Koester's proposal to explain the complicated textual history of the Gospel of Mark.[1] Taking account of what we know about the complex textual history of the Gospel,[2] Koester proposed the existence of an original Gospel. This original version of Mark was mainly characterized by the absence of the current text of Mark 6:45—8:26.[3] It was this Mark that became one of the primary sources for the Gospel of Luke. At the same time the Gospel of Matthew used an augmented version of the original Mark, one which included Mark 6:45—8:26. It was this augmented version of Mark that became the basis of the so-called *Secret Gospel of Mark*.[4] Finally, Koester argued, our

1. Sellew, "Secret Mark"; Koester, "History and Development."

2. Koester reviews, e.g., the three separate and distinct endings to Mark present in the manuscript tradition.

3. Mark 6:45—8:26 is often referred to as the "Great Omission": that is, in the classic formulation of the two source theory for the composition of the synoptic gospels, Matthew and Luke use Mark and the Sayings Gospel Q as their primary sources. Luke, however, "omits" Mark 6:45—8:26.

4. Smith, *Clement of Alexandria*.

current version of Mark, *canonical Mark*, is actually an edited version of the *Secret Gospel of Mark*.[5]

Melissa Sellew essentially agreed with her teacher with respect to the development of the tradition of the Markan Gospel, but pressed her teacher on one essential point: she argued that Mark 6:45—8:26, the great omission, should be considered as integral to Koester's proposal for an original Gospel of Mark. With typical scholarly acumen, Sellew argues her case which I present here in schematic fashion:[6]

1. There is merit in the traditional argument that Luke intentionally omitted Mark 6:45—8:26. In his use of sources Luke typically avoids duplication and repetition of similar stories, and this section of Mark contains many doublets with stories found elsewhere in Mark.

2. The section of Mark between 6:45—8:26, omitted by Luke, does fit well within the plotted narrative structure of Mark. This shows up clearly in the increasing incomprehension of the disciples along with a correspondingly progressively stern response on the part of Jesus.

    a. The disciples are mystified by Jesus' ability to walk on water, and the narrator informs the reader that their hearts were hardened.

    b. When Jesus is confronted by Pharisees and scribes in 7:1–13 he accuses them of having unclean lips and wayward hearts (Isaiah) and also accuses the disciples of sharing the Pharisees' ignorance: they are "stupid" (ἀσύνετοι).

    c. Mark constructs a whole new scene of Jesus and his disciples in the boat (8:14–21) and addresses his disciples with the same prophetic abuse he uses against outsiders at 4:11–12 and the Pharisees in 7:6–13.

Sellew concludes her argument by admitting that while thematic motifs and phrases *could* be shared by more than one writer or editor working with one basic story within a particular socioreligious situation, basic elements of a narrative plot of a writing like Mark were much more likely to be included from the start.[7] Hence Sellew concludes that there is more

---

5. Sellew, "Secret Mark," 245, has a convenient chart of this proposal.

6. Sellew, "Secret Mark," 249: "we must be very cautious about drawing overly sweeping conclusions about the history of particular sections in Mark from comparison with Matthew and Luke alone."

7. At this point in her article Sellew goes on to make two additional arguments

or less a clear trajectory from original Mark (including 6:45—8:26) to *Secret Mark* to canonical Mark. This trajectory includes Mark's portrayal of Jesus as a miracle worker and especially the mysterious nature of Jesus' speech that the disciples do not understand.

It is the latter feature of Mark's narrative plot, evident in all of the editions of Mark's Gospel, which will be the focus of this essay. Melissa Sellew's perceptive description of Jesus the teacher and his faltering "learners" (disciples) as integral to the narrative plot of Mark forces the reader of Mark to contemplate what it is that the learners within the narrative do not understand and so, conversely, what the readers of the narrative are supposed to understand.[8] And it is just here that I think there is something positive at stake for the reader. Mark does not give us the story of the disciples' lack of understanding in order to maintain an element of mystery in the narrative,[9] but to draw his readers to a particular and new understanding. And while Sellew draws our attention to the function of this mystery in the baptismal initiation rites of the Alexandrian Church in the second century,[10] I would refocus our attention on what I believe to be Mark's original understanding of the mystery revealed in the Baptismal *and Eucharistic* practices of Mark's house churches in the first century.

This mystery revealed comes to the fore precisely in the section of Mark's Gospel that Koester had argued was not part of the original Gospel, Mark 6:45—8:26, but has its roots earlier in the narrative in the first boat crossing of Mark 4:35-41. As Sellew points out there is a progression of the disciples' increasing incomprehension in this section. The disciples do not understand that it is Jesus who is walking upon the water (Mark

---

that are sound but that I will not consider further in this essay. First, Koester had argued that Mark's references to Jesus' "teaching" derive from Secret Mark. Yet Sellew points out that it is quite possible that Matthew and Mark independently removed the characterization of miracle stories as teaching. Second, Koester argued that the scene of the youth running away without his linen cloth at Mark 14:51-52 was an additional episode added at the same time the text of Secret Mark was produced. Sellew, on the other hand, convincingly points out that the reference to a "certain" young man (νεανίσκος τις) is a conscious editorial or authorial step taken to signal that the young man had not yet been mentioned in the story. See Sellew, "Secret Mark," 251-52.

8. With a nod toward Mack, *Myth of Innocence*, 78-97, Sellew posits the idea that the term οἱ μαθηταί, "learners," might have been first applied to the followers of Jesus in the circles that produced Mark's Gospel.

9. See, e.g., Kermode, *Genesis of Secrecy*.

10. Sellew, "Secret Mark," 256.

5

6:49); at Mark 6:52 the narrator informs us that "they did not *understand* (οὐ γὰρ συνῆκαν) concerning the loaves for their hearts had been hardened." Then in the discussion of meal rituals in 7:1–23 Jesus refers to the disciples as "without understanding" (ἀσύνετοι). Finally, at the conclusion of this section, and again aboard a boat, Jesus is clearly exasperated with the disciples: "do you not yet understand?" (οὔπω συνίετε; Mark 8:21).[11] For Sellew this progression of the disciples' incomprehension has to do with the development of the idea of early Christians characterizing themselves as "disciples" (learners), perhaps a distinct nomenclature developed in the Markan churches.[12] This may well be the case, but there is another aspect to the narrative portrayal of the disciples not discussed by Sellew: what is it exactly that the narrative of Mark wants its readers to learn?

The beginning and ending of this narrative progression has to do with boat travel (4:35–41; 8:14–21). The beginning is Mark 4:35–41, the so-called stilling of the storm.[13] The first two verses already point toward the perspective from which the progression begins:

---

11. In my recent book on the Gospel of Mark, Bobertz, *Gospel of Mark*, I argue that the whole of Mark's narrative (canonical Mark) can be understood as directing the ancient readers of Mark, practicing the rituals of baptism and Eucharist, toward a particular understanding of the identity of Jesus revealed in those ritual practices. This is why Mark begins with the ritual of baptism (Mark 1:1–11) and climaxes with the revelation made about Jesus with his disciples at the final ritual Eucharist ("this is my body," τοῦτό ἐστιν τὸ σῶμά μου, Mark 14:22). The movement of Jesus toward the Gentiles beginning at 4:35 ("let us cross over to the other side") and concluding with a proper understanding of the one loaf with respect to the Gentiles within the eucharistic ritual (Mark 8:14–22) sets the stage for Jesus' teaching about discipleship and the true meaning of his and his disciples' potential martyrdom.

12. Sellew, "Secret Mark," 254. Peterson, "Composition," 217, draws a similar conclusion: "The composition of Mark 4:1—8:26 depicts the unfolding of the disciples' incomprehension despite Jesus' expectations of them and despite his attempts to explain things to them."

13. Even giving a name to a pericope (a particular story within the gospel) signals a certain type of understanding of the story. This pericope is often named, "The Stilling of the Storm," which by itself places the story into the category of nature miracle and invites one to contemplate the supernatural power of Jesus (God?) to calm the storm. See, e.g., Bornkamm, "Stilling of the Storm." To read the story as I do, as an understanding of baptism (apocalyptic destruction) and resurrection (the restoration of an ordered creation) injected into the narrative story of Jesus' ministry would change how one names the pericope.

Καὶ λέγει αὐτοῖς ἐν ἐκείνῃ τῇ ἡμέρᾳ ὀψίας γενομένης, Διέλθωμεν εἰς τὸ πέραν. καὶ ἀφέντες τὸν ὄχλον παραλαμβάνουσιν αὐτὸν ὡς ἦν ἐν τῷ πλοίῳ, καὶ ἄλλα πλοῖα ἦν μετ' αὐτοῦ.

On that day when it was getting dark he said to them (the disciples), "let us depart to the other side." And leaving the crowd they placed him into the boat just as he was. And other boats were with him. (Mark 4:35-36)

There are three curious details here. First, the disciples take Jesus into the boat (παραλαμβάνουσιν αὐτόν), that is, Jesus does not climb into the boat and command the disciples to get into the boat. So the narrative invites this question from the readers: *who is this Jesus whom the disciples have invited into the boat?* This narrative situation is amplified by the second detail: the disciples take Jesus with them in the boat "as he was" (ὡς ἦν). This cannot refer to the absence of rain gear but must be a reference to the ordinary Jesus portrayed in the narrative: Jesus of Nazareth. So now the question for the reader is more obvious: *who is Jesus of Nazareth whom they have invited into the boat with them?* The third curious detail is that "other boats were with *him*" (αὐτοῦ). This is noteworthy on two counts: first, there is no further reference to these "other boats." They are simply never mentioned again in the story. The second is that the boats were with "him," when the logic of the story is that they would be with "them." After all, "they" (the disciples) placed him (Jesus) into the boat with them. Instead the phrase here matches exactly the earlier choosing of the twelve at 3:14 to be "with him" (μετ' αὐτοῦ) and the sending of them out to preach (κηρύσσειν). So besides looking backward, the readers here are also directed to look forward to the next event. The Gentile from Gerasene (the place to which the boat is going) in the next episode of the narrative also asks to be "with him" (Jesus; μετ' αὐτοῦ). But this Gentile is instead sent out to preach (κηρύσσειν) in the Decapolis, an event apparently so unusual that "all were amazed" (πάντες ἐθαύμαζον, 5:20).

The readers of the narrative are now prepared for the story that follows. Who is Jesus of Nazareth who is in the boat and has these other boats *with him*? And who is *with him* in these boats?

> And there came a great gale of wind and the waves were crashing into the boat, so that the boat was already filled. And he was in the stern, sleeping (καθεύδων) on a cushion. And they resurrected him (καὶ ἐγείρουσιν[14] αὐτόν) and said to him, "Teacher,

---

14. The Markan words for resurrection, ἐγείρω along with ἀνίστημι (Mark 8:31;

do you not care that we are being destroyed"? And having been resurrected, he rebuked the wind and said to the sea, "Silence! Be still!" And the wind ceased, and there was great calm. And he said to them, "Why are you timid? Do you not yet have faith?" And they feared with great fear and said to one another, "Who is this, that the wind and the sea obey him?" (Mark 4:37–41)

The story here intertwines apocalyptic symbols (darkness, the great gale of wind, destruction, the sea) with their enactment in early Christian liturgy.[15] In a clear allusion to a baptismal ritual, the disciples "resurrect" Jesus, as he was, from death (sleep[16]) under the water and Jesus rises to master the chaos of wind and the sea and restore great calm.[17] The creation is ordered as it should be on the Sabbath ("that day"). In addition, it is not hard for the readers of the narrative to imagine that the other boats of people "with him" (μετ' αὐτοῦ) have gone through the same experience of the storm, from immersion in the waters of death to resurrection with Christ. So here the readers might readily surmise that Mark is alluding to Gentiles now in Mark's house churches and with him in the narrative, baptized and risen with Jesus.[18]

It is also not hard for the readers of Mark to imagine the disciples' question, "Who is this, that the wind and the sea obey him?" (Τίς ἄρα οὗτός ἐστιν ὅτι καὶ ὁ ἄνεμος καὶ ἡ θάλασσα ὑπακούει αὐτῷ;) marks the relationship between Jesus "as he was" (ὡς ἦν) in the narrative and the Jesus who has now risen from death under the waters of baptism to restore the order of creation, the calm of the Sabbath day. Here the great question of faith directed at the disciples, "Why are you timid? Do you not yet have faith?" (Τί δειλοί ἐστε; οὔπω ἔχετε πίστιν) is a question that challenges any doubt that the ordinary Jesus, "as he was," is at once the resurrected Jesus, able to rise from death and conquer chaos. It is also a

---

16:6; 5:42).

15. For more discussion of Mark's use of apocalyptic symbolism and the connection to early Christian liturgy, see Bobertz, *Gospel of Mark*, 45–50; for a discussion specifically of the ritual of baptism as cosmic conflict, see Bobertz, "That by His Passion."

16. In Mark and in early Christian literature in general "sleep" is a euphemism for death (Mark 5:39; 1 Thess 4:15; Eph 5:14).

17. See Rom 6:3–5; for discussion see, e.g., Scroggs and Groff, "Baptism in Mark," 536: "Immersion into water as a participation in the death of Jesus and the emerging from it as participation, either now or guaranteed for the future, in the resurrection of Christ was apparently a widespread motif in Hellenistic Christianity."

18. I outline my arguments for the presence of Gentiles in this pericope in Bobertz, *Gospel of Mark*, 45–53.

question that challenges the readers to consider again who belongs "with him" (μετ' αὐτοῦ), Jews *and Gentiles* baptized within the community of Mark's house churches, and where this community is going. It is hard to get across this lake to a Gentile land, the forces of chaos (wind and sea) have risen against them; there is martyrdom (destruction) on this journey and so the disciples are timid. Faith in this story is faith in the reality of the resurrection of Jesus that triumphs over this chaos. It is also faith amidst the fact that some within the house churches will suffer martyrdom because of the journey.

At Mark 6:46–52 Jesus walks upon the water. Here the incomprehension of the disciples concerning the real identity of Jesus in the narrative is again connected to a story centered on the disciples and Jesus in a boat on the sea of Galilee. This episode follows immediately after the first ritual meal narrative (6:30–44). Jesus walks upon the water and apparently the reader is to understand that this event has something to do with the "loaves" (Mark 6:52). As in the previous narrative of the storm at sea, the reader is being directed to contemplate the relationship between Jesus in the narrative (Jesus of Nazareth) and the resurrected Jesus within the context of the identity, mission and ritual practices of the Markan house churches. The admixture of apocalyptic symbolism, darkness, sea and wind is again present. Again the boat is crossing in mission to the other side (πέραν, Mark 6:45). This time, however, it is Jesus who forces the disciples to get into the boat and cross to the other side toward Bethsaida (6:45). So now apparently they are supposed to be able to go out on this mission alone, that is, without Jesus: "he remained alone upon the land" (Mark 6:47). He desired to pass by them (καὶ ἤθελεν παρελθεῖν αὐτούς) as he walks upon (dominates) the chaos of the sea. He would ostensibly meet them there at their destination of Bethsaida (6:48).

Again the apocalyptic wind is against them. The disciples see Jesus walking upon the sea just before dawn, at the time of the resurrection (Mark 16:2), and conclude that Jesus must be a spirit: "They saw him walking upon the sea and they thought it was a phantom" (οἱ δὲ ἰδόντες αὐτὸν ἐπὶ τῆς θαλάσσης περιπατοῦντα ἔδοξαν ὅτι φάντασμά ἐστιν, Mark 6:49). The readers of the narrative note that the disciples did not see a phantom and cry out. Rather, they saw Jesus (αὐτόν) and thought he (Jesus) was a spirit, and then "cried out" (ἀνέκραξαν). That is, the readers understand the disciples in the story to have cried out *because* the disciples thought Jesus was a spirit (phantom). Indeed, in the story *all* the disciples saw him as a phantom and were troubled (6:50). So at this moment when

Jesus speaks with them and tells them "it is me" (ἐγώ εἰμι), it is not for the readers a moment of divine epiphany, the declaration that Jesus is actually God (the "I am" of Exodus 3:14). Rather, the immediate narrative context is centered on whether Jesus is in fact a spiritual apparition (phantom). And so Mark shows clearly that the Jesus walking upon the water is the corporeal Jesus (and not a phantom): "Jesus *rose* to them into the boat" (καὶ ἀνέβη πρὸς αὐτοὺς εἰς τὸ πλοῖον, Mark 6:51).[19] And it is only then, when this Jesus of Nazareth in the boat with them, that the wind ceases being against their progress to the other side. So once again Mark addresses the question of the relationship between Jesus of Nazareth and Jesus the resurrected one. The resurrected Jesus, the one who walks upon the water and calms the wind, is Jesus of Nazareth, the one who is now with them in the boat.

Mark is therefore using the narrative technique of portraying the incomprehension of the disciples in the narrative to focus his readers' attention on the continuity between Jesus "as he was" and "it's me" and the resurrected figure of Jesus who can calm the wind and dominate the waters. He does so, I believe, because he wants his contemporary readers to understand that Jesus of Nazareth is the resurrected Jesus present with them in the liturgical experiences, Baptism and Eucharist, of the house churches. It is not that Mark wants to relate to his readers something factual about the historical Jesus. Rather he wants to relate that the historical Jesus and resurrected Jesus are both corporeal facts. And he wants to communicate this understanding because what is at stake theologically in his understanding of Jesus as the resurrected Jesus experienced in liturgy is whether the creation itself is redeemed in the resurrection made present liturgically in the house churches. In other words, for Mark the continuity between Jesus' actual death (the death of Jesus of Nazareth) and Jesus' corporeal resurrection is front and center theologically.[20] Further, the experience of the resurrection as an eschatological reality available in the present circumstance of the ritual meal is a claim that the redeemed and restored creation itself—the gathering of the community of Jews, Gentiles, men and women—is realized within the ritual space of the communal gathering. Conversely, the claim that the resurrection itself is incorporeal (Jesus resurrected is a phantom) is a claim that the

---

19. The reader of course notes that Jesus rose (ἀναβαίνω) from the waters of baptism to begin his ministry as Jesus of Nazareth (1:10).

20. I explore this in some detail in an article: Bobertz, "Our Opinion."

created order, the physical world, is of no consequence.²¹ And in the context of the active persecution of the Markan Christians such a theology might be hard to sustain.²²

Mark's comment about the disciples in the narrative—"for they did not understand concerning the loaves, for their hearts had become hardened" (οὐ γὰρ συνῆκαν ἐπὶ τοῖς ἄρτοις, ἀλλ' ἦν αὐτῶν ἡ καρδία πεπωρωμένη, Mark 6:52)—directs the readers of Mark to understand the nature of the reality present in the previous ritual meal of the loaves (Mark 6:30–44). There when the disciples are asked by Jesus about the number of loaves they could find, the disciples discover five loaves.²³ But just here—unbidden—they also discover two fish. Hence for the readers of Mark the number seven comes to the fore (five plus two). The clear allusion is to the seventh (Sabbath) day, the ordered creation manifest in the meal. There in the house church ritual of blessing, breaking and giving, everyone, Jews *and Gentiles*, eats and everyone is satisfied (καὶ ἔφαγον πάντες καὶ ἐχορτάσθησαν, Mark 6:41–42). At the end of the meal twelve baskets are taken up, the twelve tribes of Israel are gathered into the Church. Yet the readers of Mark also note there are two fish in those baskets (καὶ ἀπὸ τῶν ἰχθύων, Mark 6:43): the Gentiles are to be a part of the final order of the redeemed and restored creation.²⁴ So in contrast to the disciples who did not understand the reality present in the ritual meal of the loaves (Mark 6:52), the readers of Mark see Jesus, the resurrected Jesus, walking upon the waters of chaos, calming the contrary winds, restoring creation and walking toward the Gentiles "beyond:" the liturgical reality of the loaves.²⁵

---

21. See, e.g., Thom 56: Jesus said, "Whoever has come to understand the world has found (only) a corpse, and whoever has found a corpse is superior to the world" (trans. Lambdin).

22. See Mark 13:9–14; Ignatius of Antioch, on the way to his own martyrdom in the early second century, articulates this theology clearly (Ignatius, *Trall.* 10.1).

23. The Jewish symbolism of this is apparent: there are five books of Torah.

24. For a full discussion of the relationship of the fish to the Gentile mission in Mark, see Bobertz, *Gospel of Mark*, 64–69.

25. Given the constraints of this paper a full discussion of Mark 7 is not possible, though again the narrative is addressing the reality of the early Christian ritual meals. At Mark 7:18 the narrative signals that the disciples are "without understanding" (ἀσύνετοι). This suggests that the readers are to contrast their understanding with that of the "stupid" disciples: everything outside of a person cannot make that person unclean. The context here is a dispute over what sort of ritual washing (according to Jewish practice) should be followed in the practice of the eucharistic meal in the Markan house churches: "And some of the scribes came from Jerusalem. And they noticed

The climax of this developing incomprehension of the disciples concerning the presence of Gentiles "with Jesus" in the rituals of Baptism and Eucharist undoubtedly is the final boat story in the Gospel of Mark:[26]

> Now they (the disciples) had neglected to bring loaves; and they had only one loaf with them on the boat. He took his disciples aside and said to them, "watch and be aware of the leaven of the Pharisees and the leaven of Herod." And they (the disciples) talked among themselves saying that they did not have any loaves. And knowing this, he (Jesus) said to them, "why are saying among yourselves that you do not have any loaves? Do you not yet know or understand (οὔπω νοεῖτε οὐδὲ συνίετε)? Is your heart hardened? Having eyes do you not see and having ears do you not hear? And do you not remember? When I broke the five loaves for the five thousand, how many baskets full of loaf pieces did you gather?" And they said to him, "twelve." "When I broke the seven loaves for the four thousand, how many very large baskets abundantly filled (πληρώματα) with loaf pieces did you take up?" And they said to him, "seven." And he said to them, "do you not yet understand (Οὔπω συνίετε)?" (Mark 8:14–21)

Once again after a ritual meal (Mark 8:1–9) the disciples find themselves in a boat: "Now they (the disciples) had neglected to bring loaves; and they had only one loaf with them on the boat" (Mark 8:14). Did the disciples have bread on this boat or not? The readers of Mark note that they did not have *loaves* but they did have the one *loaf*. So then how are these readers to understand the meaning of the disciples having one loaf with them in the boat?

In the first ritual meal in Mark (Mark 6:30–44), in a Jewish place, five loaves were broken and twelve regular-sized baskets of loaf fragments

---

that some of the disciples ate the loaves with unclean hands, that is, unwashed. For the Pharisees and all the Jews do not eat [the loaves] unless they hold their hands in a fist" (ἐὰν μὴ πυγμῇ, Mark 7:1–3). The episode here is emphatically not about the failure to practice some sort of kosher food laws in the Markan house churches, but about the validity of a particular ritual practice prior to meals which may have been a point of controversy in the house churches: "washing in a fist (πυγμῇ)." The narrative of Mark considers this practice to be a part of the Oral Torah as opposed to the Written Torah and therefore not binding on the house churches. In the narrative this episode clears the way for the second ritual meal narrative in a Gentile place (near Caesarea Philippi) that will overtly include Gentiles in the restored creation (seven loaves; seven baskets).

26. Peterson, "Composition," 196, understands the clear link in the two boat scenes at Mark 6:52 and 8:20 but surprisingly does not point out how the first boat scene (Mark 4:35–41) concerning baptism sets the stage for the next two concerning Eucharist (the loaves).

were gathered. There the gathering of the Jewish remnant of the five thousand (see Acts 4:4), five loaves (with two fish) in twelve baskets, was equated with the domination of chaos (water) by the resurrected Jesus (Mark 6:52) who rose from the waters to be in the boat with the disciples and calm the wind (Mark 6:51). In the second ritual meal (Mark 8:1–9), in a Gentile place, seven loaves were broken and seven very large baskets of loaf fragments were gathered. And here again the gathering of the Gentiles in the ritual meal, seven loaves in seven very large baskets, leads the readers of Mark to recognize the resurrected identity of Jesus of Nazareth. This time with a twist.

The narrative draws all of this together in the questions Jesus now asks his disciples about the numbers of loaves and baskets in the two ritual meals (Mark 8:19-20). The readers of Mark are quite obviously again supposed to contrast the incomprehension of the disciples with their own comprehension of what the answers to these questions convey. While the disciples still do not understand (οὔπω συνίετε) the readers come to realize the import of Mark 8:14: "Now they (the disciples) had neglected to bring loaves; and they had only one loaf with them on the boat." The readers of Mark realize, just as in the earlier episode, in which the resurrected Jesus rises into the boat with the disciples, that in having the one loaf with them in the boat they have the resurrected Jesus of Mark 4:35–41. He is present in the one loaf of their Eucharist, the inclusive meal of Jews (twelve baskets of loaf fragments) and Gentiles (seven baskets of loaf fragments) that enacts the sacred space of the Sabbath, the redemption and restoration of the creation.

There is purposeful narrative progression in Mark's portrayal of the lack of comprehension on the part of the disciples in the narrative of Mark. But this lack of comprehension is for the purpose of leading the readers of Mark toward comprehension, their understanding of the presence of the corporeal resurrected Jesus in the one loaf, the ritual gathering of the inclusive Markan house churches. Jesus, just as he was, is the one baptized under the waters of the sea and resurrected to calm the wind and the waters. Jesus walking on the waters of chaos reassures the disciples that indeed "it's me" and climbs into the boat with the disciples and calms the wind. In the meals of the five loaves and two fish and seven loaves and some fish, Jews with Gentiles, there is present the restored creation, the corporeal resurrected Jesus. So finally there is the one loaf with the disciples in the boat, the gathering of the Jews from Jewish places and the gathering of Gentiles from Gentile places into one place, the one loaf of the Eucharist of the Markan house churches. This ritual space is sacred space, the redeemed and restored creation, the destroyed and resurrected body of Christ.

My teacher and friend Melissa Sellew was absolutely right to agree with her teacher Helmut Koester in proposing that the text of Mark evolved from an original version to the versions we encounter in the second and even third centuries. And she was absolutely right to argue that certain narrative features of Mark, such as the increasing incomprehension of the disciples within large spans of the narrative, points to a very early version of Mark that encompassed the so-called great omission in Luke's use of the Mark's Gospel. Melissa Sellew's further contribution was to point out to us how the narrative of Mark manipulates the desired understanding of the readers of Mark by means of the increasing and overt lack of understanding on the part of Jesus' closest "learners." What I have offered in this short essay is a description of how this latter narrative feature, so clearly marked out by Melissa Sellew, might well have functioned within a reality created by the ritual practices of Baptism and Eucharist in the Markan house churches.

Works Cited

Bobertz, Charles A. *The Gospel of Mark: A Liturgical Reading*. Grand Rapids: Baker Academic, 2016.

———. "Our Opinion Is in Accordance with the Eucharist and the Eucharist Confirms Our Opinion: Irenaeus and the *Sitz im Leben* of Mark's Gospel." *Studia Patristica* 65 (2013) 79–90.

———. "'That by His Passion He Might Purify the Water': Ignatius of Antioch and the Beginning of Mark's Gospel." *Foundation and Facets Forum* 3 (2014) 91–98.

Bornkamm, Günther. "The Stilling of the Storm in Matthew." In *Tradition and Interpretation in Matthew*, edited by Günther Bornkamm, 52–57. Translated by Percy Scott. New Testament Library. Philadelphia: Westminster, 1963.

Kermode, Frank. *The Genesis of Secrecy: On the Interpretation of Narrative*. Charles Eliot Norton Lectures 1977–1978. Cambridge: Harvard University Press, 1979.

Koester, Helmut. "History and Development of Mark's Gospel (From Mark to *Secret Mark* and 'Canonical' Mark)." In *Colloquy on New Testament Studies: A Time for Reappraisal and Fresh Approaches*, edited by B. C. Corley, 35–57. Macon, GA: Mercer University Press, 1983.

Lambdin, Thomas O., trans. "The Gospel of Thomas." In *The Nag Hammadi Library in English*, edited by James M. Robinson, 124–38. Coptic Gnostic Library Project. 3rd ed. San Francisco: Harper & Row, 1988.

Mack, Burton. *A Myth of Innocence: Mark and Christian Origins*. Philadelphia: Fortress, 1988.

Petersen, Norman R. "The Composition of Mark 4:1–8:26." *Harvard Theological Review* 73 (1980) 185–217.
Scroggs, Robin, and Kent I. Groff. "Baptism in Mark: Dying and Rising with Christ." *Journal of Biblical Literature* 92 (1973) 531–48.
Sellew, Melissa (Philip) Harl. "Secret Mark and the History of Canonical Mark." In *The Future of Early Christianity: Essays in Honor of Helmut Koester*, edited by Birger Pearson, 242–57. Minneapolis: Fortress, 1991.
Smith, Morton. *Clement of Alexandria and a Secret Gospel of Mark*. Cambridge: Harvard University Press, 1973.

2

Figs, Pigs, and Imperial Rome

Jesus and the Barren Fig Tree in Mark 11

STEPHEN POTTHOFF

The following study investigates the symbolism behind the vexing story of Jesus withering the fruitless fig tree, an account Mark (11:12–14, 20–25) combines with the Temple-cleansing episode and places the day after Jesus' triumphal Palm Sunday entry into Jerusalem riding on a donkey. Biblical scholarship in recent decades has focused on the fig tree primarily as a symbol of the Temple, devoting relatively little attention to the fig as a symbol of Rome. Rome's sacred fig tree, the *Ficus Ruminalis*, grew at the center of the ancient city, featured prominently in Rome's foundation myth, and was reported to have withered during the reign of the emperor Nero, exactly that time frame during (or right after) which Mark is thought to have written his gospel. To the degree that the fig tree in Mark 11 represents Rome, Mark's story casts Jesus as an agent of divine judgment against Rome—its founders, its divinized rulers, and its original patron gods. As a messiah who sacrifices his own life (Mark 10:45) as "a ransom for many," Jesus' victory in Mark is not the violent, military one of either a Roman emperor or a Davidic messiah king, but rather of a peaceful prophet who proclaimed God's rule in the form of social justice, healing of the sick, feeding of the hungry, and liberation of the poor and demon-possessed from bondage.

Biblical Symbolism of the Fig Tree: Blessing and Judgment

In the literature of the Hebrew Bible, the edible common fig (*Ficus carica*) receives frequent mention and bears a host of contrasting, even contradictory symbolic meanings. A staple of the Mediterranean diet since prehistoric times, the fig tree is the first identifiable tree species mentioned by name in the Bible. After Adam and Eve eat from the tree of the knowledge of good and evil in the Garden of Eden, they recognize their nakedness and sew loincloths for themselves from the leaves of a fig tree (Gen 3:6–7). To many Jewish and early Christian interpreters, this suggests that the tree of knowledge itself was a fig tree, though the apple becomes the preferred candidate for the forbidden fruit in medieval Christianity.[1] The primeval association of the fig with sexuality and fertility is reflected not only in the story of the Fall, but also in the erotic love poetry of the Song of Solomon, in which a bride calls to her beloved: "The fig tree puts forth its figs, and the vines are in blossom; they give forth fragrance. Arise, my love, my fair one, and come away" (2:13 NRSV).

In the story of the fall, however, Adam and Eve's sexual awakening results both in the experience of shame, as well as God's cursing of Eve with the agony of childbirth and subordination to Adam. Adam, in turn, must henceforth take up agriculture, tilling the soil God has cursed with weeds. In addition, Adam and Eve's awakening results in the loss of eternal life when God banishes the primal couple from the Garden, lest they "become like one of us . . . and take also from the tree of life, and eat, and live forever" (Gen 3:22). Banned from Eden by cherubim and a flaming sword, Adam and Eve go forth to bear two sons whose rivalry, instigated ultimately by God's favoritism, introduces violence and murder into the world: After God prefers the shepherd Abel's offering of sheep to agriculturalist Cain's grain offering, Cain murders his own brother out of jealousy, and is cursed by God to wander the earth before settling in the land of Nod, east of Eden (Gen 4:1–16). In the ancient origin stories of the Hebrew people, then, the fig tree occupies a decidedly ambivalent position associated both with God's blessings of fertility and abundance, and with God's curse and judgment, which introduce pain, violence, and death into human existence. Such a polarity between blessing and curse, judgment and mercy, life and death, characterizes the

---

1. Krauss, *Das Paradies*, 75; Altman, *Sacred Trees*, 39; Telford, *Barren Temple*, 134, 190.

symbolism of the fig tree throughout the Hebrew Bible, but also, as we shall see, in the foundation myth of the city of Rome, where a nurturing fig tree is similarly eclipsed by human violence and murderous rivalry between brothers. Not surprisingly, a similar ambivalence of meaning characterizes the portrayal of fig trees in the Christian scriptures of the New Testament as well.

The long-troublesome account of Jesus cursing the fruitless fig tree in Mark's Gospel directly follows the story of Jesus' final entry into Jerusalem. While Mark splits the story into two parts to frame the well-known account of Jesus' demonstration against the money changers in the Temple, Matthew (21:18-22) locates the same story as a single narrative unit after the Temple incident, whereas Luke omits the story entirely. As Mark recounts the story:

> On the following day, when they came from Bethany, he was hungry. Seeing in the distance a fig tree in leaf, he went to see whether perhaps he would find anything on it. When he came to it, he found nothing but leaves, for it was not the season for figs. He said to it, "May no one ever eat fruit from you again." And his disciples heard it . . .
> In the morning as they passed by, they saw the fig tree withered away to its roots. Then Peter remembered and said to him, "Rabbi, look! The fig tree that you cursed has withered." Jesus answered them, "Have faith in God. Truly I tell you, if you say to this mountain, 'Be taken up and thrown into the sea,' and if you do not doubt in your heart, but believe that what you say will come to pass, it will be done for you. So I tell you, whatever you ask for in prayer, believe that you have received it, and it will be yours. Whenever you stand praying, forgive, if you have anything against anyone; so that your Father in heaven may also forgive you your trespasses." (Mark 11:12-14, 20-25)

On the surface level, Mark's story of Jesus withering the fruitless fig tree poses a host of serious problems. Why would Jesus curse a fig tree for bearing no fruit when it was not even the season for figs? In turn, even if this story serves to demonstrate Jesus' power and the power of faith in prayer, his seemingly capricious assault on an innocent fig tree hardly models the forgiveness he emphasizes at the end of Mark's account. Indeed, Jesus' outburst seems more at home in the *Infancy Gospel of Thomas*, where Jesus as a boy does not limit his withering capabilities to trees, inflicting them on an unfortunate playmate as well (*Inf. Gos.*

Thom. 3:2).² One popular nineteenth-century theory argued that Jesus cursed the fig tree for being pretentious: Since fruit buds appear on fig trees before leaves, the tree was pretending to deliver ripe figs out of season when in fact it had none to offer and therefore deserved Jesus' wrath.³ Upholding the historical reliability of the episode despite Mark's problematic note (11:13) that "it was not the season for figs," F. F. Bruce, continuing the historical-rationalist approach pursued by some nineteenth-century scholars, has suggested that Jesus, seeing no fruit on the tree from the previous season (Arabic *taqsh*), knew that the tree was infertile and therefore expendable as a symbol of Jerusalem's coming fate.⁴ Literary-critical approaches have been less concerned with, or rejected, the historicity of the account, viewing it instead as an outgrowth of Jesus' parable in Luke 13:6-9 about a vineyard owner who ordered a fig tree cut down after finding no figs on it for three years in a row.⁵ Like many biblical scholars before them, Marcus Borg and John Crossan have more recently argued that the "obvious contradiction between the two aspects of the incident is Mark's way of warning us to take the event symbolically rather than historically."⁶

Whatever the historical kernel of the story might be, however, it is easy to understand why many interpreters have chosen to focus on the more symbolic or figurative dimension of the story. In the Hebrew Bible, living, fruitful fig trees often signify God's blessing, while withered or barren fig trees signify God's judgment.⁷ Deuteronomy 8:8 lists fig trees among the many and abundant resources of the Promised Land; the prophet Micah, echoing the description in 1 Kgs 4:25 of the security and prosperity Israel enjoyed under King Solomon, promises, quoting the words of his older contemporary Isaiah, that God will bring a new era of peace out of the ruins of Jerusalem and its Temple: "they shall beat their swords into plowshares, and their spears into pruning hooks; nation shall not lift up sword against nation; neither shall they learn war any more; but they shall all sit under their own vines and under their own fig trees, and no one shall make them afraid . . ." (Mic 4:3-4, quoting Isa

---

2. *Inf. Gos. Thom.* 3:2, in Miller, *Complete Gospels*, 382.
3. Telford, *Barren Temple*, 4.
4. Telford, *Barren Temple*, 2-9; Bruce, *New Testament Documents*, 73-74.
5. Telford, *Barren Temple*, 10-15.
6. Borg and Crossan, *Last Week*, 35.
7. Telford, *Barren Temple*, 134-35.

2:3–4). Exemplifying the theme of God's judgment, Hosea (2:12) warns unfaithful Israel: "I will lay waste her vines and her fig trees, of which she said, 'These are my pay, which my lovers have given me.'" Similarly, Jeremiah (8:13) writes: "When I wanted to gather them, says the Lord, there are no grapes on the vine, nor figs on the fig tree; even the leaves are withered, and what I gave them has passed away from them." Rabbinic sources also include legends about trees uprooting themselves or bearing fruit out of season when prompted by spiritually powerful rabbis.[8]

In the Christian scriptures, fig trees are also associated with God's blessing and judgment. Luke, who presents Jesus in a strongly prophetic mold, records the aforementioned parable of the barren fig tree (13:6–9) which Jesus recounts as part of his prophetic call to repentance repeated throughout the gospel. In this parable, the gardener urges the vineyard owner to allow the fig tree, barren for the previous three years, one more year before chopping it down. In the Little Apocalypse of Mark 13 and parallels, Jesus urges his audience to heed the lesson of the fig tree: In the same way that tender springtime leaves presage the coming of summer, so the travails of the present age signify that the eschatological Son of Man is "at the very gates" (Mark 13:28–29). As in the Hebrew Bible, fig trees, then, are associated with divine judgment, but also with the promise of a new era in which God's reign will be restored.

The close association of Jesus' withering the fig tree with his demonstration in the Temple suggests, however, that his action and the story about it constitute a critique focused primarily on the Temple itself rather than Israel as a whole.[9] Though suggesting that the subsequent verses about forgiveness may be a later scribal addition, William Telford argues that the mountain-moving saying (Mark 11:23 and Matt 17:20) may plausibly go back to Jesus himself, and symbolized, for both Jesus and Mark's community, the destruction of the Temple (built on Mount Zion, the Temple Mount) Jesus predicts explicitly in Mark 13:2.[10] In their book *The Last Week*, Marcus Borg and John Crossan interpret the fig tree as a "cipher" for the Temple: Jesus' demonstration in the Temple symbolically shuts down—destroys—the Temple for its lack of fruit in the same way his curse destroys the fruitless fig tree.[11] The fruitlessness of the

8. Telford, *Barren Temple*, 187–89.
9. Ibid., 137.
10. Ibid., 59.
11. Borg and Crossan, *Last Week*, 35–36.

Temple lies not in its system of animal sacrifice or even the institution of the priesthood per se, but rather in its neglect of social justice, and its intimate ties with the foreign domination system imposed by imperial Rome. In decrying the Temple as a "den of robbers," Jesus is quoting the prophet Jeremiah (7:7), who five centuries earlier, following an already well-established prophetic tradition which demanded justice and mercy over sacrifice, had denounced Temple authorities and aristocrats for exploiting the people and taking refuge in God's house.[12]

Starting in 6 CE, Temple authorities became responsible for collecting taxes to pay the annual tribute to Rome.[13] The high priest himself was subordinate to the Roman provincial governor such as Pontius Pilate, and Herod the Great had installed a golden eagle on the gates of the Court of the Gentiles as a "symbol of Rome and its supreme divinity, Jupiter Optimus Maximus."[14] According to Josephus, the unfortunate young men who attempted to rid the Temple of such contamination were summarily executed by the Romans.[15] Some two centuries earlier, outrage over a similar "abomination that desolates" (Dan 12:11; 11:31; Mark 13:14)—the contaminating statue of Zeus that the Syrian Seleucid emperor Antiochus IV Epiphanes erected in the Temple—had sparked the Maccabean revolt. Notably, when the emperor Caligula, demanding to be worshipped as a god, sought in 40–41 CE to erect a statue of himself as Zeus in the Temple, the Jewish historian Josephus (*J.W.* 2.10.4–5) reports that this particular desecrating sacrilege by the Roman Empire was thwarted through direct, nonviolent resistance: Thousands of unarmed men, women and children offered up their lives, and refused to plant crops that year, rather than see the Temple defiled in this way.[16] Similar nonviolent direct action in the form of sit-ins at the governor's residence at Caesarea in 26 CE had forced the newly appointed Pontius Pilate to remove the Roman standards he had ordered erected around the city of Jerusalem by cover of night (Josephus, *Ant.* 18.3.1).[17]

Given the outrage many felt against the Temple's complicity in the system of foreign political and religious domination by the Roman

---

12. Ibid., 44.
13. Ibid., 18.
14. Ibid., 42.
15. Ibid., 43.
16. Ibid., 42; Ehrman, *New Testament*, 242.
17. Ehrman, *New Testament*, 242.

Empire, it is not surprising to find anti-Roman sentiments reflected in early Christian sources. While the Revelation of John, with its fairly transparent characterization of Rome as the whore of Babylon (17:9), might be the most dramatic example, Mark's tale of the Gerasene demoniac (Mark 5:1–20, with parallels in Matt 8:28–34 and Luke 8:26–39), exemplifies anti-Roman sentiment in an exorcism story containing intriguing parallels with the story of Jesus' cursing the hapless fig tree. Encountering a violently possessed man living among the tombs, Jesus forces the possessing spirits to identify themselves as "Legion," the designation for a division of over five thousand soldiers in the Roman army, subsequently casting them into an unfortunate herd of swine which careen headlong off a cliff to their deaths in the Sea of Galilee. Given that pigs were unclean animals according to kosher regulations (Lev 11:7) but the preferred sacrificial animal offered to Zeus, the Gerasene demoniac story reflects not merely anti-Roman sentiment, but also anti-Seleucid sentiment since Antiochus IV had erected an altar to Zeus in the Temple two centuries earlier.

As Ched Myers notes in his political reading of Mark's Gospel, the Gerasene demoniac story symbolizes and dramatizes Jesus' victory over Roman imperialism, and the Roman army, in multiple ways. The story itself is filled with military language and symbolism exemplified by Jesus' "dismissal" of the swine and their subsequent "charge" into the lake, an image which also recalls Yahweh's drowning of the pharaoh and his army in the sea (Exod 15:4). Myers also sees an allusion to historical events in Mark's setting of the story in the region of Gerasa. In a brutal retaliatory attack near the end of the First Jewish Revolt, Roman soldiers under Vespasian had slaughtered a thousand young men, enslaved surviving family members, then plundered and burned the town of Gerasa to the ground (Josephus, *J.W.* 4.9.1).[18] Jesus' victory over the possessing Legion, then, is for Mark both political and spiritual, as he casts out the spirits of thousands of dead Roman soldiers into the sea whose stormy waters he had just stilled before his encounter with the demoniac (Mark 4:35–41).

As Myers and others have elucidated, however, Mark challenges and undermines Rome's authority and power from the very beginning by titling his story of Jesus a "gospel." The term "gospel" (meaning good news, glad tidings, from the Greek *euangelion*) has its origins in Roman imperial propaganda which imparted divinity to Caesar, the Roman emperor whose accession to power, military victories, and announcements

18. Myers, *Binding the Strong Man*, 190–91.

were all "glad tidings" with sacred authority. By announcing the "good news of Jesus Christ, the Son of God" in his opening verse (Mark 1:1), Mark presents Jesus the anointed as the true, divinely sanctioned king, thereby "taking dead aim at Caesar and his legitimating myths."[19] Later in Mark's Gospel, a similarly subversive message underlies Jesus' clever answer to those who sought to entrap him with a question about whether it was lawful or not to pay the widely despised Roman poll tax, an ever-present reminder of Roman imperial dominion and oppression (Mark 12:13–17). Requesting his challengers produce a Roman denarius used to pay the tax, Jesus directs attention to the image and inscription of Caesar, the "August and Divine Son," on the coin. In responding (Mark 12:17) with the well-known "Give to the emperor the things that are the emperor's, and to God the things that are God's," Jesus avoids advocating either payment or nonpayment of the tax; yet, to any observant Jew, rendering anything unto the divine Caesar, rather than God, would be a violation of both the first and second commandments, which forbid the worship of other gods, and the worship of idols or images (Exod 20:3–4). Without saying it outright, Jesus reminds his Jewish audience that their allegiance and tribute belong to God and God alone.[20] Mark's glad tidings of, and about, Jesus are thus fundamentally subversive, challenging Roman imperial might, authority, and oppression with the message of an alternative empire in which the sick and possessed are healed, the hungry are fed, the poor are held up, and the captives are set free.

Ficus Ruminalis: The Fig Tree as a Symbol of Rome

While the biblical symbolism of fig trees and the anti-Roman dimension of Jesus' Temple demonstration have been thoroughly studied in recent decades, anti-imperial sentiments in Mark's Gospel and beyond suggest another dimension of meaning in the story of Jesus cursing the fig tree which might have been at play for Mark and many in his audience. As William Telford addresses in a seldom-cited follow-up article to his influential *Barren Temple and Withered Tree*, the fig tree was also a well-recognized symbol of the city and empire of Rome, figuring prominently in the story of its founders.[21] In his *Life of Romulus* (3.1–4.2), the

19. Ibid., 124.
20. Ibid., 310–12.
21. Telford, "More Fruit," 301–2.

first-century historian Plutarch (c. 46–120 CE) recounts the most well-attested version of Rome's foundation myth, which was revived and reinterpreted during the reign of Caesar Augustus.[22] Augustus founded and legitimated his authority and power as ruler by tracing his family line back to Romulus, Rome's founder, thereby also establishing his descent from both Mars, the divine father of Romulus and Remus; and Venus, mother of Aeneas and ancestor of Rhea Silvia, the twins' mother. Plutarch's version of the Romulus and Remus tale begins with Amulius and Numitor, two brothers in the royal lineage of Aeneas in competition for the throne. Amulius wins out over his brother through his superior wit and gains the kingdom, but fearing future rivals from his brother's line, he forces Numitor's daughter Ilia/Rhea Silvia to become a Vestal Virgin. Violating her vow of perpetual virginity, Rhea Silvia becomes pregnant with twin boys, but is saved from execution through the intercession of Amulius' daughter Antho. When King Amulius sees the superhuman size and beauty of the newborn Romulus and Remus, he orders his servant Faustulus to cast them in the river. Placing the infants in a trough, Faustulus goes to the river but finds it swollen and overflowing, and simply leaves the trough on the river bank, where it is swept up by the waters. As Plutarch continues:

> Now there was a wild fig-tree hard by, which they called Ruminalis, either from Romulus, . . . or best of all, from the suckling of the babes there . . . Here, then, the babes lay, and the she-wolf of story here gave them suck, and a woodpecker came to help in feeding them and to watch over them. Now these creatures are considered sacred to Mars, and the woodpecker is held in especial veneration and honour by the Latins, and this was the chief reason why the mother was believed when she declared that Mars was the father of her babes. And yet it is said that she was deceived into doing this, and was really deflowered by Amulius himself, who came to her in armour and ravished her.
> (*Life of Romulus* 4.1–2, trans. Bernadotte Perrin)

Both textual and archaeological sources testify to the significance this foundational fig tree, the *Ficus Ruminalis*, held as a symbol of the power and vitality of Rome. Like fig trees in the Hebrew Bible, fig trees in Roman culture and legend are associated with fertility and new life, the preeminent "*symbol of creative potency and fertility.*"[23] As classicist

22. Zanker, *Power of Images*, 193–95, 205.
23. Telford, "More Fruit," 278, italics original.

George Hadzsits notes, Roman historian Varro (116–27 BCE) records that shepherds in very ancient times had planted the original *Ficus Ruminalis* by a shrine to Rumina, a milk goddess associated with the suckling of animals.[24] Varro and Pliny the Elder both explain the association between Rumina and the fig tree as inspired by the milky sap fig trees produce, and Plutarch records that even in his era Rumina, as the goddess of nursing mothers, was still worshipped with milk offerings.[25] Because wild fig trees (and specifically the wasps they host) were used to artificially fertilize cultivated figs, the pairing of these trees, as reflected in the sexual pairing of Mars and Rhea Silvia in the Romulus myth, was associated with human intercourse and procreation, the wild fig viewed as male, the cultivated fig as female. This process of caprification was apparently given ritual expression in the *Nonae Caprotinae*, a Roman summer festival in which women used wild fig branches, together with the milky sap offered to Juno, as a means to promote fertility.[26] Trees and plants in Greco-Roman culture were frequently associated with divinity, as exemplified by the grape vine in the mysteries of Dionysus, or the oak at Dodona which delivered oracles of the goddess Dione, and later of Zeus through the rustling of its leaves.[27] Yet, it was not only the grapevine, but particularly the fig tree which was sacred to Dionysus, "who produced and protected its fruit and was known at times to dwell in it."[28] In his efforts to promote and ensure Rome's fertility and prosperity, Caesar Augustus supported the construction of temples dedicated both to Venus Genetrix, and to Mars. Garlands of figs, grapes and other fruits adorn the Augustan Ara Pacis (Altar of Peace), whose lovely image of the goddess of Peace/Venus/Mother Earth with infants and fruit in her lap symbolizes beautifully the fertility and abundance of the Augustan Golden Age."[29]

The Augustan era Roman historian Livy records that a statue of Romulus and Remus being nursed by the she-wolf was placed near the *Ficus Ruminalis* in 296 BCE.[30] As far back as 137 BCE, Roman coins minted under Sextus Pompeius depict the shepherd Faustulus, and the *Ficus Ru-*

24. *Res Rusticarum* 2.114.5, in Hadzsits, "Vera Historia," 305–7.
25. Hadzsits, "Vera Historia," 305, 315.
26. Telford, "More Fruit," 278–79.
27. Hageneder, *Heritage of Trees*, 89–90; Altman, *Sacred Trees*, 49.
28. Telford, "More Fruit," 289.
29. Zanker, *Power of Images*, 172–75; fig. 135.
30. Livy, *History of Rome* 10.23.12, in Telford, "More Fruit," 299n174.

minalis, with birds in its branches, shading the wolf and twins.[31] Under Caesar Augustus, the Lupercal cave at the foot of the Palatine Hill, the traditional location where the mother wolf nursed Romulus and Remus under the *Ficus Ruminalis*, was rebuilt and served as the site of ancient rituals associated with Rome's mythic early history.[32] The Ara Pacis, whose imagery promoted the new golden age of peace and prosperity under Augustan rule, included an image of Faustulus and Mars standing in wonder as they observe the miraculously rescued royal twins being nursed by the she wolf under the sacred fig.[33] The first-century Roman historian Pliny the Elder (23–79 CE) reports in his lifetime that a fig tree known as the *Ficus Ruminalis* still stood in the Roman Forum at the center of the city, and was considered sacred as a "reminder of the fig-tree under which the nurse of Romulus and Remus first tended the founders of our empire" (*Nat.* 15.77, trans. John Healy). In addition, one of the marble reliefs (known as the "Trajan Reliefs"), unearthed in the Roman Forum in 1872, depicts the sacred fig tree as well, and may have been installed during Trajan's reign (98–117 CE) as part of a balustrade surrounding the sacred tree itself.[34]

Classical archaeologist Rabun Taylor suggests that trees such as the *Ficus Ruminalis* in the Roman Forum may also have been adorned with special hanging ornaments known as *oscilla* intended as votive offerings to the divinities associated with special trees.[35] Termed "satyric images" (*saturica signa*, images of satyrs) by Pliny the Elder, such pictorial ornaments frequently adorned gardens in Pliny's day, continuing a long tradition of hanging small images in temples, sanctuaries, tombs and sacred groves.[36] At the same time, trees in the Roman world could be considered either lucky or unlucky (*arbor felix* or *arbor infelix*), the unlucky trees often understood to attract spirits of the dead who had not been given proper burial. In such cases, *oscilla* may have served an apotropaic (protective) function, driving away unhappy spirits of the dead thought to congregate around certain trees such as the elm Vergil (*Aeneid* 6.292) describes at the gates of the Underworld, which teemed with "shades of

31. Ghey et al., *Catalogue*, 235.1.1–14.
32. Zanker, *Power of Images*, 206.
33. Ibid., 205–6, fig. 158.
34. Ramage and Ramage, *Roman Art*, 204–5; Richardson, *Topographical Dictionary*, 292–93; Carter, "So-Called Balustrades," 314–15; Jenkins, "Trajan Reliefs," 77–78.
35. Taylor, "Roman Oscilla," 91.
36. Ibid., 87–90.

the restless dead."[37] Calling to mind Jesus' victory over the legion of spirits possessing the demoniac at Gerasa, the hanging of *oscilla* may thus in some cases have served an exorcistic function in the case of those trees unlucky enough to attract restless spirits of the dead. Like Vergil's elm, fig trees were also sometimes associated with the Underworld, as in the site near Eleusis in Greece named after the *Erineos* (wild fig tree) said to mark the spot where Hades had abducted Persephone and brought her down to the realm of the dead.[38]

As Telford documents, the Romans paid close attention to trees, for their health and behavior were understood to be intimately tied in with the vitality and fate of Rome and its rulers.[39] The future Augustus rejoiced in the miraculously rapid growth of a palm spared by his adopted father Julius Caesar during his campaign against republican opponents in Spain: As a symbol both of victory, and the sacred tree of Apollo, this palm, which also attracted doves to roost in its branches, prefigured for the young Octavian his future rise to power.[40] In the Roman world, Telford concludes, "the sudden blossoming or withering of a tree" served as a "portent of either good fortune or disaster, of blessing (in Jewish terms) or judgment."[41] Particularly significant for our analysis of Mark's story of Jesus withering the fig tree is Pliny the Elder's note that the *Ficus Ruminalis* "prophesies some future happening whenever it shrivels up; then it is replanted thanks to the priests" (*Nat.* 15.77). In this regard, the Roman historian Tacitus records that, in 58 CE during the reign of the emperor Nero, the withering of the *Ficus Ruminalis* was taken as an evil portent, but the tree subsequently revived (*Annals* 13.58). Given the ancient tradition that has long associated Mark with Rome and the persecution of Christians in 64 CE under Nero, the story of Jesus withering a fig tree would likely for Mark and his community have brought to mind the *Ficus Ruminalis* whose shriveling could portend Rome's downfall.[42] Some ten years later, the emperor Nero's death was understood to be foretold by the withering of an entire laurel grove.[43]

37. Ibid., 86.
38. Telford, "More Fruit," 297.
39. Ibid., 293–300.
40. Ibid., 293–94.
41. Ibid., 296.
42. Harris, *Understanding the Bible*, 334.
43. Telford, "More Fruit," 297.

Like the biblical fig, then, the *Ficus Ruminalis* could signal divine blessing, nurture, and life, or divine disfavor, disaster and death. In Plutarch's account of Rome's origins, the sacred fig embodies on the one hand maternal care, nurture, and protection by shading the she-wolf who nurses the infant twins. On the other hand, the woodpecker and she-wolf of the patriarchal war god Mars reflect the perpetual cycle of violence and bloodshed that lie at the very heart of Rome as a city and empire. Unlike Adam and Eve, Romulus and Remus are born at the center of violent conflict between royal brothers which almost claims their young lives. This violence carries over into the following generation, when the growing rivalry between Romulus and Remus ends in Remus's death after Romulus appears to be favored over his brother by the gods in a bird augury contest.[44] Like the trees of knowledge and life in the Garden of Eden, Rome's original, maternal fig tree is eclipsed symbolically by Mars, who embodies the divinely sanctioned violence at the foundation of the imperial domination system.

In the Augustan era, Mars rose to new prominence after Octavian (by this time Caesar Augustus) fulfilled his vow to build a temple to Mars the Avenger, to whom he attributed his victory over Julius Caesar's assassins in the battle at Philippi in 42 BCE. Built in the Forum of Augustus some forty years after this battle, the Augustan temple of Mars Ultor featured a statue of the war god, reinterpreted through the Romulus myth as patron god of the Julian family, together with Venus Genetrix, who brought "fertility and prosperity," and probably a statue of the deified Caesar.[45] Images of Aeneas and Romulus stood in the exedrae, with Romulus, Mars' son, celebrated as Rome's first *triumphator* for his single-handed defeat of King Akron of Caenina.[46] The poet Ovid (*Fasti* 5.533) captures the imposing impression the Mars Ultor temple made, with "mighty Mars" watching over Aeneas, Romulus, Augustus, and the Julian family, ever-ready to "unleash savage war from here."[47] Augustus, of course, allied and identified himself with other gods as well, including Jupiter, whose temple had stood on the Capitoline hill for half a millennium. After surviving a lightning strike which killed a slave lighting his

---

44. Morford and Lenardon, *Classical Mythology*, 548–49.
45. Zanker, *Power of Images*, 195–97.
46. Ibid., 203.
47. Ibid., 113.

way, Augustus built a small marble temple on the site.[48] On the famous carved onyx Gemma Augustea, Augustus is portrayed as Jupiter enthroned, the eagle of Zeus below him, with the goddess Roma admiring him to his right.[49] Through imperial portraiture and in other arenas, Caesar's successors continued to associate themselves closely with the gods, and it is these divinized rulers who are cast as the beasts in the visions of John's Revelation (chapters 13 and 17).

It was with Nero, though, that the golden age of Augustus, and the Julio-Claudian dynasty, came to an epically catastrophic and violent close. Occurring the same year that Nero killed his own mother, the withering of the *Ficus Ruminalis* would have suggested to many that Rome, through Nero's disastrous reign, had fallen out of favor with the gods who protected it. Such fears must have received dramatic confirmation when the temple of Jupiter Optimus Maximus, Rome's ancient protector, burned to the ground in the course of the civil war following Nero's death, which had been foretold by the withered laurel grove. Capturing vividly the traumatic impact of this event in the psyche of Rome's citizens, Tacitus describes the fire which claimed Jupiter's ancient temple in 69 CE as "the most lamentable and appalling disaster in the whole history of the Roman commonwealth" (*Histories* 3.72, trans. Kenneth Wellesley). Indeed, Tacitus adds, the burning of Jupiter's temple caused many in Rome "to believe that the empire was coming to an end."[50] Christians would have remembered vividly Nero's brutality following the fire five years earlier, which had destroyed a good portion of the city of Rome. Seeking a scapegoat after rumors spread that he was responsible for the fire, Nero rounded up Christians, sending them to be torn apart by dogs, crucified, and then set afire to light his gardens at night (Tacitus, *Annals* 15.44). John's Revelation (17:8–11), referring obliquely to a legend that Nero would return from the grave to exact vengeance on his enemies, promises the final destruction of this brutal emperor and the empire he had ruled.

---

48. Ibid., 108.
49. Ramage and Ramage, *Roman Art*, 133–34; Zanker, *Power of Images*, 230–31.
50. Tacitus, *Histories* 4.54, as quoted in Incigneri, *Gospel to the Romans*, 160.

Jesus of Nazareth, Vanquisher of Rome

After surveying a large body of evidence demonstrating the importance of the fig in Greco-Roman culture and history, Telford acknowledges that Gentile Christians may have seen in Jesus' withering of the fig tree a "blasting" of Dionysus, of emperor cult, or parallels with the withering of the *Ficus Ruminalis* (and laurel grove) during Nero's reign.[51] Ultimately, though, Telford upholds the conclusion he reached earlier in *Barren Tree and Withered Temple* that Mark intended this story primarily to symbolize Jesus' curse upon and rejection of the Jerusalem temple.[52] However, given the prominence of the *Ficus Ruminalis* in Rome's origin myth, Augustan iconography and propaganda, not to mention its central location in the Roman Forum, it seems evident that the fig tree continued during the first century and beyond to function as a widely recognized symbol of Rome and her empire. Given the rich symbolic and historical significance of the sacred fig, Mark's story of Jesus withering the fig tree serves to cast Jesus as an agent of divine judgment not merely against the Jerusalem temple, but against Rome itself—her ancestors, her divinized rulers, and her gods. Mark's confounding note (11:13) that "it was not the season for figs" expresses in part a conviction that the dark season of persecution under Nero and beyond, as well as Rome's dominion over Israel, was soon to end. If, as Brian Incigneri has argued, Mark was writing in Rome later in 71 CE, Jesus' withering of the fig tree signified the end of the Augustan golden age, as well as the end of a corrupt temple-state system.[53] From a literary and symbolic standpoint, Jesus' withering of the fig tree vanquishes Caesar and his empire by targeting Rome at its very roots. As an agent of the Jewish God, whose holy spirit had descended on him like a dove in the inaugural anointing through John's baptism at the beginning of Mark's Gospel, Jesus challenges and defeats the Roman Empire, its ancestors, its emperors, and ultimately Mars, Rome's original patron god. To anyone familiar with Plutarch's account, Jesus' action would have recalled his earlier victory over the spiritual Roman Legion possessing the Gerasene demoniac. In both accounts, Jesus is seen not only to reject Roman imperial power, but to conquer it.

From a narrative and literary standpoint, Jesus' withering of the fig tree serves to frame his demonstration in the Temple, but also dramatizes

51. Telford, "More Fruit," 302, 303.
52. Ibid., 303.
53. Incigneri, *Gospel to the Romans*, 362–63.

in symbolic terms the challenge to Roman imperial authority and ideology embodied in his dramatic, nonviolent entry as victorious peasant messiah into Jerusalem the previous day. Arriving at the time of the spring Passover festival, Jesus, as Borg and Crossan observe, organizes a brilliantly choreographed counterdemonstration to the virtually simultaneous arrival across town of Pontius Pilate, the Roman provincial governor, who every year processed with his military entourage into the city to maintain order and demonstrate Roman imperial power and theology.[54] Following Zechariah's prophecy, Jesus, on the other hand, intends to arrive in Jerusalem not in a battle chariot as a conquering warrior messiah in the Davidic sense, but as a peaceful messiah who will "cut off the war horse from Jerusalem ... and command peace to the nations" (Zech 9:10). At least to Gentile members of Mark's audience, then, Jesus' cursing of the fig tree embodies a challenge to imperial Rome at its very foundation: Jesus, the peaceful prophet messiah who dies "a ransom for many" (Mark 10:45) proclaiming God's imperial rule, is more powerful than Rome, its emperors, its armies, and ultimately, Mars himself, who had protected—or even fathered—the city's founders.

Whether in his conquest over the possessing Roman Legion or withering of the barren fig tree, though, Jesus also symbolically indicts, condemns, and destroys the premier tool of the Roman Empire and its original patron god: warfare and violence. For Mark and his audience, Jesus' victory over Rome, as symbolized by the palm branches spread in front of him, is a nonviolent one, and comes about through his own sacrifice. Read in a literal sense, stories of Jesus withering trees and drowning swine, while entertaining, appear morally ambiguous and problematic at best, not least of all because such violent actions violate central teachings Jesus himself delivers in the Sermon on the Mount. In the Beatitudes, Jesus proclaims: "Blessed are the peacemakers, for they will be called children of God" (Matt 5:9). In the Antitheses (Matt 5:38-41), Jesus rejects the *lex talionis*, the law of retribution. Instead of loving your neighbor and hating your enemies, Jesus commands his audience to "Love your enemies and pray for those who persecute you" (Matt 5:43). In his triumphal entry into Jerusalem riding on a donkey, and in his Temple demonstration, Jesus puts such prophetic teachings into practice, embodying the justice and peace of God's imperial rule as a radical alternative to the divinely sanctioned imperial war machine of Pilate, Caesar Augustus,

54. Borg and Crossan, *Last Week*, 2-5.

and Tiberius. As already noted, the two primary examples of effective resistance to Roman imperial assaults on the Temple both owed their success to the nonviolent tactics the Temple's defenders practiced.

Read in light of the Romulus and Remus story, however, Jesus' withering of the fig tree serves to challenge the power and legitimacy of the Roman Empire in at least one other way as well. On a geopolitical level, Rome's prosperity and vitality as an empire was established and maintained through warfare and violence in the name of Rome's patron gods, particularly Mars and Jupiter. The pairing of sexuality/prosperity and violence was enshrined architecturally in the temples Augustus built in the Forum to Venus and Mars, whose adulterous affair was well known from Greek mythology.[55] As illustrated by Nero's murder of his own mother, as well as of his pregnant wife Poppaea, matricidal rivalry and sexual violence also pervaded imperial family relations (Tacitus, *Annals* 16.5). In his account of the Romulus myth, Plutarch openly discusses doubts about the divine parentage of Rome's founding twins, suggesting that King Amulius himself may have fathered the twins through rape. Expanding on the question of the twins' ambiguous paternity, Plutarch adds the curious note that the Latin word "lupa" designates not only a she-wolf, but also a loose woman. Acca Larentia, the wife of Faustulus, the twins' foster father, was considered such a woman, and yet "in the month of April the priest of Mars pours libations in her honour, and the festival is called Larentalia" (*Life of Romulus* 4.3). Rome's complex foundation myth thus presents Rhea Silvia as the chaste virgin and victim of royal (sexual) violence on the one hand; and Acca Larentia on the other hand as the maternal, nurturing lupa/loose woman/prostitute who raised the abandoned twins under the fig tree. Early followers of Jesus in Mark's community, themselves victims of rape and sexual violence during the Neronian persecutions, might well have applauded the Revelation of John's description of Rome as the "mother of whores and earth's abominations" who is "drunk with the blood of the saints and the blood of the witnesses to Jesus" (Rev 17:5–6).

Though it required—and still requires—many to witness with their very lives, realizing the justice and peace of the divine empire Jesus proclaimed has transformed earthly nations and kingdoms. As Ched Myers notes, Mark's ultimate challenge to Roman imperial violence and power lies in his redefinition of the cross as the gateway to life and liberation.

55. Zanker, *Power of Images*, 195.

In emphasizing Jesus' exhortation to his disciples (Mark 8:34) to "deny themselves and take up their cross and follow me," Mark radically subverts and redefines the horrific instrument of capital punishment and death which lay at the root of Roman imperial power and domination.[56] Like the fig tree in Mark's story, the cross lies at the paradoxical intersection of blessing and curse, judgment and mercy, life and death. In withering the tree of Rome through his own death on the tree of the cross (Acts 5:30; 1 Pet 2:24), Jesus for Mark and other early Christians defeats not just Roman imperial might, but the very power of death itself. Explaining how Christians are baptized into new life through Jesus' death, the apostle Paul concludes (Rom 6:5): "For if we have been united with him in a death like his, we will certainly be united with him in a resurrection like his."

In the complex and paradoxical symbolism of the Revelation of John, Jesus as the sacrificial Lamb and Word of God defeats Rome and all earthly kingdoms, Death, and Hades itself, after which the New Jerusalem can descend (Rev 19-20). In the center of the New Jerusalem sits, in place of the Temple, the Lamb on the throne of God, but also the Garden of Eden. Eden's rivers water the tree of life, which bears fruit throughout the year, while its leaves bring healing to all the nations of the earth (Rev 22:1-3). John's visionary landscape, which localizes Eden in the middle of the New Jerusalem, draws its inspiration in part from the sixth-century-BCE prophet Ezekiel's vision of the Temple restored after the Babylonian destruction: Eden's rivers flowed from the Temple atop God's mountain, watering the trees beyond which feed and heal the people (Ezek 47:12). The localization of Eden at the Temple is also reflected in the palm trees and other vegetal imagery adorning the original Temple built by Solomon (1 Kgs 6:29; 35) which itself carried on a longstanding tradition in the ancient Near East of decorating temples and palaces with paradisiacal imagery.[57] Figs in particular appear as trees and fruits of Eden in the visionary journeys of the fourth and fifth-century Christian Desert Fathers and Mothers, who had moved out into the deserts of Egypt to pursue a life of asceticism and self-denial. One desert father named Patermuthius reported journeying physically to Eden, partaking of paradisiacal fruit, and returning with a giant fig, whose holy fragrance worked many a

---

56. Myers, *Binding the Strong Man*, 428.
57. Stager, "Jerusalem as Eden," 39, 43, 45-46.

cure.⁵⁸ Jesus' withering of the fig tree near the sacred space of the Temple, then, held out the promise not merely of Rome's defeat by Jesus' death on the cross, but also of a return to the Garden of Eden in which all would once again have access to the tree of life, and experience healing and restoration in the eternal presence of Christ and God.

In conclusion, taken literally, Mark's story of Jesus cursing the fig tree has posed serious questions from the very beginning. Even in the Hebrew Bible, fig trees carry a symbolic meaning, in their fruitfulness signifying God's blessing and provision, in their lack of fruit God's judgment against social injustice among the social and religious elite. Reading Mark's story symbolically in light of Rome's foundation myth highlights the extent to which Jesus' final entry into Jerusalem, and his subsequent demonstration in the Temple, targeted the divinely sanctioned military power, theology, and legitimacy of imperial Rome. Proclaiming an alternative kingdom to that of Caesar, Jesus rejected the violence that continues to be the tool of empires in the world today, instead striving to realize, ultimately through the sacrifice of his own life, the sweet fruits of healing, liberation, justice and peace promised by Isaiah, Micah, Zechariah, and many other prophets before and since.

Works Cited

Altman, Nathaniel. *Sacred Trees*. San Francisco: Sierra Club Books, 1994.
Borg, Marcus J., and John Dominic Crossan. *The Last Week: A Day-by-Day Account of Jesus' Final Week in Jerusalem*. San Francisco: HarperCollins, 2006.
Bruce, F. F. *The New Testament Documents: Are They Reliable?* 6th ed. Grand Rapids: Eerdmans, 1981.
Carter, Jesse B. "The So-Called Balustrades of Trajan." *American Journal of Archaeology* 14 (1910) 310–17.
Ehrman, Bart. *The New Testament: A Historical Introduction to the Early Christian Writings*. 3rd ed. New York: Oxford University Press, 2004.
Ghey, Eleanor, and Ian Leins, eds., with contribution by M. H. Crawford. *A Catalogue of the Roman Republican Coins in the British Museum, with Descriptions and Chronology based on M. H. Crawford, Roman Republican Coinage (1974)*. London: British Museum, 2010.
Hadzsits, G. D. "The *Vera Historia* of the Palatine *Ficus Ruminalis*." *Classical Philology* 31 (1936) 305–19.
Hageneder, Fred. *The Heritage of Trees: History, Culture and Symbolism*. Edinburgh: Floris, 2001.
Harris, Stephen L. *Understanding the Bible*. 8th ed. New York: McGraw-Hill, 2011.

---

58. *On Patermuthius* 22, in Ward, ed., *Lives of the Desert Fathers*, 85.

Healy, John, trans. *Natural History: A Selection*, by Pliny the Elder. Penguin Classics. London: Penguin, 1991.
Incigneri, Brian J. *The Gospel to the Romans: The Setting and Rhetoric of Mark's Gospel*. Biblical Interpretation Series 65. Leiden: Brill, 2003.
Jenkins, Anna S. "The 'Trajan Reliefs' in the Roman Forum." *American Journal of Archaeology* 5 (1901) 58–82.
Krauss, Heinrich. *Das Paradies: Eine kleine Kulturgeschichte*. Beck'sche Reihe 1570. Munich: Beck, 2004.
Miller, Robert J., ed. *The Complete Gospels*. 4th ed. Sonoma, CA: Polebridge, 2010.
Morford, Mark P. O., and Robert J. Lenardon. *Classical Mythology*. 5th ed. White Plains, NY: Longman, 1995.
Myers, Ched. *Binding the Strong Man: A Political Reading of Mark's Story of Jesus*. Twentieth-anniversary ed. Maryknoll, NY: Orbis, 2008.
Ramage, Nancy H., and Andrew Ramage. *Roman Art: Romulus to Constantine*. 4th ed. Upper Saddle River, NJ: Pearson, 2005.
Richardson, Lawrence. *A New Topographical Dictionary of Ancient Rome*. Baltimore: Johns Hopkins University Press, 1992.
Stager, Lawrence. "Jerusalem as Eden." *Biblical Archaeology Review* 26 (2000) 36–47.
Taylor, Rabun. "Roman Oscilla: An Assessment." *RES: Anthropology and Aesthetics* 48 (2005) 83–105.
Telford, William R. *The Barren Temple and the Withered Tree: A Redaction-Critical Analysis of the Cursing of the Fig-Tree Pericope in Mark's Gospel and Its Relation to the Cleansing of the Temple Tradition*. Bloomsbury Academic Collections. Biblical Studies. Gospel Interpretation. New York: Bloomsbury, 2015.
———. "More Fruit on the Withered Tree: Temple and Fig-Tree in Mark from a Greco-Roman Perspective." In *Templum Amicitiae: Essays on the Second Temple Presented to Ernst Bammel*, edited by William Horbury, 264–304. Journal for the Study of the New Testament Supplement Series 48. Sheffield: Sheffield Academic, 1991.
Ward, Benedicta, ed. *The Lives of the Desert Fathers*. Translated by Norman Russell. Cistercian Studies Series 34. Kalamazoo: Cistercian, 1981.
Wellesley, Kenneth, trans. *The Histories*, by Tacitus. Penguin Classics. London: Penguin, 1993.
Zanker, Paul. *The Power of Images in the Age of Augustus*. Translated by Alan Shapiro. Jerome Lectures. Ann Arbor: University of Michigan Press, 1990.

3

Double Obfuscation of Class Struggle in Luke 13:10–17

Regulation of Labor, Alienation, and Failed Revolutions

STEVEN J. FRIESEN

The brief narrative in Luke 13:10–17 is found in no other ancient Christian gospel. There are other examples of controversies involving Jesus and healing on the Sabbath,[1] but this is the only narrative in which the antagonist states his objection, which is that healing constitutes work and it is therefore not allowed on the seventh day of the week.

Since the narrative centers on the control of labor, it is perhaps surprising that commentators do not discuss labor in relation to this pericope. The narrative, they tell us, is about ideas or symbols or personal morals. But no one seems to think the pericope is about the topic it discusses—the regulation of labor. Then again, perhaps the silence of the commentariat is not surprising. In western New Testament scholarship there is a long tradition of suppressing issues of labor and economy.[2] These topics are usually assumed to be irrelevant to the study religion, or they are denigrated as part of an allegedly discredited Marxist theoretical framework. Either way, it appears to be an axiom in the discipline that religion is not affected by money or by modes of production.

---

1. See Mark 1:21–31 = Luke 4:31–39; Mark 3:1–6 = Matt 12:9–14 = Luke 6:6–11; Luke 14:1–6; John 5:1–18; 9:1–34.

2. For relevant analysis of this phenomenon, see Boer, "Marxism and the Spatial Analysis of Early Christianity."

This short pericope in Luke's Gospel, however, is full of tension over socioeconomic stratification and the control of labor, and I suspect that our inattention to issues of class struggle in this narrative suggests a reluctance on our part to consider ideology and discourse in relation to production. To get at these suppressed issues I employ Fredric Jameson's method for exploring the "political unconscious" of a narrative, and I argue that class issues were doubly obscured from view in the text, first by treating class conflicts only as disagreements about Sabbath observance and, after that, by abandoning interest in actual Sabbath observance.³ I conclude the chapter with final observations on failed revolutions and the possibilities for transcending alienation embedded in the text.

The Narrative and Recent Interpretation

Luke 13:10–17 comes in the middle of the Lukan Jesus' journey to Jerusalem, directly after the report about the Galileans killed by Pilate (13:1–5) and the parable about the fig tree that was given only one more year to produce fruit (13:6–9). The pericope itself begins like a miracle narrative that is set on a Sabbath while Jesus was teaching in a synagogue. He sees a woman bent over because she "had a spirit of weakness" (πνεῦμα ἔχουσα ἀσθενείας) that had afflicted her for eighteen years. Jesus pronounces her released from that spirit and touches her, after which she straightens up and begins to glorify God. Then the narrative transitions into a controversy as a synagogue leader (ἀρχισυνάγωγος) becomes angry and rebukes the crowd for coming for healing on the Sabbath when work is prohibited. Jesus rebukes the leader as a hypocrite whose own practice contradicts the demands he places on others, and the crowd is delighted. Two sayings about the Kingdom of God follow the pericope (13:18–19, 20–21), and then Jesus continues on his journey toward Jerusalem (13:22).

The history of scholarship related to Luke 13:10–17 distracts us from issues of class struggle, focusing our attention instead on an alleged struggle of ideas between Judaism and Christianity. Such idealist and/or supersessionist interpretation is most clear in the Christian commentary tradition, where male commentators see in this story themes such as the inability of Jews to recognize God's power in Jesus,⁴ the importance of

---

3. Scholars have mostly accepted the first and mostly ignored the second.

4. Marshall, *Gospel of Luke*, 556–59. Michael Wolter's position is less overtly derogatory than this, framed around the woman as a symbol of Jesus' mission to Israel

concern for human welfare above religious obligation,[5] the legitimacy and authority of Jesus' mission to fulfill God's purpose,[6] the way in which meticulous religious legislation can become a tool for the powers of evil,[7] and the rediscovery of the true meaning of the Sabbath as a positive command rather than as a negative prohibition.[8]

Most articles or chapters on this pericope reflect assumptions similar to those in the commentaries, but newer themes have emerged in the shorter formats, two of which deserve our attention here. One of these involves disability studies. This theme may help redirect the academic discussion in the future but so far it is underdeveloped.[9]

The second recent theme in the interpretation of this pericope deals with feminist and gender issues in the text. This trend emerged earlier than disability studies and is more central to my argument. An important early contribution came from Elisabeth Schüssler Fiorenza.[10] Schüssler Fiorenza noted that the story in Luke 13:10–17 has become a central gospel text for the women's movement among Christians, with the woman in the story serving as a symbol for the status of women in churches. She went on to advocate a more robust feminist critical theology of liberation, one that does not seek to demythologize apocalyptic or miraculous texts but rather attempts to translate them into sociopolitical language. The woman in the story, then, becomes a locus for an intersectional exploration of patriarchal domination of women within structures of class, race, gender, nationality, and religion.

(*Gospel according to Luke*, 2:183–89).

5. Fitzmyer, *Gospel according to Luke*, 1009–14; Tew, *Luke*.

6. Green, *Gospel of Luke*, 518–27; and especially Green, "Jesus and a Daughter of Abraham."

7. González, *Luke*, 173–75.

8. Bovon, *Luke 2*, 278–92. The recovery of the Sabbath's true meaning is prominent in Jeffrey's discussion as well, but with a more pastoral interest and a narrower emphasis on the alleviation of personal suffering; Jeffrey, *Luke*, 176–82.

9. Kinukawa, "Miracle Story." Kinukawa concludes that the healing in Luke challenges readers to effect a symbolic (rather than physical) miracle of healing by rejecting the biases of the abled and accepting the disabled as full members of a faith community. Parsons also touched the margins of disability studies, arguing that Luke invoked ancient physiognomic thinking—a system of assessing character through physical appearance—only to undermine such thinking by attributing the woman's disability to Satan rather than to a moral defect. See Parsons, "Ought Not This Daughter of Abraham Be Set Free?"

10. Schüssler Fiorenza, "Liberation, Unity, and Equality," esp. 59–64.

In this chapter I operate within an intersectional paradigm but argue for more attention to the category of class and the socioeconomic aspects of domination.[11] In order to relate the narrative to these class interests I turn to Fredric Jameson, who advocated an approach that connects narratives to class struggles through three phases of interpretation. The first phase is the most narrowly focused, treating the text as a narrative attempt to resolve symbolically an unresolved political conflict. The second phase broadens out to consider the text as one part of larger antagonistic social discourses. The third phase is broadest of all, treating the text and the discourses as a part of the whole historical sequence of modes of production. The residue of several modes are still embedded in the text, and these in turn give us a glimpse of a more fundamental structure: the archaic forms of alienation which still afflict us today.[12]

Labor and the Political Horizon of the Narrative

The first phase of a Jamesonian interpretation examines the text's "political horizon." This involves an analysis of the pericope as a literary creation, examining standard features such as setting, character, plot, conflict, and resolution. The difference from a standard narrative interpretation, however, is that the literary conflict is understood as a symbolic act that refracts a political conflict. This attention to the political horizon should illuminate an ultimate subtext for the narrative—a social contradiction whose resolution would require action, not thought. It should also bring to light a secondary subtext of the narrative—an ideology that attempts the impossible task of bringing closure at the level of thought to that social contradiction.[13] I turn to this first phase in the interpretation of Luke 13:10–17.

11. I employ a broad definition of class that focuses on three hallmarks. Class analysis identifies structural stratification in a socioeconomic system, it proposes asymmetrical relationships between those strata, and it connects those relationships to economic factors in some way. Cf. Vitt, "Class." For a helpful discussion of the varieties of class analysis, see Wright, *Approaches to Class Analysis*. The volume discusses Durkheimian, Weberian, Marxian, Bourdieuian, rent-based, and post-class analysis. Class analysis is different from gradational scales like the two I have published, which only measured amounts of income: Friesen, "Prospects for a Demography"; and Scheidel and Friesen, "Size of the Economy."

12. Jameson, *Political Unconscious*, esp. ch. 1: "On Interpretation: Literature as a Socially Symbolic Act."

13. Jameson, *Political Unconscious*, 74–83.

The setting of this narrative is rendered as generalized and abstract. The broader Lukan context sets the events somewhere on Jesus' journey from Galilee to Jerusalem (9:51) but no other geographic details are given. The specific location is equally vague, described simply as "in one of the synagogues" (13:10), nor are we given any temporal details beyond the statement that this took place on a Sabbath. So the setting of the story encourages readers to understand this not so much as a unique story about a particular encounter in a particular situation, but rather as an encounter involving generic issues that were manifest in some community in some synagogue on some Sabbath.

The characterization in this narrative also lacks specificity. The main character Jesus is the only one named. We then meet an unnamed woman with a chronic malady and an unnamed official described as an archisynagogos, "synagogue leader." There are references to a group of unnamed opponents of Jesus, and to an undifferentiated crowd whose positive response to Jesus is homogeneous. Most of these characters also have little complexity—a woman praises God when she is healed, a healer defends the timing and meaning of his healing, and the crowd rejoices at the deeds of the healer.

The only characters with a hint of complexity in this short narrative are the antagonists, focalized for us in the figure of the archisynagogos.[14] The denunciation of the archisynagogos and others of his ilk as "hypocrites" is our clue to the nature of their complexity—they are actors, orators, dissemblers, portraying themselves as virtuous but hiding their true selves.[15] From the point of view of the text, their hypocrisy revolved precisely around the use of religious institutions to control human labor while not subjecting themselves to those same controls.

The conflict begins when the woman is healed and the archisynagogos criticizes the crowd, saying, "There are six days on which work ought to be done (ἓξ ἡμέραι εἰσὶν ἐν αἷς δεῖ ἐργάζεσθαι); come on those days and be cured, and not on the sabbath day" (13:14).[16] Jesus' reply ends with the punchline, "Ought not this woman, a daughter of Abraham whom

---

14. The narrative is uneven at this point: "But the Lord answered him [singular] and said, "You hypocrites [plural]!" (13:15a). A source critical interpretation might see this as a sign of inept redaction. But from a narratological perspective this shift allows readers to focus on an individual character as a representative of a category of people, in this case, opponents of "the Lord."

15. See LSJ s.v. ὑποκριτής.

16. All biblical quotations come from the NRSV.

Satan bound for eighteen long years, be set free from this bondage on the sabbath day (οὐκ ἔδει λυθῆναι ἀπὸ τοῦ δεσμοῦ τούτου τῇ ἡμέρᾳ τοῦ σαββάτου)?" (13:16). The parallel use of δεῖ in these verses focuses the central normative question that separates antagonist from protagonist: What is necessary on the Sabbath—regulation of labor, or liberation?

At this point, exegetes normally divert our attention away from labor by treating the narrative as a conflict over religious ideas rather than as a class struggle involving actions and production. Exegetes do this primarily by ignoring the status of an archisynagogos as a wealthy community leader. They prefer instead an outdated reconstruction in which archisynagogos was the primary "clergy" of the synagogue, with responsibilities for liturgy, facilities, and administration.[17]

That reconstruction was thoroughly undermined by Rajak and Noy, whose review of the literary and epigraphic evidence demonstrated that the title archisynagogos was given to benefactors and patrons of a synagogue, and not to some hypothesized cleric.[18] While other writers have argued for minor adjustments to the reconstruction of Rajak and Noy,[19] there is now broad agreement that archisynagogoi were members of the wealthiest fraction of a community, men (mostly[20]) who exerted more than their fair share of influence over labor and who accumulated more than their fair share from the production. Commentators on Luke, however, consistently overlook this most distinctive feature of an archisynagogos; namely that he—or occasionally she—was a member of the small class that controlled the means of production in the ancient Mediterranean world.[21]

17. For much of the twentieth century, specialists imagined that all synagogues of the Roman period had a standardized hierarchy that included a group of elders—the *gerousia*—who made up a kind of board of trustees for a synagogue, with an *archisynagogos* as the primary official; see e.g., Schürer, *History of the Jewish People*, 2:423-53.

18. They also argued for varieties of local synagogue institutions, rejecting the theory that there was a standard hierarchy everywhere with the same sets of officers; Rajak and Noy, "*Archisynagogoi*"; Slainero, "La figura del *pater partum*."

19. Lee Levine mostly agreed with their conclusion but moved back toward a standardized notion of synagogue leadership; see Levine, "Synagogue Leadership"; and Levine, "Leadership," in *Ancient Synagogue*, esp. 415-23. Martin followed Goodman in suggesting that the an *archisynagogos* was less of a benefactor in the Jewish homeland where communities were allegedly less status-driven than in Greco-Roman urban settings; see Martin, "Interpreting the Theodotos Inscription"; Goodman, *Ruling Class of Judaea*, esp. 124-33.

20. Brooten, *Women Leaders*, 1-33.

21. On the extent of the ruling class, see Scheidel and Friesen, "Size of the

Once we note what would have been obvious to any ancient audience—the archisynagogos as benefactor or patron of the synagogue and the community—the characters and the plot take on a different hue. The antagonist is a member of the class that extracts surplus from the labor of the crowd. An itinerant teacher who is not subject to this local regime of production comes to the synagogue and heals on the Sabbath. The archisynagogos becomes angry at this infraction. Whether this is a violation of Sabbath labor rules is an open question,[22] but religious ideas are not the primary issue according to the narrative because the antagonist does not confront Jesus about contested ideologies of divine injunctions regarding labor. Rather, the primary issue is control of the laboring class, whom the antagonist does confront *en masse*.[23] He blames the crowd—not Jesus— for the threat to his authority. They are instructed to seek healing only on the six workdays of the week, even though the narrative itself does not describe anyone seeking healing at all, let alone on the Sabbath.

The protagonist responds to this attempt to regulate his labor. He is now called "Lord" (κύριος, 13:15) rather than "Jesus," emphasizing the power struggle in progress. The Lord does not simply address the individual antagonist but employs the vocative plural "hypocrites," castigating the dominant class of which the antagonist is a member.[24] They release farm animals on the Sabbath to relieve thirst, he says, but they object to the release of a daughter of Abraham on the Sabbath to relieve eighteen years of satanic constriction. This counterattack by the protagonist Lord defeats his opponents. They are put to shame and the entire crowd sides with him, rejoicing at his marvelous deeds.

Now we can begin to see the unseeable—what Jameson calls the "ultimate subtext" of a narrative, the social contradiction that "cannot be directly or immediately conceptualized by the text,"[25] the political unconscious that the narrative struggles to avoid. These few sentences in

---

Economy." For an exploration of their importance in a particular region of the Empire, see Zuiderhoek, *Politics of Munificence*.

22. For an general overview of beliefs and practices concerning the Sabbath during this period, see Sanders, *Judaism*, 208–11.

23. Kinukawa comments that in power struggles like this it is often easier for a leader to blame the powerless than to attack a rival powerful figure ("Miracle Story," 304).

24. I describe the object of Jesus' anger as the dominant class because they are distinct from "the whole crowd" (πᾶς ὁ ὄχλος) in 13:17, and they are the ones who object to the healing on the Sabbath (13:16).

25. Jameson, *Political Unconscious*, 82.

Luke 13 evince such a realm of social contradiction, one involving the existence of enforced unequal labor relationships, a mode of production that compels differentiated labor and differentiated accumulation of surplus. My articulation of that ultimate subtext is deceptively and perhaps inappropriately abstract, for the unspeakable—that which "cannot be directly or immediately conceptualized"—is always imminent in a specific and immediate context. For Luke's early audiences, the immediate context for this ultimate subtext would have been the social contradictions of urban life in the eastern Mediterranean region during the early second century CE.[26]

Since the text cannot address the question of whether its particular context of unequal labor relationships is necessary, the narrative instead moves quickly to a secondary subtext—a dispute over the correct ordering of labor inequality. In other words, rather than arguing over why it is necessary for particular groups of people to work more or harder or for less reward than others, Luke 13:10-17 has characters arguing over when it is necessary to work within this regime and whether healing constitutes work. The angry antagonist presents a dominant ideology in which the Sabbath is an instrument for the control of labor, while the protagonist presents a resistant ideology in which the Sabbath critiques the control of labor.

In this way, we approach the end of the first stage of a Jamesonian interpretation of Luke 13:10-17. So far I have argued that the text reflects an unspeakable social contradiction (inescapable inequitable labor relationships) that refracts into an ideological conundrum (the definition of the cessation of labor on the Sabbath), which generates a narrative for the literary—but not actual—resolution of the conflict. In the narrative's resolution, those who attempt to control the labor of the community by means of the Sabbath are put to shame by an itinerant teacher who performs a miraculous healing on the Sabbath and who defends his healing labor by condemning the hypocritical praxis of those who control labor.

But even within the world of the narrative there was no changed praxis, except perhaps for the daughter of Abraham who could now walk upright. The itinerant rabbi's narrative victory is an unconvincing attempt at ideological closure in the spatiotemporal setting of this synagogue/Sabbath. He departs to teach in other towns and villages (13:22), and we readers are left to assume that the crowd of people who participated in

---

26. For the dating of Luke and Acts in the second century, see Pervo, *Dating Acts*.

the class struggle in the synagogue on the Sabbath went back to work the next day.

Class Conflict within the Social Horizon of the Narrative

We now move from the political horizon of the pericope—its literary achievement as a symbolic attempt to resolve a political contradiction—to its social horizon. In this second stage of the analysis we zoom out from the particular character of the narrative and contextualize it as one statement within larger antagonistic discourses of social classes.

Jameson recommended that we begin by identifying the text's smallest units out of which the discourses are constructed. He named these "ideologemes," by which he meant the ideological "raw material" that can be used both to build narratives and to perpetuate antagonistic discourses.[27] Since Luke 13:10–17 is a very short narrative, we can attempt a complete listing of its ideologemes. My list is as follows, in the order of their appearance in the narrative: teaching, synagogue, Sabbath, woman, (spirit of) weakness, God, archisynagogos, anger, healing, crowd, work, lord, hypocrite, domestic animals, daughter, Abraham, Satan, shame, and joy. Within the political horizon of the text these ideologemes functioned as themes, characters, settings, etc. Within this second social horizon they are also the fundamental units that allow the narrative to participate in broader discourses.

Five antagonistic discourses are prominent in the narrative, all of which overlap and reinforce each other.[28] The first we encounter at the beginning of the pericope is ethnoreligious practice. It is manifest in five nouns: Sabbath (5),[29] Abraham, archisynagogos, Satan, and synagogue.

---

27. Jameson, *Political Unconscious*, 87.

28. Jameson's analysis of the social horizon of a text (i.e., this second stage of analysis) strikes me as somewhat mechanical as we shift from treating the text as an artistic production to treating the text as one "statement" in broader discourses. Specifically, the structuralist arrangement of ideologemes into opposing pairs puts a narrative's relational and personal qualities at risk. The discourses are more fluid than the structuralist's severe binaries, overflowing the channels we construct for them. For example, the verb θεραπεύω ("heal, attend to, care for") and the noun ἀσθένεια ("weakness") are part of the discourse on labor in this story, but also on disability. Discourses are pliable, tangled, and affective in their appeal, and so I put more emphasis on them and less emphasis on binary frameworks.

29. Numbers within parentheses indicate the number of times the word occurs within the pericope. If there is no number in parentheses, the word occurs once.

Abraham, Satan, and synagogue are not contested here, but Sabbath and archisynagogos surface as points of contention in the narrative, involving conflicts that are discussed below. The important point here is that as an overt framing discourse, ethnoreligious practice inflects the other discourses.

Labor is a second discourse and it overlaps in part with the first, for references to labor in the pericope occur only in relation to ethnoreligious practice. Here, work (ἐργάζομαι) describes what one does on all days except the Sabbath. Teaching (διδάσκω 2) is in the category of "not work" since it is accepted without comment as a Sabbath activity by all characters in the narrative, by the narrator, and by the implied author. Contested Sabbath activities, however, drive the narrative: healing through touch (θεραπεύω 2; ἐπιτίθημι τὰς χεῖρας); and unleashing a cow or donkey, leading them, and giving them water (λύω 2; ἀπάγω; ποτίζω; βοῦς; ὄνος).

"Heal," however, is an impoverished translation of the verb θεραπεύω in this context. The Greek verb has a semantic range covering various forms of service and care: to serve gods, parents, or masters; to treat someone medically; to train animals; to cultivate land; to prepare food; to mend garments; etc.[30] So θεραπεύειν fits easily within a discourse of labor, even if the English translation does not. The Greek verb, along with the cluster of labor ideologemes in this short narrative, participates specifically in a discourse of required labor, where one must attend to those who are more powerful or must care for those who, like medical patients and work animals, cannot care for themselves.

A third discourse is that of restriction/release, and it permeates the entire narrative. Its vocabulary includes nine of the pericope's twenty-seven verbs—to loosen (λύω 2), to stand up (ἀνακύπτω), to straighten (ἀνορθόω), to oppose (ἀντίκειμαι), to release (ἀπολύω), it is necessary (δεῖ 2), to bind (δέω), to be able (δύναμαι), and to bend over (συγκύπτω)— as well as the nouns weakness (ἀσθένεια 2) and bond (δεσμός). The dominance of this vocabulary makes this narrative part of a discourse of struggle against restraint. It also suggests that the ideological closure in the narrative revolves around release from restrictions.

Gender is the fourth discourse. It is as influential in the narrative as restriction/release, but by way of contrast gender is assumed and never rises to the level of reflection or dispute. The specific feminine vocabulary

30. See LSJ s.v. θεραπεύω.

includes woman (γυνή 2), daughter (θυγάτηρ), six pronouns, and ten verbs with female subjects. The masculine vocabulary is comprised of archisynagogos, God (θεός), Jesus (Ἰησοῦς 2), lord (κύριος), Satan, four pronouns, and thirteen verbs with male subjects.[31] In general, the one female figure is vulnerable while the male figures tend to be powerful, indicating that this narrative participates in the standard patriarchal discourses of its time.

A final crucial discourse involves emotions. These are manifest as responses to events in the narrative, and there are four examples, comprised of two pairs of contrasting responses. One pair comes in reaction to Jesus' healing activity: the restored woman glorifies (δοξάζω) God because of her liberation while the archisynagogos becomes angry (ἀγανακτέω). The other pair of emotional responses comes at the end of the narrative in reaction to Jesus' statements and deeds: his opponents are shamed (καταισχύνω) by the actions of the itinerant rabbi while the whole crowd rejoices (χαίρω). Thus, this fifth discourse overtly pits the archisynagogos against the woman, and Jesus/Lord against his opponents in struggles that are not simply over ideas.

This survey of the ideologemes and the discourses gets us to one goal of examining the social horizon of the text, for in it we begin to see this short narrative as one statement in larger antagonistic discourses.[32] The binary opposition of the archisynagogos against the woman and of the archisynagogos against the crowd takes us to the heart of the matter: the fundamental conflict in this narrative is between a representative of the dominant class and nearly everyone else.[33] In the last half of the narrative there are allusions to others in the dominant class with the plural "hypocrites" (13:15) and with the reference to other opponents of Jesus (13:17). But the author's choice to personalize this class in an individual presents readers with a powerful benefactor who is in conflict with "the whole crowd" (13:17), a dominant figure (and his allies) against the many.

---

31. Not included in these counts are ten male verbs used to indicate men and/ or women, and two pronouns used to indicate men and/or women, four impersonal verbs, and four impersonal pronouns.

32. Jameson, *Political Unconscious*, 85, 88–89.

33. "[Luke] focuses his attention on the participants in the synagogue service whom he divides up into two groups of unequal size: the opponents were not numerous but were hierarchically superior; the crowd was numerous but without much power" (Bovon, *Luke 2*, 280–81).

That binary opposition of characters in the pericope positions the story as part of larger discourses resistant to control by the dominant class. Its hero is an itinerant who injects his uncontrolled labor into a community on the Sabbath, destabilizing the relationship between those few who controlled the means of production and the many whose undercompensated labor was required for production. The angry reaction from the dominant class and its effort to enforce its control is bested by the itinerant's critique, and the crowd rejoices. In this way the text appears to participate in a counter hegemonic discourse of the laboring class. But we will need to question this preliminary conclusion below after first paying attention to the shared code of the ethnic and gendered parameters, which is another goal of the second phase of analysis.

A Shared Code for Struggle in the Text's Social Horizon

In this text, class struggle is waged within the shared code of Israel's ethnoreligious heritage, which all sides accept within the narrative. One fundamental binary that expresses the ethnoreligious parameters is God/Satan: Satan shackled the woman with a spirit of weakness for eighteen years but God removed her weakness in a moment. Another ethnoreligious binary that defines the class conflict is Sabbath/labor: there is no dispute among the characters about whether labor should cease on the Sabbath, only a disagreement about which activities violate the Sabbath. A third binary involves the national progenitor Abraham, who is drawn into an argument about Sabbath labor via the binary animal/daughter of Abraham: if beasts of burden find relief on the Sabbath, then a descendent of the legendary ancestor should certainly find relief on the Sabbath.

That last binary introduces the other crucial aspect of the text's shared code: patriarchy. While the details of implementation regarding ethnoreligious practice are contested in the narrative, the implementation of patriarchal gender norms is not. The female/male binary is not treated as worthy of discussion or dispute. The gender differential is simply accepted as self-evident. Thus, the female character is the occasion for the basic plot, but she is not central to its development or resolution. She appears on the scene chronically misshapen, constrained by a "spirit of weakness" (13:11). She is released by an itinerant male teacher-healer, and a local male leader takes issue with her restoration on the Sabbath.

The plot then runs its course with the woman offstage while the two men argue over the itinerant's therapeutic work on the Sabbath.

The itinerant rabbi referred to the woman in his clinching argument as a "daughter of Abraham" (13:16). This is an infrequent phrase in Jewish and Christian literatures but it has parallels.[34] Commentators usually treat this as a positive phrase that points toward inclusion of the woman within the traditions of Israel.[35] But as an example of a discourse on gender it is an ambiguous designation. In narrative terms, until her healing she is presented without affiliation to a male figure. Once she is healed, however, she praises Israel's male deity. More importantly, the male "Lord" then reminds his opponents and the crowd that she has always been a daughter, and therefore in a subordinate relationship to a male figure. So the narrative movement for this secondary figure is from "isolation with disability" to "full abilities with gendered dependency."

Elisabeth Schüssler Fiorenza offered another way to understand the patriarchal shared code of this text by focusing on the reception side of the narrative process. The text encourages readers to identify with the protagonist, the male figure who wins a theological debate with a local male leader. Schüssler Fiorenza broke that shared code of the text and maintained that readers should not accept such narrative closure. Female readers, who are denigrated by religious and social institutions, should instead identify with the bent over woman who maintained her praxis in spite of the patriarchal community and who asked for no help from any powerful male figure. Male readers, according to Schüssler Fiorenza, should follow Jesus' lead by recognizing individuals who have been marginalized by power structures and by working to remove those hegemonic restraints.[36] By resisting narrative closure in this way, Schüssler Fiorenza undertook analysis that rendered visible the complementary economic, religious, and gendered discourses—the shared code, in Jameson's terminology—that are at work in a text like Luke 13:10–17.

One final ethnoreligious binary involves the synagogue. It also illuminates the shared code of class struggle and patriarchial discourses in

---

34. Bovon, *Luke 2*, 289n67.

35. For examples from the malestream commentary tradition see Fitzmyer, *Gospel according to Luke*, 1013; Hamm, "Freeing of the Bent Woman"; Bovon, *Luke 2*, 289. Feminist interpretation has also claimed the woman for more liberationist agendas: Kinukawa, "Miracle Story"; Machado and Reimer, "Uma Mulher Marcada pela Opressão."

36. Schüssler Fiorenza, "Liberation, Unity and Equality," esp. 59–63.

a specific ethnoreligious context, but this binary is more subtle and requires elaboration. The entire narrative of Luke 13:10–17 is set within the synagogue form, to which there is no obvious contrast. In this pericope the synagogue is where everything occurs, the spatial terrain upon which the narrative tries to resolve symbolically a class struggle over labor. If we move beyond the pericope to the larger gospel we see that Luke deploys the synagogue form strategically. It appears more frequently than in the other three canonical gospels,[37] and the intent of its fifteen references appears to be to chart the expulsion of the disciples from this ethnoreligious form. Luke opens Jesus' public ministry with a long scene in his hometown synagogue where Jesus provokes a fight over Israel's alleged historical antipathy toward prophets. Jesus is forced out of that Nazareth synagogue and escapes a lynch mob (4:16–30). After that inaugural scene, the synagogue is an ambivalent setting in Luke's Gospel. It is a place for teaching (4:15; 4:16–30; 4:44; implied in 4:31–32), for healing (6:6–11; 13:10–13),[38] for exorcism (4:44), for hypocrisy (11:43; 20:46), for opposition and persecution (4:28–30; 6:6–11; 12:41; 13:14–17; 21:12), and for benefaction (7:5; 8:41). But our pericope in Luke 13 is the last time the author locates Jesus in a synagogue. For Luke, then, the synagogue form represents inclusion in traditional Judaism, the "inside" in the binary inside/outside. As we follow Luke through his Gospel narrative and into his Acts of the Apostles, the synagogue—the setting for Jewish insiders—is also the setting where Jesus is unwelcome and the setting his followers will abandon.

The hostility of Luke toward traditional Jewish practice takes us into one final, crucial aspect of the social horizon of this text—its gentile consumers. The shared code of ethnoreligious practice within the narrative world was not the shared code of the actual audience for the narrative. The author of Luke was writing for a mostly gentile audience in the late first or early second centuries CE, an audience that was not expected to observe the Sabbath nor to participate in a synagogue. What are we to make of this narrative's argument about true Sabbath practice in light of the fact that it was written for people who did not need to keep the Sabbath?

This feature of Luke 13:10–17 presents us with a second obfuscation of class conflict. Within the narrative's world, the struggle to control labor

---

37. Synagogues are mentioned fifteen times in Luke, 9 times in Matthew, 8 times in Mark, and twice in John.

38. But note the departure from a synagogue to a healing in a house in Luke 4:38.

plays out as a struggle over proper ethnoreligious practice within a patriarchal context. So one act of obfuscation is the narrative's focus on the ethnoreligious ideologies regarding proper control of labor rather than on the control of labor itself. But the relations between the actual author and actual audiences take us outside the narrative world and introduce a second act of obfuscation. At this level—the level of the production and consumption of Luke—class struggle is further obscured because the text's articulation of Sabbath ideologies are irrelevant to the author's audiences.[39]

So a focus only on the narrative world of Luke or of Luke 13 can be misleading. Even for the early consumers of Luke and Acts, Jesus was not the class warrior who emerges from a narrow reading of the Luke 13:10–17 itself.[40] The author first ascribed the class struggles to ethnoreligious disputes, and then left those disputes in the past. The struggle is doubly removed, first in terms of religious practice and then in terms of historical distance from that practice.

Thus, the exploration of the social horizon of Luke 13:10–17 evinces a shared code of urban Mediterranean patriarchy. Within this shared code, class struggle plays out in the tangled antagonistic discourses of Jew/gentile, householder/dependents, possession/charity, male/female, synagogue/ekklesia, incarceration/movement. As one statement in those larger discourses, the text allows class struggle to surface and then attempts to reconcile it by confining it to Jewish and nonbelieving gentile settings, and then by offering the households of believers as the solution.

---

39. The scope of this study of Luke 13:10–17 does not allow a full exploration of this topic, so I simply note four facets of the way that the literary context of Luke-Acts recasts this Lukan pericope's handling of class struggle. In Acts, the author blames class struggles on personal greed (e.g., Acts 16:16–24; 19:23–41) and on Jewish intransigence (Acts 3:1—4:4; 13:13–52; 14:8–20, esp. v. 19; 17:1–9; and 17:12–14). Regarding the alleviation of class antagonisms, the author describes an early experiment with property sharing (2:43–47; 4:32–37) but abandons it in favor of two other antidotes for class antagonisms—charity (9:36; 10:2; 11:27–30; 20:35) and the patriarchal *oikos* (9:43; 10:48; 16:15; 18:3; 18:8; 21:8; 21:15; 28:14).

40. This is not an argument about the historical Jesus and his alleged political program, and I do not claim that he was a class warrior. Whether the pericope provides any information about the historical Jesus is unknown and irrelevant. The point of this Jamesonian analysis is to identify the political unconscious of the text at the level of its production and consumption.

Modes of Production and the Historical Horizon of Luke 13:10–17

A third horizon remains in a Jamesonian interpretation—the historical horizon.[41] At this broadest level the text is viewed not only as a symbolic literary resolution of a social conflict, nor only as one statement within discourses of class struggle, but also as "a field of force in which the dynamics of sign systems of several distinct modes of production can be registered and apprehended."[42]

Before I discuss the modes of production embedded in Luke 13:10–17, two clarifications are in order. First, Jameson does not accept the notion that there are distinct modes of production isolated from each other by historical period. He proposes that we envision transitions between modes of production and overlapping modes at any given point in history. So with the historical horizon in view it is possible to talk about various modes of production that are manifest in the narrative, with some more contemporaneous than others. The older modes of production signal the formal survival of ancient forms of alienation, appearing as a kind of sedimentation in the text alongside other indicators of alienation.[43]

The other clarification is that in this last stage of interpretation we do not seek "history" as one of many possible narratives about why things happened as they did. Rather, we are looking for "History,"[44] which for Jameson is "the raw material upon which historiographic form works," the "inert chronological and 'linear' data" from which we build our histories.[45] It cannot be known directly for it is "the ultimate ground as well as the untranscendable limit of our understanding in general and our textual interpretations in particular."[46] It operates something like Althusser's "absent cause," in that it is only experienced indirectly through the failures of conflict and struggle. Thus, History is the experience of Necessity; that is, "the inexorable logic involved in the determinate failure of all the revolutions that have taken place in human history."[47]

---

41. Jameson, *Political Unconscious*, 91–102.
42. Ibid., 98.
43. Ibid., 91–98.
44. Ibid., 98–102.
45. Ibid., 101.
46. Ibid., 100.
47. Ibid., 101.

With those clarifications in mind, in Luke 13:10–17 we see traces of at least five modes of production, each of which alludes to fundamental—and in some instances archaic—forms of alienation. Perhaps the oldest is that of household agricultural production, which is presumed by the reference to proper care for a cow or a donkey on the Sabbath. This mode relies on family labor to maintain subsistence in a small-scale setting wherein labor is assigned by gender and age.

The second mode is nomadic clan patriarchy, which is embedded in the reference to Abraham. It no longer characterized the lives of Luke's consumers, but nomadic clan patriarchy was central to the ethnoreligious mythology of Israel that was being coopted by the text's gentile consumers. So this vestigial marker of a past mode of production and alienation survived in narrative and ideology.

Third, the Sabbath implies a national ordering of production for Israel, but it is difficult to link it to any specific mode. Origin theories abound for the Sabbath, but none has established itself clearly. It was part of early national life because the Sabbath is present in all strata of the Pentateuch and in most of the other strands of Israelite historical texts. Because of its long life, Sabbath instructions address rural and urban labor for domestic and corporate settings. Central to this practice is temporary abstinence from labor, and it is precisely the periodic abolition of labor relations on particular days that defines it. This periodic abolition of labor is also the factor that makes it contentious in different ways within different modes of production. The tension it produces depends on the setting, with one range of problems in a majority Jewish setting (as in the narrative world of Luke 13:10–17) and a different range of problems in majority gentile settings (more familiar to diaspora communities and to the consumers of Luke 13:10–17).

Imperial domination is a fourth mode of production of the narrative, invoked by the setting of the narrative in the synagogue. Scholarship tends to locate the origins of the synagogue form in the needs of Jewish communities during the empires of the Persian and/or Hellenistic eras.[48] It proved to be a flexible form that persisted through multiple imperial modes of production into the period of the Luke's audience and beyond.

The fifth and final mode of production is benefaction, which is suggested by the office of the archisynagogos itself. There were many ways that a synagogue could be organized. An archisynagogos was a particular

---

48. For summaries of the history of the synagogue form see Levine, *Ancient Synagogue*; Runesson et al., *Ancient Synagogue*, 1–13.

structural position designed to fit within a Hellenistic or Roman imperial mode of production. In these settings, occupational, ethnic, and religious groups usually required benefaction from members of the dominant class. Such benefactors distributed fractions of their accumulated capital to select groups and individuals among the laboring class for a variety of reasons. The structural reason for these benefactions, however, would have been to maintain their position of dominance in those particular imperial modes of production.

So when we examine the historical horizon of Luke 13:10–17, even that short narrative perpetuates several fundamental forms from the history of alienation, some archaic and some more recent. Family, clan, nation, empire, and benefaction are all present as modes of production. Each of these modes distributes labor and products in a distinctive manner and thus each of them generates distinctive forms of alienation. By bringing these aspects of the text to light, we begin to experience not just history as a narrative, but rather History that hurts, History that "refuses desire and sets inexorable limits to individual as well as collective practice."[49]

Conclusion: Alienation and Failed Revolutions

The failed revolutions of Luke 13:10–17 are crucial to my engagement with this text. I do not argue that class struggle or economy is the "real" issue in the text nor that the Sabbath and the synagogue are byproducts of the economy. I hold all of them to be crucial to the narrative and to its consumers, even though most modern western scholarship demands that we not discuss the aspects of economy and production. I argue rather that class, gender, Sabbath, synagogue, and so forth provide us with opportunities to examine the failed revolutions and forms of alienation of bygone eras that nevertheless persevere. These topics do not provide direct access to an allegedly real economic issue. Rather, they suggest indirectly the shape of History as we run up against its "inexorable limits."

The failed revolutions of this text, however, also provide us with materials to imagine the transcendence of alienation from deep within it. Three examples are central to Luke 13:10–17, beginning with the Sabbath. As a weekly abolition of unjust labor relations, this revolutionary practice and its failures point toward the parameters of History and the

49. Jameson, *Political Unconscious*, 102.

potential of transcending beyond it. A second example is the synagogue as a site for disrupting imperial domination through the declaration of peoplehood. Finally, the class warrior acts as an individual who abolishes injustice by naming the hypocrisy of contemporary modes of production.

Thus Luke 13:10–17, understood within the context of Luke-Acts and through a Jamesonian analysis, provides a method for considering class struggle in the ancient text. In so doing we are frustrated, once again, by History as an untranscendable horizon whose "alienating necessities will not forget us, however much we might prefer to ignore them."[50] Indeed, modern western scholarship has preferred to ignore those alienating necessities in the study of Luke 13:10–17 and elsewhere in early Christian literature. Rather than looking for signs of class struggle and alienation, we have taken refuge in the ideologies of mainstream interpretive traditions. In so doing our work is impoverished, at least to the extent that we acquiesce silently to the demands of Necessity and relinquish the search for the contours of History that hurts.

Works Cited

Boer, Roland. "Marxism and the Spatial Analysis of Early Christianity: The Contribution of G. E. M. de Ste. Croix." *Religion* 41 (2011) 411–30.

Bovon, François. *Luke 2: A Commentary on the Gospel of Luke 9:51—19:27*. Translated by Donald S. Deer. Hermeneia. Minneapolis: Fortress, 2013.

Brooten, Bernadette J. *Women Leaders in the Ancient Synagogue: Inscriptional Evidence and Background Issues*. Brown Judaic Studies 36. Chico, CA: Scholars, 1982.

Fitzmyer, Joseph A. *The Gospel according to Luke (X–XXIV): Introduction, Translation, and Notes*. Anchor Bible 28A. New York: Doubleday, 1985.

Friesen, Steven J. "Prospects for a Demography of the Pauline Mission: Corinth among the Churches." In *Urban Religion and Roman Corinth: Interdisciplinary Approaches*, edited by Daniel N. Schowalter and Steven J. Friesen, 351–70. Cambridge: Harvard University Press, 2005.

González, Justo L. *Luke*. Belief: A Theological Commentary on the Bible. Louisville: Westminster John Knox, 2010.

Goodman, Martin. *The Ruling Class of Judaea: The Origins of the Jewish Revolt against Rome A.D. 66–70*. Cambridge: Cambridge University Press, 1987.

Green, Joel B. *The Gospel of Luke*. New International Commentary on the New Testament. Grand Rapids: Eerdmans, 1997.

———. "Jesus and a Daughter of Abraham (Luke 13:10–17): Test Case for a Lucan Perspective on Jesus' Miracles." *Catholic Biblical Quarterly* 51 (1989) 643–54.

Hamm, Dennis. "The Freeing of the Bent Woman and the Restoration of Israel: Luke 13.10–17 as Narrative Theology." *Journal for the Study of the New Testament* 31 (1987) 23–44.

50. Ibid.

Jameson, Fredric. *The Political Unconscious: Narrative as a Socially Symbolic Act.* Ithaca, NY: Cornell University Press, 1981.
Jeffrey, David Lyle. *Luke.* Brazos Theological Commentary on the Bible. Grand Rapids: Brazos, 2012.
Kinukawa, Hisako. "The Miracle Story of the Bent-over Woman (Luke 13:10–17): An Interaction-Centered Interpretation." In *Transformative Encounters: Jesus and Women Re-viewed*, edited by Ingrid R. Kitzberger, 292–314. Biblical Interpretation Series 43. Leiden: Brill, 2000.
Levine, Lee I. *The Ancient Synagogue: The First Thousand Years.* 2nd ed. New Haven: Yale University Press, 2005.
———. "Synagogue Leadership: The Case of the Archisynagogue." In *Jews in the Graeco-Roman World*, edited by Martin Goodman, 195–213. Oxford: Clarendon, 1998.
Machado, Erika Pereira, and Ivoni Richter Reimer. "Uma Mulher Marcada pela Opressão e pela Ternura de Deus: Análise e Interpretação de Lucas 13.10–17." *Estudos Teológicos* 51 (2011) 127–37.
Marshall, I. Howard. *The Gospel of Luke: A Commentary on the Greek Text.* New International Greek Testament Commentary. Grand Rapids: Eerdmans, 1978.
Martin, Matthew J. "Interpreting the Theodotos Inscription: Some Reflections on a First Century Jerusalem Synagogue Inscription and E. P. Sanders' 'Common Judaism.'" *Ancient Near Eastern Studies* 39 (2002) 160–81.
Parsons, Mikeal C. "Ought Not This Daughter of Abraham Be Set Free? Getting the Story of the Bent Woman Straight." In *Body and Character in Luke and Acts: The Subversion of Physiognomy in Early Christianity*, 83–95. Grand Rapids: Baker Academic, 2006.
Pervo, Richard I. *Dating Acts: Between the Evangelists and the Apologists.* Santa Rosa, CA: Polebridge, 2006.
Rajak, Tessa, and David Noy. "*Archisynagogoi*: Office, Title and Social Status in the Greco-Jewish Synagogue." *Journal of Roman Studies* 83 (1993) 75–93.
Runesson, Anders, et al. *The Ancient Synagogue from Its Origins to 200 C.E.: A Sourcebook.* Ancient Judaism and Early Christianity 72. Leiden: Brill, 2008.
Sanders, E. P. *Judaism: Belief and Practice, 63 BCE–66 CE.* London: SCM, 1992.
Scheidel, Walter, and Steven J. Friesen. "The Size of the Economy and the Distribution of Income in the Roman Empire." *Journal of Roman Studies* 99 (2009) 61–91.
Schürer, Emil. *The History of the Jewish People in the Age of Jesus Christ (175 B.C.–A.D. 135)*, edited by Geza Vermes et al. 3 vols. Edinburgh: Clark, 1973–1987.
Schüssler Fiorenza, Elisabeth. "Liberation, Unity, and Equality in Community: A New Testament Case Study." In *Beyond Unity-in-Tension: Unity, Renewal and the Community of Women and Men*, edited by Thomas F. Best, 58–74. Faith and Order Paper 138. Geneva: WCC Publications, 1988.
Slainero, Raúl González. "La figura del *pater partum* como *archisynagogus* en las comunidades judías del Imperio romano." In *Visiones Mítico-religiosas del Padre en la Antigüedad Clásica*, edited by Marcos Riuiz Sánchez, 61–79. Signifer 12. Madrid: Signifer, 2004.
Tew, W. Mark. *Luke: Gospel to the Nameless and Faceless.* Eugene, OR: Wipf & Stock, 2012.
Vitt, Lois A. "Class." In *The Concise Encyclopedia of Sociology*, edited by George Ritzer and J. Michael Ryan, 65–66. Oxford: Wiley-Blackwell, 2011.

Wright, Erik Olin, ed. *Approaches to Class Analysis*. Cambridge: Cambridge University Press, 2005.
Zuiderhoek, Arjan. *The Politics of Munificence in the Roman Empire*. Greek Culture in the Roman World. Cambridge: Cambridge University Press, 2009.
Wolter, Michael. *The Gospel according to Luke: Volume II (9:54—24)*. Translated by Wayne Coppins and Christoph Heilig. Baylor–Mohr/Siebeck Studies in Early Christianity. Waco, TX: Baylor University Press, 2017.

4

"The Thoughts of Many Hearts"

Interior Characterization in the Gospel of Luke

MARK REASONER

> And his father and mother were wondering at the things spoken about him. Then Simeon blessed them and said to Mary his mother: "Behold, this one is set for the fall and rise of many in Israel and for a sign to be opposed—and a sword shall pierce your own soul—so that the thoughts of many hearts may be revealed." (Luke 2:33–35)[1]

TO OFFER A COMPLETE study of interior characterization in Luke's Gospel is no small task, and the following essay is only a preliminary study. It builds on the works of Bernhard Heininger and Melissa Harl Sellew, and it is to the latter that this essay is dedicated in friendship and thankfulness for a friendship that has spanned our professional careers.[2] From the programmatic description of Simeon's final words to Mary, it seems possible that Luke the implied author considers the revelation of many people's thoughts to be what accompanies the fall and rise of many in Israel, the way that Jesus is opposed, and the way that Mary will encounter pain in the repercussions of her son's life. To understand the revelation of many people's thoughts that seems narratively enacted in this gospel, I first

1. Author's own translations.
2. Heininger, *Metaphorik*; Sellew, "Interior Monologue."

suggest some criteria for identifying and measuring interiority in narrative, and then consider the cases where Luke tells us that Jesus knows others' thoughts, the instances where the narrator describes people's thoughts and feelings, and the way in which the passion of Jesus or division between families and the people of God over Jesus results in others' thoughts being revealed. Since a work on interiority in Luke would be incomplete without considering the causes or motives for this relatively unique characteristic of this gospel, I conclude with some suggestions for why the implied author of Luke employs interior characterization. These causes include: an imitation of the narrative techniques in Scripture and contemporaneous literature, a quest to invest his gospel with certainty, and a need to correct the hidden dimension of Mark's discourse.

Criteria for Identifying and Measuring Interior Characterization

Explicit and implicit signals combine to form the characteristic of mind-reading that the Gospel of Luke evokes for its narrator, who in most cases is indistinguishable from the implied author, and for the narrative's hero, Jesus. The presence of this signals interiority. Their presence in the absence of parallels in the other gospels confirms this interiority. The frequency of signals and connections between a given character's inner world and a νοῦς (consciousness/mind) that transcends the character allows one to measure the relative strength and depth of the interiority, in comparison to the other gospels. A glaring weakness of the following list is its vulnerability to the charge of circularity: readers may think that I have conceived of these criteria because they match characteristics of narrative interiority in Luke. My only rejoinder is that I know of no other way to offer criteria for understanding interiority in Luke. This weakness therefore seems worth the advances that these criteria and the survey of interior characterization that follows may offer for readers of Luke.

Signals of Interior Characterization

Explicit Signals:	Examples in Luke
References to emotions	2:33; 10:21, 41; 15:5–7, 9–10, 32; 23:8
References to thoughts/thinking	1:29
References to heart/mind/soul	1:51; 2:19, 35, 51b
Discourse to self	7:39; 12:17–19
Implicit Signals:	
Character's gaze or look at another	7:44; 15:20; 22:61
Character's face (πρόσωπον) as marker of intention; facial expression	9:51, 53; 24:17
Description of connection (cause, desire, or necessity) between any element of the narrative and an external νοῦς (mind)	23:41; 24:26, 44

Categories of Interior Characterization in the Gospel of Luke

Characters in Lukan Parables Talk to Themselves

The first category of interior characterization is the self-directed discourse in parables unique to Luke.[3] Heininger begins with Aristotle's *Poetics* in his consideration of monologues within parables, and notes that the genre of parable requires two or three voices for its dramatic quality, with the result that a triangular schema can usually be outlined.[4] For example, in the parable of the rich fool, the main character speaks to his soul: "What shall I do? I will build a bigger barn and say to my soul, 'Soul, you have laid up many good things for many years; be at ease,

---

3. Luke 12:12–20; 12:42–46; 15:11–32; 16:1–8; 18:2–5; 20:9–16.

4. Heininger, *Metaphorik*, 8–13. Places in Aristotle's *Poetics* that Heininger cites include 1.1–2 (1447a); 6.9, 24 (1449b 1450b); 7.3 (1450b); 11.9 (1452b); 13.1–13 (1452b–1453a); 15.1–12 (1453b–1454a).

eat drink and be merry.'" Then the voice of God completes the triangle: "Fool, this very night your soul is required of you . . ." (Luke 12:17-20).

Sellew argues that Luke narrates the inner thoughts of parable-characters in order to depict Jesus as knowing people's thoughts. Near the end of her article, Sellew summarizes: "Jesus is shown as someone who is able time after time to pierce people's hearts—to lay bare their full humanity, and thus their failings, in a mode aimed at reaching not only his fictive audiences within the Gospel drama, but us too, as the readers of the larger story."[5] Sellew thus has helpfully identified one motive for an aspect of interiority in Luke: Since Luke wants to show Jesus' ability to read others' minds, the Lukan parables' characters speak to themselves at greater frequency than parables of the other gospels.

Sellew does not, however, note the use of interior characterization in Luke's narratives. But the narratives really do contain more interior characterization than the other gospels. These include descriptions of thoughts and feelings of Jesus (e.g., 10:21; 19:41-44; 24:28b), teachings on what people should think (e.g., 3:14; 17:7-10), and descriptions of other characters' thoughts and feelings (e.g., 2:47-48; 10:29; 23:45; 24:41, 52-53), all of which are unique to the Gospel of Luke. I seek to take a step back from the good work that Sellew and Heininger have done on Luke's parables in order to discern these parables' place within Luke's literary profile.

Jesus Reads Others' Minds

The second category of interior characterization in Luke's Gospel is how Jesus knows what people are thinking. Other gospels also contain places where Jesus knows what others are thinking, but it is significant that in two cases of a triple tradition pericope—Luke 6:8 and 9:47—Luke adds material on Jesus knowing others' thoughts. Luke 19:11 and 24:38 also have clear descriptions of Jesus knowing what is going on in others' minds, statements which are not directly paralleled in the other canonical gospels. Fitzmyer claims that διαλογισμοί, or "thoughts," the last word in Luke 2:35, is to be read in light of the five other uses of the word in Luke, which occur "in a pejorative or hostile sense."[6] The usage in the other places in Luke includes the words of the disciples when they debated who

---

5. Sellew, "Interior Monologue," 253.
6. Fitzmyer, *Gospel according to Luke I-IX*, 430.

was the greatest (9:46-47), and includes the doubts of the apostles, before the resurrected Jesus appeared to them (24:38). The cognate verb is used of Mary's wondering at the angel's greeting (1:29), and the people's wondering if John the Baptist might be the Christ (3:15). Luke is definitely interested in showing that the thoughts of many will be revealed with the coming of Jesus. Bovon expresses this most succinctly: "Just as divine preparation (v. 31) awaits that of mortals, in v. 35b the ἀποκάλυψις of human hearts is juxtaposed to the divine 'revelation' (v. 32)."[7] Luke's word διαλογισμοί does have a negative connotation, but based on Luke's description of Jesus knowing these διαλογισμοί, this narrative actualizes or fulfills the prophecy of Simeon. And though the word διαλογισμοί is not used in the Magnificat, Mary's word that God "has scattered the proud in the intention of their heart" (διεσκόρπισεν ὑπερηφάνους διανοίᾳ καρδίας αὐτῶν, 1:51) fits with the mind-reading portrait of Jesus that Luke provides.

Evidence that could count against the direction of my essay is the feeding of the five thousand, where John's version tells us that Jesus knew what he was going to do, while Luke follows Matthew and Mark by not informing us of Jesus' superior knowledge before the feeding. Also, Luke does not cast his Jesus as John's Jesus who knows everything, which we learn just as Jesus is about to be arrested in John 18. In general, the differences with John seem to show that while John is concerned to show that Jesus knows everything, Luke is concerned to show that Jesus knows others' thoughts, with the connotation that these thoughts are often incomplete or misguided.

Jesus' role as mind-reader in this gospel is seen as well in Luke's unique descriptions of Jesus as looking at others. Jesus looks at the sinful woman when beginning to explain to Simon her situation (7:44). And the dramatic gaze of Jesus on Peter is certainly worth a thousand words (22:61a).

A subset of this category is that Luke portrays Jesus and also John the Baptist as concerned with people's thoughts. For example, when Luke incorporates the logion found in Matthew 5:42 into his Sermon on the Plain, he repeats the command to lend to the one who wants to borrow, but then adds, "expecting nothing in return" (Luke 6:35). Luke's Jesus develops this later by teaching that one should invite those to a meal who cannot repay (Luke 14:12-14). Luke changes Matthew's "Be perfect

7. Bovon, *Luke 1*, 105.

as your heavenly father is perfect" to "Be compassionate as your father is compassionate" (Luke 6:36; cf. Matt 5:48). We thus see that Luke has edited the Sermon on the Mount material to clarify what people should be expecting when they lend and that people should be compassionate, rather than simply being "perfect" or "complete" as Matthew's Jesus says. Luke 13:1–5 narrates Jesus telling people what not to think and what to think when they hear of random, tragic deaths. Luke 16:15 contains Jesus' teaching, unique to Luke, that God knows people's hearts: "You are those who justify yourselves before men, but God knows your hearts; for what is exalted among men is an abomination in the sight of God." In this category of concern for what people are thinking or feeling we should also note that John the Baptist's call for the soldiers listening to him to be content with their wages is only found in Luke (3:14).

Luke's Narrator Describes Characters' Thoughts and Feelings

The third category of interior characterization comes from the gospel's narrator. In the narrative episodes unique to Luke, the feelings and thoughts of characters are narrated to a degree not found in the unique material of the other gospels. For example, Zechariah is troubled and afraid when he saw the angel, while Mary is troubled and wonders what sort of greeting the angel Gabriel gives her. We are told what Mary and Joseph were thinking when leaving Jerusalem without the twelve-year-old Jesus. And we are told why the lawyer asks "Who is my neighbor?" the question that prompts the parable of the Good Samaritan. Here I part ways with Sellew, for while admitting that at "key moments the narrator can show aspects of Jesus' inner life," she still concludes that "the boundaries of distanced, third-person narration are not broken."[8]

Yes, the other evangelists can also tell us what people are thinking, as for example Matthew tells us what Joseph intends to do when he learns his betrothed is with child. And evidence against the direction of this paper is that in the story of the woman with the hemorrhage who touches Jesus when he is walking through a crowd, it is Matthew and Mark who tell us that she said ("to herself" in Matthew), "If I only touch his garment, I shall be healed" (Matt 9:21; Mark 5:28; cf. Luke 8:44). But yet Luke does add "When she saw that she was not hidden" to the narrative panel of her response to Jesus' question, "Who touched me?" (Luke 8:47). Still, Luke's

---

8. Sellew, "Interior Monologue," 252.

narration is unique among the gospel narrators for the frequency with which it relates that people are troubled, the way it drives the narrative with people's thoughts, and for its depiction of Jesus' grief and joy.

First Objection: Other Gospels Describe People's Thoughts

My readers might now be saying to themselves, "Reasoner is not fair with the evidence. As far as 'amazement' or 'astonishment,' Luke comes in behind Mark in ascribing these qualities to the crowds."[9] I will grant this, but still the evidence points to a preponderance of description of individuals' thoughts and feelings in the Gospel of Luke. One might press me by countering that the other gospels also include people's thoughts and feelings, while Luke simply narrates different thoughts and feelings. For example, in the stories of the woman anointing Jesus, Matthew, Mark, and John record at least one person present as remarking on the waste of the ointment. Luke omits this. But in Luke's version of the story, he tells us what Simon the Pharisee was thinking: "If this man were a prophet, he would know what sort of woman . . ." (Luke 7:39). This thought then prompts a story from Jesus that is unique to Luke, the story of the two men in debt (Luke 7:41–43). The implication is that Jesus knew what Simon was thinking and told the story to answer Simon's thoughts that Jesus was not a prophet. So yes, Luke omits people's response regarding the waste of the ointment, but in its place he includes Simon's skeptical thought that opens the way for the implied author to show us how Jesus can read another's mind.

And this objection also ignores Luke's narratives that are driven along precisely by key information on what people are thinking. Thus in the narrative of the 12 year old Jesus left in the Jerusalem temple, Luke makes sure to tell what Mary and Joseph were thinking when they left Jerusalem the first time. When Joseph and Mary find Jesus, they are astonished, and his mother tells Jesus how they were feeling while looking for him (2:48). In the narrative of Jesus on trial, we learn what Herod and Pilate were thinking, and we learn that they became friends on that day (23:6–8, 12).

---

9. Cf. ἐκπλήσσομαι (I am amazed) in Mark 1:22; 6:2; 7:37; 10:26; 11:18 with Luke 2:48, 4:32; 9:43; Acts 13:12. Cf. θαμβέομαι (I am astonished) in Mark 1:27; 10:24, 32 with no instances of the verb but the following instances of θάμβος (astonishment)— Luke 4:36; 5:9; Acts 3:10.

Second Objection: Luke's Interiority Only Results from His Fundamental Emphases

A second objection might be that I am framing this comparison of Luke and the other gospels in an unhelpful, overly complicated way. Luke has favorite themes, such as joy, prayer and repentance. These themes necessitate description of some thoughts and feelings, but it is not as though Luke has a special interest more than the other gospels of narrating his characters' thoughts and feelings. For example, some may say that the discourse among the three victims of crucifixion in Luke 23 is only included to underscore Luke's theme of repentance. But this objection ignores some of the specially Lukan material about thought. It is only in Luke that Simeon says that the thoughts of many hearts will be revealed, and of course only in Luke that we read that Mary treasured up these things in her heart.[10] So there is clearly more going on in Luke's narrative regarding thoughts and feelings than can be found in the other gospels.

Also, the thoughts and feelings that Luke discloses in his narratives transcend the favorite themes listed above. For example, in Luke 24:11 we are informed what the apostles thought when the women told them of Jesus' resurrection. We learn that the disciples Jesus meets looked sad (24:17). We learn that they had been hoping that Jesus would redeem Israel (24:21). And we learn that their hearts were burning when Jesus opened the Scriptures to them (24:32).

I hope that I have responded to these objections in a way that at least keeps you thinking about Luke's descriptions of people's thoughts and feelings. Let us return to reflect together on a final category of interior characterization in Luke—how its implied author connects the revelation of many people's thoughts to the sword that pierces Mary's soul.

Implied Author Connects People's Thoughts to the Sword Piercing Mary's Soul

Simeon's programmatic conclusion to Luke 2:35, "The thoughts of many hearts being revealed," seems to follow from the prediction of a sword piercing Mary's soul. If we take this expression to signify Jesus' passion,

---

10. Luke 2:19, 51b, see also Luke 1:66. The biblical parallels for this expression, LXX Gen 37:11 and LXX Dan 4:28, seem to indicate "keeping the words in mind in an effort to fathom their meaning" (Fitzmyer, *Gospel according to Luke*, 413). A similar phrase, though not a verbal parallel, is also found in LXX Dan 7:28.

we do note that a number of people's thoughts are revealed in Luke's narrative through the scenes of the last supper, Gethsemane, arrest, and crucifixion. The Last Supper opens with Jesus' words, unique to Luke, "I have earnestly desired to eat this Passover with you before I suffer (22:15). In the Last Supper scene, a dispute again arises among the disciples regarding which is the greatest. This sort of dispute has already been linked back to Simeon's words with the use of διαλογισμοί (thoughts) for a similar dispute in Luke 9:46–48 (see also Matt 18:1–5; Mark 9:33–37). Shortly after this, we have Jesus efficiently summarizing Peter's restoration and denial (22:31–34). In Gethsemane, we learn that the disciples are sleeping because of sorrow (22:45). We learn that Pilate really thinks Jesus is innocent, since Luke's Pilate says this three times. And we learn how Herod's curiosity regarding Jesus gives way to contempt (Luke 23:8, 11). Our implied author links the trials before Pilate and Herod with Psalm 2:1–2 ("Why do the heathen rage and the peoples imagine a vain thing?") in Acts 4:25–27. Verbal parallels between Psalm 2:1–2 and Luke 2:35 are non-existent, though Luke records the distress of the women who follow Jesus on the road to the cross (23:27–28) and the revealing conversation between Jesus and those crucified beside him (23:39–43). The crowd leaves Golgotha "beating their breasts" (Luke 23:48). One way of understanding the interior characterization that occurs within Luke's passion narrative is to read it in light of his addition of the "division in households" saying (12:52–53). There, Luke 12:49–50 repeats Mark's logion, "I have a baptism with which to be baptized," and joins it to Matthew's statement about not coming to bring peace but division, even division of households. Since the baptism logion is generally accepted as referring to Jesus' passion, we may conclude that among Matthew, Mark and Luke, only Luke emphasizes how Jesus' death will be a cause of division among people, such as we see between Pilate, who treats Jesus with respect, and Herod, who with his soldiers treats Jesus with contempt, the crowd before Pilate who call for Jesus' crucifixion and the crowd who follow Jesus wailing and lamenting his sentence, and those crucified on either side of Jesus. In Luke, the revelation of people's thoughts that results from Jesus' passion is communicated primarily by what people say and do when they encounter Jesus.

Fitzmyer and Juel take the prediction of a sword piercing Mary's soul more generally to signify division between people or family.[11] Most of

---

11. Fitzmyer, *Gospel according to Luke*, 430; Juel, *Luke-Acts*, 24.

the examples cited in reference to Jesus' passion would fit with this more general interpretation, especially in light of the way that Luke 12:49–50 connects Jesus' impending "baptism" with the division of households." Fitzmyer's examples are Luke 8:21 ("who is my mother and my brothers? My mother and my brothers are those who hear the word of God and do it"; see Matt 12:50; Mark 3:35), and 11:27–28 ("Blessed is the womb that bore you and . . ."). This approach to the sword that emphasizes division among the family might also explain why Luke's Jesus tells the implied reader that he must hate his own father and mother and wife and children and brother and sisters (Luke 14:26; cf. Matt 10:37). In addition, such windows into people's thoughts and feelings occur with contemplative Mary and the distracted Martha, the nine lepers who go their way while the one returns who is thankful, and Jesus' stories of the rich man and Lazarus, the Pharisee and the tax collector; all of these highlight division or separation within a household.

The Rationale behind Interior Characterization in Luke's Gospel

Simply to survey the types of interiority in Luke's Gospel seems inconsistent with Luke's own orientation toward giving a complete account. It remains for us to consider why this gospel attempts to depict the interior lives of its characters.

Interior Characterization in Contemporaneous Literature

First, it is possible that the implied author of Luke may be providing interior characterization because he is modeling his gospel after what he is reading. We can consider Luke's reading from the perspective of the Scriptures and other literature contemporary with him.

It is evident that Luke patterns parts of his narrative on the early prophets, or the history section of the LXX. Besides the literary dependence of the Magnificat on Hannah's prayer, Luke alone quotes Jesus' comparison of himself to Elijah and Elisha, and Luke narrates miracles that remind the reader of miracles these prophets performed.[12] This section of Scripture, sometimes called the Deuteronomistic History, is more

---

12. 1 Sam 2:1–10; Luke 1:46–55; 4:25–27; 7:1–17. The miracle story in 7:1–10 is of course paralleled by Matt 8:5–13 and possibly John 4:46b–54.

descriptive of its characters' thoughts than is the book of Genesis.[13] The book of Joshua opens with a command to meditate on God's law. Delilah sees that Samson told her all his heart (Judges 16:18). Hannah's distress and bitter weeping is narrated by the Deuteronomist (1 Sam 1:10-11), while no barren matriarch receives such a portrait in Genesis. God repents of making Saul king, and an evil spirit from God comes on Saul (1 Sam 15:11; 18:10). It could be that in his attempt to mimic the style of the Deuteronomistic History, Luke considers it appropriate to narrate people's thoughts and feelings. One could make a link between LXX Ps 93:11 and Luke 2:35 with the catchword διαλογισμοί (thoughts): κύριος γινώσκει τοὺς διλογισμοὺς τῶν ἀνθρώπων ὅτι εἰσὶν μάταιοι ("The Lord knows people's thoughts, that they are empty"). The designation of the thoughts as "empty" fits with Fitzmyer's description of Luke's usage of the term in a negative way.[14] LXX Ps 93:11 is a Pauline favorite, quoted in 1 Corinthians 3:20 and alluded to in Romans 1:21, but Luke does not mark the intertextuality as he does in other cases, so this connection cannot be pressed.[15]

Luke is also very taken with the role of prophet as depicted in his scriptures.[16] These writings describe prophets as divinely informed about others' thoughts and actions (1 Kgs 21:18-19; 2 Kgs 5:25-27; Isa 7:3-9; 2 Kgs 4:27—an exception that proves the rule). Luke may be including this dimension of characterization for Jesus and then for Peter and Paul in Acts (Luke 9:47; 10:41; Acts 5:3-4; 8:18-23; 13:9-10; 16:28).

As to extrabiblical literature that the implied author of Luke-Acts was reading, I suggest that the author may have received an impetus for narrating the interior lives of characters from his reading of Plutarch.[17]

---

13. Cf. Auerbach, "Odysseus's Scar," in *Mimesis*. He does not clearly distinguish between the narrative style of Genesis in the binding of Isaac, and the narrative style of the Deuteronomistic writers' descriptions of David, though he does admit that in "In the stories of David, . . . the legendary imperceptibly passes into the historical" (20).

14. Fitzmyer, *Gospel according to Luke*, 430.

15. Cf., for example, how Luke marks his own intertextual designs by narrating Elijah- and Elisha-like miracles in chapters 5 and 7 after his quotation of Jesus exegeting these prophets' significance in Luke 4:24-27, or how Acts 8 melds the foreigner and eunuch of Isa 56:3-4 with this character's reading from the same section of the Isaiah scroll.

16. Johnson, *New Testament*, 54-58.

17. In Plutarch's *Brutus* 42, for example, Plutarch tells the reader what Brutus and Cassius were thinking at the battle of Philippi, in order to explain how it was that they failed to work together and allowed Octavius Caesar to win. Plutarch's *Mark Antony*

This suggestion is based on a corollary of Richard Pervo's dating of Acts to the second century: the Gospel of Luke is also written in the second century. And Barbara Shellard's tentative decision to consider John as one of Luke's sources, partly on the basis of Luke 24:12, also coheres with this dating.[18] Pervo has noted places where Acts seems to follow narrative details from Plutarch: the means of Paul's escape from Damascus and the narrative of the textiles that healed.[19] If Plutarch spurred Luke to illumine the interior lives of his characters, it would not be the last time the wise man from Chaeronea had such an effect. James Shapiro credits Plutarch's *Lives* with a similar effect on Shakespeare.[20]

A second sort of extrabiblical literature that lies behind the interiority in Luke is New Comedy. On the way to discovering this dependence, Heininger surveys the following novels: Chariton's *Callirhoë*, Xenophon's *Ephesiaka*, and the novel of unknown authorship, *Joseph and Aseneth*. He finds that the parallels between their interior discourse and what he finds in Luke's parables do not support Luke's direct dependence on these novelists' discourse. But after examining interior discourse in New Comedy, exemplified in the works of Menander, Plautus, and Terence, he asserts that both the novelists and Luke utilized discourse conventions, e.g. the question "What shall I do?" found in New Comedy. These conventions bring the reader into the confidence of the depicted character, resulting in the reader's sense that inside access has been gained to the character's interior life.[21] This literary dependence correlates with my next suggestion

---

39, describes the lows and highs of Antony's emotions in his battle against the Parthians. Luke's use of Plutarch may also account for Luke's penchant for parallel lives, e.g. Elizabeth and Mary; Simeon and Anna; Mary and Martha, and on the macroscale, Peter and Paul in Acts. It may also account for Luke's nostalgic view of the temple.

18. Shellard, *New Light on Luke*, 258–60, 275–82.

19. Pervo, *Dating Acts*, 61, 390n54 on Paul's escape from Damascus, and Plutarch, *Aemillius Paulus* 26.2; 37–38, 383n58 on the healing textiles and Plutarch, *Sulla* 35.3–5.

20. Shapiro, *Year in the Life*, 132–35. Shapiro describes how Shakespeare began reading Plutarch's *Lives* in the first half of 1599, and how this contributed to his ability to chronicle the inward thoughts of characters in his play *Julius Caesar*: "In *Henry the Fifth* Shakespeare turns toward biography more directly than he had ever done before. And to this end, Plutarch's brief lives made available to him a model for conveying interiority, something he as yet failed to do in a sustained way in his plays. A chasm divides a revenger like Titus Andronicus from Hamlet, or even the self-revelations of Richard III from those of Brutus. Plutarch enabled Shakespeare to bridge that divide" (133).

21. Heininger, *Metaphorik*, 46–82. "What shall I do?" sorts of questions can be seen, e.g., in Menander, *Dyskolos* 190, 457; *Woman from Samos* 683–4. See Luke 12:17;

for the rationale between the interiority found in the Gospel of Luke, Luke's bid to bring certainty to readers.

Luke's Quest for Certainty

Second, we note that Luke's prologue all leads to its last word—ἀσφάλεια—or certainty. Luke is trying to give certainty to his readers. Certainty is provided by the internally open nature of his omniscient narration. If readers know what the story's characters are thinking and feeling, readers are more certain of what happens in the story. While Luke's narrative differs somewhat from Genesis, Erich Auerbach's instinctive reading of Genesis may be useful for us to understand what Luke is attempting in his gospel:

> What [the biblical narrator] produced, then, was not primarily oriented toward "realism" (if he succeeded in being realistic, it was merely a means, not an end); it was oriented toward truth. Woe to the man who did not believe it! . . . The Bible's claim to truth is not only far more urgent than Homer's, it is tyrannical—it excludes all other claims. The world of the Scripture stories is not satisfied with claiming to be a historically true reality—it insists that it is the only real world, is destined for autocracy.[22]

By giving us the thoughts of many, Luke is making the truths his readers have been taught certain for them, and Luke may be claiming that his gospel is more reliable than the others he has read.

A Correction of Mark's Gospel

Luke's quest for certainty may be a reaction or correction to the apocalyptic nature of Mark. The prologue makes it clear that Luke has read other gospels. In contrast to the hidden, apocalyptic nature of Mark, Luke is remarkably open. Mark shows people misunderstanding Jesus, but Luke connects the dots by announcing through Simeon that the thoughts of many hearts will be revealed (2:35), and then employs the same term "thoughts" when describing Jesus reading others' minds (5:22; 6:8), including those of the disciples (9:47). One place where Luke seems to be reacting to Mark is in his addition to the third passion prediction.

---

and related forms of the question in 11:5–8, 11–12; 15:17–19; 17:7–8.

22. Auerbach, "Odysseus's Scar," in *Mimesis*, 14–15.

There, Luke adds that the disciples understood nothing of what Jesus predicted, explaining that Jesus' word was hidden from them (18:34; cf. Mark 10:32–34).

The implied author in Luke enacts his story on an arena stage, in contrast to the proscenium stage of Mark's implied author. The Gospel of Luke situates events in relation to world politics (2:1–2; 3:1–2). An identification of the open, "the whole world knows" narrative mode in Luke seems to fit with the way that Luke redacts the logion found in Matthew 10:26–33. While Matthew's Jesus says "What I say to you in the darkness, speak in the light, and what your ears hear, preach on the rooftops" (Matt 10:27), Luke's Jesus emphasizes the inevitability of the public airing of all discourse: "Whatever you speak in darkness will be heard in the light, and what you say in closets will be preached on rooftops" (Luke 12:3). Similarly, in summarizing Jesus' ministry, Acts tells us that Jesus went around speaking to all Judea (Acts 10:37), and Paul claims that his own career as Jesus' apostle was not carried out in a corner (Acts 26:26).[23] Perhaps one dimension of this open, "the whole world knows" perspective, is the narration of thoughts and feelings for his *dramatis personae*. In so doing, Luke matches the breadth of his gospel narrative with a depth that similarly conveys certainty.

Conclusion

The revelation of the thoughts of many hearts appears to be literarily developed in Luke's Gospel by means of narrating what individuals are thinking and feeling to an extent not found in the other canonical gospels. Jesus the parable teller, Jesus the itinerant teacher, and the gospel's narrator all reveal others' thoughts in the Gospel of Luke. By doing so, the implied readers gain a sense that they are privy to the inmost dimensions of the characters and plot of the gospel and certainty about the things accomplished among them.

Works Cited

Auerbach, Erich. *Mimesis: The Representation of Reality in Western Literature*. Translated by Willard R. Trask. Princeton: Princeton University Press, 1953.

---

23. For further reflection on this characteristic of Luke-Acts, see Reasoner, "Open Stage."

Bovon, François. *Luke 1: A Commentary on the Gospel of Luke 1:1—9:50*. Translated by Christine M. Thomas. Hermeneia. Minneapolis: Fortress, 2002.
Fitzmyer, Joseph A. *The Gospel according to Luke I-IX*. Anchor Bible 28. Garden City, NY: Doubleday, 1981.
Heininger, Bernhard. *Metaphorik, Erzählstruktur und szensich-dramatische Gestaltung in den Sondergutgleichnissen bei Lukas*. Neutestamentliche Abhandlungen 24. Münster: Aschendorff, 1991.
Johnson, Luke Timothy. *The New Testament: A Very Short Introduction*. New York: Oxford University Press, 2010.
Juel, Donald H. *Luke-Acts: The Promise of History*. Atlanta: John Knox, 1983.
Pervo, Richard I. *Dating Acts: Between the Evangelists and the Apologists*. Santa Rosa, CA: Polebridge, 2006.
Reasoner, Mark. "The Open Stage of Luke and Acts." In *Delightful Acts: New Essays on Canonical and Non-Canonical Acts*, edited by Harold W. Attridge et al., 159–76. Wissenschaftliche Untersuchungen zum Neuen Testament 391. Tübingen: Mohr/Siebeck, 2017.
Sellew, Melissa (Philip) Harl. "Interior Monologue as a Narrative Device in the Parables of Luke." *Journal of Biblical Literature* 111 (1992) 239–53.
Shapiro, James. *A Year in the Life of William Shakespeare, 1599*. New York: HarperCollins, 2005.
Shellard, Barbara. *New Light on Luke: Its Purpose, Sources and Literary Context*. Journal for the Study of the New Testament: Supplement Series 215. Sheffield: Sheffield Academic, 2002.

5

The Pentecost Narrative of Acts

History, Tradition, and Literature

GLEN W. MENZIES

A contribution on this topic for a *Festschrift* honoring Professor Sellew might seem odd, since her work has not focused on the book of Acts. Moreover, when describing her, the appellation "historian" is not the first to come to mind. She has spent her career teaching New Testament and related subjects in a department of classical *literature*, not a history department. Nevertheless, I think this topic fits the context, and I will explain why.

Professor Sellew's scholarship has often patrolled the boundary between literature and history. I worked most closely with her during the first half of her career. As a PhD student, I absorbed all I could from an advisor who was always very generous with her time. During those years, tradition-history was her consuming passion. Building on a PhD dissertation that described the sources behind Mark's Gospel, for several years Professor Sellew participated in the (in)famous Jesus Seminar. I also remember her very thoughtful insights into the reconstruction of Q. Over the past two decades, as Professor Sellew's attention has turned more to Coptic and monasticism, she has continued to mine literature for historical insight and conversely used archaeological reconstruction to illuminate ancient literature. In other words, the *pas de deux* of literature and history dancing together in her work has persisted without interruption.

History, Literature, and Theology

Acts itself has been a battleground where scholars have fought out the competing claims of history and literature. Jerome opined that "it appears to voice bare history" (*nudam sonare videntur historiam, Epist. 53 ad Paulinim* [CSEL 463]), which more-or-less outlined the scholarly consensus until the Enlightenment. Then, in 1838, F. C. Baur, the leading light of the "Tübingen School" of biblical interpretation argued that "whatever we may think of its historical trustworthiness," Acts is fundamentally an "apologetic attempt" by its author to retroject a later theological consensus into the life of Paul and his contemporaries.[1] While Acts as history has continued to have its champions, among whom Henry Joel Cadbury, C. K. Barrett, and David Aune figure prominently, a line of scholars extending from Franz Overbeck to Martin Dibelius to Ernst Haenchen present the Acts of the Apostles primarily as proclamation or theology; its historical guise is only *pro forma*.

A mediating figure in this debate was Hans Conzelmann, who believed Luke's[2] motivations were ultimately theological, yet his tactic was to present a new theory of history. Troubled by the delay of Christ's return, he sought to reframe the two-stage promise/fulfillment scheme that had characterized the Christian vision of history with a three-stage schema that interposed a long Church Age between the bookends of promise and fulfillment. In this sense, he saw Luke-Acts as a supremely historical document.[3]

---

1. Baur, "Über den Ursprung des Episcopates," 142–145 (cited in Rothschild, *Luke-Acts and the Rhetoric of History*, 28n17).

2. Although it has been strongly challenged in recent years, I still subscribe to the idea first clearly articulated by Henry Cadbury that both Luke and Acts were written by the same person, who conceived of them as two volumes of a single work. Throughout this essay, by "Luke" I mean simply the author of Luke-Acts, not "Luke the physician" or any other individual whose name is known. I will also use masculine pronouns to accord with this convention.

3. Originally published in German (1954), Conzelmann's *Die Mitte der Zeit* was published in English under the title *The Theology of St. Luke* (1961).

More recently an additional tack has appeared that minimizes both the historical and the theological character of Acts. Best represented by Richard Pervo's book *Profit with Delight* and his commentary in the Hermeneia series, this approach emphasizes the entertainment value of the stories in Acts and treats the book as a typical piece of novelistic fiction from the ancient world.[4]

Today, few New Testament scholars find Acts as novella compelling. Instead, they identify in varying degrees both history and theology in Acts, even if the book's historical pedigree is often praised faintly as "popular history" or "apologetic history." Also, there is general recognition that the way it presents events is routinely modulated by schematization, dramatization, and tropes drawn from the larger Hellenistic literary milieu rather than the canons of modern historiography.

Before turning to an examination of the historicity of Acts 2:1-13, I will present the passage itself and a brief account of its theological contours:

> (1) When the day of Pentecost had come, they were all together in the same place. (2) And suddenly a sound came from heaven like the rush of a mighty wind, and it filled the whole house where they were sitting. (3) And there appeared to them tongues as of fire, divided and resting on each one of them. (4) And they were all filled with the Holy Spirit and began to speak in other tongues, as the Spirit gave them utterance.
>
> (5) Now there were dwelling in Jerusalem Jews, devout men from every nation under heaven. (6) And at this sound the multitude came together, and they were bewildered, because each one heard them speaking in his own language. (7) And they were amazed and wondering, saying, "Are not all these who are speaking Galileans? (8) And how is it that each of us hear them speaking in his own language with which we were raised? (9) Parthians and Medes and Elamites and residents of Mesopotamia, Judea and Cappadocia, Pontus and Asia, (10) Phrygia and Pamphylia, Rome, both Jews and proselytes, (11) Cretans and Arabians, we hear them telling in our tongues the mighty works of God. (12) And all were amazed and perplexed, saying to one another, "What does this mean?" (13) But others mocking said, "They are full of sweet new wine." (Acts 2:1-13, author's own translation)

4. Pervo, *Profit with Delight*; Pervo, *Acts*.

The Theology of Acts 2:1-13

It is axiomatic that every piece of literature from the ancient world was written with an ideological agenda. Sometimes the ideological agenda is overt and hard to miss, as is the case with the Acts. The author presents his main themes boldly, although certain ideas are subtler. And since the ideology of Acts is fundamentally religious in character, with reference to this book, the word "theology" can be substituted for "ideology."

Acts centers on the story of the growth of the Christian movement in its first decades. This growth is numeric, sociological, and geographic. Various vignettes of mass conversions are presented. The original circle of Jewish followers of Jesus expands to include God-fearing gentiles, and ultimately to pagan converts with no connection to the Synagogue. The book's focus starts in Jerusalem, on the eastern periphery of the Roman Empire, and moves relentlessly to the west, ending in Rome, the Empire's capital.

Such growth requires an explanation, and Luke's explanation is entirely theological: Empowered by the Holy Spirit, the church boldly proclaimed salvation through the risen Jesus. The words of Jesus in Acts 1:8 provides the paradigm: "But you shall receive power when the Holy Spirit has come upon you; and you shall be my witnesses in Jerusalem and in all Judea and Samaria and to the end of the earth." Acts 2:1-13 is crucial, because it describes the initial empowering by the Spirit that impels all the following narrative forward.

It is often claimed that Acts 2 describes the "birth" of the church. But this is probably a mischaracterization of Luke's presentation, since in Luke's earlier volume Jesus himself has already gathered a community around himself and selected its leadership. Acts itself starts with this leadership already bound by the Lord's instruction (1:4-5). Luke 9:1 describes Jesus sending out the Twelve, whose number represents the twelve tribes of Israel, symbolizing the totality of God's people. Similarly, in Luke 10:1 Jesus appoints and sends out the Seventy, whose number recalls that of the elders of Israel, and also represents all God's people. Even the word ἐκκλησία ("assembly" or "church") is not new, appearing nearly 100 times in the LXX, usually as a translation of the Hebrew קהל (also "assembly"), the primary designation for the collective people of Israel.[5]

---

5. That Luke does not intend Acts 2 to recount the birth of the church is suggested by the complete absence of ἐκκλησία from the chapter. In fact, the word appears nowhere in his first volume and not until 5:11 in his second volume.

The point Acts 2 makes is that at Pentecost the ἐκκλησία gathered around Christ was empowered by the Spirit to begin its new mission. As many have noted, the outpouring of the Spirit in Acts 2 parallels the baptism of Jesus presented in Luke 3:21-22. In Luke's Gospel, heaven is opened by God, who is unnamed—an example of the so-called "divine passive"—and "the Holy Spirit descends on [Jesus] in bodily form as a dove." Similarly, in Acts 2:2 a sound "comes from heaven" like a mighty, rushing wind.[6] Luke regularly emphasizes visible evidences of the presence and work of the Spirit.[7]

Verse 3 explains that "distributed tongues as of fire appeared to them" and rested on each one present. Here, the passive form ὤφθησαν ("appeared"), much as in Luke 3:21, is a divine passive, indicating that God caused the fiery tongues to appear.

This spectacular manifestation vividly makes the point that heaven has come down to earth. While the image of "tongues as of fire" seems obscure, in fact a catalogue of occurrences of similar expressions predate the book of Acts.[8] In a fragmentary work from Qumran, "tongues of fire" figure in the testing of prophets by divine consultation. In two passages from 1 Enoch, tongues of fire describe parts of the heavenly temple and its courts. The scene is especially vivid in 1 Enoch 14:9, where Enoch beholds a temple wall built of giant hailstones held together with mortar made of "tongues of fire." The impossibility of fire and ice being so conjoined in earthly spheres signals the extraordinary and supra-mundane nature of the heavenly temple. In Acts 2, rather than reprising the ascent of a human to heaven as in the Enoch literature, heaven itself is brought down to earth. The activity of the Spirit, the use of the divine passive, and the image of the tongues of fire each point in this direction.

The juxtaposition of "tongues as of fire" in v. 3 and the "other tongues" of v. 4 is striking, yet the logical connection is not obvious.

---

6. Of course, the fact that πνεῦμα like its Hebrew counterpart *ruach* can mean either "wind" or "Spirit" is a factor here, even though the word for "wind" employed in this verse is πνοή. Were a different noun not used for "Spirit" and "wind," the result would have been complete confusion; it would have seemed that the sound of wind signaled the presence of wind.

7. This characteristic of Luke's pneumatology was famously highlighted by both Hermann Gunkel, in his *Die Wirkungen des heiligen Geistes*, and by Eduard Schweizer, in his article on πνεῦμα and related words in the *TDNT*.

8. These are found in Isa 5:24, 30:27-28; 1 Enoch 14:8-25, 71:5-8; and Qumran's *Three Tongues of Fire* (reflected in 1Q29/4Q376 and possibly 1Q22 and 4Q375). For a more detailed discussion of the evidence, see Menzies, "Pre-Lucan Occurrences."

Probably the "other tongues," like the "tongues as of fire," are intended to signal the presence of the heavenly and the divine. In 1 Cor 13:1 Paul writes of "the tongues of men and angels," perhaps pointing in a similar direction, since in *Hekhalot* ("heavenly temples") literature angels often inhabit heaven.

In 1959 Eduard Schweizer made the important point that, unlike Paul's epistles or John's Gospel, "Luke adopts the typically Jewish idea that the Spirit is the Spirit of prophecy."[9] Observers may discern the presence of the Spirit wherever inspired speech is found, particularly prophecy, speaking in tongues, or the ability to proclaim a person's hidden thoughts. Luke does not present the Spirit as being active in moral transformation or in working miracles (other than speech miracles). The glossolalia of Acts 2:4 is a central example of the inspired utterance Schweizer suggests characterizes Luke's presentation of the Spirit at work.

It has become a commonplace to present the language miracle as a reversal of Babel (Gen 11:1–9). While this is probably a valid insight, the evidence is not so clear-cut as generally supposed. The chief obstacle is that in the Hebrew Bible the "lip" (שפה) is the metonym used to identify language, not the "tongue." In the LXX, "lip" (χεῖλος) also predominates, but in v. 7 αὐτῶν τὴν γλῶσσαν ("their tongue") appears where the MT has שפתם ("their lip"). Of course, even if Pentecost represents a reversal of Babel, it is only a partial reversal. Whereas Genesis 11 depicts an event with universal and sustained repercussions, Acts 2 presents a miracle that transcends normal language barriers but only for the brief moment heaven descends, in a proleptic manifestation of the eschatological hope.

Challenges to the Historicity of Acts 2:1–13

Review of the history of Acts scholarship suggests that challenges to the historicity of Acts 2:1–13 may grouped into four main categories: 1) the appearance of miracles in the account; 2) the overly convenient way this narrative fulfills John the Baptist's prophecy; 3) questions about the narrative coherence of the story; and 4) the absence of independent sources corroborating the Acts 2 story. Each challenge will be addressed in turn.

---

9. Schweizer, "πνεῦμα," 407.

The Miraculous Nature of the Story

As written, this passage contains reports of miracles. For some, this automatically marks it as fiction. Others will try to find a historical core transmitted to Luke by the sources he used. For this second group, an accompanying question is to what degree this core was modified or embellished to produce the Acts 2 account. Still others will contend that reports of miracles do not necessarily imply either creation *de novo* or the pious elaboration of more sober tradition.

Whatever judgment one makes about such considerations, it is obvious that the earliest Christians believed in miracles. While a maximally miracle-friendly position would argue for the possibility of divine intervention in the historical continuum, I will employ a more minimal standard, namely, that an event may be regarded as historical even if reports of miracles are involved, laying the deeper epistemological question aside.

The Prophecy of John the Baptist and the Desire for Closure

Although Acts 2:1–13 itself does not restate John's prophecy that "[The coming one] will baptize you in the Holy Spirit," this prophecy underlines the narrative. In Acts 1:5 John's words have already been recalled, including reference to both his own baptizing in water and the contrast of a greater Spirit baptism that was to come. Then in 1:22 John's baptism is mentioned once again.

The synoptic gospels present two forms of the Baptist's prophecy. Mark speaks of a baptism with or in "the Holy Spirit" (1:8) while Matthew and Luke (reflecting the sayings source Q) speak of a baptism with or in "Holy Spirit and fire" (Matt 3:11; Luke 3:16).[10] Surprisingly, Acts 1:5, departing from what appears in Luke 3:16, uses the shorter form,[11] as does John's Gospel (1:33). The collective weight of this evidence suggests that the earliest Christian community transmitted two forms of the logion independently.

An additional factor in this discussion is a peculiarity of biblical Hebrew. The term "Holy Spirit"—the feminine noun רוח ("spirit") modified

---

10. Matthew's wording differs slightly from Luke's. In the first gospel, John's baptism in water is specified to be "for repentance."

11. It is not clear whether Acts 1:5 relies on Mark, or if at this point Luke simply abbreviates Q.

by the feminine adjective קדושה ("holy")—never appears in the Hebrew Bible,[12] but πνεῦμα ἅγιον or the like appears several times in the LXX (e.g., Ps 50:13; Isa 63:10, 11, plus five times in the LXX books that were originally composed in Greek). Where πνεῦμα ἅγιον occurs, the usual equivalent in the Hebrew Bible is רוח קודש ("spirit of holiness"). This suggests that John, who probably preached in Hebrew or Aramaic, may have spoken of a "baptism in the Spirit of Holiness (and fire)." Nevertheless, since the reflex translation of the Hebrew "spirit of holiness" into Greek was πνεῦμα ἅγιον, this is typically what appears in the New Testament. "Spirit of holiness" only appears at two points, in 2 Thess 2:13 and in 1 Pet 1:2.

It is a generally recognized exegetical principle that sayings must make sense both in their original historical context and in any literary context in which they appear. If Luke and Acts are understood to be two parts of one project, then Acts 2 provides clarity for those who read Luke 3 and wondered what a "baptism in Holy Spirit and fire" might mean. The same closure would not be available for readers of Mark or Matthew. This has provoked considerable scholarly debate.

Since John's proclamation was apocalyptic in nature, a number of scholars have suggested that "holy" was not originally part of the tradition and that John announced a "baptism of wind and fire," connoting an impending apocalyptic judgement. The later addition of "holy" to both the Markan and Q traditions, if this actually happened, would itself constitute historical evidence for some event similar to that of Acts 2:1–13 which provoked the change. To state this differently, changing the tradition from "wind" to "Holy Spirit" would require awareness that the Christian community had experienced a "baptism in Holy Spirit."[13]

Others reckoned that "holy" was in fact always part of the tradition; the word "holy" merely implied that the fury of wind and fire was divinely appointed. Such a baptism would be entirely negative, a sign-act of judgment. As A. B. Bruce, a proponent of this approach, explains:

> The whole baptism of the Messiah, as John conceives it, is a baptism of judgment . . . I think that the grace of Christ is not here at all. The πνεῦμα ἅγιον is a strong wind of judgement, holy, as

12. In fact, no feminine form, either singular or plural, of the adjective קדוש modifying any noun at all appears in the Hebrew Bible. This is odd and suggests that perhaps the feminine form of the adjective was coined in postbiblical Hebrew.

13. The contention of some that John associated the Coming One with a baptism of fire alone seems so unlikely that I will not even bother to argue against it.

sweeping away all that is light and worthless in the nation . . .
The fire destroys what the wind leaves.[14]

Unfortunately, Bruce overlooks the clear parallel the gospels present between John's baptism in water and the coming Spirit baptism John announces. Like John's baptism in water, which was graciously offered to allow the recipient to avoid judgment, the anticipated baptism in the Holy Spirit (and fire) must convey a promise of grace to those who accepted it. In all three synoptics, the saying highlights the pronoun ὑμᾶς, emphasizing the personal aspect of these baptisms and that the same individuals may experience both: "I baptize *you* in water . . . he will baptize *you* in Holy Spirit (and fire)."[15]

An interpretation extending back to Origen suggests that two separate baptisms were implied: a baptism of blessing involving the application of the Holy Spirit; and a baptism of judgment involving the application of destructive fire. However, as James Dunn cogently argues, the way the synoptic logia are framed does not allow for two such divergent baptisms. The Markan form only mentions the one element of Holy Spirit, mooting the possibility of two divergent baptisms, and in the Q form mentioning both spirit and fire, the single preposition ἐν ("in") governs both nouns, implying the one baptism involves both elements.[16]

Having eliminated the main alternatives, what remains are two variations of a single saying promising "baptism in the Holy Spirit (and fire)" as something gracious. This does not exclude the possibility that rejection of this baptism will have negative implications, even judgement, but the basic offer is one of blessing and grace. So, how does this promise function within the context of the Baptist's proclamation or more crucially within the literary contexts of Mark and Matthew, lacking accounts of the Holy Spirit's descent to empower the church as they do?

The primary function of John's announcement of a future Spirit baptism was to draw a contrast between his own more limited role and the greater eschatological significance of the person he announced. In the Israel of John's day, there was a widespread, if not universal, sense that the Spirit was no longer so active as it had been during the time of the prophets. This sense of loss was linked with the expectation of an eschatological

---

14. Nicoll et al., *Expositor's Greek Testament*, 1:84, cited in Dunn, "Spirit-and-Fire Baptism," 82.

15. See Dunn, "Spirit-and-Fire Baptism," esp. 83–86.

16. Ibid., 83–84.

outpouring of the Spirit stimulated by the reading of certain biblical texts. Many understood Isaiah 11 to predict the rise of a new king upon whom "the Spirit of the Lord" would rest. Moses' plaintive cry in Numbers 11:29, "Would that all the Lord's people were prophets, that the Lord would put his spirit upon them," provoked dreams of such an outpouring. And the oracle delivered by the prophet Joel, "I [the Lord] will pour out my spirit on all flesh" (Joel 2:28; 3:1 [MT]) converted Moses' hope into a divine promise. Various para-biblical texts point in the same direction.

Modern exegetes place a high priority on literary closure; by their end, texts are expected to answer at least the most important questions they raise. Mark's Gospel seems not to place so much value on closure, as its original ending (at 16:8) attests. And Q, although not a gospel in the traditional sense, contains one enigma after another and very little closure. While Matthew provides more closure than either Q or Mark, on questions relating to the fulfillment of the Baptist's prophecy, it does not. Only Luke-Acts closes the loop the others leave open.

The historical-critical question is whether or not the closure Luke-Acts provides is overly convenient. Did the readerly need for closure stimulate the creation of a fictitious narrative in order to satisfy the needs and demands of the Christian community, or was an explanation based in actual events readily at hand?

The Narrative Coherence of Acts 2:1-13

As is true for all but the most turgid of narratives, in Acts 2:1-13 the reader is expected to fill in certain gaps about the story on the basis of subtle clues within the text. Who are the "all" mentioned in v. 1? Is it the group described in chapter 1 or a different group? Where do the events recounted take place? Why are there "devout men from every nation under heaven" conveniently nearby, and who are they? What sort of speech does the expression "other tongues" describe? What makes the devout men able to recognize that the speakers are Galileans? Do the other tongues sound like gibberish to the "others" of v. 13 who accuse the speakers of drunkenness?

A common scenario places these events in the temple courtyard, specifically the Outer Courtyard, also known as the Court of the Gentiles. This court would have afforded adequate space for the large crowd to which Peter speaks in Acts 2:14-42. According to this scenario, the devout "men" (ἄνδρες) were diaspora Jews who had returned to Jerusalem for the great Festival of Weeks. When these pilgrims heard the vernacular languages of their native localities and did not recognize the speakers, they made inquiries. Amazingly, they learned the speakers were Galileans. In contrast, the "others" who mock the tongues-speakers apparently do not understand what they hear; it is gibberish to them and sounds abnormal, particularly with so many languages being spoken all at once. This leads to the charge of drunkenness, which would be particularly inappropriate in the temple courtyard.

There are problems with this scenario, and these problems have received various explanations: tensions between sources; awkward editing of source material; or the basic implausibility of a concocted story. While the Court of the Gentiles fits the context of vv. 5–13, it does not fit vv. 1–4 nearly as well. The end of v. 1 states that "all" were ὁμοῦ ἐπὶ τὸ αὐτό ("together in the same place"). The precise meaning of these words is unclear, and at first glance, the verbiage seems redundant. Both the expressions ὁμοῦ and ἐπὶ τὸ αὐτό when they appear separately are normally translated "together," suggesting physical proximity. They are only rarely used together. The entire *Thesaurus Linguae Graecae* database lists only four additional independent occurrences where both expressions are used together.[17] When the two expressions are used together, they probably emphasize both temporal and physical proximity.

The emphasis that they were "all together in the same place" resets the narrative context, something that would be unnecessary if Acts 2:1–13 simply continued the context of Acts 1:15–26. Thus, there is no reason to assume either that the "all" of Acts 2:2 referred to 120 individuals or that the events surrounding the language miracle occurred in an "upper room." It does, however, indicate that the following events are the experience of the entire community of Christ followers.

Verse 2 reports that the sound like "the rush of a mighty wind filled the whole house [ὅλον τὸν οἶκον] where they were sitting [ἦσαν καθήμενοι]."

17. The relevant texts are from the third century CE (Hippolytus, *Refutatio* 4.14.4.5), the fourth or fifth century (Ps.-John Chrysostom, *In Psalmum* 100, *MPG* 55, 630, line 42), the ninth century (George the Monk, *Chronicon*, *MPG* 110, 925, line 33), and the tenth-century *Passion of the 1,003 Martyrs of Nicomedia* 3.5. In addition, the fourth-century Athanasius (in *Four Epistles to Serapion*, Ep. 1, 6.4.3) quotes this passage from Acts 2 and the seventh- or eighth-century *Epitome* of Trajan the Patrician quotes the passage by George the Monk cited above. The tenth-century *Chronicon* of Symeon Logothetes (published in Bekker, *Leonis Grammatici chronographia*, 179 line 10) quotes this passage from the *Epitome*.

Since both the Greek οἶκος and the Hebrew בית are often translated by the English word "temple," it is tempting to identify the "house" of v. 2 as the temple. But this is untenable. Both Greek and Hebrew make a distinction between a temple building (Greek οἶκος or ναός; Hebrew בית) and a holy place, which can include the surrounding courts (Greek ἱερόν; Hebrew מקדש).[18]

The events described in this passage could not have occurred inside the temple building since only priests were allowed entry. And inside the temple structure itself, where could the people mentioned have sat? Beyond this, as an author Luke is consistent in using οἶκος or ναός to refer to the temple building alone and ἱερόν to the entire temple complex.[19]

Despite these apparent problems, the references to the "house" and "sitting" are not mere redactional flotsam. Both details contribute to the larger point made explicitly in 1:7 that the remarkable events described were neither planned nor facilitated by human activity such as prayer or sacrifice. The group was simply waiting in a house, as instructed (1:4), and sitting around apparently with no agenda. Then God sovereignly moved upon them. The narrative makes no attempt to explain how the scene moves to a larger, public venue.

An additional problem with this scenario is that the "devout Jews" mentioned in v. 5 are said to be εἰς Ἰερουσαλὴμ κατοικοῦντες ("residing in Jerusalem"). This wording suggests they lived in Jerusalem on a long-term basis. If they had just been visiting, the participle παροικοῦντες ("visiting") would have been more appropriate. But perhaps this is expecting too much precision. The listing of Jews from the diaspora who had resettled in Jerusalem contains the surprising description, "residents [οἱ κατοικοῦντες] of Mesopotamia [Judea][20] and Cappadocia, Pontus and Asia . . ." Apparently, Luke considered it possible to describe the same individuals as being both κατοικοῦντες of Jerusalem and κατοικοῦντες of

---

18. An additional distinction is that a temple building can be destroyed, but a "holy place" cannot, although it can be profaned.

19. The only exception is Luke 19:46. The money changers were clearly in the courtyard, not the temple proper, but here the language is not Luke's own, but rather a quotation of both Jesus and Isa 56:7.

20. Although well supported by the manuscript evidence, the reading Ἰουδαίαν is almost certainly corrupt. Not only does it make no sense in this context, but it interrupts the pattern of listing neighboring countries in groups of two linked by καί. In addition, as Bruce Metzger has noted, Ἰουδαίαν is properly an adjective and if used substantively, it should be preceded by the definite article. See Metzger, "Ancient Astrological Geography," 133.

various foreign nations in virtually the same breath. This raises the question of how much permanence the author intended to convey.

If the historian insists on interpreting this participle very narrowly, another question emerges: Why use this problematic verb? If the narrative were entirely the creation of its author, then the author would have had the freedom to use a less problematic participle such as παροικοῦντες. However, if he felt constrained by his source, he might have reported this detail without modification. Furthermore, in the first century as today, living in Jerusalem with its temple and special status must have been attractive to "devout Jews," who wanted to participate fully in the various rites and festivals available there as nowhere else. It is certainly plausible that large numbers of diaspora Jews chose to make Jerusalem their permanent home.

At the end of the nineteenth and beginning of the twentieth centuries, when scholars habitually turned first to source criticism for answers to literary problems, it was popular to explain the tensions between vv. 1-4 and vv. 5-13 with the theory that the first four verses of the pericope were based on a written source, and the following verses, except for the list of nations found in vv. 9-11 (which was borrowed from its own source) were the creation of Luke himself. Only a single word of vv. 1-4 was judged to be a redactional addition, the word "other" that precedes "tongues." According to this explanation, the source described a meeting in a private house in which glossolalia, understood to be non-syntactic gibberish, occurred. Luke then transformed this event into something far grander, moving the location to the Outer Court of Herod's Temple and converting the gibberish into a miracle of xenolalia, speaking in known languages the speakers had never learned.

Convenient as this explanation might be, it suggests Luke both regurgitated his sources mechanically and subverted what they said. It also implies that Luke's source for vv. 1-4 already agreed perfectly with his notion that one knows the Spirit is present through visible manifestations, such as the sound from heaven, the tongues as of fire, and speaking in tongues. A more balanced assessment would minimize the degree to which Luke's sources may be reconstructed and would accord the author greater redactional/compositional skill.

Another theory, already proposed in 1936 by Ernst Lohmeyer[21] and resurrected more recently by Graham Twelftree, suggests that the events

---

21. Loymeyer, *Galilee und Jerusalem*.

of Acts 2:1–13 did not happen as presented, but rather are a pastiche of multiple encounters with the Spirit experienced by different Christian communities which for literary reasons Luke then lumped into a single account. As Twelftree summarizes,

> rather than a single story of a Spirit-focused and ecstasy inducing story that is located in Jerusalem, and that took place on the day of Pentecost, it is reasonable to suppose that early Christianity knew of a number of stories of *comings* of the Spirit or appearances of Jesus, with settings of various times and places.[22]

But the question is not, did various Christian communities have their own Pentecosts? The book of Acts itself reports as much.[23] The questions instead are these: Was there a charismatic empowering of the church in Jerusalem that defined its identity and ministry? and, As the church began to reflect on its own story, were subsequent experiences of the Spirit interpreted as further expressions of a spirituality first claimed and affirmed at Pentecost?

Lack of Independent Witnesses?

Arguments from silence are notoriously problematic, but some are hard to dismiss outright. Twelftree makes this point:

> If, as Luke portrays it, the coming of the Spirit on the day of Pentecost was such a significant event—arguably on a level with the significance of the resurrection—why has no other New Testament writer told us about it?[24]

Twelftree is correct that no other book of the New Testament mentions the event recounted in Acts 2. In fact, I would expand that statement a bit and state that no known document composed prior to Acts directly mentions this event. However, this is not to say that no other earlier document lends credence to the basic historical accuracy of the Acts 2 account. The following pages will present several New Testament passages that, when considered together, suggest something much like the Pentecost account of Acts 2 must have taken place.

---

22. Twelftree, *People of the Spirit*, 68.
23. Acts reports outpourings of the Spirit at Samaria (8:14–24), at Caesarea (10:44–48), and at Ephesus (19:1–6).
24. Twelftree, *People of the Spirit*, 65.

Acts 2 and the Primacy of Jerusalem

Even if the book of Acts had never been written, it would not be hard to discern that Jerusalem was the wellspring from which the mission of the church emerged. Dunn explains:

> It would be quite unjustified to present the origins of Christianity as a scatter of diverse and unconnected mini-Pentecosts. Two considerations in particular indicate that Luke's presentation of a determinative Jerusalem Pentecost is not without historical foundation.
>
> First, there is Paul's attitude to Jerusalem. It is quite evident from Gal 1–2 that for Paul only one centre of Christianity could lay claim to primacy; only one centre could hope to justify its claim to determine the gospel–and that is Jerusalem . . .
>
> Second, there is the significant fact that all the chief leaders of the earliest Jerusalem community were Galileans—James, Peter and John, the 'pillar' apostles. A Galilean leadership implies that the bulk of the first disciples in Jerusalem were also Galileans (cf. Acts 1.11; 2.7). If Galilee had provided a spiritual impetus of equal magnitude to a Jerusalem Pentecost why do we find so many Galileans in Jerusalem? If there were independent 'Pentecosts' in Jerusalem and Galilee, how did the Galileans gain the leadership in Jerusalem?[25]

And it is not only in Galatians that Paul acknowledges the primacy of Jerusalem. His justification for taking up a collection for "the saints of Jerusalem" also assumes that Jerusalem is the city from which the Church's missionary activity emanated: ". . . for if the Gentiles have come to share in their [the Jerusalem saints'] spiritual blessings, they [the Gentiles] ought also to be of service to them [the Jerusalem saints] in material blessings" (Rom 15:27).

Does Ephesians Allude to Spiritual Empowering at Pentecost?[26]

Having considered the location of the account described in Acts 2:1–13, what about the *timing* of the event? Do any texts suggest a connection between this seminal outpouring of the Spirit and the Feast of Weeks/ Pentecost?

25. Dunn, *Jesus and the Spirit*, 138.
26. While I believe Ephesians to have been written before Acts, at a minimum, it is independent of Acts.

The answer appears to be yes. Eph 4:7-16, especially vv. 8-11, attributes the charismatic empowering of the Church to gifts received from Christ, who has ascended to heaven (the repose of God) in triumph over his enemies, the cosmic στοιχεῖα ("demons" or "elemental forces") opposed to him. The author quotes Psalm 68:18 (MT 68:19; LXX 67:19) which describes God's ascent as a triumphant warrior to his throne on Mount Sinai, from where he bestows gifts. But why would the author connect empowering gifts with a text about Sinai as the dwelling place of God? While there are other possibilities, certainly knowledge of a tradition about the descent of the Spirit on the day of Pentecost could account for this exegetical move. While the reception of the Law at Sinai is not specifically mentioned in Psalm 68, it is implied. The psalm mentions gifts, and what greater gift did God dispense from his holy mountain than the Law? Furthermore, already in the first century, Pentecost had become linked to the giving of the Law and to covenant renewal. Any juxtaposition of Sinai and gifts would have conjured thoughts of Pentecost in the minds of many Jews.

Judaism's linkage of the Feast of Weeks with the giving of the Law was well established by the beginning of the Middle Ages. For instance, the *Babylonian Talmud*, in a saying attributed to Rabbi Eleazar ben Pedat, reports, "Pentecost is the day on which Torah was given" (*Pesahim* 68b). Much earlier evidence of this linkage comes from various Dead Sea Scrolls, especially the book of *Jubilees*. While first known to modern scholars from Ethiopic texts, the scribes of Qumran copied Hebrew manuscripts of this book, and it is now widely accepted that *Jubilees* was composed in Hebrew sometime around 150 BCE.

The book of *Jubilees* begins by announcing the date on which Moses ascended the mountain to receive the tablets of the Law (*Jub* 1:1). That date is the sixteenth day of the third month in the first year of the Exodus. Since *Jubilees* understands the Festival of Weeks to begin on the fifteenth day of the third month, this means that Moses ascended the mountain to receive the Law on the day after he had restored the eternal covenant between the Lord God and Israel by reinstituting the long-neglected festival. Why is it the day after and not the day of? As *Jubilees* presents it, Israel needed to be in a proper covenantal relationship with God before the gift of the Law could take place. Thus, *Jubilees* powerfully connects the giving of the Law with the Festival of Weeks and the renewal of the covenant it implies.[27]

27. For discussions on the distinctive calendar of *Jubilees*, see VanderKam, *Book of*

The Feast of Weeks had always commemorated God's gifts. It originally had been an agricultural festival celebrating the grain harvest and the physical bounty God provided each year. Its later association with Sinai involved a subtle but important change in the meaning of the feast. While Israel continued to celebrate this agrarian aspect, Weeks became increasingly linked to God's gift-giving in the drama of salvation-history.

The wording with which Ephesians 4:8 quotes Psalm 68:18 is puzzling. In both the MT and LXX the verbs are second-person, but they are in the third person in Ephesians. Furthermore, the verbs ἔλαβες ("you received") in the LXX and ἔδωκεν ("he gave") in Ephesians express very different ideas. The MT's לקחת ("you took") agrees with neither, and the difficulty makes various translators of the MT fudge. Most present something like, "You received gifts from people." The verb לקח normally means "he took" not "he received," but the conceptual non-sequitur of "You took gifts"—Are they given or taken coercively?—usually forces the translator's hand. Furthermore, where the LXX reads ἐν ἀνθρώπῳ ("to a person"), Ephesians reads τοῖς ἀνθρώποις ("to people"). At this point the MT reads אדם, which can be understood either as a singular or as a collective. The preposition ב prefixed to אדם is unexpected; a prefixed מ would seem more conventional if the passage meant to indicate gifts were received "from people." Marvin Tate suggests that the preposition ב might be a *beth essentiae* ("the *beth* of equivalence"). The resulting translation would be "You took/received men as gifts."[28]

An additional possibility is to understand לקח to mean not "to dispossess," but rather "to carry along," which is a well-attested meaning. This would suggest that enthroned atop Mount Sinai, Yahweh takes with him individuals, who are themselves gifts. While the exact force of this poetic language in Psalm 68 is unclear, this fits the context of Ephesians very well. The thrust of the New Testament passage is that certain individuals, fulfilling specified roles, are the exalted Christ's gifts he gives to the Church as a consequence of his triumph over the cross.

The earliest Christian confession was "Jesus [Christ] is Lord," and the fact that Jesus had received this special name was of great significance to them. Therefore, it is not surprising that Ephesians presents an account of Yahweh's gift-giving from Sinai as an explanation of the Christ's gift-giving from on high. But the fact that the specific gifts mentioned are

Jubilees; and VanderKam, "Origin, Character, and Early History."

28. Tate, *Psalms 51–100*, 166. On the *beth essentiae*, also see Waltke and O'Connor, *Introduction to Biblical Hebrew Syntax*, 198.

gifts of charismatic empowering suggests that knowledge of a tradition associating spiritual power with Pentecost may have played a role in the shaping of Ephesians 4 and its use of Psalm 68.

1 Corinthians 14:20–25:

(20) Brothers and sisters, do not be children in your thinking; be babes in evil, but in thinking be mature. (21) In the Law it is written, "'By other tongues [ἐν ἑτερογλώσσοις] and the lips of foreigners [ἐν χείλεσιν ἑτέρων] I will speak to this people, and even then they will not listen to me,' says the Lord." (22) Thus, tongues are a sign not for believers but for unbelievers, while prophecy is not for unbelievers but for believers. (23) If, therefore, the whole church assembles and all speak in tongues, and the uninstructed or unbelievers enter, will they not say you are mad? (24) But if all prophesy, and an unbeliever or uninstructed person enters, he is convicted by all, he is called to account by all, (25) the secrets of his heart are disclosed; and so, falling on his face, he will worship God and declare that God is really among you. (RSV)

Many have found this passage confusing. It suggests an Old Testament anticipation of the glossolalia that was common in the church at Corinth. Just as God had spoken through the sign of tongues long ago in ancient Israel, so also in the first century CE tongues functioned as a divine sign. At first glance, the argument seems straightforward. Then the reader quickly encounters a substantial problem.

In vv. 23 and 24 Paul clearly and strongly asserts that prophecy is better suited to evangelizing unbelievers than is tongues. So, why does he say in the preceding verse, "Prophecy is not for unbelievers"? The problem is severe enough that some commentators have claimed Paul himself got the argument tangled, having meant to say tongues was a sign for unbelievers and prophecy a sign for believers. However, this procrustean approach of customizing the evidence to fit a preordained solution is rather drastic. A better solution is available from careful consideration of the context.

Was Paul repulsed by speaking in tongues, thinking it a pagan intrusion into Christian worship with Delphi and its glossolalic Pythia lying less than fifty miles away? Clearly not. Paul not only considered tongues a genuine gift of the Spirit (both a *charisma* and a *pneumatikon*), but he also boasted that he spoke in tongues more than any of the Corinthians (14:18). Nevertheless, without accompanying interpretation, speaking in tongues was unintelligible to the Greek-speaking Corinthians and therefore was of little or no benefit to the assembled congregation. And if many spoke in tongues at the same time—the "all" of v. 23 is probably hyperbole—the gathering might look like a den of lunatics. For these reasons, prophecy was much to be preferred over uninterpreted tongues in public gatherings. Based on the model of glossolalia at Delphi, the Corinthians likely thought of it as something that could be interpreted by appropriately gifted or trained individuals; however, Paul's teaching that in public meetings glossolalia should either be interpreted or avoided altogether apparently was unknown to the Corinthians before Paul's instruction in 1 Corinthians.

Likely some or all of the Corinthians believed speaking in tongues was a divinely appointed method of evangelism. Paul wanted to disabuse them of this idea. The Corinthians may have thought glossolalia made them seem "spiritual," after the model of the world-famous Pythia, but Paul's pointed argument about which sort of *pneumatikon* was more likely to promote conversion to faith—tongues or prophecy—suggests that an evangelistic motivation also lay at the root of the controversy.

The most likely explanation for confidence in the evangelistic potential of tongues is knowledge of a tradition about the Pentecost event, or at least some event in which xenolalia led to mass conversion. While Paul nowhere gives any hint that he himself expects tongues-speech to be intelligible without exercise of the gift of interpretation, xenolalia was likely part of the picture the Corinthians visualized. "Tongues are a sign for unbelievers" may even have become a Corinthian slogan, which the apostle finds necessary to turn on its head in the course of his instruction.[29]

A clue pointing in this direction is Isa 28:11–12, the passage that Paul paraphrases in his argument. While there are substantial differences between Paul's wording and the Old Testament texts, in both the paraphrase and the apostle's source, the word "other" appears, making clear that the tongues are other known human languages. Whereas in both the MT and the LXX the word "other" appears once, Paul amplifies the point by mentioning "other" twice.[30] Paul then omits most of v. 12, including a paraphrase of only the final words of the verse.

29. This theory of a slogan is based on a discussion from years ago involving Russell P. Spittler and Alan G. Padgett.

30. There is a significant textual variant in Paul's quotation/paraphrase.

The greatest difference between the MT and the LXX is the person of the verb "speak" in v. 11. In the LXX it is the invading armies who "will speak" (λαλήσουσιν), while in the MT the verb is in the third-person singular: "he [God] will speak" (ידבר). The quotation in 1 Corinthians (λαλήσω, "I will speak") agrees perfectly with neither Old Testament text, but clearly its meaning resembles the MT more closely.

Paul emphasizes that the "other tongue" of Isaiah 28 did nothing to convert anyone to faith: "'... even then they will not listen to me,' says the Lord." Many understand the datives of v. 22 to be "datives of advantage," but this is wrong. Paul claims the sign in Isaiah 28 did not advantage the Israelites at all. But neither are the datives of v. 22 "datives of disadvantage." Prophecy as a sign does not disadvantage believers. Instead, prophecy *marks the recipients as* believers, just as tongues *marks the recipients as* unbelievers.[31] To make Paul's point by paraphrasing him, "Tongues are a sign that will not lead to belief, while prophecy is a sign that does lead to belief." If v. 22 is understood in this way, the argument of the entire of the passage flows logically. Since the Israelites did not believe as a result of the sign of tongues in Isaiah 28, it was wrong to expect pagan Corinthians to believe in Christ when they encountered tongues in church gatherings.

While Paul uses Isaiah 28 to advance his argument, it is not certain he introduced this text into the argument. Before Paul wrote 1 Corinthians, a group at Corinth may have used this text to encourage wider practice of glossolalia. Under this scenario, Paul's exegesis countered a preexisting interpretation. Whether Isaiah 28 was first introduced into the dispute by the apostle or by his flock, there is an air of proof-texting about its use. Isaiah 28 does not seem determinative of Paul's position on the proper uses of tongues and prophecy in public meetings, but rather a reactive response to a vexing problem.

Whether or not Isaiah 28 played a role in the teaching Paul corrects, 1 Corinthians provides evidence of exposition combining xenolalia, public meetings, and conversions. It is not far-fetched to suggest this was based on knowledge of a tradition about an outpouring of the Holy Spirit

---

Nestle-Aland renders the first half of the quotation as ἐν ἑτερογλώσσοις καὶ ἐν χείλεσιν ἑτέρων λαλήσω τῷ λαῷ τούτῳ ("with other tongues and with the lips of others I will speak to this people." P[46] (one of the oldest extant New Testament manuscripts) and a few manuscripts of the Western text type read ἐν ἑτερογλώσσοις καὶ ἐν χείλεσιν ἑτέροις λαλήσω τῷ λαῷ τούτῳ ("in other tongues and with other lips I will speak to this people"). In either case, the point is not essentially different.

31. Another way to state this is that all the datives of v. 22 are *datives of reference*.

in Jerusalem that also combined xenolalia, a public meeting, and conversions. Paul too was likely aware of this tradition, which he ignored, because acknowledging it would not have advanced his argument. He may have believed the Jerusalem xenolalia was *sui generis* (as it is portrayed in Acts), and therefore not a precedent for practice in the wider Church.

Conclusion

The narrative of Acts 2:1-13 has a clear theological agenda, but this does not mean its presentation was not grounded in actual historical events. Some interpretive gaps are left for the reader to fill, as is normal in literary texts. Luke almost certainly used sources, but there is no clear reason to think he tried to subvert the original message of these sources.

The most important argument against the historicity of Acts 2:1-13 is that, although it is depicted in Acts as a moment of great significance for the Church, no other earlier document directly refers to this important event. Nevertheless, I have attempted to show that other New Testament writings in less direct ways support the basic historical accuracy of the Pentecost account: 1) Jerusalem was the wellspring of Christian spirituality; 2) before the composition of Luke-Acts the Christian community associated giving of divine gifts at Sinai, and likely the Feast of Pentecost, with the charismatic empowering of its leaders; and 3) the Christian community of Corinth likely knew a tradition that combined xenolalia, a public meeting, and conversions to Christianity. Cumulatively, these testimonies powerfully support the essential historicity of Acts 2:1-13.

Works Cited

Bekker, I., ed. *Leonis Grammatici chronographia*. Corpus scriptorum historiae Byzantinae. Bonn: Weber, 1842.
Conzelmann, Hans. *The Theology of St. Luke*. Translated by Geoffrey Buswell. New York: Harper & Row, 1961.
Dunn, James D. G. *Jesus and the Spirit*. Philadelphia: Westminster, 1975.
———. "Spirit-and-Fire Baptism." *Novum Testamentum* 14 (1972) 81-92.
Gunkel, Hermann. *Die Wirkungen des heiligen Geistes, nach der populären Anschauung der apostolischen Zeit und nach der Lehre des Apostels Paulus : eine biblisch-theologische Studie*. Göttingen: Vandenhoeck & Ruprecht, 1888.
Lohmeyer, Ernst. *Galiläa und Jerusalem*. Forschungen zur Religion und Literatur des Alten und Neuen Testaments 52. Göttingen: Vandenhoek & Ruprecht, 1936.
Menzies, Glen W. "Pre-Lucan Occurrences of the Phrase 'Tongue(s) of Fire.'" *Pneuma* 22 (2000) 27-60.

Metzger, Bruce M. "Ancient Astrological Geography and Acts 2:9-11." In *Apostolic History and the Gospel: Biblical and Historical Essays Presented to F. F. Bruce*, edited by W. Ward Gasque and Ralph P. Martin, 122-33. Exeter, UK: Paternoster, 1970.

Nicoll, W. Robertson et al. *Expositor's Greek Testament*. 5 vols. New York: Dodd, Mead, 1897-1910.

Pervo, Richard I. *Acts: A Commentary*. Hermeneia. Minneapolis: Fortress, 2009.

———. *Profit with Delight: The Literary Genre of the Acts of the Apostles*. Philadelphia: Fortress, 1987.

Rothschild, Clare K. *Luke-Acts and the Rhetoric of History*. Wissenschaftliche Untersuchungen zum Neuen Testament 2/175. Tübingen: Mohr/Siebeck, 2004.

Schweizer, Eduard. "πνεῦμα." In *TDNT* 6:389-455.

Tate, Marvin E. *Psalms 51-100*. Word Biblical Commentary 20. Grand Rapids: Zondervan, 1990.

Twelftree, Graham H. *People of the Spirit: Exploring Luke's View of the Church*. Grand Rapids: Baker Academic, 2009.

VanderKam, James C. *The Book of Jubilees*. Guides to Apocrypha and Pseudepigrapha. Sheffield: Sheffield Academic, 2001.

———. "The Origin, Character, and Early History of the 364-Day Calendar: A Reassessment of Jaubert's Hypotheses." *Catholic Biblical Quarterly* 41 (1979) 390-411.

Waltke, Bruce K., and M. O'Connor. *An Introduction to Biblical Hebrew Syntax*. Winona Lake, IN: Eisenbrauns, 1990.

Part 2

Reconceiving "Gnostic" Christianity
from Corinth to Nag Hammadi

6

Contesting the Gift of *Gnosis* in 1 Corinthians

GEOFFREY S. SMITH

An early generation of commentators conceived of the controversy over knowledge in Corinth as a showdown between Paul and the gnostics. Rudolph Bultmann, for example, claimed that "already in Corinth there had been a movement of gnostic pneumatics, and Paul had to resist their influence."[1] The fullest treatment of Paul's confrontation with the so-called Corinthian gnostics came, unsurprisingly, from one of Bultmann's students, Walter Schmithals, who dedicated a monograph to the topic.[2] Yet on account of a heightened awareness of the anachronism of positing the existence of gnostics in the first century, coupled with doubts surrounding the "dubious" category of Gnosticism more generally, recent studies attempt to treat Corinthian gnosis without recourse to Gnosticism.[3] As one prominent scholar has recently put it, "Now one hears more often not of Corinthian 'gnostics' but of 'enthusiasts,' or 'spirit-people.'"[4]

Nonetheless, many aspects of the controversy between Paul and these enigmatic "enthusiasts" or "spirit-people" remain poorly understood.

---

1. Bultmann, "γινώσκω," 709.

2. Schmithals, *Paul & the Gnostics*. See also Wilkens, *Weisheit und Torheit*, who studied under Günther Bornkamm, also a Bultmann student.

3. The literature on Gnosticism as an analytical category is abundant, but in my opinion the most important works include Smith, "History of the Term *Gnostikos*"; Williams, *Rethinking "Gnosticism"*; and King, *What Is Gnosticism?*

4. Mitchell, "Paul's Letters to Corinth," 313.

97

What led some members of the Corinthian assembly to claim to be in possession of divine knowledge and wisdom? What is the nature of the knowledge and wisdom they claimed to possess? Is Paul's response to these members of the assembly best characterized as opposition? How does Paul respond to their claims? With so much unknown about those in Corinth claiming knowledge and wisdom, one wonders whether there is enough information in 1 Corinthians even to attempt such an investigation. As one commentator has recently pessimistically remarked, "The attempt to systematically reconstruct the religious attitudes represented in Corinth is fraught with great uncertainties; all attempts to interpret the thinking of the Corinthian Christians in light of phenomena that are otherwise known from a history of religions perspective must remain very vague."[5] While it is true that as an occasional letter written from Paul's perspective, 1 Corinthians does not provide us with a complete or evenhanded description of the factions within the Corinthian assembly, I do believe that all is not lost. We can sketch a profile of Paul's Corinthian rivals that is more than "extremely vague."

This article aims to advance our understanding of the controversy over knowledge in Corinth in three ways: 1) by highlighting the importance of viewing γνῶσις (gnosis, "knowledge") as one of the χαρίσματα ("spiritual gifts") practiced within the assembly, 2) by framing the controversy between Paul and the Corinthians as a contest over knowledge and wisdom, and 3) by situating this contest within the context of competitive expert performance in the first and second centuries CE. I hope to set forth a plausible explanation for the controversy over knowledge and wisdom in 1 Corinthians without recourse to the problematic notion of Gnosticism.

On the basis of a careful reading of 1 Corinthians and an awareness of the biblical and sophistic currents that likely coalesced within the first-century Corinthian assembly, I will argue that the knowers and sages were a charismatic faction within the assembly, encouraged by Apollos or someone like him to think of themselves as beneficiaries of God's eschatological gift of knowledge. Traces of their teachings survive in the form of slogans repeated back to the Corinthians by Paul. These slogans give the impression that the Corinthian knowers' teachings took the form of γνῶμαι (Lat: *sententiae*), pithy truisms delivered in support of an argument. Rather than reject Corinthian claims to knowledge outright, Paul

---

5. Lindemann, *Erste Korintherbrief*, 14. Translation is my own.

chooses to coopt Corinthian charismatic knowledge, by beating them at their own game. Paul's rivalry with the Corinthian knowers comes into fuller relief when taken as an instance of sophistic rivalry, a mode of public competition over knowledge that was alive and well in Corinth during Paul's time.

Knowledge and Wisdom in Corinth

Knowledge was one of the many spiritual gifts practiced by followers of Jesus in Corinth. Paul appeals to the "abundance of knowledge" (πᾶσα γνῶσις) among the Corinthians as proof that they do not lack any "spiritual gift" (χάρισμα, 1 Cor 1:5, 7). "Utterance of knowledge" (λόγος γνώσεως) takes its place alongside prophecy and tongues in Paul's catalogue of "manifestations of the spirit" in 12:8–10 and again in Paul's excursus on the superior ethic of love, where he contrasts the fleeting nature of prophecy, tongues, and knowledge with enduring love (1 Cor 13:8; see also 14:6.). The gift of knowledge also closely relates to the gift of "wisdom" (σοφία) in 1 Corinthians; the two may even be synonymous. Paul presents knowledge and wisdom as two kinds of rational utterance, or λόγος. In fact γνῶσις, σοφία, and λόγος form a cluster of related terms in Paul's letter. He mentions "speech and knowledge of every kind" (1:5), "eloquent wisdom" (1:17), "lofty words or wisdom" (2:1), and "plausible words of wisdom" (2:4, following the reading of Codex Sinaiticus, Vaticanus, et al.), and lists "utterance of wisdom" (λόγος σοφίας) and "utterance of knowledge" (λόγος γνώσεως) as two manifestations of "the same spirit" (τὸ αὐτὸ πνεῦμα, 1 Cor 12:8). Knowledge and wisdom are so closely related in 1 Corinthians that we should resist the urge to make a strong distinction between the two.[6] Therefore, the Corinthian assembly included not only prophets, those who speak in tongues, healers, miracle workers, and other groups traditionally recognized as charismatic, but also those who delivered wise and knowledgeable teaching to the community, groups we might refer to as the sages and knowers, or collectively as the Corinthian experts.[7]

---

6. See also the parallel notions of "wisdom" (σοφία) and "discernment/knowledge" (σύνεσις) in Paul's modified quotation of Isa 29:14.

7. I am intentionally avoiding the term "gnostic" here for two reasons: 1) the Greek adjective "gnostic" (γνωστικός) does not appear in 1 Corinthians, and 2) the term "gnostic" carries with it too much interpretive baggage.

Rehearsing the textual evidence for a cadre of Corinthian sages and knowers may seem unnecessary given the clarity with which Paul's speaks of wisdom and knowledge as χαρίσματα. Yet in comparison with prophecy and tongues, the gifts of knowledge and wisdom receive relatively little scholarly attention. Seldom are knowledge and wisdom considered among the Corinthian χαρίσματα and only infrequently are the knowers and sages conceived of as an isolatable charismatic faction within the Corinthian assembly. The lack of scholarly attention paid to the expert charismatics is even more striking given Paul's preoccupation with them in 1 Corinthians. Early in chapter 1 Paul singles out γνῶσις as a prominent gift within the assembly (1 Cor 1:5, 7). He also dedicates the bulk of chapters 1–4 to a discussion of knowledge and wisdom, before revisiting the topics in chapters 8, 12, and 14. Clearly the Corinthian experts are one of Paul's primary preoccupations in the letter. Why then has a charismatic faction of such interest to Paul received relatively little scholarly attention?

I suspect that the lack of attention paid to the charismatic knowers and sages stems in part from Max Weber's influential adaptation of the Pauline notion of *charisma*, whereby he privileges ecstatic forms of charismatic expression over and above rational ones. Weber distinguishes charisma from what he terms rational and traditional forms of authority. Whereas rational authority finds its basis in law and traditional authority in established belief, charismatic authority derives from the exceptional character of an individual. While Weber's notion of charismatic authority does not in theory preclude leaders such as the Corinthian experts, who do not make authoritative claims on the basis of law or tradition, he tends to apply the label of charismatic authority only to supernatural, superhuman, or exceptionally powerful figures such as berserks, shamans, miracle workers, prophets, and magicians. Weber's restricted application of charisma to practitioners of spiritual excess might explain why Corinthian prophets and glossolalists feature more prominently in studies of Corinthian charisma than do the knowers and sages, who offer practical instruction to the assembly by appealing to theological truths and maxims gleaned from popular philosophy. In other words, when Weber's notion of charisma overrides Paul's, the knowers and sages seem too tame to number among the Corinthian charismatics.

Another factor that has likely hampered the identification of the knowers and sages as charismatics is that many scholars of the nineteenth and twentieth centuries—those largely responsible for framing the academic study of 1 Corinthians—interpreted references to Corinthian wisdom and knowledge within the rubric of Gnosticism. Thus even though there is a longstanding interpretive tradition that associates wisdom and knowledge with a particular group within the Corinthian assembly, wisdom and knowledge have not been understood as spiritual gifts, but as hallmarks or mantras of a gnostic religious propensity, tendency, or essence. However, most scholars would now agree that those claiming knowledge and wisdom in Corinth were not gnostics, either because Gnosticism did not exist until the second century or because it never existed as an isolatable religious current at all. Yet despite the failure of the Gnostic thesis, or perhaps because it has been so widely rejected, scholars have been understandably hesitant to revisit the subject of knowledge and wisdom in Corinth. Yet when we focus upon Paul's application of the term *charisma* and move beyond the problematic notion of first-century Gnosticism we begin to recognize that the knowers and sages were a prominent charismatic faction within the Corinthian assembly.

As the passages discussed above make clear, certain members of the Corinthian assembly came to believe that God had poured forth his spirit upon them and endowed them with particular gifts. Promises of God's spiritual presence abound in the Hebrew Bible. Consider, for example, Joel 2:28–29:

> Then afterward I will pour out my spirit on all flesh; your sons and your daughters shall prophesy, your old men shall dream dreams, and your young men shall see visions. Even on the male and female slaves, in those days, I will pour out my spirit. (NRSV)

God's promise in Isaiah may have had a special appeal among the Corinthian experts: "The spirit of the Lord shall rest on him, the spirit of wisdom and understanding (πνεῦμα σοφίας καὶ συνέσεως), the spirit of counsel and might, the spirit of knowledge (πνεῦμα γνώσεως) and the fear of the Lord" (Isa 11:2 LXX).

While it is possible that the Corinthian experts emerged as leaders organically, through their own study of the scriptures of their newfound religion, I find it more likely that they came to see themselves as recipients of divine knowledge and wisdom by means of the teaching of someone well versed in the Septuagint.[8] If we are to believe Paul when he says that

---

8. Unfortunately, it is unclear whether any Jews belonged to the Corinthian

not many in Corinth were "wise by human standards" when they were "called" (1 Cor 1:26), then it is unlikely that they would have been able to conduct their own study of the Prophets. As a Hellenistic Jew well versed in the Septuagint, Paul could have been the one to introduce the notion of spiritual gifts to the Corinthian assembly, but this is unlikely for several reasons. First, Paul does not seem particularly interested in establishing leadership structures within his assemblies. Unlike the deutero-Pauline letters, where qualifications for and duties of ecclesiastical offices such as bishop, presbyter, and deacon are discussed, Paul mentions leaders in his genuine letters but never details their requirements of prescribed roles. Consider for example his letter to the Philippians, where he merely mentions "bishops (ἐπίσκοποι) and deacons (διάκονοι)" without detailing the responsibilities of these offices. When he does return to the topic of leadership within the assembly, he reverts to his preferred terminology, referring to Euodia and Syntyche simply as "co-workers" (συνεργοί, Phil 4:2–3). Paul's apparent lack of interest in expounding upon what it means to be a bishop or deacon in the Philippian assembly, coupled with the theme of disunity that runs throughout the letter, has led some to plausibly suggest that the Philippian assembly had organized its own leadership structure, and that calling out their bishops and deacons in the beginning of the letter was Paul's subtle way to call attention to the disunity that hierarchical structures can engender.[9] Regardless of Paul's reason for naming these leaders in the beginning of his letter, it is clear that he has more pressing interests than fostering leadership structures within the assembly. Additionally, it would be strange for Paul to promote one leadership structure in Philippi and another in Corinth. Paul never mentions bishops or deacons in his letters to the Corinthians, and perhaps more strikingly, with the exception of three passing references in Romans, which may suggest that the Corinthian charismatic system influenced Paul's own thinking, he never mentions charismatic gifts outside of 1 Corinthians (see Rom 1:11; 11:29; 12:6).

It is more likely that the charismatic system belonged to the teaching Apollos. Paul twice acknowledges the influence of Apollos upon some members of the assembly ("I belong to Apollos," 1 Cor 1:12; 3:4),

---

assembly. The account in Acts 18 of Paul's expulsion from the synagogue is of dubious historical value, though that Aquila and Priscilla, Jews expelled from Rome, met Paul in Corinth seems likely given his mention of them in Rom 16:3. See also Koester, "Silence of the Apostle," 340.

9. Silva, *Philippians*, 144.

and despite his mention of other factions within the assembly ("I belong to Cephas," and "I belong to Christ"), it becomes clear in the course of his letter that his primary concern is with those claiming allegiance to Apollos. In 1 Cor 3:4 and 5 Paul has reduced the sects to two, those of Apollos and those of Paul. Additionally, Paul recalls the beginnings of the Corinthian assembly with two metaphors, one agricultural and another architectural, in which there is room for only two leaders: himself and Apollos. In Paul's words, "I planted, Apollos watered," and "like a skilled master builder I laid a foundation, and someone else is building on it" (1 Cor 3:6, 10).

Paul never explicitly says that Apollos was responsible for introducing the notion of the gifts of knowledge and wisdom to the Corinthians, but the fact that in chapters 1–4 he is preoccupied with challenging notions of charismatic knowledge and wisdom and with characterizing Apollos as a teacher of secondary importance behind himself strongly suggests that Paul associates the gifts of knowledge and wisdom with the teachings of Apollos in Corinth. If, as we read in Acts 18:24, Apollos was a Hellenistic Jew from Alexandria, he would have been well versed in the Septuagint, and may well have introduced the notion of eschatological gifts to the Corinthian assembly.

But what role did these knowers and sages play in the Corinthian assembly? Here it is useful to discuss a series of sayings repeated by Paul known as the Corinthian slogans. In at least five instances Paul quotes Corinthian sayings back to them. One saying is repeated twice in the letter with slight variation.

a. 1 Cor 6:12/10:23:
All things are lawful (for me).

πάντα (μοι) ἔξεστιν.

b. 1 Cor 6:13:
Food is for the stomach and the stomach is for food, [but God will do away with both of them.]

τὰ βρώματα τῇ κοιλίᾳ, καὶ ἡ κοιλία τοῖς βρώμασιν·[ὁ δὲ θεὸς καὶ ταύτην καὶ ταῦτα καταργήσει.]¹⁰

c. 1 Cor 8:1:

---

10. I agree with Dale Martin in seeing this second sentence as part of the slogan (*Corinthian Body*, 264).

We all have knowledge.

πάντες γνῶσιν ἔχομεν.

d. 1 Cor 8:4:
There is no such thing as an idol in this world; there is no God but one.

οὐδὲν εἴδωλον ἐν κόσμῳ . . . οὐδεὶς θεὸς εἰ μὴ εἷς.

The third saying—"We all have knowledge"—leaves little doubt that the Corinthian experts were the responsible for uttering the slogans. These sayings provide us with some examples of the mode and content of the experts' teaching. The slogans may belong to an "utterance of knowledge" (λόγος γνώσεως, 12:8) delivered to the assembly by one or more members of the charismatic faction. Absent fuller context, it is impossible to say much about the genre of this "utterance of knowledge," but from the surviving slogans it is clear that the experts' teaching often took the form of γνῶμαι (Lat: *sententiae*), pithy truisms delivered in support of an argument.[11] Dale Martin provides a "minimalist sketch" of the content of these γνῶμαι: "The Strong appear to have emphasized radical freedom, at least for those wise enough to know how to use it. They claim 'gnosis,' or 'knowledge,' for themselves. That knowledge teaches them not to fear gods or daimons, and this lack of fear of the gods seems to be linked to a radical monotheism. They show no regard for purity regarding food, and this seems tied to a deprecation of the body."[12] Martin, following many others, locates the inspiration for these teachings within the popular philosophy of the day, Stoicism and Cynicism to be more precise.[13] Thus the Corinthian experts and sages likely benefitted from the dual traditions of Judaism and Hellenistic moral philosophy. In other words, they are Jesus followers who have come to think of themselves as recipients of God's eschatological gifts, and these gifts include knowledge of Hellenistic moral philosophy.

---

11. For discussions of the use of γνῶμαι in classical rhetoric, see Aristotle, *Rhetoric* 2.21; Anaximenes, *Art of Rhetoric* 11 1430a40–b1. γνῶμαι were exceptionally common in speeches in the Second Sophistic. See Philostratus and Ps. Longinus. See also the discussions of γνῶμαι in Second Sophistic rhetorical treatises (Apsines, Hermogenes, Ps.-Aristides, Anon. Seguerianus, and Ps.-Demetrius).

12. Martin, *Corinthian Body*, 70.

13. Ibid., 71–73.

As an example of the kind of ideological outlook that we find among the Corinthian experts we can point to the *Sentences* of Pseudo-Phocylides. Despite their attribution to the sixth-century-BCE Ionic poet Phocylides of Miletus, the *Sentences* were actually composed sometime between the first century BCE and the first century CE by a Hellenistic Jew likely living in Alexandria.[14] The text takes the form of a series of philosophically and theologically informed gnomic sayings addressing an array of ethical and practical matters. For example, the author declares that "Speech (λόγος) of the divinely inspired wisdom is best. Better is a wise man than a strong one; Wisdom directs the course of lands and cities and ships" (vv. 129–131). Or another example: "Eat in moderation, and drink and tell stories in moderation" (v. 69). In subject matter, this latter example echoes the slogan in 1 Cor 6:13: "Food is for the stomach and the stomach is for food." Another striking parallel with the slogans in 1 Corinthians is how the author of the *Sentences* conceives of his teachings, as a collection of wise teachings or mysteries that God has given him as a gift. The *Sentences* begin "Phocylides, the wisest (σοφώτατος) of men, sets forth these counsels of God by his holy judgments, gifts (δῶρα) of blessing," and it concludes with "these are the mysteries (μυστήρια) of righteousness . . ." While there is no direct evidence that Apollos or the Corinthian knowers and sages modeled their charismatic activities after Ps.-Phocylides, this text does exemplify the kind of self-conception that we find among the Corinthian knowers and sages and provides us with an example of the kind of philosophical and theological modes of teaching that inspired their own.

Paul was critical of the Corinthian experts. In fact the only reason we know anything about the Corinthian experts is because Paul found the content and style of their teaching objectionable and decided to criticize them in writing. Paul repeatedly challenges what he considers to be the worldly wisdom and knowledge championed by some members of the Corinthian assembly. The Corinthian knowers and sages, in Paul's opinion, are unaware of the profound epistemological reversal brought about by the death of Christ, whereby what was once considered to be genuine wisdom and knowledge is now exposed as foolishness. Paul finds support for this idea in the words of the prophet Isaiah, who long ago claimed that God would destroy the "wisdom of the wise" and thwart

---

14. Charlesworth, ed., *Old Testament Pseudepigrapha*, 2:565–73.

the "cleverness of the clever" (1 Cor 1:19).[15] Accordingly Paul reminds the Corinthians that he did not peddle worldly wisdom when he entered the city, but instead divested himself of all knowledge unaffiliated with the crucified Christ and delivered a message from God free from human inference (1 Cor 2:1-2).

Yet despite his critical stance toward Corinthian expertise, Paul does not reject the gifts of wisdom and knowledge per se. Rather he appropriates them. "Yet among the mature *we do speak wisdom*," Paul asserts (1 Cor 2:6-9). Likewise, in his discussion of eating meat sacrificed to idols in chapter 8 Paul recycles a Corinthian knowledge teaching into knowledge teaching of his own ("We know that 'we all have knowledge' ...") and limits the dissemination of knowledge to a select few ("not all have this knowledge") (1 Cor 8:1-13). Only Paul, and the select few who choose to listen to him, truly possess the divine wisdom and knowledge needed to offer authoritative theological, ritual, and ethical teaching to the assembly. By claiming these gifts as his own, Paul seeks to establish himself as the proprietor of divine wisdom and knowledge who at his discretion can broker the expert gifts to a select group of authorized teachers.

Paul's appropriation of Corinthian wisdom and knowledge makes it difficult to speak of those with whom he disagrees as "opponents." While he is critical of the Corinthian experts, he does not adopt the same polemical tone that he directs at the "super apostles" in 2 Corinthians, or the "dogs and the evil doers" in Philippi. Rather, his tone is more restrained, and his criticism is more nuanced. This point is illustrated well by his subtle relegation of Apollos to second in command behind him in his agricultural and architectural metaphors in 1 Cor 3. Paul plants the seed, but Apollos waters; Paul is the foundation, but "someone else" builds upon it. Paul does not oppose Apollos; he simply "reminds" the Corinthians that he himself is the more important leader. Paul has no opponents in 1 Corinthians, only rivals.

Thinking with the Second Sophistic

Thus the conflict in Corinth can be conceptualized as a contest over expert knowledge and wisdom between Paul on the one hand and a cadre of charismatic knowers and sages on the other. But what broader cultural

---

15. I prefer to follow the NASB in translating σύνεσις as "cleverness" rather than "discernment" as adopted by the NRSV.

framework helps us contextualize the controversy over knowledge and wisdom in Corinth?

One potentially attractive option is to follow Bruce Winter in locating the conflict in Corinth within the cultural context of the Second Sophistic, a period of renewed interest in Greek identity, rhetoric, and oratory that flourished during the second and third centuries.[16] The plausibility of Winter's contextualization of the conflict depends upon two premises: that the Second Sophistic began in the first century CE and that this sophistic revival was particularly popular in Roman Corinth. In other words, if Paul's conflict with members of the Corinthian leadership is to be understood within the context of the Second Sophistic, the cultural currents of the Second Sophistic must be shown to have been present in Corinth at the time of Paul's visit in the middle of the first century. Winter's backdating of the Second Sophistic by half a century rests in part upon a careful reading of Philostratus, the third-century sophist and biographer who coined the term "Second Sophistic (δευτέρα σοφιστική)." Although Philostratus traces the roots of the Second Sophistic to Aeschines, the fourth-century-BCE Attic orator, he understands the movement to have begun in earnest with a certain Nicetes of Smyrna, who was active during the reign of Nero, that is, during Paul's own lifetime. Winter then seeks to establish that the sophists were embraced and even emulated in Corinth by appealing to evidence from Epictetus, Dio Chrysostom, Plutarch and others who associate the sophistic revival with the city. In the words of Dio, Corinth was a place where

> one could hear crowds of wretched sophists around Poseidon's temple shouting and reviling one another, and their disciples, as they were called, fighting with one another, many writers reading aloud their stupid works, many poets reciting their poems while others applauded them ...[17]

After establishing first-century Corinth as a hub for the early sophistic revival, Winter recasts the conflict between the Corinthians and Paul as a clash between sophists and a philosopher, with the Corinthians corresponding to the sophists and Paul corresponding to the philosopher, who critiques his ostentatious opponents from outside of the sophistic tradition.

---

16. Winter, *Philo and Paul among the Sophists*.
17. Dio Chrysostom, *Or.* 8 (trans. Cohoon).

If we allow the milieu of the Second Sophistic to inform our understanding specifically of Corinthian knowledge, a topic that Winter does not discuss, then Corinthian claims to knowledge take on a new flavor. When we consider the contest between Paul and the Corinthian experts within the framework of the Second Sophistic, Corinthian claims to knowledge and wisdom appear to belong to what we might term a "rhetoric of certainty," a confident self-assurance characteristic of sophists active during the sophistic revival.[18] Consider for example Philostratus' distinction between philosophers on the one hand, who assert that they "do not yet know (οὔπω γιγνώσκειν)," and sophists on the other, who open their speeches with "I know (οἶδα)," "I am sure (γιγνώσκω)," and similar expressions that endow a speech with an air of "nobility" (εὐγένεια), "high-mindedness (φρόνημα)," and "a firm grasp on truth (κατάληψις σαφής τοῦ ὄντος)" (Lives 480). Likewise Philo speaks of the sophist as one whose "mother is wise leaning and wisdom" and who "receives training in wide learning and much knowledge."[19] Associations between sophistry and certainty are longstanding—sophistic self-assurance attracted the attention and censure of Plato centuries earlier—but authors like Philostratus and Philo suggest that sophist claims to expert knowledge were alive and well during the Second Sophistic. Perhaps then, we should contextualize Corinthian claims to knowledge within the resurgence of a rhetoric of certainty among sophists. Are the Corinthian knowers best understood as a group of sophists that number among the earliest participants in Philostratus' Second Sophistic?

In my opinion the answer to this question as stated is "no," not because the Corinthian experts do not resemble sophists in their embrace of rhetoric, but because Philostratus' category of the Second Sophistic is too narrow and self-legitimizing to serve as a cultural context relevant and proximate to Corinth in the middle of the first century. As Tim Whitmarsh correctly points out, Philostratus uses the term Second Sophistic in reference not to a period of history, as many modern scholars including Winter use the term, but to a particular rhetorical style in the tradition of the Athenian orator Aeschines, in which speeches are delivered in the persona of some other figure.[20] There is no evidence that the Corinthian

18. I am borrowing this expression from Nutton, "Galen's Rhetoric of Certainty."

19. Philo, QG 3.33, quoted in Winter, Philo and Paul among the Sophists, 69, though he does not draw a connection between sophistic knowledge and Corinthian knowledge.

20. Whitmarsh, Greek Literature and the Roman Empire, 42. Whitmarsh's

knowers assumed the persona of a hero or notorious figure from the past and declaimed before the assembly. A second problem prevents us from overlaying the cultural context of the Second Sophistic upon Paul's Corinth. Philostratus' Second Sophistic is not a neutral description of a historical phenomenon, but a self-legitimating discourse that allows Philostratus to frame himself as the inheritor of a rich sophistic tradition pioneered and handed down by a specific group of elite orators. Philostratus' construction of a circle of sophists "imagined as having an objective, self-evident reality independent of the negotiations by which it was created"—to borrow the felicitous characterization of Kendra Eshleman—says more about the self-interested aspirations of Philostratus than it does about a genuine historical phenomenon.[21] Therefore I suggest that we resist the urge to map Philostratus' narrowly defined and self-legitimating notion of the Second Sophistic onto the conflict between Paul and the experts in Corinth.

However, with careful handling, Philostratus' Second Sophistic can in fact help us situate the conflict between Paul and the Corinthian experts within a broader cultural context. Even if Philostratus' Second Sophistic does not apply directly to the situation in Corinth, it does emerge out of more fundamental shifts in the relationship between expert knowledge and performance taking place during first two centuries CE, reconfigurations that inform the conflict between Paul and the knowers in Corinth. Widespread interest in Greek identity in the first and second centuries brought with it a renewed enthusiasm for Greek rhetoric, including what Joy Connolly calls theatrical oratory.[22] It is not that there was a period of time in which knowledge wasn't performative, but in many circles during the Greek imperial period there is a heightened awareness of rhetoric and performance as metrics for gauging expert knowledge. Philostratus' rhetorical construction of the second sophistic is one outgrowth of this climate of expert performance; the conflict in 1 Corinthians, I will argue, is another.

---

comments are instructive: "The modern use of the phrase 'the Second Sophistic' is, thus, not consonant with Philostratus' use. There is nothing inherently wrong with this, but we should at least be aware that 'the Second Sophistic' is a construction of modern scholarship, formed under the disciplinary uses of the modern category, and in no sense simply a translucent window onto the 'real' practices of the ancient world" (43).

21. Eshleman, *Social World of Intellectuals in the Roman Empire*, 126.
22. Connolly, *State of Speech*.

Dio Chrysostom vividly illustrates the centrality of performance in first-century contests for knowledge and wisdom by way of appeal to the animal kingdom. In the introduction to his *Olympic Discourse* (*Or.* 12), Dio speaks of the "strange and inexplicable experience of the owl," who, despite her ordinary appearance and ostensible lack of wisdom, attracts the other birds "whenever she utters her mournful and far from pleasing note" (*Or.* 12.1). "Surely," Dio continues, "the birds ought rather to admire the peacock when they see him, beautiful and many-colored as he is, and then again truly when he lifts himself up in pride and shows the beauty of his plumage, as he struts before his hen with his tail spread out and arched all about him like a fair-shaped theater or some picture of the heavens studded with stars ... He offers himself to the spectator's gaze, quite calm and unconcerned, turning himself this way and that as if on parade; and when he wishes really to astound us, he rustles his feathers and makes a sound not unpleasing, as of a light breeze stirring some thick wood. But it is not the peacock with all this fine display that the birds want to see" (12.2–3). Instead, they flock to the owl.

Dio's owl and peacock represent respectively the philosopher and the sophist, who compete for the attention, affection, and allegiance of the people. He puzzles over the fact that despite the throng of wise and peacock-like sophists strutting about town, his audience still chooses to flock to him, "a man who knows nothing and makes no claims to knowing" (*Or.* 12.5. See also 9, 13, 14, 15). Dio's disavowal of expert knowledge is intertwined with self-deprecating remarks about his unimpressive bodily appearance and lack of rhetorical skill: "You have been eager to hear a man who is neither handsome in appearance nor strong, and in age is already past his prime, one who has no disciple, who professes ... no art or special knowledge either of the nobler or of the meaner sort, no ability as a prophet or sophist, nay, not even as an orator or a flatterer, one who is not even a clever writer, who does not even have a craft deserving of praise or of interest, but who simply wears his hair long" (12.15). Yet Dio's disavowal of knowledge is offset by his own coy intimations that he is in fact wiser and more knowledgeable than his ostentatious rivals. He says that the owl may "in fact possess some superior sagacity" (12.6) and that birds flock to her "as to one possessing all knowledge" (12.8). The crowds mistake Dio's foolishness for wisdom and his ignorance for knowledge.

Dio's avian analogy highlights the highly performative nature of expert knowledge in the first century CE. He presents both the philosopher and the sophist as acutely aware that knowledge and wisdom must be embodied and performed before audiences, even if the philosopher and the sophist perform their knowledge and wisdom in different ways. The peacock-sophist conforms to recognized standards of beauty, grace, and elegance. The owl-philosopher, however, rejects these stands and adopts a countercultural persona; he is weak, scruffy, and inarticulate. From the perspective of onlookers, the philosopher and sophist are opposites. Yet the two have more in common than they would care to admit. Both the sophist and the philosopher are performers. Dio's owl is in reality a peacock. Both agree upon the same premise, that expert knowledge must be embodied and performed in relation to the cultural standards of their audiences, either in conformity to or in contrast with these expectations. Both modes of performance pivot on the same fulcrum. Or perhaps Philostratus said it better: a "spirit of rivalry ... is always directed against one's competitors *in the same craft*" (*Lives* 491). For this reason, the distinction between sophists and philosophers often maintained rigidly among modern scholars risks obscuring a host of similarities between the two.

Now let us return to 1 Corinthians with Dio's characterization of expert competition in mind. We can conceive of the confrontation in 1 Corinthians as a contest over knowledge and wisdom between the Corinthian peacocks and Paul the owl. Paul gives the impression that rhetorical performance was a central component of the teaching by Corinthian experts. They appear to have delivered their wisdom and knowledge with "preeminence" (ὑπεροχή), a term which, as scholars have noted, is used by Aristotle to describe the rhetorical "superiority" of the eloquent over and above less articulate rivals (1 Cor 2:1. Aristotle, *Rhetoric* 2.2.7).[23] Paul also suggests that the Corinthians' teachings were crafted in such a way to be persuasive (πειθός, 1 Cor 2:4). As discussed above, I would not be surprised if the Corinthian experts received rhetorical training from Apollos, a rhetorically sophisticated man (ἀνὴρ λόγιος) according to Acts 18:24.

Paul, like Dio, presents himself as the inverse of his rivals. He is the austere and unrefined owl who avoids eloquence and techniques of persuasion and disavows possession of knowledge and wisdom. It is Paul the owl who speaks in 1 Cor 2:1–5:

---

23. See Winter, *Paul and Philo among the Sophists*, 150.

> When I came to you, brothers and sisters, I did not come proclaiming the mystery of God to you in lofty words or wisdom (καθ' ὑπεροχὴν λόγου ἢ σοφίας). For I decided to know nothing among you (οὐ γὰρ ἔκρινά τι εἰδέναι ἐν ὑμῖν) except Jesus Christ, and him crucified. And I came to you in weakness and in fear and in much trembling. My speech and my proclamation were not with plausible words of wisdom (οὐκ ἐν πειθοῖς σοφίας λόγοις), but with a demonstration of the Spirit and of power, so that your faith might rest not on human wisdom (μὴ ᾖ ἐν σοφίᾳ ἀνθρώπων) but on the power of God.

At the same time, however, Paul like Dio's owl, makes sly grabs at knowledge and wisdom. As already mentioned he claims a hidden wisdom in 1 Cor 2:6, and in 8:1 he transforms a Corinthian slogan about knowledge into a slogan of his own ("We know that 'we all have knowledge' . . ."). Despite his explicit rejection of the use of persuasive rhetoric, Paul's letter to the Corinthians is loaded with Greek rhetorical *topoi*, as Margaret Mitchell and many others have demonstrated.[24] Thus despite claims to the contrary, Paul is engaged in an expert performance contest with his Corinthian rivals. Paul deploys a rhetoric of non-rhetoric and resorts to coy claims to wisdom and knowledge.[25] He calls to mind figures such as Hippodromus, Marcus of Byzantium, and other sophists who adopted antisophist personae in order to find success by, in the words of Tim Whitmarsh, "[making up] their own rules within the received syntax of sophistic deportment."[26] By moving away from the heuristic of the Second Sophistic and situating Paul and the Corinthian knowers and sages within the context of performative expert competition, we not only better approximate the cultural context of first-century Corinth, we also begin to see the similarities between Paul and the Corinthian experts. In their struggle for possession of knowledge and wisdom, both Paul and the Corinthian experts make use of similar strategies of performance. Paul is implicated within the system he denounces. Thus, in the end Paul like Dio is not an owl, but a peacock, "beautiful and many-colored" who "lifts himself up in pride and shows the beauty of his plumage, as he struts before his hen with his tail spread out and arched all about him like a fair-shaped theater . . ." (*Or.* 12.2–3).

24. See, e.g., Mitchell, *Paul and the Rhetoric of Reconciliation*.

25. I am drawing upon the notion of the rhetoric of antirhetoric in Hesk, "Rhetoric of Anti-Rhetoric."

26. Whitmarsh, *Second Sophistic*, 29.

Works Cited

Bultmann, Rudolf. "γινώσκω." In *TDNT* 1:689-719.
Charlesworth, James H. *The Old Testament Pseudepigrapha*. Vol. 2. Peabody, MA: Hendrickson, 2010.
Cohoon, J. W., trans. *Discourses 1-11*, by Dio Chrysostom. LCL 257. Cambridge: Harvard University Press, 1932.
———, trans. *Discourses 12-20*, by Dio Chrysostom. LCL 339. Cambridge: Harvard University Press, 1939.
Connolly, Joy. *The State of Speech: Rhetoric and Political Thought in Ancient Rome*. Princeton: Princeton University Press, 2007.
Eshleman, Kendra. *The Social World of Intellectuals in the Roman Empire: Sophists, Philosophers, and Christians*. Greek Culture in the Roman World. Cambridge: Cambridge University Press, 2012.
Hesk, Jon. "The Rhetoric of Anti-Rhetoric in Athenian Oratory." In *Performance-Culture and Athenian Democracy*, edited by Simon Goldhill and Robin Osborne, 201-30. Cambridge: Cambridge University Press, 1999.
King, Karen L. *What Is Gnosticism?* Cambridge, MA: Belknap, 2003.
Koester, Helmut. "The Silence of the Apostle." In *Urban Religion in Roman Corinth: Interdisciplinary Approaches*, edited by Daniel N. Schowalter and Steven J. Friesen, 339-49. Harvard Theological Studies. Cambridge: Harvard University Press, 2005.
Lindemann, Andreas. *Der Erste Korintherbrief*. Handbuch zum Neuen Testament 9/1. Tübingen: Mohr/Siebeck, 2000.
Martin, Dale. *The Corinthian Body*. New Haven: Yale University Press, 1995.
Mitchell, Margaret M. "Paul's Letters to Corinth: The Interpretive Intertwining of Literary and Historical Reconstruction." In *Urban Religion in Roman Corinth: Interdisciplinary Approaches*, edited by Daniel Schowalter and Steven Friesen, 307-38. Cambridge: Harvard University Press, 2005.
———. *Paul and the Rhetoric of Reconciliation: An Exegetical Investigation of the Language and Composition of 1 Corinthians*. Hermeneutische Untersuchungen zur Theologie 28. Tübingen: Mohr/Siebeck, 1991.
Nutton, Vivian. "Galen's Rhetoric of Certainty." In *La rhétorique médicale à travers les siècles: actes du colloque international de Paris, 9 et 10 octobre 2008*, edited by Joël Coste et. al., 39-49. Hautes études médiévales et modernes 104. Geneva: Droz, 2012.
Schmithals, Walter. *Paul and the Gnostics*. Translated by John Steely. Nashville: Abingdon, 1971.
Silva, Moisés. *Philippians*. Baker Exegetical Commentary on the New Testament. Grand Rapids: Baker, 1992.
Smith, Morton. "The History of the Term *Gnostikos*." In *The Rediscovery of Gnosticism: Proceedings of the International Conference on Gnosticism at Yale, New Haven, Connecticut, March 28-31, 1978*, edited by Bentley Layton, 2:796-807. 2 vols. Studies in the History of Religions: Supplements to Numen 41. Leiden: Brill, 1981.
Whitmarsh, Tim. *Greek Literature and the Roman Empire: The Politics of Imitation*. Oxford: Oxford University Press, 2001.
———. *The Second Sophistic*. Greece & Rome: New Surveys in the Classics. Oxford: Oxford University Press, 2005.

Wilkens, Ulrich. *Weisheit und Torheit.* Beiträge zur historischen Theologie 26. Tübingen: Mohr/Siebeck, 1959.

Williams, Michael Allen. *Rethinking "Gnosticism": An Argument for Dismantling a Dubious Category.* Princeton: Princeton University Press, 1996.

Winter, Bruce. *Philo and Paul among the Sophists: Alexandrian and Corinthian Responses to a Julio-Claudian Movement.* 2nd ed. Grand Rapids: Eerdmans, 2002.

7

"Why Can't a Woman Be More Like a Man?"

Making Mary Male (Thomas 114) in the Gendered World of Antiquity

STEPHEN J. PATTERSON

In the Louvre are two very different depictions of the ancient god/dess Hermaphroditus. They illustrate two very different ways of thinking about androgyny in the ancient world. One, the more famous of the two, is called *Hermaphroditus endormi*, the "sleeping Hermaphroditus," the other, *Hermaphroditus stante*, the "standing Hermaphroditus," as it were. One of these androgynous images is all about love; the other is all about power. One of them offers an interpretive framework for understanding Thomas 114; the other does not. When Jesus says to the disciples in this notorious saying, "Look, I will guide her along so as to make her male, so that she too may become a living spirit similar to you males," and then "for every woman who makes herself male will enter the kingdom of heaven," is he talking about love or about power?

The Resting Hermaphrodite

Hermaphroditus endormi[1] is lying on a mattress made for her/him by a seventeenth-century Italian sculptor (Gian Lorenzo Bernini), but the

---

1. No. d'inventaire: Ma 231. To view an image, visit https://www.photo.rmn.fr/

figure itself was created by a now-forgotten early Roman-era artist. It was, however, not an original but a copy of an earlier Hellenistic work, possibly the one mentioned by Pliny the Elder and ascribed to Polycles in *Natural History* (34.80). This Roman copy is usually called the Borghese Hermaphroditus, so named for the seventeenth-century Cardinal Scipione Borghese, who claimed it for his personal collection when it was discovered during the construction of Santa Maria della Vittoria. He paid Bernini to carve a proper bed for it and installed it in a dedicated room in his villa. This copy actually inspired many other Roman-era copies, some of which survive: one is housed today in Rome's Museo Nazionale, another in Florence, another in the Vatican Museum, and one in the Hermitage in St. Petersburg. The bronze version in the Met is a seventeenth-century copy—one among many later renderings.

The Borghese Hermaphroditus lays almost prone on his/her mattress. Approaching from behind, your first impression is all feminine, her comely derriere, part of a breast discretely revealed, her face and feminine hairstyle, all suggesting an ancient ideal of female beauty. She sleeps with one leg drawn up, however, raising her left hip ever so subtly, so that as you perambulate the sculpture to the right you are suddenly confronted with an unexpected surprise: there tucked beneath that left thigh is a delicate set of male genitalia. Who is this unusual god/dess?

One version of his/her story is found in Ovid's *Metamorphoses* (4.274–388). It is told as a tall tale by Alcithoe, one of the daughters of King Minyas, whom Bacchus later turns into a bat on account of her impiety on his holy day. It goes like this: Hermaphroditus (now *he*) was the son of Hermes and Aphrodite. One day, while wandering in the land of the Carians, he comes upon an enchanted pool, home to the water nymph, Salmacis. Hermaphroditus is a handsome lad and Salmacis is smitten at once. "Are you married?" she asks. Silence. "Then marry me! No? Just a little kiss then?" Silence, still. So she comes out of the pool and starts to ply him with an embrace. But he recoils. "Stop that!," he insists. "If you're going to be like that," she pouts, "then I'll just go away!" And she does. Now, the day is hot and the pool is cool, so Hermaphroditus, now alone, strips down and slips into the placid waters to enjoy a bath. But alas, Salmacis has not gone after all! She is only hiding in the bushes. Out she jumps and into the pool to wrap herself around the beautiful boy! As they struggle, Salmacis sends this prayer up to the gods: "Grant me this,

archive/13-555827-2C6NU054FWC9.html/.

"WHY CAN'T A WOMAN BE MORE LIKE A MAN?"

ye gods, and may no day ever come that shall separate him from me or me from him" (*Metam.* 4.370-72). The gods hear her prayer, but in response, grant her a most unusual marriage: there as they wrestle and writhe in the pool, the bodies of Salmacis and Hermaphroditus gradually merge and become one form, both feminine and masculine—a hermaphrodite.

Odd as it may seem to modern sensibilities, the *Hermaphroditus endormi* embodies a kind of unusual love story. In it, two people are bound to one another, never again to be parted. Today in the land of the ancient Carians (southwestern Turkey), every local museum seems to have at least one small statuette of Hermaphroditus, just about the right size to serve as a nice wedding gift. What the gods have joined together, let no one pull asunder.

There must have been various iterations of this mytheme—the androgyne as a marriage of the male and female forms, drawn together out of desire for one another. The very name, Hermaphroditus, suggests a basic myth of origins involving the merging of the male (Hermes) and the female (Aphrodite)—though if such a tale existed, it does not survive in literature. Other versions do, however. The best known, perhaps, is Aristophanes' creation myth, related in Plato's *Symposium* (189d-92e): In the beginning, when human beings first walked the earth, they were unlike our modern species. They were round, and instead of one set of arms, legs, one face, one set of genitals, and so forth, each had two sets, as it were: four arms, four legs, two faces, etc. Thus they rolled about deftly on four arms and four legs, and with two faces they could see both forward and backward, and each could pee, alas, both forward and backward. Aristophanes explains that some of these original human beings were male, some female, but some were a third gender, having one male side and one female. These, he says, were ἀνδρόγυνοι—androgynes, both male and female.

These original human beings were very powerful in their fullness, though, and the gods feared them. So Zeus intervened and, with his thunderbolt, divided them each in two. Now each person had but two arms and two legs, one face, and one set of genitalia—more or less as human beings do now. But the splitting of them was too harsh. Each halfperson pined for its other half, and they all began to waste away. So, once again the gods intervened, and with a little anatomical rearranging, made it possible for the two halves of each whole to come together once again— by making love. Those who had originally been male-male wholes, came together male to male, and those original female-female wholes, female to female, and those who had originally been androgynes, came together male to female. Thus, Plato (Aristophanes) accounts for the various love lives of all those around him: love drives two people together, each seeking his/her other half in relationships reflecting their original nature. So, whether male or female, this primordial splitting is what causes each to desire another, to be "joined and fused with [a] beloved, that the two might be made one" (*Symp.* 192e).

The Jewish version of this mytheme is found in Genesis. There it is said that Adam, created originally as both male and female (Gen 1:27; 5:2), was later divided into male and female versions, when God brought forth Eve from Adam's side (Gen 2:21-23). Far-fetched? Not at all to the rabbis, some of whom read Genesis with what seems to have been at least a passing knowledge of Aristophanes' tale. Thus, *Genesis Rabbah*:

> R. Jeremiah b. Leazar said: When the Holy One, blessed be He, created Adam, He created him an hermaphrodite, for it is said, "Male and female created He them and called their name Adam" [see Gen 5:2]. R. Samuel b. Nahman said: When the Lord created Adam, He created him double-faced, then he split him and made him of two backs, one back on this side and one back on the other side. (*Gen. Rab.* 8.1)

Then Genesis adds: "That is why a man leaves his father and mother and cleaves to his wife, and they become one flesh" (Gen 2:24). The Jewish Middle Platonist,[2] Philo of Alexandria, comments on this coming together of the two:

> But when woman too had been made, beholding a figure like his own and a kindred form, [Adam] was gladdened by the sight, and approached and greeted her. She, seeing no other living thing more like herself than he, is filled with glee and shamefastly returns his greeting. Love supervenes, brings together and fits into one the divided halves, as it were, of a single living creature, and sets up in each of them a desire for fellowship with the other with a view to the production of their like. (*Creation* 152, LCL)

Philo bemoaned these primordial developments as the lustful beginnings of everything evil. But others saw in them a clue to salvation, when *Endzeit* would recapitulate *Urzeit* and the two halves of the primordial human would come together once again to form a single androgynous whole. Among these were the nascent Christians who once practiced

---

2. On Philo's Middle Platonism, see Dillon, *Middle Platonists*, 139-83.

the now forgotten ritual of the "Bridal Chamber," one of the five rituals mentioned by the author of the Gospel of Philip, who says this about it:

> If the woman had not separated from the man, she should not die with the man. His separation became the beginning of death. Because of this, Christ came to repair the separation, which was from the beginning, and again unite the two, and to give life to those who died as a result of the separation, and unite them. But the woman is united to her husband in the Bridal Chamber. Indeed, those who have been united in the Bridal Chamber will no longer be separated. (*Gos. Phil.* 70:9–22, trans. Isenberg)

Here is an ascetical twist on the mytheme, where normal sexual desire and the estrangement from which it comes are overcome by a deeper, mystical, ritual reunification through the sacrament of the Bridal Chamber. No one can be certain what this ritual entailed or the life changes it initiated,[3] but it is likely that it involved celibacy and perhaps the practice "spiritual marriage," in which two people lived together in chaste matrimony.[4]

For soloists, baptism, too, might have been understood by some nascent Christians as a pathway back to Adam's prelapsarian innocence as the original androgyne. In this they found an interpretive foothold in the fate of Adam and Eve after they had tasted of the forbidden fruit in the garden. Genesis says that after they had eaten, the primordial pair became aware of their nakedness, so they sewed for themselves garments of leaves for an apron. Later the Lord God replaced these flimsy clothes with more permanent "garments of skins" (Gen 3:21). Jews with a Platonizing bent, like Philo, could see no reason for the Holy One's interest in clothing, per se, and assumed, therefore, that the meaning must be metaphorical. In the Platonic world, of course, the body as a suit of clothes to cover the bare-naked soul was a metaphorical commonplace. So, these "garments of skins" must actually have been the new, flesh and blood, gender-specific bodies that God gave to Adam and Eve to clothe their souls.[5] This tradition of speculative exegesis offered an opening to nascent Christians who would interpret the elements of baptism in Platonizing terms. The disrobing of the initiate came to symbolize the shedding of the old, gendered body of sin, in preparation for the new,

---

3. Discussion: Uro, "Bridal Chamber."
4. See esp. *Acts Thom.* 10–15.
5. See, e.g., *QG* 1.53; 4.78.

androgynous identity of the newly baptized.[6] As Dennis MacDonald has shown, this is the significance of an ancient dominical saying from the lost Gospel of the Egyptians quoted by Clement of Alexandria in the late second century:

> When Salome asked when the things about which she had inquired would be made known, the Lord said, "When you (pl.) trample upon the garment of shame and when the two become one and the male with the female is neither male nor female."[7]

Is this, then, the mythic and religious framework for understanding the idea that women should become men in Thomas 114? That these ideas were in the mix among those who wrote and used this gospel seems beyond doubt. According to the Gospel of Thomas, people "enter the Kingdom" when they "make the two into one . . . ," so as to "make the male and the female into a single one, so that the male will not be male and the female will not be female" (saying 22). This distinctly Platonic language clearly echoes the hermaphroditic tradition. Elsewhere Thomas speaks of celibates (*emmonakhos*) who enter the Bridal Chamber (saying 75), and initiates who "trample upon the garments of shame" (saying 37). Consequently, many students of the passage have argued that Thomas 114 should also be understood against this backdrop of primordial androgyny.[8]

But the plain sense of the saying itself seems to rule this out. It does not speak of undoing the separation of female from male, of erasing the distinction, so that "the male will not be male and the female will not be female." There is no marriage theme here, metaphoric, symbolic, or literal, no coming together to create a greater, more complete whole. Most importantly, there is no sense that gendered existence generally is a problem to be overcome, ritually or otherwise. To the contrary, the female gender alone is the problem—there is nothing wrong with the male gender. The solution to the problem, then, is not the merging of the

---

6. MacDonald, *There Is No Male and Female*, 50-63; see also Smith, "Garments of Shame."

7. *Gospel to the Egyptians*, fragment quoted by Clement of Alexandria, *Stromateis* 3.13.92 (text and translation in Stoker, *Extracanonical Sayings of Jesus*, 12).

8. The proposals are many and by no means monolithic, yet, most presume some version of this tradition of primordial androgyny: Grant and Freedman, *Secret Sayings of Jesus*, 84-85; Ménard, *L'Évangile selon Thomas*, 216; Buckley, "Interpretation of Logion 114"; DeConick *Seek to See Him*, 18; Hedrick, *Unlocking the Secrets*, 186; Gagné, "Conaissance, identité, et androgynéité" ("male androgyny"), etc.

two, but the transformation from one into the other. Jesus offers Mary spiritual guidance that will do just that: he will lead her away from the spiritual deficiencies of the female and improve her lot by "making her male." None of this is consistent with the ideas that find expression in Thomas 22 and the Jewish Platonic exegesis of Genesis that lay behind it. It is, rather, a distinct and different idea. Thomas 114 is about something else, something male that Peter assumes Mary, as a woman, does not have or cannot be. That should take us now back to the Louvre and another very different sculpting of Hermaphroditus.

The Erect Hermaphrodite

The *Hermaphroditus stante*[9] is a very different kind of Hermaphroditus. It stands erect, but there are versions of the amorous Hermaphroditus— *Hermaphroditus endormi*—that are actually not sleeping, but standing. What is distinctive about the *Hermaphroditus stante* is the *way* she/he is standing. One is meant to experience this sculpted image as a full-frontal encounter. She (the figure is iconographically female) faces you as, with her two hands, she lifts her *chiton* high above her waist in what is known as the *anasyrma* pose. This is the gesture, known through the ages as powerfully apotropaic—a woman exposing herself to an opponent in an attempt to ward off the would-be evildoer.[10] But in this case, what the female exposes is male—and not just the male member in flaccid repose, but a firm, erect phallus of the sort Romans came to see as synonymous with male power. This is the erect phallus one sees carved onto city gates, door posts, and scrawled onto the walls of shops and baths, intended also as a display to ward off the evildoer. Thus, the apotropaic powers of the *anasyrma* pose itself are doubled. Here is an erect Hermaphroditus, a woman daring to expose others to her male power. Where does this idea come from?

Women, Power, and Plato

The arresting quality of the *Hermaphroditus stante* derives from the fact that most people in antiquity—as in Western civilization generally—did

9. No. d'inventaire 4866; to see an image visit https://www.photo.rmn.fr/archive/10-504886-2C6NUoQ9VDL4.html/.

10. See Suter, "Anasyrma."

not think that women could be equal to men or have anything like male power. But Plato most famously did. The issue comes up in the *Republic* (5.451c–457b), where a question arises as to whether women could be trained to serve alongside men in the role of "Guardian" of the state. This was the state's highest calling, an office that could be held only by the ablest of the Republic's citizens, men filled with the qualities that made them suitable for this task: athletic (γυμναστική), warrior-like (πολεμική), lovers of wisdom (φιλοσοφική), and "spirited" (θυμοειδής) (2.375a–b). Could women become "Guardians" too?

This is the same question posed by Thomas 114. At issue is a role, the highest role. Because it is the highest role, most will have assumed that it was available only to men, on the further assumption, of course, that men are generally superior to women. But Plato confounds this thinking. He does not doubt the general principle of male superiority, but his hero, Socrates, argues that some women do have these superior qualities. They are more common in men, and better developed in the best men than in the best women. But some women do have them, even while some men do not. In that sense, particular women can be equal (or superior) to particular men.[11] These women, he maintains, must be trained as Guardians and take their place among the male Guardians. Together they will beget Guardian children, who will grow up to protect the community from its enemies. They are like guard dogs: male, females, pups—there are differences between the males, the females, and the pups, but they are all guard dogs just the same.

In the 1960s and 70s all of this sparked something of a controversy among scholars over Plato's view of women.[12] Was he a feminist? The female Guardians in Socrates' ideal Republic seemed to suggest that he was. But in the *Timaeus* (41d–42d), Plato's famous astrologer gives an account of the rebirth of souls that would suggest otherwise. There he says that women are men, who, in a former existence, had proven cowardly or immoral (42b; 90e). Women, it would seem, are like the animals and other lesser forms, each of them a reincarnate man who showed lesser qualities in a former life: birds, formerly light-minded men; beasts, formerly beastly men; fishes, formerly stupid men, etc. (91–92c). The continuum thus implied is, needless to say, far from feminist, and at odds with the *Republic*. Or is it?

---

11. Calvert, "Plato and the Equality of Women," 236–39.
12. Discussion: Allen, "Plato on Women."

"WHY CAN'T A WOMAN BE MORE LIKE A MAN?"

Plato lived in an androcentric and patriarchal world. As such, his illustrations and images often depend on these basic social structures, including the inferiority of women. But in his metaphysics, Plato was exploring new and somewhat novel territory: all human beings are *essentially* the same. One sees this on a closer reading of the *Timaeus*, even in that very sexist passage where Plato's astrologer speaks of how human beings come to have souls (*Tim.* 41d-42b). After creating the Universe and imbuing it with soul, the creating Father returns to the mixing bowl wherein He had created this soul and finds in it some leftover residue. Now, says Timaeus, He dilutes this leftover soul and creates enough of it to give each star a little bit, which rides that star like a chariot until it is deposited in a living creature to live out its earthly existence. If in that existence it lives wisely, it shall return to its native star in the heavens, but if not, it must start all over again—metempsychosis. All souls, says Timaeus, begin their sojourn in a man. But if as a man they fail to attain a just life, in their next life they enter the form of a woman, and failing there, into some bestial form, until, at last, that soul shall "yield himself to the revolution of the Same," that is, conform itself to the ways of the divine in the Universe by living justly and wisely (*Tim.* 42c). The salient point here is that the soul is in each incarnation *essentially* the same. And in each round of existence the soul has the possibility to recover its original divine nature. Timaeus (Plato) does not say why the soul, after failing in a man, passes into a woman. Is the soul being punished? Or is it that, in the role of a woman, the soul has a better chance of regaining its original divine habits? Again, Plato does not say. But this much is clear: the soul of a woman is the same as the soul of a man, and that selfsame soul, whether in a man or in a woman, is expected and destined to rediscover its original divine nature and return to the heavens from whence it came.

This underlying metaphysics comes into play in Plato's attempt to convince his reader that women may become Guardians of the Republic.[13] There he argues that the differences one may clearly observe between men and women are superficial to the role of Guardian. Women bear and nurse children, for example. Should this disqualify them? Not at all. Why? Because some women, as well as some men, have the qualities that all had earlier agreed were essential to the role of Guardian: athletic (γυμναστική), warrior-like (πολεμική), lovers of wisdom (φιλοσοφική), and "spirited" (θυμοειδής) (*Republic* 456a). Plato's hero does not go on to

---

13. Allen, "Plato on Women," 135-36.

say that these are qualities of the divine soul, or mind, dwelling within women as well as men. Some of them, by ancient lights, would probably not be warrior-like, for example; others certainly are φιλοσοφική, for example. The point, though, is this: in Plato's new world women and men may both ascend to the highest calling of "Guardian" because they are in the most essential respect the same. Physical differences are not decisive in a world where people have bodies and souls, and character is a function of the soul, not the body. To bring it out in a person, one needs only the right inclination and education.

There is, then, an awkward tension in Plato's view of women: as women they are generally inferior in every respect to men, but as human beings they can embrace their essential divine nature and achieve the same spiritual heights as men. Plato does not, so far as I can see, reify maleness as the divine nature, per se. True, his most technical term for the divine soul is νοῦς, a masculine noun, but just as often he refers to it simply as the soul—ψυχή, a feminine noun. He simply assumes that because men are generally superior to women, they will be better at and more apt to achieve enlightenment. But women can, and do become enlightened, and when they do, they are superior to those men who do not.

This tension did not sit well with everyone in Plato's world. Most considered it subversive. Even within Plato's own orbit, Aristotle proved a fatal defection. He considered the issue in terms of a more explicit metaphysics, in which women cannot serve in the highest capacities, ruling over men, because they simply do not have the temperament for it. Women do have souls, he granted, and they even have that part of the soul that engages in deliberation and decision-making (the βουλευτικόν). However, while in men this part of the soul is—or can be—sovereign (κῦρον) over the rest, in women it is not sovereign (ἄκυρον). In women, it is overruled by other parts of the soul. This is not necessarily a bad thing, he thinks. Women are well suited to other things—just not ruling. That is a job for men, and women should not try to be like men (*Politics* 1259–60).[14]

Jews, Gender, and Plato

In the period of Christian origins, Jews who became interested in Plato also began to entertain some of his ideas about women. The best known

---

14. Discussion: Smith, "Plato and Aristotle on the Nature of Women," 475.

of them is Philo. As with Plato, Philo embraces the view, common to his time and western civilization generally speaking, that women generally are inferior to men. So, for example, when exegeting the story of Eve's creation from Adam side, Philo asks why she was formed from his side, and not from the earth, as Adam himself was. He explains:

> First, because woman is not equal in honor with man. Second, because she is not equal in age, but younger. Wherefore, those who take wives who have passed their prime are to be criticized for destroying the law of nature. Third, he wishes that man should take care of woman as a very necessary part of him, but woman, in return, should serve him as a whole. Fourthly, he counsels man figuratively to take care of woman as of a daughter, and woman to honor man as a father. (*QG* 1.27)

So, Philo is a fairly typical man of his time, with fairly typical patriarchal ideas about men and women. In his philosophical work, these patriarchal assumptions and structures are also quite apparent.

This is true, even when Philo is dealing with matters of central importance to his Platonic foundations. Consider, for example, what he says about the mind (νοῦς) when waxing allegorical on the meaning of the Jewish sacrifices. The victim of the holocaust offering is to be male, he says,

> ... because the male is more complete, more dominant than the female, closer akin to causal activity, for the female is incomplete and in subjection and belongs to the category of the passive rather than the active. So too with the two ingredients which constitute our soul (ψυχή),[15] the rational and the irrational; the rational, which belongs to the mind (νοῦς) and reason, is of the masculine gender, the irrational, the province of sense (αἴσθησις), is of the feminine. Mind (νοῦς) belongs to a genus wholly superior to sense (αἴσθησις) as man is to woman. (*Spec. Laws* 1.200–201)

The Platonic categories are pretty clear here: the highest faculty of the soul, mind (νοῦς), is masculine, whereas the function relating to the world and sense perception (αἴσθησις), is feminine. So, one might easily

---

15. ψυχή ("soul"). Colson renders "life principle" here, but this risks confusing the term with Plato's use of ψυχή to mean "life force" in the *Timaeus*. In this passage Philo is rearranging Plato's terminology to describe in his own way Plato's notion that the highest faculty has a rational and an irrational aspect.

jump to the conclusion now that for Philo, men are essentially νοῦς and women are essentially αἴσθησις. But this would be a mistake.

As Sharon Mattila has shown, Philo is best understood when we bring in a little modern theory and make a distinction between sex and gender.[16] Philo seldom discusses with literal concern the physical differences between men and women (sex). Rather, he uses the perceived differences between men and women metaphorically, reifying certain characteristics as either masculine or feminine. Male is active, female, passive, for example; νοῦς is male, αἴσθησις, female, as above. But note—and here is Mattila's point—both men and women are actually both active and passive; both (more importantly) have both mind and sense perception. Here, for example, is how Philo introduces the discussion referred to above about why Eve was created from Adam's "side":

> The literal sense is clear. For by a certain symbolical use of "part" it is called half of the whole, as both man and woman, being sections of nature, become equal in one harmony of genus, which is called man. But in the figurative sense, man is a symbol of mind ... and sense perception ... is symbolized by woman. (*QG* 25)

That is, every member of the genus "man" shares in the whole. Men and women are both complete, each one endowed with mind and sense perception—the "masculine" and "feminine" parts of the soul, each with the capacity for "masculine" reason and "feminine" unreason, and so forth. Here is the same tension we saw in Plato. Philo operates in a symbolic universe in which men and maleness are superior, women and femaleness inferior. But his metaphysics told him that women, too, have the capacity to be rational, holy and chaste. Mattila thus speaks of Philo's "gender gradient," whereby both men and women can be more and less masculine *and* feminine at the same time. For both, spiritual progress is made when the feminine gives way to the masculine:

> For progress is indeed nothing else than the giving up of the female gender by changing into the male, since the female gender is material, passive, corporeal, sense-perceptible, while the male is active, rational, incorporeal and more akin to mind and thought. (*QE* 1.8)[17]

---

16. Mattila, "Philo's Gender Gradient."

17. See Davies, *Gospel of Thomas*, xxxviii–xxxix (citing Ehrman, *Lost Christianities*, 265).

"WHY CAN'T A WOMAN BE MORE LIKE A MAN?"

So, for Philo, *a woman can be more like a man*. Consider Julia Augusta, the great grandmother of Gaius Caligula, whom Philo mentions in the *Embassy to Gaius*.[18] She, Philo points out, was very pious and made elaborate and expensive gifts to the Jewish temple. Why? Even though "the judgments of women as a rule are weaker...,"

> she, through training (παιδεία) of exceeding purity in both nature and practice, excelled her sex in this as in everything else, by becoming male with respect to her reasoning power (ἀρρενωθεῖσα τὸν λόγισμον),[19] which gained such clarity of vision that it grasped the things of the mind (τὰ νοητά) better than the things of sense perception (τῶν αἰσθητῶν) and considered the latter to be mere shadows of the former. (*Embassy* 320, trans. author)

So, a woman can "become male" through παιδεία—training, education. This is not a modern feminist take on women, but an exception to the general ancient (male) perception of women, carved out by dint of metaphysics. Women, Philo believes, have the capacity to grasp the "things of the mind" (τὰ νοητά), even if usually they don't. This capacity is a function of the soul, namely its power to reason and comprehend the "things of the mind."

A similar idea appears in the odd theory Philo had about virgins.[20] For Philo, the problem with women is that their very existence causes human sexual desire, which he views as corrupting. He thinks that when a virgin has sex, it defiles her and "turns her into a woman," unfit for converse with God. A true virgin, in his view, is a person who is not corrupted by sex, either because she has not had sex, or because she has passed through menopause and (so he assumes) is no longer interested in sex. Here is what he says about all this in his allegorical reflection *On the Cherubim*:

> For the union of human beings that is made for the procreation of children turns virgins (παρθένους) into women (γυναῖκας). But when God begins to consort with the soul, He makes what was before a woman into a virgin again, for he takes away the

18. See Mattila, "Philo's Gender Gradient," 107n22.

19. The phrase loses its significance when translated more periphrasically, as Colson gives it. The sense of the participle is circumstantial to Julia herself, explaining how it was that she excelled all others of her γένος: *she* becomes male, not her reasoning powers (τὸν λογισμόν), as Mattila ("Philo's Gender Gradient," 107n22) implies.

20. Mattila, "Philo's Gender Gradient," 106–7.

degenerate and emasculating passions by which it was made female (ἀνάνδρους ἐπιθυμίας, αἷς ἐθηλύνετο)[21] and plants instead the native growth of unpolluted virtues. Thus, He will not talk with Sarah till she has ceased from all that is after the manner of women, and is ranked again as a pure virgin. (*Cher.* 50, trans. author)

So, sex transforms a virgin into a woman, but consorting with God can change her back again. The transformation comes through the soul and involves freeing it from the "emasculating passions" (ἀνάνδρους ἐπιθυμίας) that are aroused by sex. This curious phrase implies that the corrupted soul is the feminized soul, while a pure soul is one that is properly masculine. This is true for women as well as for men.

Thus, Philo's ideas about men and women, male and female, are fairly comprehensible within a historical Platonic framework. Philo, the Jewish Middle Platonist, believed that women, like men, had souls (variously called: mind, soul, thought, spirit),[22] and this made them able to rise above their generally accepted, socially inferior status and roles. This did not come naturally to Philo, and his examples are exceedingly rare (the women among the *Therapeutrides*, for example). The key is a lifestyle (virginity) that makes converse with God possible.

Every Woman Who Makes Herself Male

We may now return to Thomas 114 with a fairly clear framework for understanding its peculiar valence. Like the Platonic desiderata we have been examining, it presumes the patriarchal structures of the world in which it was coined. Women are inferior to men, and yet, here is Mary among the apostles. Can women share in the honored role some now presume to be the province solely of men? Plato posed the same question about women in his Republic—could they occupy roles one would assume belong only to men? The answer to this question hinged on how one imagined the inner makeup of a woman. Plato imagined that women, like men, possessed a soul, a "mind," and thus could exhibit the same qualities of mind that men do, with proper training and education.

---

21. Again, a more literal rendering of the Greek adds clarity. It is not that the soul's masculinity is removed (thus, Colson's "which unmanned it"), but that the emasculating passions make it into a woman.

22. To straighten out Philo's sometimes confusing terminology and equally confusing anthropology, see Wolfson, *Philo*, 1:360–423 (esp. 393–95).

"WHY CAN'T A WOMAN BE MORE LIKE A MAN?"

Aristotle disagreed. Women had souls, yes, but their souls were different from men's souls: the reasoning function of the soul was regnant in men, but not in women. Philo, the latter-day Middle Platonist, believed that women had (masculine) souls, but they were emasculated by the passions of sexual activity. Nevertheless, the souls of women could be made male again if they chose to refrain from sex and lent themselves instead to converse with God.

This is the conversation into which saying 114 clearly fits. The problem is not the existence of two genders and their desired reunion. Saying 22 and other sayings in the Gospel of Thomas do indeed hinge on that question, but 114 does not. The question is whether the perceived differences between men and women justify excluding women from certain roles—precisely the question Plato raises in the Republic. Peter lobs the question in and Jesus answers like a good Platonist: yes, she can. She can "become male." The language is peculiar, but not unprecedented, as we have seen with Philo. It reflects the notion, also seen in Philo, that to be open and receptive to God is to be "male," while to be distant and distracted by passionate feelings is to be "female." Julia Augusta "became male" through superior education that strengthened the reasoning function of her mind. Virgins are restored to spiritual masculinity by their chastity and by God's direct consort with their souls. As in these examples, "becoming male" in Thomas 114 is a metaphor for enlightenment, whatever practical implications that might also have carried.[23]

How is Mary to become male? Jesus "will bring her along ..." (*tinasōk ᵉmmos*). The phrase has always puzzled, and Crum offers only a little help: *sōk* + *na* might mean to "draw aside" or "induce"/"in zeal,"[24] so, perhaps, to encourage in some special way, to mentor. That it should lead to "life," and transformation into a "living spirit" is consistent with the soteriology of the Gospel of Thomas, generally speaking. In this gospel Jesus is "the living one" (saying 59), and whoever "lives from the living one will not taste death" (saying 111). Indeed, anyone who works to understand these sayings "will not taste death" (saying 1); "blessed is the one who has struggled and found life" (saying 58). The student is enjoined to "seek the place of life and ... live!" (saying 4). This is what Mary is to do—what she *can* do, and what any woman can do to become a "living

---

23. I once suggested that asceticism was probably the point of this saying (in the *Gospel of Thomas*, 153–55). The saying may well have also carried these practical implications for women, but the more significant valence is enlightenment.

24. Crum, *Coptic Dictionary*, 326B.

spirit" and enter the kingdom of heaven. The saying intends to cast the entire collection in this light: both men and women can study the sayings of this gospel with the expectation of finding enlightenment and life.

The saying can now also be placed easily within the history of early Christianity. As is well known, in the later decades of the first century, men began to challenge women occupying leadership roles in the churches in an effort to see the church conform more to the prevailing social conventions of their world. One sees this already in the *Haustafeln* of the Deutero-Pauline epistles (Col 3:18; Eph 5:21–33), but then more explicitly contested in the Pastoral Epistles, on the one side (esp. 1 Tim 2:11; 5:3–16), the Acts of Paul and Thecla and the Gospel of Mary, on the other. In the Gospel of Mary, the fictive surrogates for the "for and against" sides of the debate are, as in Thomas, Mary and Peter. That text also shares with Thomas a Middle Platonic interpretation of the Jesus tradition.[25] So did Tatian, who shared Thomas' Edessene homeland and also championed the role of "wise women" in his community (*Oration to the Greeks* 33). When men began to challenge women in roles of spiritual leadership within the early church, the Platonizing theology of the Gospel of Thomas, the Gospel of Mary, and other texts and their champions, offered a metaphysical rationale for pushing back. Women could be leaders: prophets, "widows," ascetics, and patrons. In the Platonic tradition, women have all the masculine spiritual equipment that men have and, with training, can "become male." Thomas 114 was part of that pushback. This saying is not about love; it is about power—male power manifest in enlightened women.

Conclusion

The history of patriarchy in Christianity also includes a history of resistance and pushback, but always in an idiom at home in the patriarchal culture from which it sprang. In the ancient world, this pushback did not normally take the modern feminist form of celebrating the difference between men and women and holding them up as equals. Rather, the question was framed as it is in Thomas 114: can a woman be like a man? Most people, of course, said no. A woman in the role of a man was a monster, an Amazon to be defeated and put in her place. Women might try to be like men, but in the end, they cannot prevail. And yet, one also finds little

---

25. See King, *Gospel of Mary of Magdala*, 41–47, *et passim*.

Amazon dolls among the grave goods of young females—the playthings of little girls who dreamt of growing up to become a great warrior?[26] Amazonian tombs were purportedly venerated throughout the ancient world, including in Athens itself.[27] And there were people like Plato, who ventured out of the cave of cultural convention and saw women in a brighter light. He knew of extraordinary women, including Diotima, whose powerful intellect and character made them "leaders among men," dispelling the notion that all leaders must be male (*Symposium* 201d-212b).

Western civilization is not really very far removed from this question and the patriarchal way in which it is answered in our ancient texts. Can a woman be a leader among men? Yes, but she'll do better if she lowers the timbre of her voice, coifs her hair short, and wears suits rather than dresses. A woman must still become a man to occupy roles that were only recently reserved for men. And men who chafe at this instinct and instead abandon the code of masculinity for a more feminine mien are greeted with wonder and astonishment. Men who became women were rare in ancient Christianity, but not unknown. Women who became men were more common, and probably quite common before the end of the second century, when the patriarchy of ancient Roman culture finally pressed them to the margins, even in a movement that once reveled in bending gender to the limits.

Works Cited

Allen, Christine Garside. "Plato on Women." *Feminist Studies* 2 (1975) 131–38.
Buckley, Jorunn Jacobsen. "An Interpretation of Logion 114 in the Gospel of Thomas." *Novum Testamentum* 27 (1985) 245–72.
Calvert, Brian. "Plato and the Equality of Women." *Phoenix* 29 (1975) 231–43.
Colson, F. H., and G. H. Whitaker, trans. *Philo*, vol. 1. LCL 226. Cambridge: Harvard University Press, 1929.
Crum, W. E. *A Coptic Dictionary*. 1939. Reprint, with a new foreword by James M. Robinson. Ancient Language Resources. Eugene, OR: Wipf & Stock, 2005.
Davies, Stevan L. *The Gospel of Thomas and Christian Wisdom*. 2nd ed. Oregon House, CA: Bardic, 2005.
DeConick, April. *Seek to See Him: Ascent and Vision Mysticism in the Gospel of Thomas.* Supplements to Vigiliae Christianae 33. Leiden: Brill, 1996.
Dillon, John. *The Middle Platonists (80 B.C. to A.D. 220)*. Rev. ed. Ithaca, NY: Cornell University Press, 1996.

---

26. Mayor, *The Amazons*, 33.
27. Pausanias, *Description of Greece* 1.2.1

Ehrman, Bart. *Lost Christianities: The Battles for Scripture and the Faiths We Never Knew*. Oxford: Oxford University Press, 2003.
Freedman, H., trans. *Midrash Rabbah: Genesis*. 2 vols. London: Soncino, 1951.
Gagné, Andre. "Conaissance, identité, et androgynéité: conditions du salut dans l'Évangile selon Thomas." In *Pratiques et constructions du corps en christianisme: actes du 42ième congress de Société canadienne de théologie*, edited by M. Allard et al., 131-47. Héritage et projet 75. Montreal: Fides, 2009.
Grant, Robert M., and D. N. Freedman. *The Secret Sayings of Jesus*. Garden City, NY: Doubleday, 1960.
Hedrick, Charles W. *Unlocking the Secrets of the Gospel according to Thomas*. Eugene, OR: Cascade Books, 2010.
Isenberg, Wesley W., trans. "The Gospel of Philip." In *The Nag Hammadi Library in English*, edited by James M. Robinson, 139-60. Coptic Gnostic Library Project. 3rd ed. San Francisco: Harper & Row, 1988.
King, Karen. *The Gospel of Mary of Magdala*. Santa Rosa, CA: Polebridge, 2003.
Lamb, W. R. M., trans. *Lysis, Symposium, Gorgias*, by Plato. LCL 166. Cambridge: Harvard University Press, 1925.
MacDonald, Dennis R. *There Is No Male and Female: The Fate of a Dominical Saying in Paul and Gnosticism*. Harvard Dissertations in Religion 20. Philadelphia: Fortress, 1987.
Mattila, Sharon Lea. "Wisdom, Sense Perception, Nature, and Philo's Gender Gradient." *Harvard Theological Review* 89 (1996) 103-29.
Mayor, Adrienne. *The Amazons: Lives and Legends of Warrior Women across the Ancient World*. Princeton: Princeton University Press, 2014.
Ménard, Jacques-É. *L'Évangile selon Thomas*. Nag Hammadi Studies 5. Leiden: Brill, 1975.
Miller, Frank Justus, trans. *Metamorphoses*, books 1-8, by Ovid. Revised by G. P. Gould. LCL 42. Cambridge: Harvard University Press, 1977.
Patterson, Stephen J. *The Gospel of Thomas and Jesus*. Foundations & Facets. Reference Series. Sonoma, CA: Polebridge, 1993.
Smith, Jonathan Z. "The Garments of Shame." *History of Religions* 5 (1966) 217-38.
Smith, Nicolas D. "Plato and Aristotle on the Nature of Women." *Journal of the History of Philosophy* 21 (1983) 467-78.
Stoker, William D. *Extracanonical Sayings of Jesus*. Society of Biblical Literature Resources for Biblical Study 18. Atlanta: Scholars, 1989.
Suter, Ann. "The Anasyrma: Baubo, Medusa, and the Gendering of Obscenity." In *Ancient Obscenities: Their Nature and Use in the Ancient Greek and Roman Worlds*, edited by Dorota Dutsch and Ann Suter, 21-43. Ann Arbor: University of Michigan Press, 2015.
Uro, Risto. "The Bridal Chamber and Other Mysteries: Ritual System and Ritual Transmission in the Valentinian Movement." In *Sacred Marriages: The Divine-Human Sexual Metaphor from Sumer to Early Christianity*, edited by Martti Nissinen and Risto Uro, 457-86. Winona Lake, IN: Eisenbrauns, 2008.
Wolfson, Harry A. *Philo: Foundations of Religious Philosophy in Judaism, Christianity, and Islam*. 2 vols. Structure and Growth of Philosophic Systems from Plato to Spinoza 2. Cambridge: Harvard University Press, 1947.

8

The *Gospel of Judas* and the End of Sethian Gnosticism

DAVID BRAKKE

Throughout her career Melissa Harl Sellew has made outstanding contributions to the study of Christian apocryphal gospels, especially the *Gospel according to Thomas* and the so-called *Secret Gospel of Mark*. In an important essay of 2001, she questioned how scholars have used the *Gospel of Thomas*, the *Book of Thomas the Contender Writing to the Perfect*, and the *Acts of Thomas* to reconstruct a community of "Thomasine Christians" in second- and third-century Syria. She expressed skepticism about the possibility of reconstructing social groups from narratives about Jesus and the apostles, and she warned against reducing a "masterly romance" like the *Acts of Thomas* to "the archival level of community records."[1] On the other hand, the assignment of the Thomas works to a "School of St. Thomas" did remove them from the category "Gnosticism," which neither accurately characterizes their shared theology nor provides them with useful contextualization. Reconstructing a "Thomas Christianity" sought to produce a more variegated social history of ancient Christianity, one less dependent on a binary contrast of "proto-orthodoxy" and "Gnosticism," and to envision how even a novel about an apostle might have communicated religious meaning to people who gathered to celebrate the rituals it portrays.[2]

---

1. Sellew, "Thomas Christianity," 35. I am grateful for the opportunity to offer this essay in honor of Melissa Harl Sellew, who introduced me and many others to the Greek of the New Testament and thus to the pleasures and challenges of studying early Christian literature.

2. This approach follows Sellew's and my shared teacher, Helmut Koester, in

The appearance of the *Gospel of Judas* in 2006 likewise presents an opportunity to consider the significance of a non-canonical gospel for the social history of early Christianity, particularly its relationship to Gnosticism. When the *Gospel of Judas* became available to scholars, a debate immediately broke out over whether the character of Judas in this remarkable work is a positive or negative figure. Scholars have discussed almost as intensely, if less publicly, the question of whether the *Gospel* is "Sethian" in its teachings and sectarian origins. This question is at least as urgent to historians of ancient Christianity as that of Judas's character because Sethianism or Sethian Gnosticism has become one of the most important categories for the reconstruction of the social and intellectual history of Gnosticism and for the interpretation of gnostic texts. By gathering a set of works within a larger group, historians believe that we better understand the individual writings and that we have uncovered a particular group or school of gnostics (or persons formerly known as "gnostics"), whom we call "Sethians." In turn, we have often fit individual texts into our reconstructed history of this larger Sethian tradition by dividing them into multiple sources. The appearance of the *Gospel of Judas* has led scholars to ask, Does it belong to the Sethian text group? And if so, how does it fit into our understanding of Sethianism and its development?

Nearly all scholars have said, Yes, the *Gospel* somehow belongs to the tradition of Sethianism, but the work's failure to conform to important features of that tradition has led some scholars to say that it comes from very early in Sethian history, others to say that it comes from a very late period in that history, and still others to say both (by dividing the gospel into different sources and layers). This disagreement raises a more profound question that historians have not addressed: maybe the *Gospel of Judas* does not fit into our understanding of Sethian Gnosticism because our understanding of Sethian Gnosticism is wrong.

In this essay I shall briefly explain the origins, characteristics, and functions of the category "Sethianism" in modern scholarship. Then I shall describe how three scholars have approached the question of whether and how the *Gospel of Judas* belongs to this category. Finally, I shall make the argument to which my title refers: not that the *Gospel of Judas* should bring to an end the scholarly practices of gathering texts into literary traditions or of creating social categories, which I consider

---

Koester and Robinson, *Trajectories*.

essential to the history of early Christianity, but that *Judas* should lead historians to discard the present category "Sethianism" and its reconstructed history and instead to create a new one, called "the Gnostics," and start over on its history.

What Is Sethianism?

The current scholarly category of Sethianism was born in 1974 when Hans-Martin Schenke published an essay titled "The Sethian System according to the Nag Hammadi Manuscripts."[3] The discovery of so-called gnostic manuscripts near Nag Hammadi in Egypt in 1945 had brought a flood of new data for scholars of Gnosticism to examine. They could compare these new primary sources with the accounts that the ancient heresiologists give of so-called gnostic groups, which include descriptions of "Sethians." Schenke noted that the heresiological descriptions of the Sethians, which first appear in the third century, are contradictory, although they share the assertion that the Sethians celebrated their connection to Seth, Adam and Eve's third son. Moreover, none of the newly discovered Nag Hammadi texts precisely matches the church fathers' accounts of Sethians. Therefore, Schenke concluded, our category of Sethianism cannot be that of the church fathers.

Schenke then noted that several texts from Nag Hammadi likewise shared a preoccupation with Seth, and that several of them spoke of God's elect, the truly saved religious people, as "the seed of Seth" or descendants of Seth. Moreover, several of these works seem to narrate, refer to, or presuppose the same mythological system. In his original article of 1974 and his expanded discussion of 1981, Schenke developed a list of mythological motifs and characters that he considered not only characteristic of but also distinctive of the Sethian system.[4] These include such aeons as the Invisible Virgin Spirit, the Barbēlō, and the self-originate aeon and its four attendant luminaries; the identification of the saved as the seed of Seth; and a baptismal ritual of "five seals." Schenke recognized that these motifs and characters could occur in works that were not Sethian, just as, say, the Christian characters Jesus and the Virgin Mary might appear in the Qur'an or other Muslim texts, but it was *how* such motifs

---

3. Schenke, "Das sethianische System." For a longer and better account of the category's history, see Rasimus, *Paradise Reconsidered*, 28–41.

4. Schenke, "Phenomenon and Significance."

and characters function within an overall mythological system that was decisive. Moreover, Schenke admitted that few if any Sethian works would feature *all* of the listed motifs. For reasons of genre and purpose, no Sethian work would necessarily feature the entire system, just as we would not expect every writing produced by a Presbyterian theologian or group to contain the entire body of Presbyterian doctrine and practice. Sethian works include the *Secret Book (Apocryphon) according to John*, the *Revelation of Adam, First Thought in Three Forms, Zōstrianos*, and others.

Schenke included in his list of Sethian evidence not only writings from Nag Hammadi and other manuscript hoards, but also testimonia from the church fathers that appear to describe the same mythological system. Of the heresiological reports that Schenke included, only Epiphanius of Salamis attributes the system to a group called "Sethians," and Schenke did *not* include other descriptions of so-called "Sethians" because the systems they report did not match his reconstructed Sethian mythology. The touchstone of what is genuinely Sethian is the system found in Schenke's text group, not the reports of ancient authors about Sethians.

For Schenke the value of creating this constellation of texts was twofold:

> The texts of this group shed light upon one another if compared synoptically; and the proportion and relationship of common, shared material to special, unique material permits a process of deduction that leads to considerable insight not only into the development of the teaching they contain, but also into the history of the community that transmitted them.[5]

In other words, first, at the level of the individual work, placement in the text group allows the reader to solve exegetical difficulties and simply to understand the story better through reference to other works in the group. Someone will understand and appreciate the *Revelation of Adam* more if she has read the *Secret Book according to John*. Second, as a group the texts give us access to the religious community that produced and transmitted them and allow us even to reconstruct their history. The Sethian group of *texts* gives us access to a Sethian group of *people*.

The method of gathering a set of ancient works into a text group and hypothesizing a community behind them is, as Melissa Harl Sellew

---

5. Schenke, "Phenomenon and Significance," 589.

noted in 2001, standard in the study of early Christianity. For example, in New Testament studies, we group together the Gospel of John and the three Letters of John (but not the Apocalypse of John) into a group called "Johannine literature." Our understanding of 2 John is enhanced by comparison of it with the Gospel and 1 John, and we posit a community, "Johannine Christianity," as the source of these works. Scholars have used these works to reconstruct a history of Johannine Christianity, and they have even discerned redactional layers in the Gospel that reflect this history. Scholars may quarrel with specific arguments, but this is standard operating procedure when we lack better evidence for religious groups and their development. Moreover, we may ask, what is an ancient author, if not a text group that we attribute to a single human being?[6]

In the case of Sethianism, only very few scholars have questioned the basic textual group that Schenke created. There have been and doubtless will continue to be debates about whether specific texts should be included and whether and how the text group should be related to other text groups and individual works. But nearly all scholars of Gnosticism have recognized the utility of Sethianism for illuminating the frequently puzzling mythological details in individual works. This includes even the scholars who have been most critical of the prevailing concept of Gnosticism, such as Michael Williams and Karen King.[7]

There has been more substantial disagreement about the extent to which we can move from the text group to a religious community that existed in the second and third centuries. Schenke was very optimistic that his text group reflected the beliefs, experience, and ritual life of an actual gnostic community, and he believed that he could trace the history of that community, albeit sketchily. Other scholars, however, are less sanguine about the reconstruction of a second-century religious group from pseudepigraphic works of mythology that primarily discuss the nature of God and events before the great flood of Noah. Or, like Sellew in the case of the Thomas literature, they are skeptical of the entire project of assigning ancient texts and people into reified social groups. Such scholars may be more comfortable speaking simply of a literary tradition, which may have originated among like-minded individual authors who riffed off each other's writings much as authors of fan fiction do today.[8]

---

6. See Foucault, "What Is an Author?"
7. Williams, "Sethianism"; King, *What Is Gnosticism?*, 158–62.
8. See Scott, "Churches or Books?"

Most historians, however, have agreed that, despite the mythological character of the works, the Sethian text group must have come from a religious community of some kind. They point to such features as sectarian self-identifying language and references to a shared ritual of baptism. A standard view of Sethian origins and development has emerged, based on Schenke's own hypothetical reconstruction of the sect's history. The orthodox scholarly narrative of Sethian history has had a crucial effect on how we understand the origin and character of Gnosticism and its relationship to Christianity.[9]

The Sethians, most scholars agree, did not originate within Christianity. Rather, Sethianism most likely first emerged among Hellenized Jews in the late first century or early second century CE. For political and/or philosophical reasons, these learned Jews became disenchanted with the God of Genesis and speculated instead about a higher divinity and its relationship with Seth, the third son of Adam and Eve. After they had developed their basic mythology and a baptismal ritual, they encountered Christian teachings about Jesus. The Sethians then incorporated Jesus and other Christian elements into their system. This Christianization of Sethianism brought the sect to the attention of heresiologists like Irenaeus of Lyons, who had available to him a version of the *Secret Book according to John* when he wrote his *Against the Heresies* around 180 CE.

By the late second century, then, the Sethians were one among the many groups that might be called Christian, but the Christian character of Sethianism was mostly superficial and did not really transform the essentially non-Christian heart of its mythology. It was, then, Valentinus and his students who created the first genuinely Christian gnostic myth. Meanwhile, the work of bishops like Irenaeus helped to promote an emerging "proto-orthodoxy" among Christians, and the Valentinian school of Christian thought provided gnostically inclined Christians with a much more fully Christian form of mythological gnosis. By the middle of the third century, therefore, Sethians had turned away from Judaism and Christianity and engaged more with mystical forms of non-Christian Platonism connected with Plotinus and others. Sethian works from this period emphasize modes of mystical ascent to contemplation of God and play down the biblically inspired mythology of earlier works.

---

9. The standard narrative of Sethian history originated in the articles of Schenke and has been most fully, precisely, and persuasively articulated by John D. Turner in several works, especially Turner, *Sethian Gnosticism and the Platonic Tradition*. It appears briefly in textbooks: e.g., Pearson, *Ancient Gnosticism*, 99–100.

By the fourth century, people with Sethian interests likely dispersed into various countercultural or mystical movements of the post-Constantine era (desert monasticism, theurgic Neoplatonism, and the like), although a few Sethian Christians may have survived in Egypt to give us the Nag Hammadi codices.

Scholars argue about details of this account, but most agree on Sethianism's non-Christian origin and essence. Christian elements of Sethian mythology, such as references to Jesus and the apostles, were secondary, added after the development of Sethianism's basic ideas. Thus, the Sethians easily shed them when being "Christian" became less viable or attractive. This hypothesis holds great explanatory power at the level of the text group, for it enables scholars to place Sethian texts in a rough chronological order, and it invests their unity in mythological features that undeniably appear throughout the text group, in which however the prominence of indisputably Christian motifs conspicuously varies.

Moreover, this hypothesis liberates Gnosticism from its identity as a Christian heresy (perhaps to become a Jewish heresy). Sethian Gnosticism does not represent a rebellion against specific Christian doctrines, but arises, on the one hand, from a profound sense of alienation from the created world as it is, including its political structures and its God, and, on the other, from a profound confidence in the divine nature of humanity and the solidarity of the ultimate God with human beings.

Nevertheless, Christian motifs do appear in nearly all of the Sethian works—and most importantly, they appear in the *Secret Book according to John*, which must be one of the earliest works in the text group because Irenaeus knew some version or source of it in 180. Thus, an originally non-Christian Sethianism requires source criticism, the detection of sources or layers in certain texts in the group that would reflect the community's origin in Hellenized Judaism and subsequent Christianization. In the case of the *Secret Book according to John*, this surgery is fairly easy to perform, for the most explicitly Christian elements occur only in a frame story. The *Secret Book* opens with the disciple John confused and dismayed over the crucifixion of Jesus. After John has a short conversation with an unsympathetic Pharisee, the Savior, presumably Christ, appears to John. The Savior's lengthy revelation to John is interrupted by questions only a few times. It covers the complex nature of the godhead, which includes a divine figure called the anointed or Christ, and it retells the events in the first six or so chapters of Genesis, without any references to Jesus or unambiguous citations of or allusions to explicitly Christian literature (so it is argued). The frame story returns at the conclusion of the Savior's discourse, and in two of the four manuscripts the author proclaims that Jesus is the Christ.

Most scholars have concluded that an editor has taken an originally non-Christian mythological discourse based on Genesis, Plato's *Timaeus*, and other non-Christian works and secondarily framed it with a dialogue between Jesus and the disciple John. This hypothesis finds further support in Irenaeus's summary of part of the *Secret Book*, which mentions neither Jesus as the revealer of the myth nor John as its recipient. The placement of a non-Christian gnostic discourse within a Christian frame would reflect the Sethians' origin as a non-Christian movement, which then later became Christianized. Other Sethian works, such as the *Revelation of Adam* and *Three Steles of Seth*, lend themselves to this kind of source analysis, especially if the historian seeks to reconstruct a highly precise literary and thus social history of Sethianism.

In addition to identifying suspicious seams within texts, source criticism of Sethian works has depended upon the easy identification of different religious traditions, not only Jewish vs. Christian vs. pagan, but also of traditions within these larger complexes. For example, even within Judaism, speculation on the role of Wisdom (Sophia) in the created order can be distinguished from interest in retelling the stories of Gen 1–6, which in turn can be distinguished from eschatological visions. Scholars understand these diverse mythological traditions to be indications of separable modes of religiosity, which can be the basis for discerning different literary traditions, and so different sources, and then even different religious communities or stages in the development of a single community.

To be sure, some scholars have criticized both the standard narrative of Sethian history and the source critical analyses that support it.[10] For example, some have challenged the interpretation of the *Secret Book according to John* that identifies the frame story as secondary and the revelation discourse as lacking Christian elements.[11] At the level of social and religious history, all three ancient non-Sethian authors who (according to the hypothesis) show knowledge of Sethian mythology or literature (Irenaeus of Lyons, Porphyry of Tyre, and Epiphanius of Salamis) identify the writers and readers of this literature as Christians—false Christians, say

---

10. Burns, *Apocalypse of the Alien God*; Rasimus, *Paradise Reconsidered*.
11. Pleše, *Poetics of the Gnostic Universe*; Dubois, "La tradition johannique."

Irenaeus and Epiphanius, but Christians nonetheless. We have no external evidence that confirms the existence of a non-Christian Sethian community. Finally, one of the most distinctive features of Sethian mythology is that it does not depict the God of Genesis, the God who created this universe, as merely a lower demiurgic deity, inferior to the ultimate first principle—nearly all philosophically inclined Jews and Christians of the first centuries of our era did that. Rather, they identify him as an evil, malicious, and ignorant being, named Ialdabaōth or Saklas—that is, as satanic. How likely is it that thoughtful Jews, no matter how influenced by Platonism or how discouraged by political events, would make this kind of identification? Is it not more plausible to imagine an intermediary step toward such a conclusion, such as the proclamation of the temporary nature and inferior status of the Law in the preaching of Paul or the sharp contrast between Moses and Jesus found in the Gospel of John (1:17), in which Jesus tells skeptical Jews that their father is Satan (8:44)?

Even the skeptics of the standard narrative of Sethian history and of the practice of source criticism that supports it, however, have seldom questioned the contents and utility of the Sethian text group or its connection to an actual religious community in the second and third centuries. But the *Gospel of Judas* may suggest the need for a new approach to the category. I turn now to the new gospel and its significance for the category and history of Sethianism.

Judas in the History of Sethian Gnosticism

Scholars noticed the Sethian features of the *Gospel of Judas* as soon as it appeared.[12] The work identifies the ultimate god as "the great invisible spirit" and includes the Barbēlō aeon, the Self-Originate and its four attendants, the divine Adamas, and the race of Seth in its godhead—all distinctively Sethian ideas. This world is created by Saklas, who is distinct from Ialdabaōth, but there is precedent for this in Sethian literature. Moreover, like the *Secret Book according to John*, the gospel contains a revelation discourse that focuses on the complexity of the godhead and the creation of humanity, embedded within a dialogue between Jesus and a disciple, here Judas. Finally, also like the *Secret Book*, Irenaeus seems to confirm the existence of the *Gospel of Judas* in the middle of the second century. He gives its title, and his brief and sketchy description of its

---

12. I have made my own translations from the edition of Jenott, *Gospel of Judas*.

contents matches the gospel that we have fairly well. I shall return to this point below.

On the other hand, *Judas* differs from other Sethian works in important ways. It does not give any role to the aeon Wisdom (Sophia) in the generation of Saklas, the creation of this world, and the salvation of humanity—in sharp contrast to the *Secret Book* and some, but not all, other Sethian works. It does not discuss explicitly an advent of a savior figure, such as First Thought or the Great Seth, as one finds elsewhere, and there is no reference to the distinctive Sethian baptismal ritual. In addition, the *Gospel of Judas* is very Christian. In the *Secret Book according to John*, the Christian frame story is short: the vast majority of the work consists of the allegedly non-Christian revelation discourse. In the *Gospel of Judas*, however, dialogues between Jesus, Judas, and the other disciples constitute most of the work, while the allegedly non-Christian revelation discourse is rather short and serves as a kind of climax to the preceding dialogues. Judas's handing over of Jesus to Jewish leaders then concludes the gospel.

No scholar who has examined the gospel's place in the history of Sethianism has found that it undermines the standard narrative of Sethian history. Indeed, the example of another seemingly non-Christian revelation discourse placed within a Christian story has only confirmed the superficial relationship between Christianity and Sethianism. But scholars have disagreed markedly about how to fit *Judas* into the historical development of Sethianism. Its Sethian character appears either to be underdeveloped or merely tacked on, so the options seem to be very early in Sethian history or very late.

On the one hand, Marvin Meyer argued that the *Gospel of Judas* comes from, as he put it, "when the Sethians were young."[13] He accepted that Irenaeus knew pretty much the text that we have, and he believed that the revelation discourse comes from Sethianism's origins outside Christianity, in what he called "Jewish Gnosis." Its underdeveloped version of the Sethian myth, moreover, suggests that it may be even older than what we find in the *Secret Book according to John*. Both works, however, show how the Sethian myth was secondarily Christianized—and quite early.

On the other hand, Gesene Schenke Robinson and John Turner argue that the *Gospel of Judas* was originally Christian, but was secondarily

---

13. Meyer, "When the Sethians Were Young."

Sethianized and must come from the third century.[14] Both, then, must claim that the *Gospel of Judas* known to Irenaeus in 180 cannot be the text that we now have; rather, Irenaeus must have known an earlier version of the *Gospel of Judas* or even a different text altogether. In part, they make this claim based on what Irenaeus does *not* say about the gospel; that is, both argue that if Irenaeus had known in Greek the text that we have in Coptic, he would have summarized and/or criticized certain features about which he is silent. These include the gospel's highly negative portrayal of the disciples other than Judas and the specifically Sethian aspects of the gospel's mythology.

Turner dates the *Gospel of Judas* to the second quarter of the third century. He suggests that in the history of Sethianism, the gospel's highly charged criticism of clergy who make claims to apostolic succession indicates that it comes after Sethian works, such as the *Revelation of Adam*, which criticize the baptism and Christology of other Christians. And yet it must come before works like *Zōstrianos*, which originated in the later third century, when the Sethians turned away from Christianity to pagan Platonism. Turner does not attempt a precise account of the literary sources and stages of the gospel, except to say that the current gospel must be a revision of a non-Sethian work that depicted Judas's handing over of Jesus in the way Irenaeus describes it.

Schenke Robinson, in contrast, presents a detailed hypothetical history of the gospel's redaction. I leave aside the source-critical details here; rather, the most important point is this:

> The *Gospel of Judas* is a distinctive Christian-Gnostic, albeit anti-orthodox, text, whereas Sethianism was basically a non-Christian, Jewish-Gnostic movement. Although Sethianism did come in contact with Christianity, and its texts were subjected to various degrees of Christianization, its focal point or main thrust never had a specifically Christian-Gnostic perspective; it was always more typified by an inner-Jewish tension. Sethian writings generally deal with notorious Old Testament figures by means of reinterpreting their purpose and function in the Hebrew Scriptures, and reassessing their reputation in Judaism; they do not employ New Testament characters. Non-Sethian Christian-Gnostics, in contrast, favor personages who are marginalized in the orthodox church and give them a different role and meaning—as, for instance, the case with Mary in the *Gospel of Mary*. Hence rather than being a document whose Sethian

14. Schenke Robinson, "*Gospel of Judas*"; Turner, "Sethian Myth."

themes are not yet fully developed, the *Gospel of Judas* in its present form appears to be a quite late and distant offshoot of Sethianism.[15]

Schenke Robinson reaches the exact opposite conclusion from that of Meyer: *Judas* does not represent underdeveloped Sethianism, as Meyer claims, but a late and distant offshoot of Sethianism. Nonetheless, Schenke Robinson, and Meyer, along with Turner, attempt to fit the *Gospel of Judas* into the history of Sethianism as we know it—that is, into the history of a community that originated in non-Christian Judaism, that subsequently had a brief, highly conflicted, and yet ultimately superficial relationship with Christianity, and that finally became alienated from increasingly orthodox Christianity and drifted into pagan mystical Neoplatonism. In this history, the deeply Christian and less deeply Sethian *Gospel of Judas*, must come rather early—at the start of the Sethians' contact with Christians—or rather late—as that contact was coming to a bitter end.

Seemingly forgotten in this debate is the constructed nature of both Sethianism and its history. Sethianism is a modern category, a text group that we scholars have created. That these texts belong together, that they can be placed in a chronological order, and that they reflect the religious history of a specific group of people are all ideas that we have invented. These are powerful ideas, which have made the surviving texts easier to understand and contextualize—but again, Sethianism and its history are modern creations.[16]

I propose that instead of deciding how to fit the *Gospel of Judas* into our current theory of Sethianism and its history, we should use this new piece of data to see whether this category still works and whether the history we have created from it still makes sense.

The End of Sethian Gnosticism

As polemical and distorted as it is, one of our few anchors for dating and sorting so-called gnostic teachers, texts, and groups is Irenaeus of Lyons' *Against the Heresies* from around 180. As I have said, Irenaeus mentions a

---

15. Schenke Robinson, "*Gospel of Judas*," 89.

16. Jenott criticizes the notion of "'fully developed' and 'genuine' Sethian thought" and eschews any "unilinear model of development" of the Sethian myth (*Gospel of Judas*, 71–74).

Gospel of Judas. It is not clear whether he has read the book or has merely heard about it. His description of its contents is very brief and sketchy.

> And furthermore—they say—Judas the betrayer was thoroughly acquainted with these things; and he alone was acquainted with the truth as no others were, and (so) accomplished the mystery of the betrayal. By him all things, both earthly and heavenly, were thrown into dissolution. And they bring forth a fabricated work to this effect, which they entitle *The Gospel of Judas*.[17]

Irenaeus reports three things about the *Gospel*. First, Judas knew "these things": it is not clear which of the many things Irenaeus has just described Judas knew. Some of the mythological motifs and stories Irenaeus has narrated in the preceding sections are found in our *Gospel of Judas*, but many more or not, including the things that Irenaeus attributes to the "others" just before he mentions *Judas*. It may be relevant on this point that our *Judas* is a relatively short work. Second, Irenaeus says that Judas "alone was acquainted with the truth as no others were, and accomplished the mystery of betrayal." Our *Gospel of Judas* repeatedly emphasizes Judas's knowledge of Jesus' true identity and origin and the ignorance of the other disciples, and it concludes with his agreement to hand Jesus over to Jewish leaders. Third, Irenaeus says that by Judas's act "all things, both earthly and heavenly, were thrown into dissolution." In our gospel, after Jesus tells Judas that he will sacrifice the human being he inhabits, he announces that "[. . . the thrones] of the aeon have been [defeated, and] the kings have become weak, and the races of the angels have groaned, and the evils that [. . .] the ruler is destroyed" (*Gos. Jud.* 57:4–10). This sounds very much like what Irenaeus describes—the dissolution of the present world order, both earthly and heavenly.

Brief as it is, then, Irenaeus' description of the *Gospel of Judas* that circulated before 180 matches our newly discovered work. He does not say anything about the work that rules out our gospel. Any hypothesis, therefore, that argues against identifying our *Gospel of Judas* as a Coptic translation of the Greek work known to Irenaeus must rely on Irenaeus' failure to mention other aspects of the gospel. It seems to me, then, that we ought to identify our gospel as a translation of that known to Irenaeus unless other evidence from antiquity compels us to do otherwise.[18]

---

17. Irenaeus, *Against Heresies* 1.31.1 (in Layton, *Gnostic Scriptures*, 181).
18. See Jenott, *Gospel of Judas*, 5-6.

Irenaeus mentions the *Gospel of Judas* toward the end of the first book of *Against the Heresies*, which is devoted to a genealogy of heretical teachers and groups, the purpose of which is to expose the diabolical origins of the Valentinian school of Christianity. Irenaeus does not present these heresies in chronological order, but he concludes his catalogue of heresies with his account of "a multitude of Gnostics," whom he identifies as the immediate intellectual predecessors of Valentinus and his school. Irenaeus first narrates what "some of them" say (1.29), then what "others" of them say (1.30), and finally what still "others" say (1.31). Later heresiologists concluded that Irenaeus was in fact describing three distinct groups and gave them specific names, but Irenaeus seems to see all of them as related manifestations of the group whose teachings Valentinus adapted, a group that he earlier refers to as "the Gnostic school of thought (or heresy)" (1.11).

Scholars have long recognized that in the first portion of this discussion Irenaeus narrates a mythological account of divine emanations that matches that in the *Secret Book according to John*. Some version of this work must have appeared no later than the middle of the second century, most likely earlier if, as Irenaeus claims, Valentinus and his students knew its teachings. Irenaeus, then, provides us with the basis for attributing both the *Secret Book according to John* and the *Gospel of Judas* to the gnostic school of thought that he says influenced Valentinus. In other words, these two works may serve as the foundation or, better, the nucleus for a new text group, a group of texts that we might call "Gnostic." That is, after all, the term that Irenaeus uses. This plan may be superior to borrowing the name "Sethian" from certain heresiological reports and then having to explain that some of these heresiological reports are not truly "Sethian."

This new text group would most probably look very similar to the old "Sethianism," but here the *Gospel of Judas* forms part of the nucleus of the group, rather than being a text that we must somehow find or not find a place for in a preexisting group. It would help to define the key features of the text group, rather than be measured against such features. Moreover, we would have to reconstruct the origins and history of this group differently and reconsider what it means for the relationship between "Christianity" and so-called "Gnosticism."

Consider the most significant features that the *Secret Book according to John* and the the *Gospel of Judas* share. First, they both feature a revelation dialogue between Jesus or Christ and a disciple, which provides information about God, the origin of the cosmos, the structure and population of the heavens, and the origin and early history of humanity. In each case, the divine revealer departs at the conclusion of the dialogue.

Second, both gospels are related intertextually to the Fourth Gospel. The *Secret Book* makes John, the purported author of the gospel, its main character, and Johannine elements appear in both the frame story and the revelation dialogue.[19] *Judas* shows knowledge of Matthew and Luke,[20] and its dramatic opening scene of Judas's "confession" is clearly modeled on the "confession" of Peter in the synoptic gospels (Matt 16:13–20 and parallels). Still, the gospel's scenario, showing Judas just outside the location of the Last Supper, seems to presuppose the departure of Judas from the guest room in John 13:30.[21]

Third, they share a set of theological or mythical motifs that they arrange into a similar story. An unknowable ultimate source, the Invisible Spirit, emanates two other divine hypostases, the Barbēlō (or a "luminous cloud") and the self-originate aeon, the latter of which has four attendants.[22] From these emanate multiple other divine aeons, among which are heavenly prototypes of Adam and the posterity of his son Seth. The universe in which we live, in contrast, is created and ruled by a hostile power, named Ialdabaōth and/or Saklas, who is identified as the god of Genesis. At the top of the hierarchy within this cosmos preside twelve rulers, doubtless corresponding to the twelve signs of the Zodiac, for both works closely identify the power structure of this universe with the heavenly bodies. Five names of rulers occur in both works in the same order—only five because that is as many as the *Gospel of Judas* names (*Gos. Jud.* 52:3–14; *Ap. John* [BG] 40:5–9).

Fourth, both works identify the saved people as a *genea*, a "race"— for example, "the immovable race" in the *Secret Book* and "the mighty and holy race" in the *Gospel of Judas* (*Ap. John* [BG] 73:9-10; *Gos. Jud.* 36:25-26). Both works place in the spiritual realm an archetypal progeny

---

19. Dubois, "La tradition johannique."

20. Gathercole, "Matthean or Lukan Priority?"

21. Emmel, "Presuppositions and the Purpose."

22. Judas's statement to Jesus early in the gospel—"I know who you are and where you have come from. You have come from the aeon of the Barbēlō, the immortal (aeon). But as for the one who sent you, I am not worthy to proclaim his name" (35:17–21)—refers explicitly to the Barbēlō and obliquely to the Invisible Spirit. In his later cosmological revelation, Jesus refers explicitly to the Invisible Spirit and obliquely to the Barbēlō ("a luminous cloud") (47:14–21).

of Seth: "the seed of Seth" in the *Secret Book* and "the incorruptible race of Seth" in the *Gospel of Judas* (*Ap. John* [BG] 36:3-4; *Gos. Jud.* 49:5-6). Neither, however, explicitly identifies human beings in the material realm as the descendants of Seth. The name "Seth" appears only three times in the entire *Secret Book* (*Ap. John* [BG] 35:21; 36:3-4; 63:14), and the *Gospel of Judas* speaks of a final exaltation of (perhaps a portion of) "the great race of Adam" (*Gos. Jud.* 57:11-12). Given the prominence of Adam in both works and the lesser role of Seth, the name "Sethian" does not seem the most apt choice for these materials.[23]

Finally, both works refer to "the perfect (*teleios*) human being," with whom the saved are associated, early in the narratives. In the *Secret Book* the Savior tells John to share what he is about to reveal with persons from "the immovable race of the perfect human being" (*Ap. John* [BG] 22:15-16; II 2:24-25). In his first dialogue with the disciples, Jesus challenges them to "bring forward the perfect human being" (*Gos. Jud.* 35:3-4).

The two works also differ in significant ways, as I mentioned above. In the *Gospel's* opening dialogue, Judas makes a confession of Jesus' identity similar to Peter's confession at Caesarea Philippi in the synoptic gospels: "I know who you are and where you have come from. You have come from the aeon of the Barbēlō, the immortal (aeon). But as for the one who sent you, I am not worthy to proclaim his name" (*Gos. Jud.* 35:15-21). Despite the prominence of the Barbēlō in this important statement, the *Gospel of Judas* gives remarkably less attention to that aeon in its theology than does the *Secret Book*, leaving it unnamed as a "luminous cloud" in Jesus' later revelation (*Gos. Jud.* 47:14-21).

Even more significant, however, is that the two works differ in how the rulers of this cosmos originated. Famously, in the *Secret Book*, Ialdabaōth comes into being when the aeon Wisdom attempts to think without the consent of her male consort: Ialdabaōth is a kind of glitch in divine thought, an error. In the *Gospel of Judas*, however, one of the immortals, most likely Ēlēlēth, calls Ialdabaōth and his fellow rulers into being (*Gos. Jud.* 51:3-15). This scenario appears also in the *Holy Book of the Great Invisible Spirit*, which shares other key features with *Judas* (*Gos. Eg.* III 56:22-59:9).[24] In other words, the error and fall of the aeon Sophia, which scholars have tended to highlight as a central feature of

---

23. Schenke remarked on the artificial nature of the name "Sethian": his text group could, he wrote, be called simply the "X-group" ("Phenomenon and Significance," 590).

24. See Jenott, *Gospel of Judas*, 94-99.

Gnosticism, was only one of seemingly two possible gnostic explanations for how the imperfect lower divinities originated from the serene perfection of the Entirety.

If we jettison the category "Sethianism" and its standard history and instead try to develop a category "Gnostic" from the new evidence that the *Gospel of Judas* presents us, then we can see that this movement developed in close interactions with competing Christian claims to revelation and authority, claims in which literary depictions of the original disciples of Jesus figured prominently. Both the *Secret Book according to John* and the *Gospel of Judas* are revelations (apocalypses), akin in their literary forms to the Revelation to John in the New Testament and the *Shepherd of Hermas* outside of it. Theologically they participate in the lively debate among second-century Christians over how to relate the new revelation of Jesus to the Septuagint, the Jewish Law, and the God of Genesis—a debate that the teachings of Paul and the Gospel of John inspired and that Christians ranging from Basilides to Marcion to Valentinus and Justin took up with vigor. The narrative of secondary and superficial Christianization appears much less plausible.

Gnostic Christianity, I suggest, did not originate in some particularly grave sense of alienation from this world and its God, but in the very elements that generated diversity and debate among second-century Christians—the nature of authority and the legacy of the original apostles, the practice and meaning of rituals like baptism and the eucharist, the persistence of or end to revelatory experiences of the Savior, the status of the Jewish Scriptures and their God when the Law is no longer observed among Gentile believers. To be sure, the gnostics lie at one "extreme" end of the spectrum of Christian approaches to these questions, but they do lie on that spectrum.

This proposal modifies, in light of the appearance of *Judas*, the method for identifying evidence for the gnostic school of thought that Bentley Layton first articulated in 1995, well before the appearance of the *Gospel of Judas*, and which I defended in my book of 2010.[25] In his original essay Layton advocated placing at the center of any historical reconstruction of the gnostics Irenaeus's account of the myth of the so-called gnostic school of thought as well as the literature that he and Porphyry associate with the people whom they call gnostics: the *Secret Book according to John*, *Zōstrianos*, *Foreigner (Allogenēs)*, and the *Book of*

---

25. Layton, "Prolegomena"; Brakke, *Gnostics*.

Zoroaster (excerpted in the *Secret Book*). For Layton's scheme, Schenke's Sethian hypothesis provided a crucial step by which the data assigned to the gnostics could be expanded beyond that which Irenaeus and Porphyry provide: because the works gathered from Irenaeus and Porphyry teach or assume Schenke's Sethian myth, the remaining works in the Sethian text group could be assigned to the gnostics (hence the works in the section "Classic Gnostic Scripture" in Layton's *The Gnostic Scriptures*).[26] I argued for this proposal in my own book on the gnostics, but unlike Layton, I wrote after the appearance of the *Gospel of Judas* and should not have fallen victim to the error of assessing whether *Judas* belongs within the Sethian group.[27] I failed to realize that the text group itself needs to be revised in light of this new piece of data.

To be sure, some historians would abandon the project that I advocate. Instead, they justly fear the creation of reified categories and groups that would obscure the hybridity and fluidity of pre-Nicene Christianity.[28] I am sympathetic to this position, but I am reminded of the question some feminist historians asked in the 1980s and 1990s: Why, just as historical women were being rediscovered, did the academy decide to do away with subjectivity and so with women? In a similar way, I am worried that, just as sources have appeared that allow us to reconstruct better the teachings and practices of the so-called "heretics," we will deprive them of much of what we consider the essentials of religion in general and of Christianity in particular, that is, community, ritual, patterns of authority, and tradition.

If historians of pre-Nicene Christianity are going to make any progress in reconstructing the social and intellectual history of Christians, then we must make use of groups of literary works that seem to reflect the same religious and social traditions. But, as Melissa Harl Sellew argued about Thomas Christianity, we must recognize also that the categories that we create we have in fact created. We must be open to the possibility that new data may require the dismantling of old textual groups, the creation of new ones, and the revision of our theories of historical development. Some of us have concluded that the Nag Hammadi treatises should lead us to discard the category "Gnosticism." Now I suggest that the *Gospel of Judas* should lead us to reconsider the category "Sethianism." I am

26. Layton, "Prolegomena," 342–43.

27. Brakke, *Gnostics*, 37–41.

28. I take this to be King's position in King, *What Is Gnosticism?*; and King, "Which Early Christianity?"

not ready, however, to give up categories altogether: whether the Judas of this new text is a hero or a villain, he might be able to teach us a few things about the history of the diverse groups that made up what we call early Christianity.

Works Cited

Brakke, David. *The Gnostics: Myth, Ritual, and Diversity in Early Christianity*. Cambridge: Harvard University Press, 2010.
Burns, Dylan M. *Apocalypse of the Alien God: Platonism and the Exile of Sethian Gnosticism*. Divinations: Rereading Late Ancient Religion. Philadelphia: University of Pennsylvania Press, 2014.
DeConick, April D., ed. *The Codex Judas Papers: Proceedings of the International Congress on the Tchacos Codex Held at Rice University, Houston Texas, March 13-16, 2008*. Nag Hammadi and Manichaean Studies 71. Leiden: Brill, 2009.
Dubois, Jean-Daniel. "La tradition johannique dans l'*Apocryphe de Jean*." *Adamantius* 18 (2012) 108-17.
Emmel, Stephen. "The Presuppositions and the Purpose of the *Gospel of Judas*." In *The Gospel of Judas in Context: Proceedings of the First International Conference on the "Gospel of Judas,"* edited by Madeleine Scopello, 33-39. Nag Hammadi and Manichaean Studies 62. Leiden: Brill, 2008.
Foucault, Michel. "What Is an Author?" In *Language, Counter-Memory, Practice: Selected Essays and Interviews by Michel Foucault*, edited by Donald F. Bouchard, 113-38. Translated by Donald F. Bouchard and Sherry Simon. Ithaca: Cornell University Press, 1977.
Gathercole, Simon. "Matthean or Lukan Priority? The Use of the NT Gospels in the *Gospel of Judas*." In *Judasevangelium und Codex Tchacos*, edited by Enno Edzard Popkes and Gregor Wurst, 291-302. Wissenschaftliche Untersuchungen zum Neuen Testament 297. Tübingen: Mohr/Siebeck, 2012.
Jenott, Lance. *The "Gospel of Judas": Coptic Text, Translation, and Historical Interpretation of the "Betrayer's Gospel."* Studien und Texte zu Antike und Christentum 64. Tübingen: Mohr/Siebeck, 2011.
King, Karen L. *What Is Gnosticism?* Cambridge, UK: Belknap, 2003.
———. "Which Early Christianity?" In *The Oxford Handbook of Early Christian Studies*, edited by Susan Ashbrook Harvey and David G. Hunter, 66-84. Oxford Handbooks in Religion and Theology. Oxford: Oxford University Press, 2008.
Layton, Bentley. *The Gnostic Scriptures*. Garden City, NY: Doubleday, 1987.
———. "Prolegomena to the Study of Ancient Gnosticism." In *The Social World of the First Christians: Essays in Honor of Wayne A. Meeks*, edited by L. M. White and O. L. Yarbrough, 334-50. Minneapolis: Fortress, 1995.
Meyer, Marvin. "When the Sethians Were Young: The *Gospel of Judas* in the Second Century." In *Codex Judas Papers: Proceedings of the International Congress on the Tchacos Codex Held at Rice University, Houston Texas, March 13-16, 2008*, edited by April D. DeConick, 58-74. Nag Hammadi and Manichaean Studies 71. Leiden: Brill, 2009.

Pearson, Birger A. *Ancient Gnosticism: Traditions and Literature*. Minneapolis: Fortress, 2007.
Pleše, Zlatko. *Poetics of the Gnostic Universe: Narrative and Cosmology in the "Apocryphon of John."* Nag Hammadi and Manichaean Studies 52. Leiden: Brill, 2006.
Rasimus, Tuomas. *Paradise Reconsidered in Gnostic Mythmaking: Rethinking Sethianism in Light of the Ophite Evidence*. Nag Hammadi and Manichaean Studies 68. Leiden: Brill, 2009.
Robinson, James M., and Helmut Koester. *Trajectories through Early Christianity*. 1971. Reprint, Eugene, OR: Wipf & Stock, 2006.
Schenke, Hans-Martin. "Das sethianische System nach Nag-Hammadi-Handschriften." In *Studia Coptica*, edited by Peter Nagel, 165–73. Berliner byzantinistische Arbeiten 45. Berlin: Akademie, 1974.
———. "The Phenomenon and Significance of Gnostic Sethianism." In *The Rediscovery of Gnosticism: Proceedings of the International Conference on Gnosticism at Yale, New Haven, Connecticut, March 28–31, 1978*, edited by Bentley Layton, 2:588–616. Studies in the History of Religions: Supplements to Numen 41. Leiden: Brill, 1981.
Schenke Robinson, Gesine. "*The Gospel of Judas*: Its Protagonist, Its Composition, and Its Community." In *The Codex Judas Papers: Proceedings of the International Congress on the Tchacos Codex Held at Rice University, Houston Texas, March 13–16, 2008*, edited by April D. DeConick, 75–94. Nag Hammadi and Manichaean Studies 71. Leiden: Brill, 2009.
Scott, Alan B. "Churches or Books? Sethian Social Organization." *Journal of Early Christian Studies* 3 (1995) 109–22.
Sellew, Melissa (Philip) Harl. "Thomas Christianity: Scholars in Quest of a Community." In *The Apocryphal Acts of Thomas*, edited by Jan N. Bremmer, 11–35. Studies on Early Christian Apocrypha 6. Leuven: Peeters, 2001.
Turner, John D. *Sethian Gnosticism and the Platonic Tradition*. Bibliothèque copte de Nag Hammadi 6. Sainte-Foy, Québec: Les presses de l'Université Laval, 2001.
———. "The Sethian Myth in the *Gospel of Judas*: Soteriology or Demonology?" In *The Codex Judas Papers: Proceedings of the International Congress on the Tchacos Codex Held at Rice University, Houston Texas, March 13–16, 2008*, edited by April D. DeConick, 95–133. Nag Hammadi and Manichaean Studies 71. Leiden: Brill, 2009.
Williams, Michael. "Sethianism." In *A Companion to Second-Century Christian "Heretics,"* edited by Antti Marjanen and Petri Luomanen, 32–63. Supplements to Vigiliae Christianae 76. Leiden: Brill, 2005.

9

The Persistence of Crafted Memories

The Nag Hammadi Cartonnage, Upper Egyptian Monasticism, and the Literary Sources[1]

JAMES E. GOEHRING

The recycled papyrus documents or cartonnage used to stiffen various of the Nag Hammadi codices have been a subject of debate among scholars over the years, particularly with respect to their use to date and provenance the codices themselves. While several monastic texts found among them have been used to support the codices' monastic origin, other documents have been seen to point away from this conclusion. Among Nag Hammadi scholars, the debate is well known.[2] While the divide is often sharp, I would suggest that the various sides still accept, albeit to varying degrees, a basic understanding of Egyptian monasticism and its relationship with the surrounding cultural world, an understanding drawn from the literary sources and pervasive in the history of western scholarship. This paper seeks to further loosen the literary sources' traditional hold on the understanding of Egyptian monasticism in an effort to better appreciate monastic scribes' access to the discarded documents

[1]. It is a pleasure to offer this small contribution in honor Melissa Harl, whose kindness, friendship, and scholarship has enhanced my experience of the academy through many years. Thank you, Melissa.

[2]. For a recent summary of the debate, see Lundhaug and Jenott, *Monastic Origins*, 104–11; cf., Goehring, "Provenance."

used in codex construction. The argument hinges on a notion of greater interaction than usually assumed between monks and their surrounding communities.

The cartonnage offer evidence independent of the literary content of the codices with respect to the date and provenance of the latter's production. They include a mix of seemingly secular texts (commercial and official documents, contracts, and tax receipts), fragments of Genesis, and monastic correspondence. Three documents from Codex VII dated in the 340s suggest a production date for the codices from the latter half of the fourth into the fifth century. More important to the issue at hand, however, is the mix of secular and monastic texts. The codices, discovered in 1945 by peasants digging for fertilizer near the Upper Egyptian city of Nag Hammadi, preserve a remarkable collection of heterodox and so-called gnostic texts.[3] Their content hardly comports with the reading material one would expect to find in an Egyptian monastic setting as it was traditionally understood, namely withdrawn from the world, biblically based, and orthodox.[4] Had the codices come into the hands of scholars apart from any indication of their geographical provenance, one suspects that the traditionally understood divide between "heretical" texts and "orthodox" monks would have kept the notion of any such connection remote at best. Their discovery, however, in fairly close proximity to two monasteries of the well-known Pachomian federation, including its central monastery, raised the question of their possible connection.

The possibility of such a connection, suggested initially by James Robinson in 1974,[5] gained considerable momentum in 1975 with John Barns' posthumous preliminary publication on the cartonnage.[6] He revealed that a number of names found in the monastic letters preserved in the cartonnage of Codex VII occur in the Pachomian literary dossier, and pointed to one text in particular that seemed to offer a "smoking gun" connecting the codices to the Pachomian monastic movement. Though fragmentary, the text begins, "To my beloved father Pachômě, Papnoutě, greetings in the Lord," which Barns interpreted as a letter from the Pa-

---

3. Robinson, "Introduction."

4. Jean Doresse, one of the first individuals with access to the codices, assumed the boundary between monks and heterodox texts, asserting in 1958, "Already the contents of these Gnostic collections had led us to suppose that, whoever may have possessed them, they cannot have been monks" (*Secret Books*, 135).

5. Robinson, *Nag Hammadi Codices*, 3–4.

6. Barns, "Greek and Coptic Papyri."

chomian federation's *oikonomos*, or chief economic officer, Paphnutius to Pachomius, the founding head of the movement. While Barns did not assume that the heterodox texts in the codices meant that the Pachomians or some subset thereof actually believed them, he did conclude that the codices belonged to the Pachomians, used perhaps for heresiological purposes.[7]

When Barns died suddenly in 1974, work on the critical edition passed to G. M. Browne and John Shelton. In the introduction to the critical edition published in 1981, Shelton thoroughly rejected Barns's conclusion with respect to the codices' Pachomian provenance. He argued that many of the texts were secular in nature and included commercial contracts (one of which mentions a chairman of an oil workers' guild); official accounts of the sort one might find from a government office; and accounts mentioning quantities of wine, wheat, and barley that seemed too high for a monastic setting.[8] As for the monastic letters, he rejected the evidence of the names as simply coincidental due to their common use in Egypt, and found the letter from a woman to the monk Sansnos inconsistent with a Pachomian milieu. Far from a smoking gun, the cartonnage, as one might expect, could be read and interpreted differently by different scholars. In the ongoing debate over the origin of the codices, the cartonnage continue to be used both in favor of and against the argument of their Pachomian provenance.

It is not necessary for my argument to follow the subsequent path of this debate in detail. I am interested only in the argument used by those opposed to a Pachomian connection that various secular documents among the cartonnage, both commercial and official, point to the codices' non-Pachomian origin. In order to make that case, however, an additional supposition, often hidden, is assumed, namely, that the Pachomian's separation from the world precludes their possession of such documents for use in manuscript production. Lundhaug and Jenott, who supply the most recent summary of the debate, addressed this issue in a section of their book on the "Acquisition of Cartonnage."[9] Rejecting the notion that all of the documents came from a single source, such as a town dump, they maintain that "there is no reason to posit that whoever

---

7. Ibid., 15–16; cf. Säve-Söderbergh, "Holy Scriptures or Apologetic Documentations?"

8. For a more recent detailed account of the various cartonnage texts that seeks to counter Shelton's assertions, see Lundhaug and Jenott, *Monastic Origins*, 104–45.

9. Ibid., 139 42.

made the covers would have acquired all the papyri from one place or through one person."¹⁰ They imagine that a monastic organization like the Pachomian federation would have gathered some recycled documents from within its communities (biblical fragments, monastic letters, and so forth) and others from outside, brought into the community when new members joined. They point in particular to Petronius who, when he joined the monastery, brought along everything he had, which in the various sources includes sheep, goats, cattle, camels, donkeys, carts, boats, and all sorts of gear.¹¹ Their point is well taken.

I would argue, however, that they do not go far enough. The notion that nonmonastic documents came into the monastery with individuals who brought such documents from their premonastic life with them when they joined the community remains wedded to the traditional notion, however tenuously, of the separation between the ascetic and the secular world. It retains the separation by linking the acquisition of all the cartonnage fragments to monastic ownership, even if some were acquired by a monk in his previous secular existence. I would argue that while the nature of the traditional literary sources fosters the notion of such a separation, the reality was quite other. Given the rapid growth of the Pachomian communities within or in close proximity to the villages and towns in the area, that is, not separated from them by the desert,¹² surely local townsfolk, with whom they interacted and who knew of the monks' need for scrap papyri, would have brought it to them. The fact that this possibility has not made it into the discussion of the origin of the cartonnage underscores the power of the desert myth in early Egyptian monasticism. The problem, of course, lies in the nature and function of the literary sources, both in their original setting in late antiquity and their subsequent use in the creation of Christian history.

Outside of the letters and catecheses (instructions), which appear to go back to the early leaders of the Pachomian federation, the descriptive sources on which the portrayal of the movement is most often based, namely the various versions of the *Life* and *Rules*, are notoriously difficult to date and organize.¹³ All versions of the *Life* necessarily postdate

10. Ibid., 140

11. Ibid., 140–41; SBo 56; G¹ 80; Veilleux, trans., *Pachomian Koinonia*, vol. 1, *The Life of Pachomius and His Disciples*, 77, 252. SBo refers to the Coptic Sahidic-Bohairic compilation as translated in Veilleux; G¹ refers to the first Greek life or *Vita prima*.

12. Goehring, "Withdrawing from the Desert."

13. For introductions and English translations of most of the Pachomian dossier,

Pachomius' death (346–47 CE), and most, if not all, the death of Theodore (368 CE). Likewise, while some of the rules may go back to Pachomius' era, it seems impossible to find general consensus on which, while it is clear that many portions stem from later periods.[14] As a result the reconstruction of the federation's early years depend on products produced in later years and designed to promote the movement as it was then understood. Memory of the past necessarily aligned it over time with the monastic patterns of the present, an unconscious process that transformed the early figures from human leaders to be followed into monastic saints to be emulated.[15] As guidebooks, the *Lives* required saints whose lives corresponded to the ideals that the later authors and editors sought to instill in their readers.

It is worth noting in this context the impact of Athanasius and his *Life of Antony* in the production of the Pachomian vita tradition.[16] The earliest Greek version, known as the *Vita prima* or G¹, explicitly references in its opening (G¹ 2) Athanasius' composition as the source of its comparison of Antony with Elijah, Elisha, and John the Baptist (all associated with the desert). The corresponding section in the Coptic versions (SBo 2) retains the same comparisons though it does not identify the source. One suspects that the Greek author simply chose to identify it. Later in both versions (G¹ 134 = SBo 134), after Pachomius' death, Theodore recalls Pachomius' words extolling Athanasius, Antony, and the Pachomian monastic community to the brothers. The passage in the *Vita prima* reads as follows:

> I [Theodore] heard, and you ancients were also present, when our father said, "In our generation in Egypt I see three important things that increase by God's grace for the benefit of all those who have understanding: the bishop Athanasius, the athlete of Christ contending for the faith unto death; the holy Abba Antony, the perfect model of anchoritic life; and this *Koinonia*, which is a model for all those who wish to assemble souls in God, to succor them until, they be made perfect."[17]

---

see Veilleux, trans., *Pachomian Koinonia*.

14. For the most recent discussion, see Joest, *Mönchsregeln der Pachomianer*.

15. Goehring, "Encroaching Desert"; Goehring, "Remembering for Eternity."

16. Athanasius, *Life of St. Antony*; Brakke, *Athanasius and the Politics of Asceticism*, 201–65.

17. Veilleux, trans., *Pachomian Koinonia*, 1:395.

The reference to the ancient ones suggests those few that remain from the earliest generation at some point after Pachomius' death (346–47 CE) and before Theodore's (368 CE), since he delivers the passage. Both sources, however, continue on through Theodore's death, which suggests that a later author fashioned the episode either from a memory or out of whole cloth. In either case, the episode reflects the ascetic faith and practice of the federation at the time of the author's writing. To what degree that corresponds with the earlier period of the federation's origins remains an open question. While it makes perfect sense that Theodore might extoll Pachomius' monastic innovation after Pachomius' death, it seems doubtful that Pachomius would equate his life's work with the efforts of Athanasius and Antony. The story reflects rather a later view within the federation.

The influence of the *Life of Antony* on the Pachomian tradition offers but a more immediate example of its broad impact on the understanding of Egyptian monasticism both within Egypt and beyond. Athanasius' *Life* served a political purpose, namely to align the monastic movement more closely with the agenda of the Alexandrian patriarchate.[18] He accomplished this aim by shaping the story's hero and thus the understanding of monasticism in general through three idealized motifs. First, Athanasius correlates Antony's ascetic prowess with his withdrawal into the desert. The account of his early ascetic life involves a series of moves ever further into the desert, each adding further to his ascetic stature and spiritual power.[19] The underlying message links the ascetic goal of withdrawal from the traditional patterns of human existence (family, food and drink, sex, and so forth) and from the sphere of the church to the ascetic's retreat to the desert. The image proved immensely powerful for it captured in simple spatial terms the more complex spiritual notion of separation from the world.

Second, the *Life of Antony* emphasized the role of the biblical narrative in monastic self-understanding. This element was, of course, fundamental to the movement from its inception. Athanasius, however, set the emphasis on the Bible over against the import of traditional education by presenting his hero as unlettered. Antony turned to asceticism on hearing the scripture read in church and following the literal command to sell all that you have and give to the poor. No deeper philosophy here.

---

18. Brakke, *Athanasius and the Politics of Asceticism*.
19. Goehring, "Origins of Monasticism," 18–19.

The image again offered a powerful mythic notion of the Bible's influence apart from any education of philosophical exploration (*Sola scriptura*) that might lead one to such an interpretive move and lifestyle change. The pattern finds its way into the Pachomian literary sources, where for example Cornelios and Theodore outshine in debate a visiting philosopher (SBo 55; G¹ 82). The Coptic version makes the equation explicit by having Cornelios assert:

> "Well, we are the salt; we have come here to salt you, for you are more insipid than most people in the world. For you pride yourselves on being teachers and now what you say is vain. All discourse of this sort is bad." Hearing this, they [the philosophers] retired, greatly put to shame, because by their vain learning they could not overcome those who possess the true knowledge of the Lord dwelling in them.[20]

Finally, Athanasius brings the perfected Antony, after his final withdrawal to an abode by the Red Sea, back into the city to support the archbishop's anti-Arian agenda. He thus fashions the ideal monk as one who has withdrawn from the sphere of the church into the desert, renounced philosophy and traditional education, and yet remains active in support of the archbishop's political goals. Ecclesiastical politics and theological interpretation belong to the purview of the archbishop; the proper role of monks, like Athanasius' Antony, is to act in support of the archbishop's agenda.

Historical scholarship on early Egyptian monasticism has over the last few decades increasingly challenged Athanasius' portrayal.[21] While there surely were individual ascetics who withdrew to the desert, even for those most remote, some form of contact with the world remained essential for survival. Most monks, however, remained in closer proximity to the world, and many, as the papyrological evidence has established, practiced their asceticism within and near the cities, towns, and villages of Egypt.[22] When one turns to Upper Egypt in general, and the milieu of the Pachomian movement in particular, the equation becomes even more problematic. Pachomius embarked on the ascetic life under Apa Palamon, who resided with his disciples within the fertile valley beside the village of Šeneset (SBo 10; G¹ 6). When Pachomius set out to establish

---

20. Veilleux, trans., *Pachomian Koinonia*, 1:75.
21. See especially, Rubenson, *Letters of St. Antony*.
22. Goehring, "World Engaged"; Wipszycka, "Le monachisme égyptien."

his own community, he built his first monastery, Tabennēse, in a deserted village near the Nile. The monks' renewal of the village in turn brought local people back for whom the monks built a church (G¹ 29). When the monastic community grew too large, Pachomius founded a second monastery, Pbow, in another nearby deserted village well within the fertile valley (SBo 49; G¹ 54). By the time of his death in 346-47 CE, the federation numbered ten monasteries (9 male and 1 female). It added an additional four monasteries (3 male and 1 female) under Theodore, who died in 368 CE (G¹ 134). There is every reason to believe that all of these were situated in or near towns and villages within the fertile valley.[23] Pachomian monasticism, far from being a desert movement, arose and remained within the inhabited world of Upper Egypt, a world it shared with the local lay population and the church.

The parallel Upper Egyptian monastic federation of Shenoute, while somewhat later in date and smaller in scope, followed remarkably similar patterns.[24] Although Shenoute's three monasteries were in fact constructed in the desert, they lay at its edge, up against the fertile valley near the village of Atripe (modern Sohag; 3.5 km distant) and across the river from the city of Panopolis. While Shenoute withdrew alone further into the desert from time to time, he also ventured into Panopolis to contend with opponents and support his political agenda. The example of Shenoute's federation simply confirms the pattern with respect to the desert established by the Pachomian federation; namely, Upper Egyptian monasticism in this area was neither remote nor withdrawn from its surrounding lay community. Ascetic prowess was not gained, as Athanasius suggests, by withdrawal into the desert and separation from the broader lay community, the government, and the church. Although scholars now recognize Athanasius' linkage of asceticism with the desert and its concomitant separation from the *oikoumene* as a politically inspired cultural myth, its power as myth continues to shape general understandings and portrayals of Egyptian monasticism. Too often still early monasticism is simply described as a desert movement with Antony and Pachomius as the primary examples of its solitary (anchoritic) and communal (coenobitic) forms.

---

23. Goehring, "Withdrawing from the Desert."

24. The corpus on Shenoute is large and growing. For good introductions, see Brakke and Crislip, trans., *Selected Discourses of Shenoute*; Layton, *Canons of Our Fathers*.

In the remainder of this paper, I want to reconsider in a similar fashion Pachomian monasticism's relationship to Athanasius' second idealized motif, namely, the unlinking of monasticism from traditional education and philosophy. It is incumbent in this regard to consider Pachomius and his early movement in light of the later evidence offered in Shenoute's *Canons* and *Discourses*. The latter offer primary witness to Shenoute's thought and his federation's practices, and as such supply an important lens through which to view the secondary literary accounts of Pachomius and his movement. In general, scholars have rightly viewed Pachomius and his early movement as less involved with the surrounding political and ecclesiastical world than Shenoute. I would contend, however, that rather than seeing Shenoute's more aggressive practices as something new and strikingly different, his behavior represents a natural evolution of the socially embedded and educationally oriented monasticism in Upper Egypt evidenced in the Pachomian sources. Once again, it is Athanasius' fabled account of Antony as a desert monk, in this case coupled with his anti-traditional education agenda, which clouds the historical picture.

In truth, we know little to nothing of Pachomius' early life. While the sources indicate that his parents were pagan (SBo 3; G¹ 2), later references to an older brother named John and a sister named Mary (SBo 19, 27; G¹ 14) raise doubts about the claim. The following sections present his youth in legendary form, including miraculous accounts of demons fleeing from the young Pachomius, his vomiting out wine poured in sacrifice, and his rejection of a young woman's request to sleep with him ("he was horrified because he hated that") (SBo 4–6: G¹ 3).[25] As a result, most modern accounts begin their narrative of Pachomius' life with his conscription in the war between Licinius and Maximin Daia in 312–313 CE, during which he was befriended by Christians who brought food to the conscripts in prison and converted to Christianity. Upon his release, he was instructed in the faith and baptized in the village of Šeneset, where he remained for three years serving the community. He then embraced more fully a monastic life, joining the anchoritic community led by Apa Palamon on the outskirts of the village. Some years later he began his own communal form of monasticism (coenobitism) in the nearby deserted village of Tabennēse.

25. Translation from Veilleux, *Pachomian Koinonia*, 1:26.

In all of this there is no indication of any formal education. The absence of evidence, however, given the nature of the childhood stories and agenda of the vita tradition, offers no data from which to draw any conclusion in this regard, certainly not to align Pachomius with Athanasius' unlettered Antony. In fact, when one reads the Pachomian sources in their entirety, the assumption or even expectation of literacy is readily apparent. The dossier includes eleven letters and two catecheses authored by Pachomius, indicative of his literary abilities. While the catecheses appear to have been elaborated after his death by his successors,[26] the letters, which incorporate a mysterious alphabetical code, suggest a capable, creative author.[27] Furthermore, the vita tradition indicates literary correspondence between Pachomius and Athanasius (SBo 96). While the account of this correspondence may be legendary, it nonetheless underscores the community's understanding of their founder as a literate person.

Given the early stages of the monastic movement in Upper Egypt when Pachomius embarked on his ascetic career, one assumes that he acquired his education prior to it. The vita tradition, in fact, suggests his ability from the start of his ascetic endeavors under Palamon. The Coptic life reports his practice of reciting lengthy passages in order from the books of scripture, which the Greek account expands to "When he began to read and to write by heart the words of God" (Bo 15; G^1 9).[28] While one might argue that the clear evidence of literacy in the Greek life is secondary, the Coptic's indication of his desire to keep the lengthy passages from the books of scripture in their proper sequence, suggests the use of a written source as well.

The Pachomian rules, while expanded and elaborated after his lifetime, underscore the federation's interest in literacy. Sections of the *Precepts* associated with Pachomius indicate that each house within the monastery kept books in an alcove from which individuals could borrow them to read (*Praecepta* 25, 100–101; G^1 59; *Praecepta et Instituta* 2). Additionally, in a section likely added after Pachomius' death (*Praecepta* 139–40), the rule asserts the requirement that all in the monastery be able to read. A system of daily instruction existed to bring illiterate individuals who entered the monastery up to speed. The educational program was

26. Joest, *Über den Geistlichen Kampf.*
27. Joest, *Die Pachom-Briefe.*
28. Veilleux, trans., *Pachomian Koinonia*, 1:304

strict, emphasizing that "even if he [the student] does not want to, he shall be compelled to read" (*Praecepta* 139).[29] While the written codification of this requirement appears to postdate Pachomius, it surely represents an orientation towards learning within the federation that goes back to him, as witnessed in his own literary abilities. His interest in learning is confirmed by the account of his effort to learn Greek so as better to serve the Greek speaking brothers who joined his community (SBo 89; G^1 95). Pachomius established an expectation of literacy from the start on which the federation built over time.

The draw of the expanding federation offers additional support for the learned nature of the movement. While it attracted members from a broad cross-section of society, the leadership, as far as we can tell, came from the wealthy literate class. Petronius, Pachomius' immediate successor as head of the federation, for example, came from a wealthy, well-placed family in the diocese of Hiw (Diospolis parva). His parents' sizeable land holdings allowed him to fulfill his ascetic calling by withdrawing to a portion of their land away from people where he built his own monastery. He eventually brought his monastery into the Pachomian federation, converting his family in the process, who brought with them into the federation "sheep, goats, cattle, camels, donkeys, carts, boats, and all sorts of gear" (SBo 56; G^1 80). His abilities led Pachomius to appoint him initially as the head of the federation's northern cluster of monasteries around the city of Šmin, and eventually as his chosen successor to lead the federation as a whole.

Theodore, who quickly became Pachomius' favorite and eventually his most famous successor, likewise came from a prominent family. The Coptic Bohairic life reports his early schooling after which he embarked on the monastic life in a monastery in the diocese of Snē (Latopolis) before joining the Pachomian community (SBo 31; G^1 33). Beyond his authorship of letters and catecheses, the Pachomian sources report his debate with visiting philosophers (SBo 55; G^1 82), his receipt and reading of a letter from Antony (*Letter of Ammon* 29), and his composition of a letter concerning the Arian persecutions (*Letter of Ammon* 32). Less is known about Horsiesius, who both preceded and succeeded Theodore as head of the federation. He appears suddenly in the vita tradition shortly before his appointment by Petronius as head of the federation (SBo 121;

---

29. Veilleux, trans., *Pachomian Koinonia*, 2.166.

G¹ 114).³⁰ Nonetheless, Horsiesius' literary ability seems clear. Four letters attributed to him and a lengthy testament, described by Armand Veilleux as "one of the most beautiful pieces of Pachomian literature,"³¹ survive. In addition, a number of instructional fragments and a series of regulations attributed to Horsiesius, while less secure as products of his pen, bear witness to the tradition's understanding of his learning. As such, the vita tradition reports a letter from Athanasius to Horsiesius (SBo 210; G¹ 150), and a later source preserves letters from the archbishop Theophilus, one of which requests Horsiesius to bring a copy of the *Life of Pachomius and Theodore* with him when he comes to Alexandria.³²

The creation of a Greek-speaking house of foreigners in the federation's central monastery of Pbow further substantiates this pattern. It arose when a reader from the Alexandrian church named Theodore elected to join the Pachomian movement. Born into a pagan family, he converted to Christianity at seventeen (SBo 89; G¹ 94).³³ Athanasius baptized him and made him a reader in the church, suggesting his earlier education. While serving as a reader,³⁴ he came into contact with Pachomian monks who were visiting the archbishop and returned with them to become a monk. One suspects that the draw depended in part on his recognition that the Pachomians would appreciate his education. When he arrived at Pbow, he was initially placed with an older Greek monk, who taught him Coptic (G¹ 94) and eventually put in charge of the house of foreigners. This house included Alexandrians and Romans (SBo 91). Its very existence underscores the federation's link to Alexandria and as such sets it apart from other monastic organizations in Upper Egypt, including Shenoute's federation. The connection to Alexandria brought numerous monastic recruits to the federation (SBo 107).³⁵ One suspects that many, like the Alexandrian Theodore, came with an education.

---

30. An earlier reference to Horsiesius in SBo 91 simply connects an earlier practice to Horsiesius's time.

31. Veilleux, trans., *Pachomian Koinonia*, 3.8.

32. Crum, *Papyruscodex*, 65–76.

33. The Coptic Bohairic life lists his age a twenty-seven. The age seventeen, given in two Sahidic versions (S4 and S5), seems more likely; cf., Veilleux, trans., *Pachomian Koinonia*, 1:281.

34. SBo 89 indicates he served in this capacity for twelve years, though given its suggestion of his age at conversion, one might well question this time frame.

35. Goehring, "Pachomian Federation."

Ammon, who eventually composed the *Letter of Ammon*, offers another later interesting case in point.³⁶ He too converted to Christianity in Alexandria, embraced the ascetic life, and was steered by his priest to the Pachomians circa 351 CE (*Letter of Ammon* 2). There he was received into the house of foreigners (*Letter of Ammon* 7) where the Alexandrian Theodore translated from Coptic into Greek for him. He remained with the Pachomians for three years, after which, upon learning of his parents' grief, he returned to Lower Egypt where he dwelt as an ascetic in the Mountain of Nitria. He eventually became a priest in the Alexandrian church, where he composed the *Letter of Ammon* in response to a request from the archbishop Theophilus. Ammon's Alexandrian origin, his eventual service as a priest in the church, and his composition of the *Letter of Ammon* suggest an educated background likely gained prior to his embrace of an ascetic life.

While there can be no doubt that the Pachomian federation attracted from across a broad spectrum of Egyptian society, including literate and illiterate individuals, the evidence seems clear that from its inception literacy played an important role. The organizational structure of the individual monasteries and eventually of the federation's far flung monastic establishments, while occasionally attributed to experience gained by Pachomius during his stint in the army, is better explained, I would suggest, by his educational background and social class; he served after all as a forced conscript for but a brief time. While I do not mean to imply that Pachomius' education placed him among the philosophically elite, I would argue that he arose from within the educated class in Upper Egypt where Sahidic Coptic served as the primary language. He would have been able to read and write, had learned at least some Greek, and would have been familiar with general philosophical and ecclesiastical systems and ideas of his day. In this regard, his origin and status in life parallels that of Antony as recovered and promoted by Samuel Rubenson.³⁷ As with Antony, one suspects that it was precisely Pachomius' origin in the educated class that facilitated his interest in and eventual embrace of the monastic life. So too it fostered a connection with others of similar background in the surrounding society from whom he drew recruits who could further his dream of an educated monastic federation.

36. Goehring, *Letter of Ammon*.
37. Rubenson, *Letters of St. Antony*.

I suspect, given this background, that monks in the Pachomian federation interacted rather regularly with those with similar backgrounds outside of the community. Their monasteries were located in or near towns and villages, and they frequently enough traveled outside of their monasteries for agricultural and commercial dealings. The federation had monks from the beginning who oversaw the sale of the community's products and the purchase of things needed (SBo 26; G^1 28). It sent products by boat to and from Alexandria as part of this economic exchange (G^1 113), and a late source reports negotiations with a neighboring village for supplies during a period of famine (*Paralipomena* 21–22). Such commercial activity necessarily involved frequent contact with surrounding lay dealers and tradesmen, and one suspects eventually caught the federation up in matters of government regulation and taxation.[38] In this regard, the Pachomian federation parallels the later neighboring federation of Shenoute. The latter, as evidenced in his writings, actively engaged the economic and religious politics of the surrounding community. His discourses reveal his involvement in ecclesiastical issues, his opposition to local pagan activity, his preaching to nonmonastic audiences in the monastery's basilica, his forceful confrontation of wealthy landowners and local magistrates, and his federation's housing of refuges in time of famine. The evidence of Shenoute underscores the growing prestige and power of monasticism in Upper Egypt in the fifth century.

The case of Shenoute, however, should not be set in opposition to that of Pachomius. In the conclusion to his excellent study of Shenoute's uses of poverty, Ariel López offers such an assessment. With reference to Shenoute, he writes:

> The contrast with the stars of the Egyptian monastic tradition—Antony, Pachomius, the monks of Nitria and Scetis—is clear. Notwithstanding their reputation and prestige, most of these monks were, in comparison with Shenoute, relatively harmless. Neither Antony nor Pachomius is known to have been involved in economic and religious struggles with the surrounding countryside. Neither seems to have had enough power in local society to threaten wealthy landowners. They rarely if ever preached about social injustice or the behavior of magistrates. In fact, they rarely preached to nonmonastic audiences. As far as we know, they never felt powerful enough to publicly attack paganism. To put it briefly, an Egyptian who lived in any town

---

38. Goehring, "World Engaged," 46–52.

> near Antony's outer mountain or near a Pachomian congregation could have led his life—if he chose to—in complete ignorance of the fact that there were monks living nearby. This was not possible around Panopolis, for Shenoute made sure that everybody in the area knew that *he was there* and that he had an opinion about them, an opinion that—if necessary—he might try to impose on them.[39]

While I agree that Shenoute engaged with and wielded more power in the surrounding ecclesiastical and political world than Pachomius, I am less convinced as to the degree of the Pachomian federation's invisibility to those in the area who chose not to see it. Its expanding geographical presence up and down the Nile from its central monastery of Pbow, much greater in this regard than Shenoute's rather parochial organization, surely did not escape the notice of ecclesiastical and governmental authorities. Its economic activity necessitated frequent contact with the local population. Over time its expanding wealth increased its prestige and power. It gained support from the archbishop to construct a great basilica at its central monastery of Pbow in the fifth century, a basilica that parallels in size and shape the one still standing at Shenoute's White Monastery. Over the course of its existence, its boats plied the Nile River between its monasteries and Alexandria, from which it brought Greek and Latin speaking recruits to its monasteries in Upper Egypt. Its growing connections with Alexandria increasingly enhanced its relationship with the patriarchate, which in the early fifth century encouraged the federation to establish a monastery in the Alexandrian suburb of Canopus (Metanoia). The latter became a source of pro-Chalcedonian archbishops in the ecclesiastical conflicts of the latter half of the fifth century, a clear indication of the federation's involvement by that time in ecclesiastical politics.[40]

While I would agree that such involvement developed over time and that Pachomius, as far as the sources allow us to know, was much less engaged in rhetorical and physical conflict with those outside of the monastery than Shenoute, the evidence indicates his organization's outreach to and involvement with the surrounding world from its inception. The difference with Shenoute I would argue lies not in the interaction with the surrounding world itself, but with the nature of that interaction.

---

39. López, *Shenoute of Atripe*, 127.

40. Goehring, "Remembering Abraham of Farshut"; Goehring, *Politics, Monasticism, and Miracles*, 50–67.

It represents the growing power of Christianity in the Roman world, the increasing influence of the Alexandrian patriarch, and the growing desire and capability to enforce religious and doctrinal purity. Lopez, following the passage quoted above, argues that "the best parallels for Shenoute's public life are not to be found in Egypt but elsewhere, among Christian bishops all over the Roman Empire and, above all, among the monks of Syria and Constantinople."[41] I would suggest that this is a byproduct of the nature of our surviving sources and the era in question. The fifth-century Pachomian archimandrite Victor corresponded with the Alexandria archbishop Cyril, whom he accompanied along with Shenoute to the Council of Ephesus in 431 CE. If we knew more about the Pachomians and their leaders in this era, or had sources from say Victor similar to those from Shenoute, I suspect that they too, though not perhaps to the degree of Shenoute, would have played a greater role in the promotion of Christian dominance in the region.

Apart from the question of such forceful involvement in the surrounding community, however, the evidence seems clear that the Pachomian federation engaged with the surrounding world and its players from the start. Its educational orientation, its recruitment of experienced literate leaders, its draw of recruits from Alexandria, and its steady growth established it as an important player in the local economy. Their leaders, like Shenoute, would have been at home among the literate, economic class of the world in which they lived. While the world was not yet such that they engaged them harshly as political rivals or attacked them as purveyors of economic and social injustice, engaged them they did. It is in this context that Shenoute's harsher rhetoric and political actions can be understood in continuity with the earlier Pachomian example. Certainly one must recognize Shenoute's idiosyncrasies and will to power, but his and his community's interaction with the surrounding community follows naturally from the Pachomian precedent.

Returning in conclusion to the question of the Nag Hammadi cartonnage, it should now be apparent why the question of their origin has no relevance to the question of the codices' provenance. The interaction of the Pachomian federation with the surrounding world, which included considerable economic activity, offered ample opportunity to acquire used papyri for book binding purposes. Given the monks' educational level and social standing, one suspects that their interactions with

---

41. López, *Shenoute of Atripe*, 127.

nonmonastic players often involved individuals with similar educational and class backgrounds. Such could easily account for the monks' acquisition of receipts and other documents that seem non-monastic. If their interactions were not hostile, unlike Shenoute's, their interlocutors would have no reason to deny a request for used papyri. Responding to the request, or independently offering to fulfill a recognized need, might in fact be seen as part of a general economic strategy. Creating good working relationships with one's economic partners has and always will be an important aspect of any business. My point here is only that those papyrus fragments whose monastic origins seem problematic need not be explained as somehow monastic or as brought into the monastery among the belongings from an earlier lay life by a prospective monk. The exchange between monks and laypersons offered ample opportunity for the acquisition of such materials.

This fact then raises the issue of probability with respect to whose access to the variety of papyri in the cartonnage, a collection of clearly monastic texts alongside others that seem non-monastic, seems most likely. If one envisions educated non-monastic urban scribes working in cities and towns, there is little difficulty in imagining their ready access to numerous non-monastic sources of used papyri to stiffen the bindings.[42] At the same time, while certainly not impossible, their access to or need of used or discarded monastic texts seems less probable. When one turns to the idea of monastic scribes on the other hand, given the assessment of this paper, the availability of the various document types in the cartonnage seems more readily apparent. While the evidence does not exist that allows a definitive answer with respect to the production of the codices, in terms of the cartonnage, the probability seems to lean, if in any direction, in that of their monastic origin.

I would further suggest that the shift evident in Upper Egypt in Shenoute's more forceful imposition of a particular brand of Christianity represents the broadening of a more general shift in Christian attitudes towards pagans and heretics associated with the religion's increasing dominance in the Roman world. The eventual forcing of heterodox codices out of homes and monasteries would simply represent part of this process. If the origin of monasticism, as Rubenson argues in the case of Antony, emerged among a literate class familiar with common Origenist ideas, and if Upper Egyptian monasticism as evidenced in the case of

42. Khosroyev, *Bibliotheque von Nag Hammadi*. One acknowledges that urban monks existed from whom such scribes might have acquired the monastic documents.

the Pachomians drew from such a literate class, one can well imagine an interest in such literature among some elements within monastic communities at a stage where the pull of one's devotion to asceticism, community building, expansion, and economic growth drew more immediate and necessary attention than enforced doctrinal purity. As the role of the bishops and abbots conjoined over time (recall López's statement that "the best parallels for Shenoute's public life are to be found ... among Christian bishops all over the Roman Empire"), however, the push against paganism and heterodoxy would have increasingly impacted everyone, including those within the monasteries. One can see the beginning of this process in Pachomian monasticism during Theodore's tenure as head of the federation.[43] It is not hard to imagine in the later context the purging of libraries, both non-monastic and monastic, whether forcibly from above or surreptitiously from below by those who wished to preserve anathematized texts. While we may never know with certainty who owned and eventually buried the Nag Hammadi codices, I for one remain decidedly unpersuaded by the arguments put forth to date that they could not have belonged to monks in general, or for that matter to Pachomian monks in particular.

Works Cited

Athanasius, Saint. *The Life of St. Antony*. Translated by Robert T. Meyer. Ancient Christian Writers 10. New York: Newman, 1950.

Barns, John W. B. "Greek and Coptic Papyri from the Covers of the Nag Hammadi Codices: A Preliminary Report." In *Essays on the Nag Hammadi Texts in Honor of Pahor Labib*, edited by Martin Krause, 9–18. Nag Hammadi Studies 6. Leiden: Brill, 1975.

Brakke, David. *Athanasius and the Politics of Asceticism*. Oxford Early Christian Studies. Oxford: Clarendon, 1995.

Brakke, David, and Andrew Crislip, trans. *Selected Discourses of Shenoute the Great: Community, Theology, and Social Conflict in Late Antique Egypt*. Cambridge: Cambridge University Press, 2015.

Crum, W. E. *Der Papyruscodex saec. VI–VII der Phillippsbibliothek in Cheltenham*. Schriften der wissenschaftlichen Gesellschaft in Strassburg 18. Strassburg: Trübner, 1915.

Doresse, Jean. *The Secret Books of the Egyptian Gnostics: An Introduction to the Gnostic Coptic manuscripts discovered at Chenoboskion*. Translated by Philip Meiret. New York: Viking, 1960.

Goehring, James E. *Ascetics, Society, and the Desert: Studies in Early Egyptian Christianity*. Studies in Antiquity and Christianity. Harrisburg, PA: Trinity, 1999.

---

43. Goehring, "New Frontiers."

———. "The Encroaching Desert: Literary Production and Ascetic Space in Early Christian Egypt." *Journal of Early Christian Studies* 1 (1993) 281–96. Reprinted in *Ascetics, Society, and the Desert: Studies in Early Egyptian Christianity*, by James E. Goehring, 73–88. Studies in Antiquity and Christianity. Harrisburg, PA: Trinity, 1999.

———. *The Letter of Ammon and Pachomian Monasticism*. Patristische Texte und Studien 27. Berlin: de Gruyter, 1986.

———. "New Frontiers in Pachomian Studies." In *The Roots of Egyptian Christianity*, edited by Birger A. Pearson and James E. Goehring, 236–57. Philadelphia: Fortress, 1986. Reprinted in *Ascetics, Society, and the Desert: Studies in Early Egyptian Christianity*, by James E. Goehring, 162–86. Studies in Antiquity and Christianity. Harrisburg, PA: Trinity, 1999.

———. "The Origins of Monasticism." In *Eusebius, Christianity, and Judaism*, edited by Harold W. Attridge and Gohei Hata, 235–55. Detroit: Wayne State University Press, 1992. Reprinted in *Ascetics, Society, and the Desert: Studies in Early Egyptian Christianity*, by James E. Goehring, 13–35. Studies in Antiquity and Christianity. Harrisburg, PA: Trinity, 1999.

———. "The Pachomian Federation and Lower Egypt: The Ties that Bind." In *Christianity and Monasticism in Northern Egypt: Beni Suef, Giza, Cairo, and the Nile Delta*, edited by Gawdat Gabra and Hany N. Takla, 49–60. Christianity and Monasticism in Egypt 7. Cairo: American University in Cairo Press, 2017.

———. *Politics, Monasticism, and Miracles in Sixth Century Upper Egypt: A Critical Edition and Translation of the Coptic Texts on Abraham of Farshut*. Studien und Texte zu Antike und Christentum 69. Tübingen: Mohr/Siebeck, 2012.

———. "The Provenance of the Nag Hammadi Codices Once More." *Studia Patristica* 35 (2001) 234–53.

———. "Remembering Abraham of Farshut: History, Hagiography, and the Fate of the Pachomian Tradition." *Journal of Early Christian Studies* 14 (2006) 1–26.

———. "Remembering for Eternity: The Ascetic Landscape and Cultural Discourse in Early Christian Egypt." In *Ascetic Culture: Essays in Honor of Philip Rousseau*, edited by Blake Leyerle and Robin Darling Young, 201–28. Notre Dame: University of Notre Dame Press, 2013.

———. "Withdrawing from the Desert: Pachomius and the Development of Village Monasticism in Upper Egypt." *Harvard Theological Review* 89 (1996) 267–85. Reprinted in *Ascetics, Society, and the Desert: Studies in Early Egyptian Christianity*, by James E. Goehring, 89–109. Harrisburg, PA: Trinity, 1999.

———. "The World Engaged: The Social and Economic World of Early Egyptian Monasticism." In *Gnosticism & the Early Christian World: In Honor of James M. Robinson*, edited by James E. Goehring et al., 134–44. Forum Fascicles 2. Sonoma, CA: Polebridge, 1990. Reprinted in *Ascetics, Society, and the Desert: Studies in Early Egyptian Christianity*, by James E. Goehring, 39–52. Studies in Antiquity and Christianity. Harrisburg, PA: Trinity, 1999.

Joest, Christoph. *Die Mönchsregeln der Pachomianer*. Corpus scriptorum Christianorum orientalium 660. Subsidia 134. Leuven: Peeters, 2016.

———. *Die Pachom-Briefe: Übersetzung und Deutung*. Corpus scriptorum Christianorum Orientalium 655. Subsidia 133. Leuven: Peeters, 2014.

———. *Über den geistlichen Kampf: Katechesen des Mönchsvaters Pachom*. Weisungen der Väter 9. Beuron: Beuroner Kunstverlsag, 2010.

Khosroyev, Alexandr L. *Die Bibliotheque von Nag Hammadi: Einige Probleme des Christentums in Ägypten während der ersten Jahrhunderte.* Arbeiten zum spatantiken und koptischen Ägypten 7. Altenberge: Oros, 1995.

Layton, Bentley. *The Canons of Our Fathers: Monastic Rules of Shenoute.* Oxford Early Christian Studies. Oxford: Oxford University Press, 2014.

López, Ariel G. *Shenoute of Atripe and the Uses of Poverty: Rural Patronage, Religious Conflict, and Monasticism in Late Antique Egypt.* Transformation of the Classical Heritage 50. Berkeley: University of California Press, 2013.

Lundhaug, Hugo, and Lance Jenott. *The Monastic Origins of the Nag Hammadi Codices.* Studien und Texte zu Antike und Christentum 97. Tübingen: Mohr/Siebeck, 2015.

Robinson, James M. "Introduction." In *The Nag Hammadi Library in English*, edited by James M. Robinson, 1–25. San Francisco: Harper & Row, 1977.

———. *The Nag Hammadi Codices: A General Introduction to the Nature and Significance of the Coptic Gnostic Codices from Nag Hammadi.* Claremont, CA: Institute for Antiquity and Christianity, 1974.

Rubenson, Samuel. *The Letters of St. Antony: Monasticism and the Making of a Saint.* Studies in Antiquity and Christianity. Minneapolis: Fortress, 1995.

Säve-Söderbergh, Torgny. "Holy Scriptures or Apologetic Documentations? The 'Sitz im Leben' of the Nag Hammadi Library." In *Les Textes de Nag Hammadi*, edited by Jacques É. Ménard, 9–17. Nag Hammadi Studies 7. Leiden: Brill, 1975.

Veilleux, Armand, trans. *Pachomian Koinonia.* 3 vols. Cistercian Studies 45–47. Kalamazoo: Cistercian, 1980–1982.

Wipszycka, Ewa. "Le monachisme égyptien et les villes." *Travaux et mémoires* 12 (1994) 1–44.

Part 3

Soundings from Jewish
and Greco-Roman Culture

10

Messianism in Septuagint Amos?

W. EDWARD GLENNY

It is suggested by some that there is an evolution or development of messianic belief in the Septuagint (LXX) that goes beyond its Hebrew *Vorlage*.[1] Others, however, have greeted this suggestion with caution, and there is no consensus of opinion on the issue.[2] The "minimalist" position is championed by Johan Lust, who "argues for a [more] nuanced exegesis of those passages in the Septuagint for which a messianic interpretation has been claimed," and the "maximalist" view is represented in the writings of William Horbury and Joachim Schaper, who make a case for a broader application of messianic interpretation in the LXX.[3] In this chapter I will introduce some of the issues related to the question of a development of messianism in the LXX in one of the passages that is sometimes presented as an example, LXX-Amos 4:13. To begin the discussion I will present a

---

1. The term "Septuagint," comes from the Latin *septuaginta*, meaning "seventy," and it is generally understood to refer to the translation of the Hebrew Bible and some related texts into Koine Greek. The Roman Numerals LXX (seventy) are often used as an abbreviation for Septuagint. *Vorlage* refers to the hypothetical Hebrew source text used by the translators. The Masoretic Text (MT) is the Medieval Hebrew and Aramaic text upon which most modern English translations are based.

2. Although this was the main question addressed at the fifty-third Colloquium Biblicum Lovaniense held in Leuven in 2004, it appears that little if any consensus of opinion emerged from the proceedings. See the summary of the discussion in Knibb, "Introduction," esp. xx–xxi.

3. Knibb, "Introduction," xiv. See Lust, *Messianism and the Septuagint*; Horbury, *Jewish Messianism*; and Schaper, *Eschatology in the Greek Psalter*. The focus of this discussion is the close examination of relevant passages in that variegated collection of translations and revisions of the Jewish Scriptures in Greek we call the LXX.

basic definition of messianism and a suggestion for what constitutes messianic interpretation in the LXX; then I will give an overview of the LXX rendering of Amos 4:13 and the evidence for messianic development in that verse and in LXX-Amos; and subsequently I will address a related issue, the question of the *Vorlage* of this LXX rendering.

Definition of *Messianism*

Craig Evans offers a basic definition of *messianism* as,

> the expectation of a coming anointed person or persons who will redeem Israel and/or the church. The appearance of this anointed figure is usually understood to be part of a larger eschatological drama whereby human activity on earth is appreciably altered. At that time God's will on earth will be more tangibly and perhaps permanently experienced, often under the rubric, "kingdom of God." It is usually believed that this anointed figure is part of the climax of human history and will not be succeeded by other anointed figures.[4]

Evans mentions two main elements: an anointed figure, and an eschatological drama or context, of which the anointed figure is a part. Horbury and Lust are more detailed in their descriptions of the anointed figure, and they both connect messianism with Davidic promise and kingship and a deliverer of Israel.[5] However, Horbury does not require a specifically eschatological (or endtime) context for messianism; he allows that it could simply point to the future and be applied to rulers, like the Maccabees.[6]

Now turning more specifically to the issue of messianism in the LXX, Knibb offers four criteria to determine whether or not the Septuagint has introduced a messianic reference. They are: (1) significant differences between the Hebrew and the Greek; (2) an eschatological thrust in the context; (3) the messianic figure has a kingdom and is a military

---

4. Evans, "Messianism," 698.

5. See for example, Horbury, "Monarchy and Messianism," esp. 126–28; and Lust, *Messianism and the Septuagint*, 142.

6. Horbury, *Jewish Messianism*, 6–7; and Knibb, "Septuagint and Messianism," esp. 10.

leader; and (4) the Dead Sea Scrolls offer a more or less contemporary interpretation of the passage, which construes it messianically.[7]

Knibb's first two criteria are helpful. His third criterion that the messianic figure has a kingdom and is a military leader is a useful guide, but I would question whether both ideas must be present in messianic interpretation. Is there no room for a development in the concept or a reference to part of the picture of the messiah in some contexts? Finally, his criterion that the Scrolls offer a more or less contemporary interpretation of the passage, which takes it messianically, limits messianic interpretation in the LXX to passages treated in the Scrolls.[8] Therefore, to require all of his suggested criteria be present in messianic interpretation (or translation) seems idealistic and overly restrictive for general use in the LXX. Certainly some criteria are necessary, but one wonders if changes in the rendering of the text resulting in references to eschatology and a messianic (i.e., Davidic) figure would not be sufficient to signal messianism on the part of the translator? The other criteria he suggests could then certainly serve as collaborative evidence. We will now test our tentative definition and criteria on Amos 4:13.

LXX-Amos 4:13

I would render LXX-Amos 4:13 as follows: "For behold I am the one who strengthens thunder and creates wind and proclaims to humans his Anointed, who makes daybreak and misty dark and treads on the high places of the earth: the Lord, the God, the Almighty One, is his name!"[9]

This verse is the first of three doxologies in the book of Amos (see also 5:7–9 [MT 5:8–9] and 9:5–6), and they all stand apart from their contexts in regards to participles extolling the actions of the Lord and an identification of the Lord ("His name is . . ."). The emphasis on the might and power of the omnipotent God of creation in 4:13 follows naturally the warnings of judgment and the admonition to prepare to call upon him in the previous verse. The subject of this verse is apparently the Lord,

---

7. Knibb, "Septuagint and Messianism," 18.

8. This basically leaves Amos out of the picture except for 5:25–27 and 9:12, since these are the only verses in Amos interpreted in the Scrolls.

9. The LXX text of Amos 4:13 in the Rahlfs and the Göttingen edition is, διότι ἰδοὺ ἐγὼ στερεῶν βροντὴν καὶ κτίζων πνεῦμα καὶ ἀπαγγέλλων εἰς ἀνθρώπους τὸν χριστὸν αὐτοῦ, ποιῶν ὄρθρον καὶ ὁμίχλην καὶ ἐπιβαίνων ἐπὶ τὰ ὕψη τῆς γῆς· κύριος ὁ θεὸς ὁ παντοκράτωρ ὄνομα αὐτῷ.

who refers to himself in the first person in the LXX (with the rendering ἐγώ at the beginning of the verse), which strengthens the connection between 4:13 and the Lord's admonition in the first person in 4:12. In the references to "his Anointed" and "his name" later in the verse the Lord is apparently describing himself in the third person.[10] The use of the first person pronoun (ἐγώ) to refer to the Lord at the beginning of 4:13 and then the use of two third-person pronouns (αὐτοῦ and αὐτῷ) to refer to him later in the same verse is awkward. And it is noteworthy that the first person pronoun is not found in many LXX manuscripts, including Venetus and the text of Vaticanus; nor does Swete include it in his version.[11] However, even if the first person pronoun is included at the beginning of 4:13, as most modern editions of the LXX do, the variation in persons referring to the Lord in the same context is not unusual in biblical prophecy. The same kind of variation occurs in LXX-Hosea 13:14-15, and that passage involves a reading in the LXX that differs from the Hebrew.[12] There are many other examples in the prophets of this kind of variation of persons referring to the Lord,[13] and thus the variation in persons in the

10. Dafni, "Παντοκράτωρ in Septuaginta-Amos," 448-50 discusses the parallelism of παντοκράτωρ and χριστός in LXX-Amos 4:13. In order to understand these two names as parallel and referring to the same person αὐτοῦ in τὸν χριστὸν αὐτοῦ must refer to the Lord (ἐγώ), and αὐτῷ in κύριος ὁ θεὸς ὁ παντοκράτωρ ὄνομα αὐτῷ must refer to the anointed (τὸν χριστὸν αὐτοῦ) mentioned earlier in the verse. This seems unlikely for several reasons. First, it requires the two third-person personal pronouns to refer to different referents. This seems especially unlikely since they are separated by two participle phrases; if the second clause ("the Lord the God, the Almighty One is his name") followed directly after the first ("his anointed"), it would be more natural for "his name" to refer to the "anointed." Second, in the other two doxologies in LXX-Amos (5:7-9 [MT 5:8-9] and 9:5-6), the title παντοκράτωρ refers to the Lord, who is the subject of the participles, and thus it likely does here also.

11. See Glenny, *Amos*, 22 and 84-85, for an illustration from Vaticanus of a text where there is no clash between first- and third-person pronouns in 4:13. The rendering of the first part of 4:13 in this commentary on the text of Vaticanus is, "For he who strengthens thunder and creates wind," and the implied subject agrees with the third-person pronouns that follow, all referring to the Lord.

12. In 13:14 the Lord speaks in the first person, and in 13:15 "the Lord" is described as speaking in the third person and the LXX changes the second line of 13:15 to make the Lord the speaker (i.e., "the wind of the Lord" [ESV] is changed to "the Lord will bring a hot wind" [NETS]).

13. I will give a few examples of this phenomenon elsewhere in the Twelve Prophets. See the change of persons in Hosea 8:1 where the Lord is speaking and he refers to the "house of the Lord" and "my covenant." In Hos 8:12-13 the Lord speaks as "I" in 8:12, and he is referred to as "the Lord" and in the third person in 8:13. In Hos 8:14 the Lord is referred to as "Israel's maker" and speaks as "I." Hos 12:9 and 13 repeat the

LXX rendering of Amos 4:13 cannot be used to prove that the translator was incompetent or did not know what he was doing when he rendered Amos 4:13. Furthermore, the LXX rendering here with ἐγώ could have been influenced by LXX-Hosea 13:4, which has many parallels to LXX-Amos 4:13 and also begins with a first person personal pronoun referring to the Lord.[14] We will say more about the possible influence of the rendering of Hosea 13:4 on the translation of Amos 4:13 in what follows.

There are three important differences between the LXX and the Hebrew in Amos 4:13. First, as mentioned above, the LXX has ἐγώ at the beginning of the verse, identifying the Lord as the speaker. There is no explicit pronoun in the Hebrew, and the Hebrew participle construction is normally rendered with a third person pronoun. Second, instead of the Hebrew plural noun "mountains" (הרים), in the first participle phrase "who forms the mountains" (NRSV), the LXX has "makes the thunder strong" (NETS), apparently reading "mountains" (הרים), as "the thunder" (הרעם). This reading involves changing the *yod* (י) in the Hebrew plural suffix with "mountains" to an *ayin* (ע). This variation in the understanding of the word could have been caused by confusion of the two letters, but it is also possible that the translator was influenced by the long LXX addition in Hosea 13:4 in his rendering of this phrase. That addition contains direct speech by the Lord, addressed to idolatrous Israel, contrasting the Lord, the one who "makes the heaven firm and creates the earth" (NETS), with idols and false gods, specifically referring to Baal in the context (13:1). Furthermore, that verse uses the same two participle forms (in the phrases "establishing the heaven and creating the earth") that are found in the first two participial phrases in Amos 4:13 ("the one who strengthens thunder and creates wind"). Thus, it is possible that the polemic in the addition to Hosea 13:4 was on the mind of the translator, and he replicated language from that anti-Baal or anti-Zeus argument in the similar context of Amos 4:13.[15] Such anti-Baal polemic is common in the Old Testament (Pss 77:18; 18:13–15), and its authors often show that

---

same idea, and one time it is "I" and another it is "the Lord" who brought Israel up from Egypt.

14. I have rendered LXX-Hosea 13:4 "But I am the Lord your God who establishes the heaven and creates the earth, whose hands created all the host of the heaven. And I did not reveal these things to you to follow after them. And I brought you up from the land of Egypt, and you shall not know a God except me, and there is no savior beside me"; see Glenny, *Hosea*, 61.

15. See the discussion of this in Glenny, "Hebrew Misreadings," 545. See also Glenny, *Finding Meaning*, 177–78.

Yahweh and not Baal is the God of creation, and thunder and lightning are his weapons, not the weapons of Baal. However, it is not necessary to have anti-Baal polemic in Hosea 13:4 for it to influence Amos 4:13; both passages also contain praise of God for his creative activity.

Finally, and especially important for this study, is the third main difference from the Hebrew in LXX-Amos 4:13; in the third participle phrase the Hebrew which reads "what is his thought" (מה־שחו) is rendered "his Christ" or "his anointed" (τὸν χριστὸν αὐτοῦ). The translator apparently read the radicals מהשחו as the homograph משחו ("his anointed"). Such a scenario is very likely. The Hebrew noun שח ("thought") is a hapax legomenon, and would have been very difficult for the translator; it is more commonly found in the form שיח or שיחה ("complaint, musing") related to the verb שיח ("to muse, talk"). Also, the Hebrew texts the early translators of the LXX employed would have differed greatly from the Hebrew Bibles we have today. They would have been largely consonantal, with no vowel points to guide the translator in his pronunciation. And it is possible the consonants *aleph, heh, waw,* and *yod,* which are used to represent vowel sounds, would not have been used in them (i.e., *scriptio defectiva*).[16] Furthermore, word divisions would not have always been clearly marked, and perhaps sometimes not marked at all. Thus, it is very easy to see how the Greek translator, who was trying to make sense of the difficult passage, could have rendered a Hebrew text like the one in the MT as it is in the LXX. It is also very likely that theological concerns could have influenced him in the translation.[17] And if that is what happened, LXX-Amos 4:13 would be evidence of a developing messianism in the LXX text. As with all suggested messianic development in the LXX, we must consider briefly if there is evidence to support such a development in this LXX text and its context.

Let's begin with the immediate context. The "anointed" in LXX-Amos 4:13 could be a High Priest, which fits well with the cultic connections in 4:4–5 and the issues concerning the high priesthood in Israel in the second century BCE. If "anointed" refers to a High Priest worthy of God, then that would also make sense with the modifying pronoun αὐτοῦ. If the "anointed" is a king, the phrase could refer to promises made in the past, especially to the Davidic dynasty or to a general announcement of

16. These *matres lectionis* were added sporadically and inconsistently by the scribes to facilitate further the laity's study of the unpointed text.

17. See support for reading this as a theological interpretation in Glenny, *Finding Meaning*, 238.

his anointed to "humans," perhaps here gentiles. However, several pieces of evidence suggest that the phrase is more universal in its intention and it indicates belief in the coming of an eschatological figure.[18] First, the words, "proclaims to humans his anointed" suggest a broad and public announcement of this information. This is consistent with the translator's emphasis that the Lord God is ὁ παντοκράτωρ ("the almighty one," 4:13b; and 9:15) and that the gentiles are going to seek him (esp. 9:12). The language is similar to 9:12, which in a context of Davidic fulfillment speaks of "those remaining of humans and all the nations" (οἱ κατάλοιποι τῶν ἀνθρώπων καὶ πάντα τὰ ἔθνη) seeking the Lord in the last days. In LXX-Amos 4:13 the translator employs the same noun, "humans" (ἄνθρωπος), apparently to refer to gentiles as it does in 9:12. Thus, both of these passages are naturally taken to refer to a messianic figure who is part of the Lord's program for the gentiles. And if that connection is intended, it suggests that 4:13 also has eschatological implications, i.e., the Lord's proclamation to gentiles concerning his anointed finds its consummation in them seeking the Lord in the future time of Israel's promised restoration and blessing, as described in 9:12 (see also 9:13–15).

It is also generally assumed that theological factors influenced the translator in his rendering of Amos 4:13. Satterthwaite notes that at the very least the LXX translation is a "concretization" compared to the MT.[19] He classifies this as a "theological" interpretation, agreeing with Park, who comments, "this reading is most likely intentional in light of the inclusion of gentiles into the Jewish religion."[20] Jobes and Silva conclude this reading "certainly reflects a Messianic perspective on the part of the translator."[21] It is difficult to discern whether the Messianic/theological perspective and concern of the translator were the cause of the rendering or whether the initial cause was the difficulty he encountered with the *hapax* שׂח, which required adaptation on his part and opened the way for him to express his theology. Here we are wrestling with the problem of distinguishing the translation technique of the translator from his theology, and they are very difficult if not impossible to distinguish. Knibb posits, "The unintentional as well as the deliberate changes introduced by a translator, often simply to clarify obscurities in the original, inevita-

---

18. See the discussion in Dines, "Septuagint of Amos," 155.

19. Satterthwaite, "Translators as Imperialists," 25. Thanks to Dr. Satterthwaite for sharing this paper with me.

20. Park, *Book of Amos*, 151.

21. Jobes and Silva, *Invitation to the Septuagint*, 338.

bly betray something of the historical and social circumstances, and the intellectual and religious milieu in which the translation was made."[22] In the words of the old cliché, "all translation involves interpretation," and it is ultimately impossible to clearly separate the translation technique of the translator from his theology.[23]

Furthermore, the manipulation of the Hebrew text that would have taken place to change the *Vorlage* from "what is his thought" to "his anointed" is consistent with the translator's changes to the text elsewhere in the book, and I will give some relevant examples from the broader context of LXX-Amos.[24] The translator of Amos clearly had eschatological interests, and a royal Messiah would be consistent with such interests. The free rendering "Gog" in 7:1 is especially important in this regard. This figure, whom the translator introduces into 7:1 as the leader of the enemies of God, is in the LXX "the messianic opponent" already in Numbers 24.[25] In Ezekiel 38 he leads the opponents of God and Israel when Israel has been reestablished in the land and is living in peace (38:8, 11, 12, 14), apparently as a new nation under the rule of a Davidic king (34:23; 37:15-28). It is in the climactic battle with Gog that God intervenes for Israel and annihilates the invaders.

Also, the description in LXX-Amos 9:11-12 of the rebuilt "tent of David" must have some reference to a Davidic dynasty/kingdom,[26] and it is likely that it refers to a messianic figure.[27] Therefore, especially in view of the references to gentiles in both contexts (4:13 and 9:12; "humans" employing ἄνθρωπος; 9:12 also has πάντα τὰ ἔθνη), it is likely that the translator of LXX-Amos intended "his anointed" in 4:13 to refer to the same eschatological, messianic figure, who represents the Almighty God, and is described in 9:11.

22. Knibb, "Septuagint and Messianism," 9.

23. Ibid.; interestingly the participants at the Colloquium on messianism at Leuven in 2004 were not able to distinguish clearly between the theology and translation technique of the LXX translators (Knibb, "Introduction," xx).

24. Elsewhere in LXX-Amos the translator felt free to make free renderings of the Hebrew when he did not understand the *Vorlage*; see Glenny, *Finding Meaning*, 71-148.

25. See the discussion of 7:1 in Glenny, *Finding Meaning*, 202-7; and in Horbury, *Jewish Messianism*, 61.

26. Also, it is worth noting that connected with its description of an eschatological Davidic Messiah, 2 Kingdoms 23:3 (in Vaticanus) uses language similar to Amos 4:13 (Ἐν ἀνθρώπῳ πῶς κραταιώσητε φόβον χριστοῦ;).

27. See Glenny, "Septuagint and Apostolic Hermeneutics."

Questions Concerning the Vorlage of LXX-Amos 4:13

An important factor in determining if there is evidence of messianism in the LXX rendering of Amos 4:13 is the issue of the LXX's *Vorlage*. Two seasoned LXX scholars have recently questioned whether the Septuagint text in Amos 4:13 is a translation of a Hebrew text like the one found in the MT. Siegfried Kreuzer argues that the reference to the Lord's anointed in LXX-Amos 4:13 was found in the LXX's *Vorlage*, which he argues is the earliest text we have of Amos 4:13, and thus the LXX reading of Amos 4:13 is not a "messianic interpretation" nor is it a result of "Christian editing" of the text.[28] He notes that שח in the MT's מה-שחו ("what is his thought") occurs only this one time in the MT, and elsewhere in Scripture it is "always written *plene* (שיח)." Furthermore, the *plene* form is "used only for people (not used with god), and describes (with the possible exception of Ps 104:34) only negative 'ideas' in the sense of worries or grief, which does not fit the context."[29] Thus, apparently because שח is a difficult reading in the MT and because it is not a normal word for the Hebrew authors, he feels it does not reflect the original, but may be instead "an antimessianic change" in the MT made in an apparent revision of the Hebrew. Kreuzer theorizes that at the time of the formation of the later MT reading, "what is his thought," the earlier reading, "his anointed, messiah," would have been separated, in keeping with the rabbinic rule of Notarikon, which allows the breaking up of words or transposition of letters in words, to create a new sense.[30] And the addition of the *maqqep* in the MT joining the two words in the new reading would have assured that the two words were read separately and not joined again in the context of *scriptio continua*.[31] Kreuzer thinks such a scenario could have been a reaction against a Christian understanding of Amos 4:13, but it "could also have been the product of an inner-Jewish rejection of messianic apocalyptic tendencies after 70 CE and after 135 CE."[32]

28. Kreuzer, "Origin and Development," 27-28.

29. Ibid., 28.

30. Kreuzer, "Origin and Development," 27, defines *Notarikon* as a rabbinic rule that "allows for the new separation of words or within words in order to 'discover' new meanings in the text that (and this is presumed in this understanding) are already contained in the text because this sacred text is perfect and complete." Kreuzer notes that this is "one of the thirty-two rules of scriptural interpretation from Rabbi Eliezer" (27n79). Rashi (Middle Ages) is well known for the employment of this rule.

31. Kreuzer, "Origin and Development," 27.

32. Ibid., 28.

Kreuzer's argument, based on the changes he suggests in the transition from "his anointed" (משיחו) to "what is his thought" (מה־שחו), is intriguing, but for several reasons I do not find it convincing. First, the meaning of the *plene* form of שח in Ps 104:34 ("May my meditation (שיחי) be pleasing to him"), does not describe a negative idea, and its meaning in this verse would make good sense in the context of Amos 4:13. Second, if "his anointed" (משיחו) were the original why would the scribe who is responsible for the text found in the MT choose שח, a word that occurs nowhere else in the Hebrew Bible, in the revision of the Hebrew text? Why would the reviser, who is supposedly responsible for the text found in the MT remove the *yod* in משיחו if he could leave it in his rendering and have a more common word, i.e., שיחו (the *plene* form, which is found five times in MT) rather than use a word that occurs nowhere else (שחו)? Thus, the problems Kreuzer suggests a translator would have encountered in rendering a text like the MT into the LXX are not as great as the problems in explaining why a reviser would render the retroverted LXX text into the text form found in the MT. Furthermore, the purpose of a *maqqep*, such as the one that connects מה and שחו in the MT of Amos 4:13, is to show that two words are connected, not to keep them divided. And as far as the rabbinic rule *Notarikon* applies, Kreuzer explains elsewhere that the rule allows one to achieve new meaning in a text "by dividing or combining words differently"; thus it could apply in changing a text like the MT to a retroversion of the LXX or also in moving from a retroversion of the LXX to a text like the one in the MT.[33] Finally it should be noted that Kreuzer's discussion of Amos 4:13 is in a context in his article that is explaining the Jewish exegetical tradition reflected in the LXX and most specifically the rule of Notarikon, which is crucial to his understanding of Amos 4:13.[34] In fact, he employs LXX-Amos 4:13 in his article to illustrate this rule, but the rule could be employed to argue against his proposal as well as to support it. In summary, I do not find his evidence convincing, and since there is no textual evidence to support his theory I find it insufficient. (I will explain the textual evidence below.)

Martin Karrer also argues for the priority of the reading found in the LXX of Amos 4:13, and he especially bases his argument on his reconstruction of the reception history of the text.[35] He theorizes that the

33. Ibid., 29.

34. The rule of *Notarikon* is very important for Kreuzer's thesis concerning the Antiochene Text in the book in which the article is found.

35. Karrer and Kraus, "Umfang und Text der Septuaginta," 56–59. He develops

reading in the LXX developed in Judaism, and the Old Greek was then revised to its present form based on a text form found in a popular updating of the proto-MT. The reference to "his messiah" in Amos 4:13 in its original Jewish context, as one reading among several for this text, probably referred to God's announcement of a coming king. At about the end of the second century CE when their ideas of the Messiah began to solidify, Christians received this text and started to use it (as evidenced in the writings of Tertullian). And the reading in the MT was the creation of a new meaning by word separation (Notarikon). The messianic reading in the LXX was then cast off,[36] perhaps because of the refutation of the idea in the Jewish revolts. Karrer commends this reconstruction in spite of its complications, because of the absence of proof that Amos 4:13 played any part in the early Jewish messianic discussions from the second century BCE until the middle of the second century CE (at the time of Bar Kochba) and the fact that it was not employed by Christians until about 200 CE.[37] Furthermore, since the Greek words "thunder" (βροντή) and "anointed" (χριστός) are not found elsewhere in the LXX of the Twelve Prophets, he thinks it is unlikely that the translator would have employed them and they are more likely original. However, in response to Karrer the Hebrew noun for "thunder" (רעם) is not found in the Hebrew of the Twelve either, so there would be no occasion where the translator would be required to use the corresponding Greek noun. And χριστός ("anointed") would surely have been a word that the translator knew and would have been free to use whether it occurred elsewhere in his translation of the Twelve or not. As far as the absence of the LXX version of Amos 4:13 in the reception history until about 200 CE, that is difficult to explain, but it is an argument from silence and the LXX version of Amos 4:13 does not provide much information about the Lord's anointed for Jews or Christians nor does it provide theological support for Christianity. It basically states that God has a messiah, and he is making him known to humans. Finally and crucial for the discussion, the messianic reading in the LXX is not found in any Hebrew manuscripts

---

further Kreuzer's suggestion concerning the history of this text in his argument for the priority of the reading found in the LXX of Amos 4:13.

36. Apparently he means it was cast off in the received Hebrew texts.

37. Tertullian, *Against Hermogenes* 32.2, uses the LXX of Amos 4:13 in a context of creation. In Tertullian, *Against Praxeas* 28.9, he uses LXX-Amos 4:13 to show that Christ is not the Father. Dines ("Septuagint of Amos," 150–56) discusses the use of Amos 4:13 by the fathers and other possible Greek influences on LXX-Amos 4:13.

or in the Aramaic (Targum) or Syriac (Peshitta) translations, which are based on the Hebrew. Nor is there evidence supporting it in the other Greek versions, as one would expect if it was in the *Vorlage* of the LXX. Therefore, Dines comments that the only way that the messianic reading could possibly have been in the *Vorlage* of the LXX is if the reading was an isolated tradition, or else if it disappeared very rapidly.[38] Both of those possibilities are unlikely for a rendering concerning a messianic figure. Thus, in view of the evidence we have concerning the text of Amos 4:13 the absence of the LXX form of that text in messianic discussions until the latter part of the second century does not convince me that the messianic reading found in the LXX was also in the *Vorlage* of the LXX. It is simpler and more likely that the LXX translator is responsible for the messianic reading in LXX-Amos 4:13.

In summary, the reading "announcing his anointed to humans" in LXX-Amos 4:13 is best understood to be a translation of a Hebrew text similar to the MT and to be evidence of a "messianic perspective on the part of the translator."[39] There are several indications of this messianic perspective in the LXX text: (1) There are significant differences between the Hebrew and Greek texts; (2) One of those differences in the LXX is a reference to a specific messianic figure ("his messiah," which could be a reference to the final and ultimate Davidic Messiah); (3) There are several other eschatological passages in the LXX rendering of Amos (esp. 7:1; 9:11–12), and one of them, 9:11–12, connects an end time Davidic kingdom/dynasty with gentiles, echoing themes from 4:13.[40] Thus, there is evidence to see messianism in LXX-Amos 4:13 and to call the rendering messianic. This messianic reading from LXX-Twelve, which was likely translated into Greek in the latter half of the second century BCE, is evidence of an interest in messianism in that period, and more than that of an interest in gentiles knowing about the Jewish Messiah.

Works Cited

Dafni, E. G. "Παντοκράτωρ in Septuaginta-Amos: Zur Theologie der Sprache der Septuaginta." In *The Septuagint and Messianism*, edited by Michael A. Knibb, 443–

---

38. Dines, "Septuagint of Amos," 154. See ibid., 149–156, for her discussion of LXX-Amos 4:13.

39. Jobes and Silva, *Invitation to the Septuagint*, 338.

40. See Knibb's four criteria to determine whether or not the Septuagint has introduced a messianic reference and the discussion of them earlier in this article.

54. Bibliotheca Ephemeridum theologicarum Lovaniensium 195. Leuven: Leuven University Press, 2006.

Dines, Jennifer Mary. "The Septuagint of Amos: A Study in Interpretation." PhD diss., University of London, 1991.

Evans, Craig. "Messianism." In *Dictionary of New Testament Background*, Craig A. Evans and Stanley E. Porter, 698–707. Downers Grove, IL: InterVarsity, 2000.

Glenny, W. Edward. *Amos: A Commentary Based on Amos in Codex Vaticanus*. Septuagint Commentary Series. Leiden: Brill, 2013.

———. *Finding Meaning in the Text: Translation Technique and Theology in the Septuagint of Amos*. Supplements to Vetus Testamentum 126. Leiden: Brill, 2009.

———. "Hebrew Misreadings or Free Translation in the Septuagint of Amos?" *Vetus Testamentum* 57 (2007) 524–47.

———. *Hosea: A Commentary Based on Hosea in Codex Vaticanus*. Septuagint Commentary Series. Leiden: Brill, 2013.

———. "The Septuagint and Apostolic Hermeneutics: Amos 9 in Acts 15." *Bulletin for Biblical Research* 22 (2012) 1–26.

Horbury, William. "Monarchy and Messianism in the Greek Pentateuch." In *The Septuagint and Messianism*, edited by Michael A. Knibb, 79–128. Bibliotheca Ephemeridum theologicarum Lovaniensium 195. Leuven: Leuven University Press, 2006.

———. *Jewish Messianism and the Cult of Christ*. London: SCM, 1998.

Jobes, Karen H., and Moisés Silva. *Invitation to the Septuagint*. 2nd ed. Grand Rapids: Baker Academic, 2015.

Karrer, Martin, and Wolfgang Kraus. "Umfang und Text der Septuaginta." In *Die Septuaginta—Texte, Kontexte, Lebenswelten*, edited by Martin Karrer et al., 8–63. Wissenschaftliche Untersuchungen zum Neuen Testament 219. Tübingen: Mohr/Siebeck, 2008.

Knibb, Michael A. "Introduction." In *The Septuagint and Messianism*, edited by Michael A. Knibb, xiii–xxxi. Bibliotheca Ephemeridum theologicarum Lovaniensium 195. Leuven: Leuven University Press, 2006.

———. "The Septuagint and Messianism: Problems and Issues." In *The Septuagint and Messianism*, edited by Michael A. Knibb, 3–19. Bibliotheca Ephemeridum theologicarum Lovaniensium 195. Leuven: Leuven University Press, 2006

Kreuzer, Siegfried. "Origin and Development of the Septuagint in the Context of Alexandrian and Early Christian Culture and Learning." In *The Bible in Greek*, edited by Sigfried Kreuzer, 3–46. Society of Biblical Literature Septuagint and Cognate Studies 63. Atlanta: SBL Press, 2015.

Lust, Johann. *Messianism and the Septuagint: Collected Essays*, edited by K. Hauspie. Bibliotheca Ephemeridum theologicarum Lovaniensium 178. Leuven: Leuven University Press, 2004.

Park, Aaron W. *The Book of Amos as Composed and Read in Antiquity*. Studies in Biblical Literature 37. New York: Lang, 2001.

Rahlfs, Alfred, and Robert Hanhart, eds. *Septuaginta*. Stuttgart: Deutsche Bibelgesellschaft, 2006.

Satterthwaite, Philip E. "Translators as Imperialists: And Other Aspects of the Septuagint Translation of the Book of the Twelve." An expanded version of an unpublished paper given to the Cambridge University Old Testament Seminar, October, 1997.

Schaper, Joachim. *Eschatology in the Greek Psalter.* Wissenschaftliche Untersuchungen zum Neuen Testament 2.76. Tübingen: Mohr/Siebeck, 1995.

Ziegler, Joseph, ed. *Septuaginta: Vetus Testamentum Graecum.* Vol. 8, *Duodecim prophetae.* 3rd ed. Göttingen: Vandenhoeck & Ruprecht, 1984.

11

Jewish-Christian Relations in Smyrna

Rhetoric, Reality, and the Limits of Historical Knowledge

MICHAEL W. HOLMES

The cast of characters who make an appearance in the early Christian document known as the *Martyrdom of Polycarp*[1] (*Mart. Pol.*) includes, in addition to the expected groups of Roman officials, pagan crowds, and Christian supporters, one unexpected entry: Ἰουδαῖοι, "Jews" (or perhaps "Judeans"[2]), who are mentioned three times in all. In 12.2, they are mentioned as part of "the entire crowd, Gentiles as well as Jews living in Smyrna" (ἅπαν τὸ πλῆθος ἐθνῶν τε καὶ Ἰουδαίων τῶν τὴν Σμύρναν κατοικούντων), who "cried out with uncontrollable anger and with a loud shout" against Polycarp: "This is the teacher of Asia,[3] the father of the Christians, the destroyer of our gods, who teaches many not to sacrifice or worship." In the second instance, in 13.1, they (Ἰουδαίων) are character-

---

1. For text, translation, and introduction, see Holmes, *Apostolic Fathers*; for introduction, see also Parvis, "Martyrdom of Polycarp," 126-46; Buschmann, "Das Martyrium des Polykarp," 147-69 (ET, 135-57); for commentaries, see Buschmann, *Das Martyrium des Polykarp*; and Hartog, *Polycarp's Epistle*.

2. Cf. BDAG, "Ἰουδαῖος, αία, αῖον," esp. 2c; see also Boyarin, "Semantic Differences," 67-71.

3. The text is uncertain: Ασιας km Eusebius L] ασεβιας abcpsv. For the text and the abbreviations, see Holmes, *Apostolic Fathers*, 318; 302-3; for discussion see Hartog, *Polycarp's Epistle*, 304, who favors, however, the other reading.

189

ized, rather emphatically, as "being especially eager to assist" in carrying out Polycarp's execution, "as is their custom"—a statement that functions as "an indication of a fundamental element of social identity."⁴ In the third passage (17.2–18.1), the cremation of Polycarp's body by the centurion and his associates is attributed to the "instigation" (ὑποβαλλόντων), "insistence" (ἐνισχυόντων), and "opposition" (φιλονεικίαν) of this same group (here τῶν 'Ιουδαίων twice). Moreover, "Their activity is even parallel to, or perhaps the earthly counterpart of, that of the 'evil one who opposes the race of the righteous' [17.1]; just as he 'incited' (ὑπέβαλεν) Nicetas, so they too are all the while inciting (ὑποβαλλόντων) these things."⁵ In short, the portrayal of the Jews in *Mart. Pol.* goes from bad to worse to worst as the narrative unfolds.

This negative portrayal of "Jews" in *Mart. Pol.* has, traditionally and more recently, often been read as an accurate (or at least generally accurate) description of their role in the circumstances and events leading to the death of Polycarp in mid-second-century Smyrna, a reliable narrative, in other words, that offers (at least relatively) unmediated access to the event.⁶ Description, however, does not occur apart from interpretation, and a number of considerations, general as well as particular, raise questions regarding this positivistic reading of these passages.

In particular, a number of details entail what at least seems to be unlikely "Jewish" behavior. These include (1) the reference to "our gods" and idol sacrifice (12.2);⁷ (2) Jewish attendance at a pagan festival on

---

4. Cobb, *Dying to Be Men*, 83.

5. Lieu, *Image and Reality*, 67.

6. See, e.g., Lightfoot, *Apostolic Fathers*, 2.1.468–70; Harnack, *Mission and Expansion*, 1:57–59; Cadoux, *Ancient Smyrna*, 361–62 ("degenerate Jews . . . showed their usual bitter hostility to the Christians"); Frend, *Martyrdom and Persecution*, 272 ("Jews cooperating gleefully with the pagans in having a common enemy removed"); for Asia in general, ibid., 259 ("In the persecutions which were to wrack Asia in the reign of Marcus Aurelius the Jew was often in the background. For nearly another century he continued to stir up trouble wherever he could"). Others use the material more cautiously but still handle it in an essentially positivist manner: e.g., Trebilco (*Jewish Communities in Asia Minor*, 29, 32, 35); Robert (*Le martyre de Pionios*, 55, 58, 81); Bowersock (*Martyrdom and Rome*, 44, 56); Litfin (*Early Christian Martyr Stories*, 61n 15). Rokeah (*Jews, Pagans, and Christians*, 9, 66), whose overall thesis is that the Jews played no role in pagan-Christian polemic, nevertheless attempts to offer an explanation for "the strong animosity" against Polycarp attributed by *Mart. Pol.* to the Jews in Smyrna—accepting, in other words, the assumption of its historicity.

7. On Jewish rejection of alien, pluralist, and iconic cultic activities as a distinctive social marker, see Barclay, *Jews in the Mediterranean Diaspora*, 429–34.

a "great Sabbath" (8.1, 21.1);[8] (3) the gathering of wood on a Sabbath (13.1, particularly interesting inasmuch as wood collection is "among the few acts specifically prohibited by Torah on the Sabbath");[9] and (4) the intense Jewish interest in the disposition of a Christian body (17.2). These four elements are not of equal weight, of course, and the cogency of points 2 and 3 depends to a great extent on how one envisions Jewish life in the Diaspora in the second century (e.g., does one take the emerging rabbinic view of Jewish life as typical or ideal,[10] or does one acknowledge that some Diaspora Jews assimilated to their surrounding culture to one degree or another,[11] and thus these behaviors might not always have been seen as problematic in some way?). Nonetheless, the four together do raise the question as to whether the overall portrait of Jewish activity in *Mart. Pol.* accurately reflects events as they unfolded.

In general, the portrayal of active Jewish involvement in the persecution of Christians in Smyrna stands in no small degree of tension with what is known from other sources: with regard to the second century CE, "actual evidence of Jewish instigation of persecution ('stirring up trouble') is hardly to be found."[12] For example, of all the Christian mar-

---

8. The meaning of this phrase remains a matter of uncertainty; see the discussions in Lieu, *Image and Reality*, 71-77; Lane Fox, *Pagans and Christians*, 486-87 (Purim and Dionysia coinciding); Hartog, *Polycarp's Epistle*, 191-99.

9. Gibson, "Jews and the Christians," 152 (citing Exod 35:3 and Num 15:32-36). On Jewish observance of the Sabbath as a distinctive social marker, see Barclay, *Jews in the Mediterranean Diaspora*, 440-42.

10. Cf., e.g., the summary statement of Kraemer ("Mishna," 313): "Perhaps, then, the Mishnah represents the early rabbinic vision of a restored, Torah-perfected, 'messianic' world. [. . .] The Temple and its cult are central to this world. Israel lives on its own land and Jews are their own masters." For a recent overview of the rabbinic movement and its influence in the second century see Alexander, "Rabbis and Their Rivals."

11. For documented examples and a taxonomy of various degrees of Jewish assimilation, see Barclay, *Jews in the Mediterranean Diaspora*, 320-35. Cf. also Rajak, "Mediterranean Jewish Diaspora."

12. Lieu, *Image and Reality*, 91; cf. Parkes, *Conflict of the Church and the Synagogue*, 121-50; Simon, *Verus Israel*, 115-25; similarly Taylor, *Anti-Judaism*, 91-97, who stresses "the paucity of the references," and notes further the "retrospective character" of nearly all of these few references. Many of the classic patristic statements traditionally cited as "evidence" of widespread Jewish persecution, such as Tertullian's infamous comment that the Jewish synagogues are "fountains of persecution" (*Scorpiace* 10:10, *synagogas Iudaeorum, fontes persecutionum*), in fact refer to the time of Jesus and the apostles, and inform us not at all about later times. See for a discussion of this and similar texts Schreckenberg, *Die christlichen Adversus-Judaeos-Texte*, 171-225; MacLennan, *Early Christian Texts*; Taylor, *Anti-Judaism*; Lieu, *Image and Reality*.

tyrdoms we know of from the time of Domitian through Decius, Jews are said to play an active role in exactly two, both of which happened in Smyrna: those of Polycarp in the mid-second century and of Pionius in the mid-third.[13] In short, the role attributed to Jews in *Mart. Pol.* is both intrinsically problematic and extrinsically anomalous; that is, the actions and attitudes attributed to "the Jews" do not seem to square with the portrait of second-century Asia Minor as determined via other sources.

If, in light of these considerations, one is inclined to conclude that "the world of the document is not identical with the world of the events it purports to describe,"[14] it becomes necessary to ask what has generated this negative portrayal of Jewish activity in Smyrna, and why the narrator has drawn attention to the Jews in this particular manner.[15] A number of suggestions have been offered, of which the more plausible include the following.[16]

Miriam Taylor, drawing attention to the well-documented tendency of the document to highlight parallels between the stories of Jesus and Polycarp,[17] argues that all the references to Jews in *Mart. Pol.* are purely literary features that were created solely for the sake of the story, and have no point of contact with or reference to the historical situation in Smyrna at the time of Polycarp's death. That is, "the references to the Jews ... can be explained as forming part of a story that clearly aims to glorify the tradition of the '*imitatio Christi*.'"[18] Indeed, in her estimation "the influence of the gospel accounts is so all-persuasive that it seems highly probable that Jews were included in this account to make the parallels with Christ's death all the more complete"; in other words, "these references are clearly

---

13. See Robert, *Le martyre de Pionios*; Lane Fox, *Pagans and Christians*, 460–92.

14. Lieu, *Image and Reality*, 94.

15. For the historiography of the larger issue behind the specific incident addressed here, which in current discussion has largely centered on the question of whether and/or how and/or when the emerging Christian and Jewish movements "parted ways," see Burns, *Christian Schism*, 19–60; Paget, *Jews, Christians and Jewish Christians*, 1–24; Jacobs, "Lion and the Lamb," 97–108; also Reed and Becker, "Introduction."

16. Approaches that eliminate the problem by attributing the passages in question to a later interpolator, or by asserting, for example, that "If any so-called 'Jews' acted in the manner described in the *Martyrdom of Polycarp*, they were altogether alien in mind and conduct from any actually known class to whom the name 'Jews' might be accurately applied" (Abrahams, *Studies in Pharisaism*, 69) will not be considered in the present context.

17. For a standard list of Jesus-Polycarp parallels, see Cobb, "Polycarp's Cup," 224.

18. Taylor, *Anti-Judaism*, 102.

interpolations that form part of the attempt by the writer to bring out the resemblances between Polycarp's martyrdom and the passion of Christ."[19]

In reaching this conclusion Taylor echoes the earlier view of I. Abrahams: "the narrative is patently unhistorical ... this is embellishment, not history."[20] This perspective—which in effect detaches completely the rhetoric from any connection with the reality of the circumstances—is plausible, but not persuasive, if only because, as Lieu points out, "It is unlikely that the imitation theme has created the presence of the Jews entirely—if it had, more explicit verbal echoes could be expected."[21] Furthermore, it is not clear why a community would accept a fictionalized account of its revered hero that stood so at odds with their own (on this view, quite different) experience.[22] Such an approach also runs the risk, from a historiographic perspective, of devaluing the unusual on the basis of the typical.[23]

Stephen G. Wilson, while agreeing that "there is little doubt that this account is affected by the desire to make the death of Polycarp conform to that of Jesus," to the extent that it includes an "exaggerated role for the Jews," nonetheless is reluctant to cut as completely as Taylor does the connection between text and reality. The presence of the parallels in the narrative, he argues, "does not entirely undercut its veracity," and so the account "may in fact reflect the local conditions in Smyrna."[24]

The tension here between the perceived need to acknowledge the rhetorically exaggerated treatment of the Jews and the desire to retain nonetheless the document as a source of historically useful information (it "may in fact reflect the local conditions") is also evident in the essay by E. Leigh Gibson. After arguing that the references to the hostility of Jews are devoid of any historical value, she then hypothesizes that "Jews" are really only a surrogate for the author's real target, "Judaizing Christians"—i.e., "followers of Jesus who also embraced observance of

---

19. Ibid., 103. For an appreciation and detailed critique of Taylor's work, see Paget, *Jews, Christians and Jewish Christians*, 43-73.

20. Abrahams, *Studies in Pharisaism*, 67-69 (here 67).

21. Lieu, "Accusations," 288.

22. Cf. ibid., 291.

23. For a discussion of the challenge of dealing with unique events, see Tucker, "Unique Events."

24. Wilson, *Related Strangers*, 174. Earlier scholars taking a similar line include Parkes (*The Conflict of the Church and the Synagogue*, 137, 148) and Simon (*Verus Israel*, 121-23).

Jewish law"—and concludes with the surprisingly positivistic claim that the document "demonstrate[s] the exchange of ideas between Jews and Christians."[25] In the case of both Wilson and Gibson, one is left with the impression of trying to have one's cake and eat it too.

Perhaps the most developed and nuanced attempt to bridge the gap between the "world" created by the rhetoric of the text and "the world of the events it purports to describe" is offered by Judith Lieu.[26] She affirms that in light of the importance of the "imitation" theme for the narrative, it is not surprising to find the Jews portrayed as "active in ensuring the carrying out of the death sentence. Yet the imitation theme is hardly likely to have created the Jewish presence, nor is it sufficient explanation of the highlighting of their contribution to the mob action at this point."[27] Rather, the role attributed to the Jews "is one which must have been rooted in *perceived* experience."[28] Thus in her estimation "the recognition of the theological significance of the presentation of the Jewish role in the martyrdom of Polycarp ... demands rather than replaces a historical interpretation";[29] it "demands of the modern interpreter a path between a simple historicism and a sceptical dismissal of theological fantasy."[30]

Lieu finds a basis for a historical interpretation in the "impression of rivalry" between Jews and Christians that she finds hinted at in *Mart. Pol.* 17.2—18.1. Specifically, she notes "the issue of contention or rivalry [φιλονεικία[31]] ... in the city context of the time," involving matters of "rights, privilege and influence"[32]—in other words, two minority groups struggling to maintain, on the one hand, or achieve, on the other hand, a place within the civic structure of Smyrna as they competed for status and/or civic standing.

Her attractive and well-developed thesis, however, while plausible, is unpersuasive.[33] Certainly civic strife, both within cities and between cities, of the sort suggested by Lieu was not at all uncommon in the cities

25. Gibson, "Jews and Christians," 157–58.
26. Lieu, *Image and Reality*, 94.
27. Ibid., 64.
28. Lieu, "Accusations," 291.
29. Lieu, *Image and Reality*, 70.
30. Lieu, "Accusations," 291.
31. Melito of Sardis reported an outbreak of anti-Christian φιλονεικία from around the same time (Eusebius, *Hist. eccl.* 4.26.6).
32. Lieu, *Image and Reality*, 91, 93, 94; cf. 68.
33. Cf. similarly Gibson, "Jews and Christians," 158.

of Asia Minor in the second century CE. Further, there is widespread evidence of Jews playing an active and public role in the "life of the city," whether in Alexandria in the time of Philo, for example, or Caesarea,[34] or in various cities in Asia Minor in the second century CE.[35] In Aphrodisias, they even had their own seating section in the Odeon.[36]

This sort of public engagement was possible because the Jewish community had two things the Christian community did not: an ancient and respected tradition, and recognized legal status and protection.[37] As Andrew Jacobs observes,

> Jews enjoyed a cultural and political legitimacy (as tenuous as it may have been) that Christians did not. Their odd and sometimes unsettling beliefs and practices (such as monotheism and circumcision) had legal protection, and Jews had the benefit of a long and rich ethnic history to grant them some cultural legitimacy.[38]

That is, it was these "extraordinary privileges and exemptions granted uniquely to Jewish communities in virtue of the ethnicity and antiquity of their own ancestral way of life," as Fredriksen and Irshai point out, that "in turn allowed Hellenistic Jews, without compromising those things fundamental to their own religious identity, to attain their remarkable degree of social and cultural integration in the ancient city."[39]

The Christian communities, on the other hand, lacked both of these elements, and furthermore were perceived as a threat to civic well-being due to their seeming atheism[40]: "a nuisance cult whose members were

34. On Philo and Alexandria, see Barclay, *Jews in the Mediterranean Diaspora*, 48–81, and for Caesarea, ibid., 252–58.

35. Cf. Trebilco, "Jews in Asia Minor."

36. Cameron, *Circus Factions*, 79 ("At Aphrodisias, after τόπος Ἑβρέων and τόπος νεωτέρω(ν), τόπος Βενέτων can still be read on a bench in the Odeum"). For a similar inscription (τόπος Εἰουδέων τῶν καὶ θεοσεβίον) from the theater in Miletus (dated "probably in the second century or the beginning of the third century CE") and discussion of it, see Trebilco, *Jewish Communities*, 159–62.

37. For the legal status of Jews in general, see Linder, "Legal Status of the Jews," esp. 128–44.

38. Jacobs, "Lion and the Lamb," 110.

39. Fredriksen and Irshai, "Christian Anti-Judaism," 997–98.

40. That Christians were viewed by pagans as "atheists" is a widely held truism, for which *Mart. Pol.* 9.2 is a foundational text. For the argument that "the accusation of atheism develops primarily within a Christian discourse rather than being levelled at Christians from the outside," see Whitmarsh, "'Away with the Atheists!'"

considered potentially disloyal citizens because of their allegiance to Christ" rather than to Caesar.[41] Indeed, in surviving mid-second-century documents nominally directed towards an external audience (e.g., the apologies of Justin, or Melito),[42] the Christian community is portrayed as being more concerned about its survival than about acquiring or exercising civic rights within the *polis*.[43] That is, Christians purportedly addressed letters and petitions to emperors seeking relief from persecution and/or redress of wrongs done to them and/or acknowledgement of the right to exist as a lawful and law-abiding element of Roman society, primarily, it seems, so they could be left alone to go about their business.[44]

Evidence from Asia Minor of Christians seeking to play an active role in the civic life of a Greco-Roman city in the early to mid-second century seems to be lacking.[45] The most Lieu can offer in the case of *Mart. Pol.* is the impression of rivalry for the ear of Nicetes, who seemingly has influence with his son Herod, the *eirenarch* or police captain.[46] But this is surely an ambiguous reference: there is no indication that on the Christian side this is any more than a matter of a private intervention, made possible by the circumstance that Alce, the sister of Nicetes, was a Christian (17.2; cf. Ignatius, *Smyrn.* 13.2; *Pol.* 8.3). In short, their very different social contexts make it unlikely that the synagogue and the church were competing with each other for civic status and position.[47]

41. Tabbernee, "Asia Minor and Cyprus," 302-3.

42. See, respectively, Minns and Parvis, *Justin, Philosopher and Martyr*; and Eusebius, *Hist. eccl.*, 4.26.4-11.

43. Similarly Horbury, "Church and Synagogue," 78-81, who discusses Justin and Melito, among others.

44. On this contrast between the political or civil status of Jews and Christians, cf. Horbury, "Church and Synagogue," who, after noting the similarities and differences in the respective situations of each group, concludes with the observation that "A contrast remains between relative Jewish security, and relative Christian insecurity" (ibid., 87); that is, "the liberty of the synagogue ... seems to stand in contrast with the precarious political situation of Christians" (ibid., 86).

45. There is epigraphic evidence "by the middle of the third century" for "a surprisingly large number of Christians in Asia Minor" serving as "local city councilors or senators" (Tabbernee, "Asia Minor and Cyprus," 317), but not, apparently, for the second century.

46. Lieu, *Image and Reality*, 88, 90-91, 94.

47. In offering the preceding argument, this essay runs, of course, the same risk (of devaluing the unique on the basis of the typical) it noted earlier with respect to the work of others.

More persuasive is the suggestion that it was not contention for civic "rights, privilege and influence," but competition for the allegiance of adherents—together with the accompanying need to define more clearly what one believed and how one behaved—that provides a plausible historical context for the "anti-Jewish" statements in *Mart. Pol.*[48] This competition for allegiance and the work of identity construction played out on both inter-group and intragroup levels, and both deserve notice.[49]

On the intergroup level, from at least as early as the time of Ignatius of Antioch (*Magn.* 8; *Phld.* 6) to the time of John Chrysostom, Christian writers testify to the attractiveness of the synagogue to Jesus followers.[50] The synagogue had rights and privileges (sketched above) that the Christian community lacked; one thing it did share with the Christianity community—the Jewish Scriptures—were the subject of contentious disputes about who had the right reading of the story narrated therein. Furthermore, the Quartodeciman version of Christianity found throughout Asia Minor (one of whose best-known leaders was Polycarp) was dependent on the synagogue for its liturgical calendar. Thus the continuing existence of the synagogue was a powerful challenge to the legitimacy of the growing Christian movement, both socially and theologically, especially as Christianity was in a socially marginal position throughout the second century and the boundaries between the Jewish and Christian communities remained permeable.

On the intragroup level, *Mart. Pol.* reveals rather clearly that the Smyrnean Christian community was caught up in a debate about the meaning and practice of martyrdom (cf. 1.1–2). Sometimes (as in ch. 4) the debate is in the open, but other times one side of the internal debate seems to have been projected on outsiders, Jewish in particular, the better not only to critique but to distance oneself from them.[51] Thus the Jewish community plays a double role: it is an external threat in its own right, and a surrogate for internal threats. In such circumstances (particularly in light of the Christian movement's tradition of *adversus Judaeos* literature) it is not surprising to find disparaging remarks directed towards the

---

48. Cf., e.g., Lieu, "Accusations," 290; Lieu, "'I am a Christian.'"

49. For an overview of identity construction in theory and practice see Cobb, *Dying to Be Men*, 1–32.

50. See, e.g., Wilken, *John Chrysostom and the Jews*; Drake, *Slandering the Jew*, 78–98.

51. Cf. Lieu, *Image and Reality*, 67, 94; Gibson, "Jews and Christians," 158.

Jewish community that have little if anything to do with the community itself, and much more to do with the community of origin.[52]

Hypothesizing that intra-Christian rivalry is the more likely genesis of the negative portrayal of Jews in *Mart. Pol.* still leaves on the table the question of the relationship between the rhetorical portrayal and actual experience: if the gap between the way Jews are portrayed in the document and the perceived experience of its intended readers is too great, the rhetorical tactics could well backfire.[53]

Here it may be fruitful to explore the possibility that the charges against "the Jews" are rooted in the difference between an insider's and an outsider's view of the synagogue's membership. In Aphrodisias, inscriptional evidence indicates that the synagogue encompassed three groups: Jews, proselytes, and "God-worshippers" (θεοσεβεῖς). The latter were, apparently, Gentiles who, on the one hand, were "attached in some definite way to the Jewish community ... a subsection of the whole," and, on the other hand, were still highly assimilated to the pagan ethos of the city; indeed, nine were βουλευταί ("city councilors").[54] From an "inside the synagogue" perspective, this group was on the margins of the Jewish community, having a status inferior to that of the other two groups, whereas someone outside the synagogue may well have perceived the group as representative figures. If so, it is plausible that some of the behavior that the author of *Mart. Pol.* attributes to the Jews, and which some scholars find impossible to imagine as the behavior of anyone who was "truly Jewish," may reflect the conduct of those who, from the synagogue's perspective, were on the margins of the synagogue, but who, from an outsider's perspective, were perceived as representative of the group. In short, it may be that the author of *Mart. Pol.* is attributing the behavior of a minority of the group to the group as a whole.

The hypothesis that intra-Christian rivalry is the more likely genesis of the negative portrayal of Jews in *Mart. Pol.* is at least plausible; one could argue that it is also a more probable hypothesis than others that have been discussed. But no matter how plausible or probable one may judge this proposal to be, it is, like the suggestions of Gibson and Lieu, only a hypothesis (not data or evidence). In seeking to understand the "historical Polycarp" and the circumstances surrounding his death, one

---

52. Fredriksen and Irshai, "Christian Anti-Judaism."
53. Lieu, "Accusations," 291.
54. Trebilco, *Jewish Communities in Asia Minor*, 152-54.

encounters the same conundrum encountered by those seeking after the "historical Jesus": there is no unmediated access to that history. Instead, we must acknowledge the hermeneutical consequences of the circumstance that our only access is mediated through documents written by their followers.[55]

So where does that leave us? In the absence of any other contemporary evidence from or about Smyrna bearing on the question of "Jewish-Christian" relations in that city, the possibility (however small) must be left open that the circumstances portrayed in *Mart. Pol.* are an anomaly in the otherwise-uniform picture (sketched above) of Jewish-Christian relations in Asia in the second century. To do otherwise risks using the typical to erase the possibly unique. There may have been in Smyrna some indeterminate number of people with whom the label "Jew" could not unreasonably be associated who had the opportunity and inclination to attend the civic pagan games when the opportunity presented itself, and who on this occasion perhaps did join a similarly indeterminate number of their fellow citizens in calling for the arrest and execution of Polycarp.

On the other hand, though the absence of other evidence from Smyrna requires the acknowledgement of the possibility of such an atypical scenario (or something similar), it is nonetheless clear that the uniform portrait presented by the evidence for the rest of Asia Minor as a whole—namely, that Jews were not involved in anti-Christian activities—suggests rather strongly the higher probability of a different scenario: that the origin of the portrait of Jewish behavior conveyed by *Mart. Pol.* lies not in any actual Jewish behavior but within the Christian community. That is, the references to Jews in *Mart. Pol.* probably reveal far more about the circumstances, issues, and opinions of Christians in Smyrna than they do about the behavior of Jews (however defined) in that town.

In the end, the attempt to sort out the relationship between rhetoric and reality, between the world of the text and the world of the events for which it is our only witness, ultimately reminds us of the limits of our historical knowledge.

---

55. As Lane Fox (*Pagans and Christians*) seems to recognize: cf. 446 ("In the 150s, the Jews of Smyrna were said to have retained Polycarp's corpse for fear that Christians would start a cult of it"); and ibid., 481 ("In the 150s, Christians believed that the city's Jews had persuaded the pagan notables to petition the Roman governor and deter him from releasing Polycarp's corpse. Whatever their truth, these beliefs are evidence for the Jews' high contacts in the city's life").

Works Cited

Abrahams, I. *Studies in Pharisaism and the Gospels*. Second Series. Cambridge: Cambridge University Press, 1924.
Alexander, Philip. "The Rabbis and Their Rivals in the Second Century CE." In *Christianity in the Second Century: Themes and Developments*, edited by James Carleton Paget and Judith Lieu, 57–70. Cambridge: Cambridge University Press, 2017.
Barclay, John M. G. *Jews in the Mediterranean Diaspora: From Alexander to Trajan (323 BCE—117 CE)*. Edinburgh: T. & T. Clark, 1996.
Bowersock, Glen W. *Martyrdom and Rome*. The Wiles Lectures Given at the Queen's University of Belfast. Cambridge: Cambridge University Press, 1995.
Boyarin, Daniel. "Semantic Differences; or, 'Judaism'/'Christianity'." In *The Ways That Never Parted: Jews and Christians in Late Antiquity and the Early Middle Ages*, edited by Adam H. Becker and Annette Yoshiko Reed, 65–85. Texts and Studies in Ancient Judaism 95. Tübingen: Mohr/Siebeck, 2003.
Burns, Joshua Ezra. *The Christian Schism in Jewish History and Jewish Memory*. New York: Cambridge University Press, 2016.
Buschmann, Gerd. *Das Martyrium des Polykarp*. Kommentar zu den Apostolischen Vätern 6. Göttingen: Vandenhoeck & Ruprecht, 1998.
———. "The Martyrdom of Polycarp." In *The Apostolic Fathers: An Introduction*, edited by Wilhelm Pratscher, 135–57. Waco, TX: Baylor University Press, 2010.
Cadoux, Cecil John. *Ancient Smyrna: A History of the City from the Earliest Times to 324 A.D.* Oxford: Blackwell, 1938.
Cameron, Alan. *Circus Factions: Blues and Greens at Rome and Byzantium*. Oxford: Clarendon, 1976.
Cobb, L. Stephanie. *Dying to Be Men: Gender and Language in Early Christian Martyr Texts*. Gender, Theory, and Religion. New York: Columbia University Press, 2008.
———. "Polycarp's Cup: Imitatio in the *Martyrdom of Polycarp*." *Journal of Religious History* 38 (2014) 224–40.
Drake, Susanna. *Slandering the Jew: Sexuality and Difference in Early Christian Texts*. Divinations: Rereading Late Ancient Religion. Philadelphia: University of Pennsylvania Press, 2013.
Fredriksen, Paula, and Oded Irshai. "Christian Anti-Judaism: Polemics and Policies." In *The Late Roman-Rabbinic Period*, edited by Steven T. Katz, 997–1034. The Cambridge History of Judaism 4. Cambridge: Cambridge University Press, 2006.
Frend, W. H. C. *Martyrdom and Persecution in the Early Church*. Oxford: Blackwell, 1965.
Gibson, E. Leigh. "The Jews and Christians in the *Martyrdom of Polycarp*: Entangled or Parted Ways?" In *The Ways That Never Parted: Jews and Christians in Late Antiquity and the Early Middle Ages*, edited by Adam H. Becker and Annette Yoshiko Reed, 145–58. Texts and Studies in Ancient Judaism 95. Tübingen: Mohr/Siebeck, 2003.
Harnack, Adolf von. *The Mission and Expansion of Christianity in the First Three Centuries*. 2 vols. 2nd ed. London: Williams & Norgate, 1908.
Hartog, Paul, ed. *Polycarp's Epistle to the Philippians and the Martyrdom of Polycarp*. Oxford Apostolic Fathers. Oxford: Oxford University Press, 2013.

Holmes, Michael W., ed. and trans. *The Apostolic Fathers: Greek Texts and English Translation*. 3rd ed. Grand Rapids: Baker Academic, 2007.
Horbury, William. "Church and Synagogue vis-a-vís Roman Rule in the Second Century." In *Christianity in the Second Century: Themes and Developments*, edited by James Carleton Paget and Judith Lieu, 78-87. Cambridge: Cambridge University Press, 2017.
Jacobs, Andrew S. "The Lion and the Lamb: Reconsidering Jewish-Christian Relations in Antiquity." In *The Ways That Never Parted: Jews and Christians in Late Antiquity and the Early Middle Ages*, edited by Adam H. Becker and Annette Yoshiko Reed, 95-118. Tübingen: Mohr/Siebeck, 2003.
Kraemer, David. "The Mishna." In *The Late Roman-Rabbinic Period*, edited by Steven T. Katz, 299-315. The Cambridge History of Judaism 4. Cambridge: Cambridge University Press, 2006.
Lane Fox, Robin. *Pagans and Christians*. New York: Knopf, 1987.
Lieu, Judith M. "Accusations of Jewish Persecution in Early Christian Sources, with Particular Reference to Justin Martyr and the *Martyrdom of Polycarp*." In *Tolerance and Intolerance in Early Judaism and Christianity*, edited by G. N. Stanton and G. G. Stroumsa, 279-95. Cambridge: Cambridge University Press, 1998.
———. "'I am a Christian': Martyrdom and the Beginning of 'Christian' Identity." In *Neither Jew Nor Greek? Constructing Early Christianity*, edited by Judith Lieu, 211-31. Studies of the New Testament and Its World. London: T. & T. Clark, 2002.
———. *Image and Reality: The Jews in the World of the Christians in the Second Century*. London: T. & T. Clark, 1996.
Lightfoot, J. B. *The Apostolic Fathers*. 5 vols. 2nd ed. London: Macmillan, 1889-1890.
Linder, Amnon. "The Legal Status of the Jews in the Roman Empire." In *The Late Roman-Rabbinic Period*, edited by Steven T. Katz, 128-73. The Cambridge History of Judaism 4. Cambridge: Cambridge University Press, 2006.
Litfin, Bryan. M. *Early Christian Martyr Stories: An Evangelical Introduction with New Translations*. Grand Rapids: Baker Academic, 2014.
MacLennan, Robert S. *Early Christian Texts on Jews and Judaism*. Brown Judaic Studies 194. Atlanta: Scholars, 1990.
Minns, Dennis, and Paul Parvis. *Justin, Philosopher and Martyr: Apologies*. Oxford Early Christian Texts. Oxford: Oxford University Press, 2009.
Paget, James Carleton. *Jews, Christians and Jewish Christians in Antiquity*. Wissenschaftliche Untersuchungen zum Neuen Testament 251. Tübingen: Mohr/Siebeck, 2010.
Parkes, James. *The Conflict of the Church and the Synagogue: A Study in the Origins of Antisemitism*. 1934. Reprint, Philadelphia: Jewish Publication Society, 1961.
Parvis, Sara. "The Martyrdom of Polycarp." In *The Writings of the Apostolic Fathers*, edited by Paul Foster, 126-46. London: T. & T. Clark, 2007.
Rajak, Tessa. "The Mediterranean Jewish Diaspora in the Second Century." In *Christianity in the Second Century: Themes and Developments*, edited by James Carleton Paget and Judith Lieu, 39-56. Cambridge: Cambridge University Press, 2017.
Reed, Annette Yoshiko, and Adam H. Becker. "Introduction: Traditional Models and New Directions." In *The Ways That Never Parted: Jews and Christians in Late Antiquity and the Early Middle Ages*, edited by Adam H. Becker and Annette Yoshiko Reed, 1-24. Texts and Studies in Ancient Judaism 95. Tübingen: Mohr/Siebeck, 2003.

Robert, Louis. *Le martyre de Pionios, prêtre de Smyrne*. Ed. Glen W. Bowersock and C. P. Jones. Washington DC: Dumbarton Oaks Research Library and Collection, 1994.

Rokeah, David. *Jews, Pagans and Christians in Conflict*. Studia post-biblica 33. Jerusalem: Magnes, 1982.

Schreckenberg, Heinz. *Die christlichen Adversus-Judaeos-Texte und ihr literarisches und historisches Umfeld (1.-11. Jh.)*. 2nd ed. Europäischen Hochschulschriften: 23, Theologie: 172. Frankfurt: Lang, 1990.

Simon, Marcel. *Verus Israel: A Study of the Relations between Christians and Jews in the Roman Empire (135-425)*. Translated by Henry McKeating. The Littman Library of Jewish Civilization. Oxford: Oxford University Press, 1986.

Tabbernee, William. "Asia Minor and Cyprus." In *Early Christianity in Contexts*, edited by William Tabbernee, 261-320. Grand Rapids: Baker Academic, 2014.

Taylor, Miriam. *Anti-Judaism and Early Christian Identity: A Critique of the Scholarly Consensus*. Studia Post-biblica 46. Leiden: Brill, 1995.

Trebilco, Paul. *Jewish Communities in Asia Minor*. Society for New Testament Studies Monograph Series 69. Cambridge: Cambridge University Press, 1991.

———. "The Jews in Asia Minor, 66-c. 235 CE." In *The Late Roman-Rabbinic Period*, edited by Steven T. Katz, 75-82. Cambridge History of Judaism 4. Cambridge: Cambridge University Press, 2006.

Tucker, Aviezer. "Unique Events: The Underdetermination of Explanation." *Erkenntnis* 48 (1998) 59-80.

Whitmarsh, Tim. "'Away with the Atheists!' Christianity and Militant Atheism in the Early Empire." In *Christianity in the Second Century: Themes and Developments*, edited by James Carleton Paget and Judith Lieu, 281-93. Cambridge: Cambridge University Press, 2017.

Wilken, Robert L. *John Chrysostom and the Jews: Rhetoric and Reality in the Late 4th Century*. The Transformation of the Classical Heritage 4. Berkeley: University of California Press, 1983.

Wilson, Stephen G. *Related Strangers: Jews and Christians, 70-170 C.E.* Minneapolis: Fortress, 1995.

12

Could Luke Read Latin? New Evidence That He Did

DENNIS R. MACDONALD

Previous answers to the question posed in this title have focused on Latin loan words. Several of Luke's transliterations of Latin are sufficiently common that they add little to the discussion: ἀσσάριον (*assarius*, "penny," Luke 12:6), δηνάριον (*denarius*, "denarius," Luke 7:41; 10:35), Καῖσαρ (*Caesar*, "Caesar," Luke 2:1; Acts 25:8), κράβαττος (*crabattus*, "mat," Acts 5:15; 9:33), λεγιών (*legio*, "legion," Luke 8:30, cf. Mark 5:9), μόδιος (*modius*, "basket," Luke 11:33), πραιτώριον (*praetorium*, "praetorium," Acts 23:35), σουδάριον (*sudarium*, "cloth," Luke 19:20; Acts 19:12).

The following, however, are less common: Εὐρακύλων (a compound of Εὖρος and *Aquilo*, "Euroclydon," a northeast wind, Acts 27:14), κολωνία (*colonia*, "colony," Acts 16:12), φόρον (*forum*, Acts 28:15), λιβερτῖνος (*libertinus*, "freedman," Acts 6:9), σιμικίνθιον (*semicinctium*, "handkerchief," Acts 19:12), σικάριος (*sicarius*, "assassin," Acts 21:38), ταβέρνα (*taberna*, "inn," Acts 28:15), and χῶρος (*corus*, "north-west," Acts 27:12). In addition, occasionally one finds grammatical Latinisms, such as τὸ ἱκανὸν λαμβάνειν (cf. *satis accipere*, "to take security," Acts 17:9).

One might account for these data without attributing them to Luke's knowledge of Latin. In this essay in honor of Melissa Harl Sellew—whose facility with Greek, Latin, and Coptic is exemplary—I wish to reconsider Luke's Latin with three additional arguments in favor of it: (1) the likely dating of Luke-Acts to the second century and its relationship to the so-called Second Sophistic, (2) parallel imitations of the Homeric epics in

Vergil's *Aeneid* and Luke-Acts, and (3) the name Scevas for a Jewish high priest in Acts 19.

The Dating of Luke-Acts

Several scholars, most ardently Richard I. Pervo, have argued for Luke's composition around 115 CE, while others have placed his two-volume work among writings often called the Second Sophistic.[1] Authors identified with this movement included Latin-speakers, but even Greek-speakers were conversant in Latin; many of them held prestigious administrative positions in the Empire.[2] Quintilian (d. ca. 95 CE) provides a brilliant portrayal of bilingual education in Rome.[3]

Parallel Homeric Imitations in the *Aeneid*

In several publications I have argued that the Markan Evangelist imitated the *Iliad* and the *Odyssey*, most of which appear also in the Gospel of Luke.[4] The following list, however, includes only passages where Luke likely imitates the same passages in the *Iliad*, the *Odyssey*, the *Homeric Hymns*, and Euripides' *Bacchae* that Vergil earlier had imitated in the *Aeneid*. Although Luke could have been aware of Vergil's Homeric debts without having read the *Aeneid* himself, the parallels are so extensive and sophisticated that the most economical source of his knowledge would be his reading of the Latin epic himself.

1. The Annunciations of the Births of John, Jesus, and Aeneas (Luke 1:5–80; *Homeric Hymn to Aphrodite*; and *Aen.* 1.305–406)

2. Three Flying Visitors: The Spirit, Athena, and Apollo (Luke 3:21–22; *Od.* 1.88–324; and *Aen.* 9.656–660)

---

1. Pervo, *Dating Acts*. On Luke and the Second Sophistic, see, for example, Nasrallah, *Christian Responses*; and Carhart, "Acts and the Second Sophistic."

2. See especially Swain, *Hellenism and Empire*, 17–45. Swain discusses at length Plutarch, Dio of Prusa, Arrian, Appian, Aristides, Lucian, Pausanias, Galen, Philostratus, and Cassius Dio. See also Holford-Strevens, "*Utraque lingua doctus*"; Rochette, *Le Latin dans le monde grec*.

3. See MacDonald, "Luke's Antetextuality."

4. The most important of these publications are MacDonald, *Gospels and Homer*; Macdonald, *Luke and Vergil*; and Macdoanld, *Luke and the Politics of Homeric Imitation*.

3. The Divine Bloodlines of Jesus and Aeneas through Their Fathers (Luke 3:23-38; *Il.* 20.203-241; and *Aen.* 7.219-221)

4. Two Lords of Winds: Jesus and Aeolus (Luke 8:22-25; *Od.* 10.28-77; and *Aen.* 1.50-63)

5. Two Monsters in Caves: The Gerasene and Polyphemus (Luke 8:26-39; *Od.* 9.142-531; and *Aen.* 3.569-676)

6. Turning Soldiers into Swine: Jesus and Circe (Luke 8:31-33; *Od.* 10.135-465; and *Aen.* 7.10-20)

7. Jesus, Apollo, and Venus Stanch Hemorrhages (Luke 8:40-56; *Il.* 16.433-683; and *Aen.* 12.318-429)

8. Jesus, Nestor, and Evander Feed Multitudes (Luke 9:10-17; *Od.* 2.427—3.68; and *Aen.* 8.90-185)

9. The Transfigurations of Jesus, Odysseus, and Aeneas (Luke 9:28-36; *Od.* 16.172-303; and *Aen.* 1.588-613)

10. The Courage of Jesus, Achilles, and Aeneas (Luke 13:31-33; *Il.* 9.410-416; 18.95-121; and *Aen.* 10.467-469)

11. Two Rich Men in Hades (Luke 16:19-31; *Od.* 11.465-590; and *Aen.* 6.603-611)

12. The Untriumphal Entries of Jesus, Odysseus, and Aeneas (Luke 19:28-38; *Od.* 6.251—7.135; and *Aen.* 1.305-497)

13. Jesus, Priam, and Latinus Weep for Cities about to Fall (Luke 19:41-44; *Il.* 22.33-65; and *Aen.* 12.19-45)

14. Daughters of Jerusalem and Trojan Women (Luke 23:26-31; *Il.* 22.79-89; and *Aen.* 12.54-63)

15. Rescuing Corpses of Jesus and Hector: Joseph of Arimathea and Priam (Luke 23:50-53a; *Il.* 24.322-798; and *Aen.* 12.930-36)

16. Flesh and Bones: Jesus but not Anticleia, Creusa, and Anchises (Luke 24:37-40; *Od.* 11.204-22; and *Aen.* 2.793-94 and 6.700-702)

17. Bodies Snatched up into the Sky: Jesus, Aeneas, and Romulus (Luke 24:49-53; Acts 1:8-11; *Aen.* 1.257-59; 12.794-95; and Livy 1.16.1-7)

18. Two Outbreaks of Divine Madness: Jerusalem and Thebes (Acts 2:1-11; *Bacch.* 1-166; *Homeric Hymn to Apollo* 156-164; and *Aen.* 7.385-405)

19. Three Heroes with Radiant Heads: Stephen, Achilles, and Aeneas (Acts 6:8–7:60; *Il.* 18.205–275; and *Aen.* 10.270–275)

20. Cures for Two Aeneases (Acts 9:32–35; *Il.* 5.302–515; and *Aen.* 12.385–429)

21. Dorcas, Penelope, and Dido (Acts 9:36–42; *Od.* 2.1–128; and *Aen.* 4.63–73, 262–264, and 665–669)

22. Dreams to Military Commanders: Cornelius, Agamemnon, and Turnus (Acts 10:1–8; *Il.* 2.1–71; and *Aen.* 7.408–432)

23. Portents of Birds and Reptiles (Acts 10:9–11:18; *Il.* 283–335; and *Aen.* 2.199–227 and 5.84–103)

24. Miraculous Escapes: Peter, Priam, and Aeneas (Acts 12:1–17; *Il.* 24.431–801; and *Aen.* 4.238–594)

25. Three Councils and Embassies (Acts 15:1–35; *Il.* 9.1–88; and *Aen.* 9.224–449)

26. "Then We Set Sail" (Acts 16:9–12; *Od.* 9.1–42; and *Aen.* 3.4–17)

27. Four Fallen Young Men: Eutychus, Elpenor, Palinurus, and Misenus (Acts 20:5–12; *Od.* 10.551–574; 11.51–80; and 12.1–5; and *Aen.* 5.835–871; and 6.156–371)

28. Brave Heroes and Tearful Farewells: Paul, Hector, and Aeneas (Acts 20:13–38; *Il.* 6.360–502; and *Aen.* 2.671–789; and 12.430–43)

29. We-Voyages (Acts 27:1–8; *Od.* 9.1–61; and *Aen.* 3.1–18)

30. Shipwrecks (Acts 27:9–44; *Od.* 5.269–454; and *Aen.* 1.34–119)

31. Terra Firma and Friendly Natives (Acts 28:1–10; *Od.* 5.467—6.244; 13.63–72; and *Aen.* 1.173–613)

32. Three Reconciliations and Two New Kingdoms in Italy (Acts 28:11–31; *Od.* 24.426–548; and *Aen.* 12.820–37)

In several passages, Luke seems to imitate the *Aeneid* directly. For example, frequently in the Latin epic Olympian visitors inform Aeneas that it is his fate to settle the Trojan exiles in Italy (*Aen.* 2.270–781; 3.116–505; and 4.274–361). Similarly, heavenly visitors inform Paul that he must go to Rome (Acts 23:11 and 27:23–24). Acts' apparent incomplete ending—with Paul awaiting execution in Rome—resembles the abrupt ending of the *Aeneid*—with the death of Turnus that anticipates the Trojan victory in Italy.

To be sure, some of these analogous imitations between Luke-Acts and the *Aeneid* are stronger than others, but many are secure. Even if one grants only a few of them, one must ask how Luke knew of Vergil's debts to Homer. Marianne Palmer Bonz proposed that Luke knew the *Aeneid* from a Greek translation ascribed to C. Iulius Polybius, but this is highly unlikely insofar as the translation, which has not survived, obviously was less accessible than the Latin text itself.[5] The most obvious answer is to assume that Luke could read Latin, whether or not he could speak it.

The Case of Scevas

Few episodes in Luke-Acts are stranger than this:

> (13) Some itinerating Jewish exorcists attempted to name the name of the Lord Jesus on those who had evil spirits and said, "I adjure you by Jesus whom Paul preaches!" (14) Seven sons of a certain Scevas, a Jewish high priest, kept doing this. (15) When the evil spirit responded, it said to them, "I know Jesus and have knowledge of Paul, but who are you?" (16) The man in whom was the evil spirit lunged after them, subdued them all, and so overpowered them that they fled from that house naked and wounded.
>
> (17) This became known to all the Jews and Greeks who resided in Ephesus. Fear fell over them all, and they magnified the name of the Lord Jesus. (18) Many of those who believed began confessing and disclosing their [occult] practices. (19) Quite a few practitioners of the magical arts collected their books and burned them publicly. They assessed their value and found it to be fifty thousand silver [*drachmae*]. (20) By the power of God the word thus grew and strengthened." (Acts 19:17–20, author's translation)

This passage bulges with military imagery: ἐφαλόμενος, "lunged," κατακυριεύσας, "subdued," ἴσχυσεν, "overpowered," ἐκφυγεῖν, "fled," τετραυματισμένους, "wounded," κράτος, "power," and ἴσχυεν, "strengthened." It is "the evil spirit" who inflicts the violence.

The name Scevas (Σκευᾶς) never appears in lists of Jewish high priests and is a most unlikely name for a Jew.[6] It comes from the Latin

---

5. Bonz, *Past as Legacy*, 64.

6. Codex Bezae omits references to both Scevas and his sons as Jews; Scevas is simply called a priest, not a high priest. The density of textual variants for these eight

scaeva, "left-handed," which appears in a Greek inscription discovered in western Turkey to describe a left-handed gladiator; similar inscriptions with *scaeva* describe fighters in Latin.[7] Scevas is "Lefty." To understand the mimetic import of this name and the weird story about his seven sons one must turn to the *Iliad*.

Soon after Achilles returned to the fight, he faced an ambidextrous Trojan and seven of his allies. Homer's hero "holding his long-shadowy spear / lunged for Asteropaeus, eager to kill him" (*Il.* 21.139–140, author's translations). The Trojan, also eager for the fight, held two spears, one in each hand. Achilles asked him who he was, implying that his opponent had insufficient pedigree to make such a stand. "Who among men are you, and from what stock such that you dare to come against me? / Those who oppose my might are children of unfortunate parents" (21.150–151).

Asteropaeus responded by delineating his noble lineage—which included a river god—and by throwing two spears at once, "for he was ambidextrous [περιδέξιος]" (21.162–163). The Achaean then "leaped on him enraged" (21.174).

> He struck him in the stomach, beside the navel, and all his guts
> poured out to the ground.[8] Darkness hid his two eyes
> as he gasped. And jumping on his chest,
> Achilles stripped off his armor and gloated. (21.180–183)

He left the naked corpse at the shore of the Scamander, where "eels and fish attended to him, / biting and ripping the fat that covered the kidneys" (21.203–04). Immediately Achilles pursued and slew seven more warriors cowering in fear (21.209–210).

Compare the following:

Il. 21.139–210	Acts 19:14–17
Ambidextrous Asteropaeus claimed to be a descendant of a river god. (157–160)	"Seven sons of a certain Scevas [i.e., Lefty], a Jewish high priest," exorcised by using the name of Jesus as an apotropaic. (14)

---

verses reveals scribal consternation about this episode.

7. Robert, *Gladiateurs dans l'Orient grec*, 70–72 and 180–82. LSJ: "σκευᾶς, Lat. *scaeva*, gladiator fighting with his left hand" (supplement, 276).

8. Luke uses a similar expression to describe Judas's death in Acts 1:18.

Achilles taunted Asteropaeus: "Who among men are you [τίς . . . εἰς], and from what stock such that you dare to come against me?" (150)	"When the evil spirit responded, it said, 'I know Jesus and have knowledge of Paul, but who are you [τίνες ἐστέ]?'" (15)
Achilles "lunged [ἐπᾶλτο] for Asteropaeus, eager to kill him," and inflicted a lethal blow. His intestines spilled to the ground; Achilles stripped off his armor. (139–141, 180–185)	"The man in whom was the evil spirit lunged after [ἐφαλόμενος] them, subdued them all, and so overpowered them that they fled from that house naked and wounded." (16)
Achilles then found seven other foes "cowering in fear [πεφοβήατο]" from watching their comrade so brutally slain. He killed them as well. (206–210)	The flight of the sons of Scevas "became known to all the Jews and Greeks who were living in Ephesus, and fear [φόβος] fell on them all." (17a)

Nowhere else in the New Testament does one find the verb ἐφάλλομαι, "I leap on." It appears three times in the LXX, all in 1 Samuel with the spirit of God as the subject (10:6; 11:6; and 16:13). But the word is common in Homer, especially in the *Iliad*, to describe the aggression of fighters, as here in the Asteropaeus episode. A similar construction appears just before the kill: Achilles "leaped on him [ἆλτ' ἐπί οἱ] enraged" (21.174). The evil spirit does not slay Scevas' sons; it merely wounds them and puts them to flight naked.

A reader familiar with Roman history may have related Scevas to the most famous Roman lefty of all, Scaevola. Livy and other Latin authors told the tale of a Gaius Mucius, a Roman soldier who failed in a daring attempt to slay the Etruscan Porsenna and defiantly boasted to his captors of Roman valor. To illustrate his point, he thrust his right hand into a blazing fire until it crackled. Astonished by this demonstration of courage, Porsenna released Mucius, who from that time on was known as Lefty, *Scaevola* (Livy 2.12.1—13.1).

Silius Italicus, Luke's Roman contemporary, incorporated a descendent of Mucius Scaevola into his account of the Second Punic War. This Mucius Scaevola, "not unworthy of the right hand [*dextra*] of his ancestors," carried a shield that depicted his ancestral namesake burning his hand: "fire blazed on the altar; / Mucius stood in the center of the camp of the Tyrrhenians, as his rage / was turned against himself" (*Punica* 8.385–87). The shield also portrayed Porsenna "fleeing the burning right hand [*dextram*]" of his captive (8.389). In book 9, the younger Scaevola sought to die with heroism matching that of his older namesake.

Silius modeled the death of Scaevola after the death of ambidextrous Asteropaeus in *Iliad* 21, the very text that informed Luke's account of the seven sons of Scevas! Silius' Scaevola rushed forward to attack and, ironically, lopped off the right hand of one of his opponents. A Carthaginian named Nealces, "lunged forward, / prodded to do so all the more because of the famous name" Scaevola (8.393–394). With a boulder he crushed Scaevola's face; another Roman soldier stripped the corpse of its armor (410). Silius surely recognized similarities between the legend of Mucius Scaevola and Homer's ambidextrous Asteropaeus, from which he created his mimetic hybrid.

As far as I have been able to determine, the inscription in Turkey is the only other Greek transliteration of the Latin sobriquet *scaeva*. All other references to Mucius Scaevola and to other left-handers with the root *scaev*- are in Latin. One might expect that Dionysius of Halicarnassus, when retelling Livy's account of Mucius in Greek would have used the word Scaevola, but he does not (*Roman Antiquities* 5.27–30). For the wordplay to succeed in Acts as a flag to Homer's ambidextrous Asteropaeus, Luke and his readers would need to know at least that the name of the Jewish high priest was "Lefty" in Latin. The implications of Luke's knowledge of Latin extend well beyond observations concerning his linguistic and literary competence insofar as they encourage an investigation into his debt to popular Latin literature such as Livy's *Ab urbe condita libri* and especially Vergil's *Aeneid*.

Works Cited

Bonz, Marianne Palmer. *The Past as Legacy: Luke-Acts and Ancient Epic*. Minneapolis: Fortress, 2000.

Carhart, Ryan James. "Acts and the Second Sophistic: The Politics of Imitation and Self-Presentation." PhD diss., Claremont Graduate University, 2010.

Holford-Strevens, L. "*Utraque lingua doctus*: Some Notes on Bilingualism in the Roman Empire." In *Tria lustra: Essays and Notes Presented to J. Pinsent*, edited by H. D. Jocelyn and Helena Hurt, 203–13. Liverpool Classical Papers 3. Liverpool: Liverpool Classical Monthly, 1993.

MacDonald, Dennis R. *The Gospels and Homer: Imitations of Greek Epic in Mark and Luke-Acts*. New Testament and Greek Literature 1. Lanham MD: Rowman & Littlefield, 2014.

———. *Luke and the Politics of Homeric Imitation: Luke-Acts as a Rival to the Aeneid*. Lanham, MD: Rowman & Littlefield, 2018.

———. *Luke and Vergil: Imitations of Classical Greek Literature.* New Testament and Greek Literature 2. Lanham MD: Rowman & Littlefield, 2014.

———. "Luke's Antetextuality in Light of Ancient Rhetorical Education." In *Ancient Education and Early Christianity*, edited by Matthew Ryan Hauge and Andrew W. Pitts, 155–63. Library of New Testament Studies 533. London: T. & T. Clark, 2016.

Nasrallah, Laura. *Christian Responses to Roman Art and Architecture: The Second-Century Churches amid the Spaces of Empire.* Cambridge: Cambridge University Press, 2010.

Pervo, Richard I. *Dating Acts: Between the Evangelists and the Apologists.* Santa Rosa, CA: Polebridge, 2006.

Robert, Louis. *Les Gladiateurs dans l'Orient grec.* Bibliothèque de l'Ecole des hautes études, IVe section, Sciences historiques et philologiques 278. Amsterdam: Hakkert, 1971.

Rochette, Bruno. *Le Latin dans le monde grec: recherches sur la diffusion de la langue et des lettres latines dan les provinces hellenophones de l'empire romain.* Collection Latomus 233. Brussels: Latomus, 1997.

Swain, Simon. *Hellenism and Empire: Language, Classicism, and Power in the Greek World, AD 50–250.* Oxford: Clarendon, 1996.

13

The House Gathering and the Poor in the Gospel of Mark

DENNIS E. SMITH

In a seminal study published in 2004, Steve Friesen argued that the overwhelming majority of early Christians came from the ranks of the poor.[1] This is based partially on studies of the ancient world that conclude that most of the inhabitants of the Roman Empire were poor.[2] His study was focused primarily on the letters of Paul. But his data also fits the Gospel of Mark.

A close reading of Mark reveals that the idealized membership profile of Mark's community did not include the wealthy. The wealthy are like the seed planted among the thorns for whom the "lure of wealth" chokes off the word (4:18–19). They cannot enter the kingdom of God; their only chance is to sell off their possessions and give it all to the poor (10:17–23). To be sure, it is *possible* for the wealthy to enter the kingdom of God (10:23–27), but Mark tends to view the wealthy as outsiders while celebrating the poor and those who have sacrificed to care for the poor as the core membership of the community (10:28–31).

Just as the membership profile did not include the wealthy, so also its gathering space was not the synagogue. In specific contrast to the synagogue, the Gospel of Mark glorified the house. We find this contrast

---

1. Friesen, "Poverty in Pauline Studies."

2. See also Knapp, *Invisible Romans*, esp. 1–4, where he distinguishes between the 0.5 percent who made up the elites and the 99.5 percent that made up the rest of the population in the Roman world.

at the very beginning of Jesus' ministry, when he returns to Capernaum and goes first to a synagogue and then to a house.

> They went to Capernaum; and when the sabbath came, he entered the synagogue and taught.... Just then there was in their synagogue a man with an unclean spirit, and he cried out, "What have you to do with us, Jesus of Nazareth? Have you come to destroy us? I know who you are, the Holy One of God." But Jesus rebuked him, saying, "Be silent, and come out of him!" And the unclean spirit, convulsing him and crying with a loud voice, came out of him. (1:21-28 NRSV)

Here the synagogue is characterized as corrupt, as indicated by the presence of an "unclean spirit." The very existence of uncleanness in the synagogue is a symbol of its corruption. Jesus responds by casting the unclean spirit out of the man, and therefore out of the synagogue, just as later he will cleanse the temple (11:15-17). But he is unable to save either institution. Later in the story, when Jesus preaches in his hometown synagogue, he is rejected and he can only marvel at their unbelief (6:1-6).

In contrast to the synagogue, Jesus next enters the more welcome space of a house:

> As soon as they left the synagogue, they entered the house of Simon and Andrew, with James and John. Now Simon's mother-in-law was in bed with a fever, and they told him about her at once. He came and took her by the hand and lifted her up. Then the fever left her, and she began to serve them. (Mark 1:29-31)

The literary contrast between synagogue and house is clearly intentional, since they enter the house "as soon as they left the synagogue."[3] There is no unbelief or uncleanness to be found in the house, only an illness that prevents the appropriate hospitality from being offered. Once Jesus heals Simon's mother-in-law, she is able to carry out her role in the household, namely, "to serve them" (1:31; Greek: διακονέω, "serve at table"). She has a necessary role in order for the household to function as it should, and Jesus, by healing her, empowers her to carry out that role, that is, to offer hospitality.

In 2:15-17, the house is the location for a pivotal story that defines in idealized terms the social formation of the Markan community.

---

3. See also Boring, *Mark*, 65-66.

And as he reclined in his house, many tax collectors and sinners were also reclining with Jesus and his disciples—for there were many who followed him. When the scribes of the Pharisees saw that he was eating with sinners and tax collectors, they said to his disciples, "Why does he eat with tax collectors and sinners?" When Jesus heard this, he said to them, "Those who are well have no need of a physician, but those who are sick; I have come to invite (Greek: καλέω) not the righteous but sinners." (NRSV with modifications by the author)

Notice that this is a group gathered by Jesus; it is he who extends the invitation to the meal (2:17). Indeed, according to the logic of the story, the house, identified in the Greek only as "his house," is assumed to be Jesus' house. The story defines the group so gathered as engaged in community formation, which is the symbolism of "reclining together." The ancient banquet was universally understood to be a ritual moment for social bonding.[4] For the Markan community, therefore, the ritual of eating together in a formal, reclining banquet was where the magic happened, where the community was formed, and where redemption happened. Thus the concluding words of Jesus define this event as more than a mere meal: "Those who are well have no need of a physician, but those who are sick; I have come to invite (Greek: καλέω) not the righteous but sinners" (2:17). The Greek term καλέω functions here as a pun. It is both the standard term for an invitation to a banquet and a term for a religious calling. The invitation of Jesus to the meal represents symbolically an invitation into the community of God.

The story therefore connects the offering of hospitality in the house with the social formation of Jesus followers. As such, it fits with what we know about the ancient house from archaeological data. The house was designed so that guests in the home were to be received in the dining room where the host would be expected to offer the finest of his hospitality.[5] A standard dining room contained a *triclinium* or three-couch arrangement with the couches arranged in a "Π" or "U" shape. Each couch could hold, at minimum, three diners, so that nine diners would be the standard number for a triclinium setting. This was the standard size even for the most luxurious of settings in the houses of the elite.[6]

4. Smith, *From Symposium to Eucharist*, esp. 8-12, 16-17.

5. Clarke, *Houses of Roman Italy*, 1; see also Smith, "House Church as Social Environment," 9-10.

6. See examples in Smith, *From Symposium to Eucharist*, 17; and "Hospitality, the

For the Mark community, as idealized in the story, houses in which they would have met would not have been equivalent to elite houses of the type found in Pompeii and Ephesus. How then might we imagine a reclining meal in a simple non-elite house? They would not have had couches and luxurious place settings; therefore we should probably not imagine a triclinium-style banquet. More likely is the *stibadium* style in which diners were arranged in a Greek "sigma" or semi-circular shape. Such an arrangement is pictured in figure one. Here the diners appear to be reclining on cushioning arranged on the floor. This may be the style implied in the description of the room where Jesus and his disciples ate the last supper according to Mark. The room is described as a large upstairs room that had already been prepared for dining: "He will show you a large room upstairs, furnished and ready" (14:15) for a meal where they would be reclining (14:18; Greek: ἀνακειμένων αὐτῶν, "while they were reclining;" NRSV: "when they had taken their places"). The Greek term translated "furnished" in verse 15 is στρώννυμι, which literally means "to spread something." While it could mean to provide cushioning for couches, it could just as likely mean to spread the floor with cushioning. That is a style that makes sense of the kinds of modest house settings where the community of Mark would gather. It would be in a room that was not specifically designed for dining but which could be adapted for that purpose.

Reclining was a custom that marked social status. In the Greek tradition, only free male citizens reclined. If women, children, slaves, or social inferiors were included in the meal, they would normally sit. In the Roman period, it became more common for reclining to be made available to those who might traditionally be excluded. In such cases, reclining continued to carry the symbolism of status.[7] Thus when tax collectors and sinners are pictured as reclining together with Jesus, it represents a symbolic acceptance of them as being given equal status within the community of God.

Of course, tax collectors and sinners are not specifically the poor. Rhetorically, the term stands for a category of individuals who in Mark 2:15–17 are being vilified by "the scribes of the Pharisees" as being unacceptable. Their rhetorical status therefore is "not Pharisees." Also among the "not Pharisees" were the poor, as exemplified by the poor widow

---

House Church, and Early Christian Identity"; see also Dunbabin, *Roman Banquet*.

7. Smith, *From Symposium to Eucharist*, 16–17, 42–46.

(12:41-44), who is specifically contrasted with the scribes "who like to ... have the best seats in the synagogues and places of honor at banquets!" and who "devour widows' houses" (12:38-40).

Another text which symbolically pictures the community gathering is the multiplication of the loaves story in chapter 6:

> As he went ashore, he saw a great crowd; and he had compassion for them, because they were like sheep without a shepherd; and he began to teach them many things. When it grew late, his disciples came to him and said, "This is a deserted place, and the hour is now very late; send them away so that they may go into the surrounding country and villages and buy something for themselves to eat." But he answered them, "You give them something to eat." They said to him, "Are we to go and buy two hundred denarii worth of bread, and give it to them to eat?" And he said to them, "How many loaves have you? Go and see." When they had found out, they said, "Five, and two fish." Then he ordered them to get all the people to sit down (Greek: ἀνακλιθῆναι, "recline") in groups (Greek: συμπόσια συμπόσια, "symposia by symposia") on the green grass. So they sat down (Greek: ἀνέπεσαν, "reclined") in groups of hundreds and of fifties. Taking the five loaves and the two fish, he looked up to heaven, and blessed and broke the loaves, and gave them to his disciples to set before the people; and he divided the two fish among them all. And all ate and were filled; and they took up twelve baskets full of broken pieces and of the fish. Those who had eaten the loaves numbered five thousand men. (6:34-44)

Just prior to this story is this reference: "The apostles gathered around Jesus, and told him all that they had done and taught" (6:30). This takes the reader back to an earlier text where Jesus sent them out two by two with these instructions: "Wherever you enter a house, stay there until you leave the place. If any place will not welcome you and they refuse to hear you, as you leave, shake off the dust that is on your feet as a testimony against them" (6:10-11). Note that their mission included fostering the practice of hospitality in the house.

Between the sending out of the apostles and their return to report to Jesus was found the story of a banquet given by Herod "for the leading men of Galilee." This was a banquet of such debauchery that it resulted in the death of John the Baptist (6:14-29).

In specific contrast to the banquet of Herod, Jesus' banquet is held in "a deserted place" (6:31). Instead of the elite who attend Herod's banquet

(6:21), Jesus' guest list is made up entirely of a motley group identified only as "a great crowd" (6:34). Later in Mark's story the difference between these two meal scenes will be emphasized: "Watch out—beware of the yeast of the Pharisees and the yeast of Herod" (Mark 8:15). That is to say, one's identity is defined by the meal community of which one is a part—you are who you eat with.

The multiplication of the loaves story draws on the theme of hospitality. The crowd serves as the stranger in the hospitality equation. The disciples want to send them away to find food on their own, but Jesus commands "you give them something to eat" (6:37) which is what they eventually do (6:41). The disciples are thereby being instructed in the practice of hospitality.

There is more at stake here than simple hunger. This is clear when Jesus commands that the people are to recline in separate dining groups, "symposia by symposia" (6:39).[8] This is tantamount to saying, "have the people prepare themselves for a banquet." Here in the rural countryside Jesus has convened a series of substitute house churches, with each dining group symbolically representing a separate house church. Then he prepares for them a sumptuous meal with the appropriate ceremonial prayers.

The command that all should recline can be compared with Jesus' meal with tax collectors and sinners in which they all reclined together with Jesus. This is an important component of the way in which the Markan meal community was intended to function. It has an effect similar to the Mishnah's rule regarding the Passover: "even a poor man in Israel does not eat until he reclines."[9]

The Social Structure Supporting the House Church

A house church required a supportive social structure. First, someone needed to be available who could provide a house in which to meet. Such an individual would function culturally as a benefactor, which would suggest some degree of social stratification in the Markan community.

---

8. Collins points out that the division of the reclining groups into "hundreds and fifties" (6:40) is a reference to the divisions of the eschatological community as described in the *Damascus Document*. She acknowledges, however, that this is a shift in imagery from the description in 6:39 that they reclined "symposia by symposia" (*Mark*, 324–25).

9. *Mishnah Pesahim* 10.1, as quoted in Smith, *From Symposium to Eucharist*, 147.

However, there is no reason to posit a very high degree of social stratification nor should one assume that they would have met in grand houses. Rather, while often it is primarily the grand houses that survived for archaeological investigation, there are enough examples of modest housing for us to imagine where the less-than-elite might have lived.[10]

One character whom Mark may have idealized as a literary stand-in for a host is Levi, the tax collector (2:13–14). Interpreters have often noted how anomalous his story is, for, unlike every other named character who is "called," Levi is not included in Mark's list of the twelve.[11] In the context, he is addressed by Jesus with the single phrase, "follow me." Immediately after this, Jesus hosts other tax collectors and sinners in a banquet in "his house." Matthew and Luke both interpret the house to belong to Levi; following their lead the NRSV translates "Levi's house" in Mark 2:15. That is a misleading translation, however, since the Greek simply reads "his house" (2:15), and, given the logic of the story in which Jesus serves as the host, the author appears to assume that the house belongs to Jesus. When Jesus says to Levi, "follow me," we are to imagine that, by observing and participating in the meal that follows, Levi is being instructed in the proper way to host Jesus' followers in one's house. Similarly, when in chapters 6 and 8 Jesus multiplies the loaves to feed the crowd, these stories function as teaching stories for the disciples. Jesus tells them to feed the crowd, then demonstrates how it is to be done. After arranging the crowd into dining groups and ceremonially blessing the food, he then gives it to the disciples to serve. It is as if the Jesus of Mark is saying to the community leaders: "this is how hospitality in the house is to be practiced."

At any reclining banquet, it was necessary that there be servants. Normally those servants were slaves, and normally they would go unnoticed by the diners. In Mark, those who serve the meal are singled out as important figures in the community, ranging from Peter's mother-in-law (1:31) to the disciples at the multiplication of the loaves stories (6:41, 8:6). This is not entirely unprecedented. After all, in the classic hospitality story from the Hebrew Bible, Abraham himself serves his guests (Gen 18:8). On the other hand, in the Pauline communities, while he mentions the existence of slaves, he never defines their roles at the meals (compare 1 Cor 7:21–26 with 11:17–34). In Mark, however, perhaps because there

---

10. See examples in Hirschfeld, *Palestinian Dwelling*; see also Smith, "House Church as Social Environment," 7–8.

11. Boring, *Mark*, 80; Collins, *Mark*, 190–91.

is a greater consciousness of the underclass as the core members of the community, serving at the table is an honorary task, as seen especially in the use of the term διακονέω to describe the action of Peter's mother-in-law (1:31), a term whose basic meaning is "to serve at table." This idea became embedded in Christian tradition through the preservation of the term "deacon" as a designated task and position of honor at the community gatherings.

Normally, it was the householder who served as host of the meal and controlled the guest list. That is the model Jesus embodies when he dines with tax collectors and sinners. However, on the symbolic level, that story implies that, whoever may host the meal on the earthly level, Jesus is the one who invites. At that level, the story is parallel to other cultic meals of the day, in which the god is the one who invites to the banquet.[12]

Conclusion

The narrative of the Gospel of Mark privileges the house as a gathering place for the followers of Jesus, especially in opposition to the synagogue. It also privileges the poor as the primary members of the house gathering. An archaeological and social analysis of the Greco-Roman house as a gathering place illustrates the importance of the banquet as the focal point for such gatherings. The social environment of the house gathering, which was marked by hospitality at the banquet, became a means in the narrative for social formation and for embedding the poor in the community as full and equal members.

Works Cited

Boring, M. Eugene. *Mark: A Commentary*. New Testament Library. Louisville: Westminster John Knox, 2006.
Clarke, John R. *The Houses of Roman Italy, 100 B.C.—A.D. 250: Ritual, Space, and Decoration*. Berkeley: University of California Press, 1991.
Collins, Adela Yarbro. *Mark: A Commentary*. Hermeneia. Minneapolis: Fortress, 2007.
Dunbabin, Katherine M. D. *The Roman Banquet: Images of Conviviality*. Cambridge: Cambridge University Press, 2003.
Friesen, Steven J. "Poverty in Pauline Studies: Beyond the So-Called New Consensus." *Journal for the Study of the New Testament* 26 (2004) 323–61.

12. Compare the second-century inscribed invitations of *Zeus Panamaros* from Caria in Asia Minor, in which the standard phrase is "the god invites you to the sacred feast" (Smith, *From Symposium to Eucharist*, 80–84).

Hirschfeld, Yizhar. *The Palestinian Dwelling in the Roman-Byzantine Period*. Collectio minor (Studium Biblicum Franciscanum) 34. Jerusalem: Franciscan (Israel Exploration Society), 1995.

Knapp, Robert. *Invisible Romans*. Cambridge: Harvard University Press, 2011.

Smith, Dennis E. *From Symposium to Eucharist: The Banquet in the Early Christian World*. Minneapolis: Fortress, 2003.

———. "Hospitality, the House Church, and Early Christian Identity." In *Mahl und religiöse Identität im frühen Christentum*, edited by Matthias Klinghardt and Hal E. Taussig, 103–18. Texte und Arbeiten zum neutestamentlichen Zeitalter 56. Tübingen: Francke, 2012.

———. "The House Church as Social Environment." In *Text, Image, and Christians in the Graeco-Roman World: A Festschrift in Honor of David Lee Balch*, edited by Aliou Cissé Niang and Carolyn Osiek, 3–21. Princeton Theological Monograph Series 176. Eugene, OR: Pickwick Publications, 2011.

14

Jesus and Sympotic Desire

DAVID H. SICK

In the year 46 BCE, the Roman orator and statesman Marcus Tullius Cicero accepted a dinner invitation. It was not a momentous event. The one-time leader of the republic was in internal exile, living "in letters," as he says, and Julius Caesar was surging, almost at the apex of his political power (*Ep.* 9.26.1). Yet the social event signified mores and structures of power. Cicero found himself at "that type" of party. *Epistulae ad Familiares* 9.26 chronicles his surprise when he discovered that the mime actress and lover of Mark Antony, Volumnia Cytheris, was a fellow guest at the home of Volumnius Eutrapelus, and she was reclining on a couch next to the host no less! The surprise may be feigned, but the consequences and context all too real. Cicero would rail against Antony in the *Philippics* three years later, and the triumvir would reply by demanding and literally receiving the greatest Latinist's hands and head.

The reader may recognize the difficulty of Cicero's social situation. We often must make decisions about the parties or dinners we will attend. A guest cannot be certain what or whom exactly he or she may encounter on any specific evening. If only in youth, many have made choices about sexual activities and mind-altering substances at a party. A host, moreover, may have sufficient economic or political or social clout to demand attendance or at least make rejection risky. These considerations are noted in Cicero's letter: he makes reference to the "servitude" (*Ep.* 9.26.1) under which he must operate and claims that sexual enticements, "such things" (9.26.2) in the conservative language of the author, then sixty years old, did not move him even as a young man. The letter does not mention the amount of wine consumed at the *cena* "dinner," but Mark Antony, not present that evening, was infamous for his heavy drinking, and these partiers were members of his crew.

A modern audience may even recognize some of Cicero's strategies in dealing with the situation. He takes a place on a couch between two of his close friends (9.26.1), bulwarks against easy approach. He furthermore alleges that the letter itself is a reaction: he composed it while reclining just before the dinner began—perhaps the first Tweet in Western history. He explains to his friend Paetus, the addressee, "My god—I did not suspect that she would be here" (9.26.2).[1] Yet it strains credulity that Cicero could compose a five-hundred-word, disparaging letter while reclining and without anyone questioning him. More notably, the defender of the republic did not depart, but he was not at liberty to do so without offending the host who was a client of Antony then in political ascendancy with Caesar. Yet Cicero notes the long relationship between philosophers and courtesans (9.26.2) and confesses the pleasure he takes from the conversations at *convivia* "dinner parties" (9.26.3), in which, in his own mind at least, he excelled. He points to examples of clever thinkers who have turned such tense social situations to their advantage: "I change groans into the greatest laughs" (9.26.3).

The anecdote has much to commend it to students of the character Jesus in the gospels, which are full of comparable social situations. Should one dine with the powerful but corrupt? Certainly the allegation that he dined with sinners and tax collectors raises that question. Whom should one invite to a dinner party? The numerous parables about inviting random folks on the street forces the audience to confront the conventional practice (Matt 22:1-10; Luke 14:15-24). Where should one sit at dinner parties? Jesus answers the disputes among the disciples about their relative importance in sympotic terms (Luke 22:24-30). How should a diner react when one of the guests is of questionable morals, at least in conventional terms? The entrance of the sinful woman to Simon the Pharisee's home epitomizes that issue in a personal way (Luke 7:36-51). How much should one drink and eat? The wedding at Cana (John 2:1-12) inverts the former, and Jesus' own symposium (Mark 6:39) of fish and bread nullifies the latter.

What is more, there is now a general but certainly not universal consensus in New Testament studies that dining scenes in the New Testament

---

1. All translations from Greek and Latin are my own.

are portrayed in keeping with those of the classical tradition. Members of the Meals in the Greco-Roman World Seminar of the Society of Biblical Literature, including Kathleen Corley, Matthias Klinghardt, Dennis Smith, and Hal Taussig, have encouraged these advances in interpretation and effected much of the work themselves.[2] The most important contributions of the last three scholars are included in the bibliography below. Whether the classically influenced portrayals are the consequence of the agenda and perspectives of the evangelists or reflect actual historical events continues to be debated, and we will address the difficulty of resolving that question in this essay as well. A claim for dining in keeping with the customs of the larger Mediterranean does not, however, deny Jesus' Jewish background, because such dining practices and attitudes were adopted within the communities of Hellenistic Judaism well before the first century. In fact, those scholars, such as Craig Blomberg, who oppose the classical reading of the dining scenes tend to argue against Hellenistic influence in general, limiting Graeco-Roman culture to the elite. In this context opponents must go so far as to claim that Greek verbs meaning "to recline" at a meal in the New Testament are actually shorthand for "to sit."[3]

Social commentary on dining in classical literature dates back to the Greek lyric authors if not Homer himself, and in making that statement we do not deny a parallel vibrant tradition of commentary in Hebrew literature, found in texts such as Proverbs, the Wisdom of Ben Sira, and legal documents. The most famous, even paradigmatic, classical sympotic writings were by two students of Socrates—Plato and Xenophon, most famously in their respective works entitled *Symposium*. For many of these sympotic works, but especially for Plato and Xenophon, sex and love are associated with the symposium or cena, both because of literary precedent but no less because of cultural tradition. To give an interpretative example, Greek, Roman, and Hebrew poets wrote love poems where the setting is supposed to be a dinner party, but sometimes actual poets did recite poems to their lovers, or, more vulgarly, sex partners, at actual dinners. Cicero himself noted the association of prostitutes, or at least dancing girls, with classical dinner parties, while he both attended and participated in the party described above. We will develop this connection between literature and social practice further below.

2. See Corley, *Private Women*; Klinghardt, *Gemeinschaftsmahl und Mahlgemeinschaft*; Smith, *Symposium to Eucharist*; Taussig, *In the Beginning*.

3. Blomberg, *Contagious Holiness*, 95 96, with earlier citations.

Our thesis for this essay will combine two premises—the sexual and the sympotic—but neither can be sufficiently examined here. We ask the reader to accept the premises for the sake of the argument. If dining scenes in the New Testament are presented in keeping with classical literary genres if not actual social practices, and if literary and historical symposia and cenae are sites of social tension with regard to love and sex, we should expect that love and sex are issues for the dining scenes of the New Testament. Our method for proving this doubly premised thesis will be to examine closely several dining scenes from different canonical gospels, both in John and the synoptics, as well as one saying from the non-canonical Gospel of Thomas. In this examination we will propose sources, mainly classical but with some attention to the Judaic as well, that treat similar social phenomena, literary topoi, or philosophical and theological ideas. Once we have completed the close reading of these scenes, we will interpret the themes that emerge from a synthetic reading of the passages. The primary objective of the essay is to reorient the educated readings of the texts concerned with commensality in the New Testament, but because the dining scenes are spread across the ancient sources on Jesus, our conclusions should have implications for the modern understanding of the historical Jesus as well.

The Sinful Woman of Luke 7:36-51

In chapter 7 of the Gospel of Luke (7:36–51), a woman, identified by the narrator as "some woman who was a sinner in the city" (7:37) enters the home of Simon the Pharisee, where Jesus is reclining as a guest at dinner. The uninvited guest proceeds to kiss Jesus' feet and anoint them with a mixture of perfume and her own tears, wiping them with her hair. Because of the assessment of the authorial voice and because of her very actions at the dinner, an ancient, if not a modern, audience might conclude that her sins are of a sexual nature, and, consequently, the same audience might wonder about Jesus' participation in a banquet where such activities occurred.

Kathleen Corley in her book *Private Woman and Public Meals* investigates thoroughly those women who are documented at banquets with Jesus in the synoptic gospels. For the most part, women who associate with Jesus in Luke assume a subservient role in keeping with traditional mores of upper-class Hellenistic society, Corley concludes, but the sinful woman of Luke 7 is an exception. Corley believes that she is a prostitute or lower-class wage earner.[4] Her exact crimes are not important to our study—only the implication that they were of a sexual nature. She is a sinner of some sort, because Jesus forgives "her many" sins in vv. 47 and 48. The expression "some woman who was a sinner in the city" would imply public exposure and, from an ancient perspective, a lack of modesty and thus heightened sexuality. Criticism of women in the ancient Mediterranean tended toward the sexual because males controlled the media and the gender of women defined them as distinct from men according to the conventional male perspective. So whatever the woman's crimes, sexual impropriety would easily be assumed by the male diners at the banquet.[5] Whether the unnamed woman was a prostitute, adulterer, promiscuous, or even if her crimes were non-sexual, the consequence for Jesus would be the same. The public of his own time and the audience of Luke would want to know why the master would attend a party where such a woman was present. In fact, the host of the banquet raises that question, albeit oddly, since he is the host and the party is in his home: "The Pharisee who had invited (Jesus) said to himself, 'If this man were a prophet, he would know what sort of a woman was touching him'" (7:39). One might respond by pointing out the host's own hypocrisy: "Well, if you, Simon, are a Pharisee, why is this sexy Sally, as you allege, at your own party in your own home?" If the host was wealthy enough to put on splendid feast, then he was sure to have had a costly house with slaves to watch the door, such as we see at the famous dinners of Agathon, Callias, and Trimalchio in Plato (*Symp.* 174e, 212d), Xenophon (*Symp.* 1.11), and Petronius (28–30) respectively. The guest-list was the host's responsibility, but any explanation for the woman's entrance must necessarily be speculative.[6]

The sensual quality of the encounter between Jesus and the woman would only intensify the concern of the audience, and the possible sexual connotations of her actions would be obvious from either a Near Eastern or a Graeco-Roman perspective. The unnamed woman looses her hair to wipe Jesus' feet, which are wet with her tears; as she performs this act she begins to kiss his feet and concludes by anointing them with myrrh (Luke 7:38). Although the act is surely an unusual one, especially because of the

---

4. Corley, *Private Women*, 108–46.

5. See, for example, Richlin, "Invective against Women in Roman Satire"; Henderson, "Satire Writes 'Woman'"; Dixon, *Reading Roman Women*, 36–40; and Corley, *Private Women*, 53–66.

6. See Derrett, *New Resolutions*, 124; LaGrange, *Evangile*, 228; Gallo, "'Peccatrix in civitate,'" 85.

weeping, the meaning of this complex of actions should be understood in the social context of the banquet at which they occur. That qualification is key: these events are taking place at a banquet. We should first try to understand the ostensible meaning from the immediate context and then turn to implied meanings from other contexts, such as burial or religious cult. The latter interpretative contexts are necessarily metaphorical or allegorical.[7]

For a woman to unbind her hair in public was a sign of extreme emotion, a setting aside of normal etiquette. Among the possible emotions demonstrated was sexual desire, but also grief and religious ecstasy.[8] The first of these is the most likely to occur at a Graeco-Roman banquet. The second-century writer Apuleius probably provides the best examples of the sexual significance of unbound hair from Graeco-Roman literature. In his novel the *Metamorphoses*, the main character asserts that a bald Venus, despite all her other alluring qualities, would go unwanted (*Metam.* 2.8). When this same character pleads with his mistress to fulfill his desires, he summarizes the request with these words: "loose your locks in a torrent and return loving embraces with your hair flowing in waves" (*Metam.* 2.16). To turn to Judaic custom, J. F. Coakley has assembled a collection of rabbinic sources that condemn women for appearing in public with head uncovered or hair unbound, and a few verses from the Song of Solomon (4:1; 5:11; 6:5; 7:5) argue for the voluptuousness of loose, long hair.

The kissing of Jesus' feet by a sinful woman has an obvious sexual implication, even if we are correct to set aside an actual euphemism of feet for penis, as is possible in Hebrew, because of the public context.[9] The act additionally demonstrates subservience, and such subservience is easily transferable to sex in an ancient context. Derrett notes an exchange between the philosopher and one-time slave Epictetus and his students. The philosopher cites kissing the feet of a beloved as an act done out of some coercion, implying that the lover is enslaved by love.[10] A similar

---

7. The other evangelists place the pericope closer to Jesus' passion, and Jesus himself references his coming burial (Matt 26:12; Mark 14:8; John 12:7). The immediate context in all cases is a meal.

8. Cosgrove, "Unbound Hair," collects many examples of women with unbound hair. He concludes that a first-century audience would *not* interpret the sinful woman's act sexually (688), although in my view he underestimates the consequence of the sympotic context.

9. See examples at Exod 4:25; Isa 7:20; Ruth 4:3, 7.

10. Derrett, *New Resolutions*, 126; Epictetus, *Diatr.* 4.1.17.

theme may be found in the writings of the Latin elegists, who occasionally describe their pleading at the feet of their beloved.[11] A pertinent example from a sympotic context is found in Ovid's *Amores* (1.4). The poet describes a banquet in which he himself, his mistress, and her husband are all guests. Ovid, or at least his poetic voice, pleads with his lover to touch his feet furtively as she passes, as a sign of her love. The reclining posture of the banquet, with dangling, exposed feet would provide such an opportunity, as it does in the episode in Luke 7.[12]

The washing and even anointing of feet was a custom of hospitality in both Graeco-Roman and Near Eastern cultures, with the washer or anointer almost always in the subservient position, but these perfumes were also used as a prelude to romance, as is demonstrated again by the Song of Solomon (1:3, 12, 13; 3:6; 4:6, 10, 13; 5:1, 5, 13), and social servitude may at times be transferred to the servitude of love or sexual attraction.[13] Athenaeus, in his long catalogue of dining practices, offers four examples of prostitutes or slaves massaging the feet of patrons with perfumes. Three are included in a section on decadence; the best excerpt comes from a comedy by the fourth-century Attic poet Antiphanes:

> And so, aren't I right to be a lady's man and enjoy all the call girls? Because, first off, this thing you're doing right now, that is, rubbing my feet with your soft, beautiful hands, how is that not respectable?[14]

The issue of pleasure and propriety to which the courtesan's patron alludes is very similar to the one which Simon the Pharisee ponders to himself and Jesus subsequently divines. Foot-washing is socially acceptable, even necessary, but one must be careful not to slip into hedonism or sexual desire.

Luke 7:36-51 in the Context of Sympotic Sexuality

As I implied above, this scene in Luke contains many of the conventional elements of a Graeco-Roman symposium or cena and the genre of

11. See Ovid, *Am.* 1.7.61-2; Propertius 4.8.72; Tibullus 1.9.30.

12. Note κατεκλίθη in v. 36.

13. See Thomas, *Footwashing in John 13*, and the lists of Coakley, "Anointing at Bethany," 247-48; Thomas deemphasizes any sexual connotation of footwashing, even in his own examples.

14. Athenaeus 13.553c-d; the other examples are at 6.257a, 12.553a, and 13.583f.

literature related to that social custom. The interpretative structure has been supplied by several scholars, most thoroughly by J. Delobel and E. Springs Steele.[15] It is important to note that Jesus himself, when he addresses the group, also interprets the acts of the woman as a part of the hospitality of a banquet: Simon did not provide water for foot-washing, the woman used tears. Simon did not kiss him in welcome; the woman kissed his feet. Simon did not anoint his head with perfumes; the women anointed his feet (7:44–46). In each case, Simon fails to demonstrate a heart-felt reception for his guest, while the sinful woman's actions indicate her deep gladness at Jesus' presence at the banquet. A kiss of greeting between two adult males would be viewed as emotional and affectionate in Mediterranean cultures, inappropriate unless in extreme circumstances, and Luke's use of the verb καταφιλέω ("to kiss," 7:38, 45), with the preposition used intensively, agrees with this standard for the custom. There are three other instances in the Lukan corpus where males kiss one another: the betraying kiss of Judas (22:47), the return of the prodigal son (15:20), and the rescue of Paul from the shipwreck (Acts 20:37)—all obviously emotionally charged events.[16] The anointing of the head was more common than the feet; at Petronius 70.12, the anointing of the feet is called in hyperbole "an unheard of custom" (*inauditus mos*). The fragrance was viewed as a formal, albeit luxurious, preparation for the celebration.[17]

The Graeco-Roman dinner party was fraught with or delighted in sexuality; one might say that the expectation of the sensual was the default setting of any such gathering. The employment of beautiful slaves to serve at the event was a sign of social rank.[18] Flirtation or even couplings between guests, either male-male or male-female, was not uncommon, as the example from Ovid given above evinces. In fact, lovers are stock characters of the sympotic genre of literature.[19] The traditional entertainments were risqué—scantily clad dancers or musicians of both genders,[20]

---

15. Delobel, "L'onction"; Steele, "Luke 11:37–54."

16. See Delobel, "L'onction," 431.

17. Clarke, "Jewish Table Manners," 262. See also Horace, *Carm.* 2.7.7–8; or Josephus, *Ant.* 14.54, 19.58; and Josephus, *Ag. Ap.* 2.256 for other ancient examples.

18. See D'Arms, "Slaves at Roman Convivia"; Dunbabin, "Waiting Servant"; Roller, *Dining Posture in Ancient Rome*, 30–34.

19. Martin, *Symposion*, 113–16.

20. Starr, "Evening with the Flute Girls"; Davidson, *Courtesans & Fishcakes*, 81–83; Fear, "Dancing Girls of Cadiz."

and prostitutes were accustomed to attend or even host dinners and symposia for their patrons.[21] The symposium of Xenophon, at which the guests decide to pursue philosophic conversations, still ends with a pantomime dance by a handsome maiden and youth, dressed as Ariadne and Dionysus respectively. At the end of the performance the unmarried male guests vow to marry, and the married ride home quickly to make love to their wives (*Symp.* 9).

The influence of the paradigmatic symposia of Xenophon and Plato should not be underestimated in this regard, since love, in its various forms, was a topic of conversation at both. It is the main topic of conversation in Plato's account; it is discussed several times at Xenophon's (*Symp.* 5, 8, *et passim*). Many later accounts of sympotic gatherings either model themselves after these paradigms or at least respond to them.[22] Plutarch lists them at the head of eight famous literary symposia written by philosophers,[23] and Lucian's *Symposium* provides striking examples of both the literary and social influences of the earlier masterpieces. His tale of philosophers invited to a wedding banquet uses a narrative technique similar to one employed by Plato. Both works begin with professed confusion about the actual attendees at the affair, and thus there is a question about whose account can be trusted. More intriguing is the uninvited guests' use of a phrase from Homer in both works: they reference *Iliad* 2.408, where Menelaus arrives at a feast of Agamemnon without direct invitation.[24] Lucian's narrator alleges that the excuse is now something used commonly (ἐκεῖνο τὸ κοινόν), implying that the literary device has made its way into social practice. From a modern context and a different artistic register, one might compare toga parties on college campuses to the form itself found in the film *Animal House*. Because of the priority of Plato and Xenophon, both historically and artistically, and the prominence of theme of love and sex in their sympotic creations, later authors

---

21. See Corley, *Private Women*, 34–52; Keuls, *Reign of the Phallus*, 160–70; Davidson, *Courtesans & Fishcakes*, 1–97, 104–8. Athenaeus devotes much of book 13 (555a–599c) of his treatise on dining to anecdotes about famous prostitutes.

22. Martin, *Symposion*, 1, notes two subdivisions within the genre: the first focuses on the food and accompanying entertainments, such as Athenaeus' *Deipnosophistae*; the second focuses on the conversation, in keeping with Plato and Xenophon.

23. Plutarch *Quaest. conv.* 1 proem. (612e): "Plato, Xenophon, Aristotle, Speusippus, Epicurus, Prytanis, Hieronymus, and Dio of the Academy."

24. See Plato, *Symp* 174c, and Lucian, *Symp.* 12.

who ventured into the same or similar genres had to confront those same topics.

Let me be clear: not all symposia and cenae were wild or even mild orgies, but one had to be careful to make the distinction. The banquets of philosophers or guilds or for religious commemorations would have their own proper characteristics, but they cannot be neatly or easily separated from the traditional conventions, and sexuality is a component of the tradition. If a symposium is to *exclude* sexual pursuits, the hosts and guests must be clear about that revision of convention. Some examples may help to convince. Before they begin their philosophic conversations and rhetorical performances, the guests at both Plato's and Xenophon's symposia must "say goodbye to the flute-girl."[25] The musicians and dancers have been hired; they perform briefly according to custom, but the audience of intellectuals intervenes and turns the entertainment in a new direction. These versions again set the model by which later ones must respond. The limited treatment of sexuality by the philosophers in Plutarch's sympotic dialogues is a consequence of that model. In his *Sympotic Questions* (3.6), the assembled philosophers respond to a statement made in the *Symposium* of Epicurus, namely that it is better to have sex before dinner, during the day, than after dinner at night. The intertextualities of the discussion are stunning: philosophers at a symposium discuss a matter proposed in a literary account of an earlier philosopher's symposium, which, in turn is probably responding to an incident in an even earlier sympotic antecedent, namely the conclusion of Xenophon's work, mentioned above. That conclusion is, in fact, referred to in Plutarch's account (653c). Moreover, all of these works allege to be historical records of actual convivial gatherings. Hence, Plutarch, who without doubt wants to wrest the sympotic genre away from decadence and award it to philosophy, must be very careful here.[26] An uninhibited conversation about having sex after dinner, especially with young men present, might incite the discussants to actions in keeping with sympotic sexuality, and, thus, the company first must agree that the topic is decent for a philosophic gathering. The company concludes that it cannot be shameful to say or hear anything useful about intercourse, even while drinking (653e).[27]

---

25. Plato, *Symp.* 176e; Xenophon *Symp.* 3.1–3.
26. Again, see Plutarch, *Quaest. conv.* 1.1.
27. See the comments of König, *Saints and Symposiasts*, 164.

The most pertinent example to a first-century Judaic context comes from Philo's description of the feasts of the Therapeutae (*Contempl.* 40–90), ascetics who resided communally on a hill above Lake Mareotis near Alexandria, Egypt.[28] The συμπόσια of these φιλόσοφοι (both terms that Philo uses throughout the work) were very different from most Hellenic or Hellenistic examples, although the account is surely idealized. To start with, wine was not served, only water, and the only foodstuffs were bread, salt, and hyssop (37, 73–74). Wine, the narrator alleges, may not only incite desire but even animalistic cannibalism (40–43, 74). Both male and female members of the community (68–69) attended these symposia held every seventh sabbath (65), but they reclined separately on opposite sides of the room, separated by a wall that did not reach the ceiling. One diner reclined on each simple couch made from planks and strewn papyrus (69). There were no beautiful slaves serving the reclining diners (50–52), for young members of the community assumed these duties (71–72). According to Philo, these are the true philosophers, not Xenophon and Plato, for the latter permitted various forms of sensuality at their famous gatherings:

> They [the symposia of Xenophon and Plato] were recorded as worth remembering for what examples of proper conduct in symposia posterity should use, they supposed, but if compared to those (of the Therapeutae), who have embraced the contemplative life, they will seem to be a joke, for each contains pleasures ... (57–58)

Philo must acknowledge yet deny the earlier philosophic paradigms, for even though they prohibited sexual activity, some degree of pleasure was allowed (58–63). The flute girls played before dismissal, and there was frequent talk of erotic desire. The difference in atmosphere of the symposia of this community and that of the banquet at the home of Simon the Pharisee seems clear. No female member of the community would sneak to the other side of the room and anoint a man's feet with myrrh and dry them with her hair, at least no man or woman from the perfect world outlined by Philo.

---

28. The identity of the Therapeutae (male) and the Therapeutrides (female), to what extent they were Jewish and of what sect, to what extent they were a community, and even whether they existed at all, continues to be debated. See Niehoff, "Symposium of Philo's"; Taylor, *Jewish Women Philosophers*; Taylor and Davies, "So-Called Therapeutae."

The sinful woman's mere presence at the feast of Simon, not to mention her actions, would be signs that the event would fit with other sensuous examples. The responsibility for the atmosphere of the party lies primarily with the host, however, as we have noted. A guest could not be certain what exactly he or she would encounter on any specific evening, as Cicero indicated to his readers above. One might, of course, choose to leave a symposium if the entertainments or atmosphere proved inappropriate. Pliny the Younger, later in the first century CE, received a letter from the teacher of rhetoric Julius Genitor, who left a dinner when various types of clowns were introduced as the entertainment. Pliny calls one troupe *cinaedi* (*Ep.* 9.17.1, 2), an insult applied to effeminate males, so sexual humor or sensuous dance was probably a part of their routine. In his response Pliny pleads with Genitor, whom elsewhere he describes as "even a little too rough and harsh for the license of the times," to be more accepting of others' tastes.[29]

In comparison to the reactions of Cicero and Genitor, Jesus is much more indulgent. Conservative moralists might even suggest that he use Cicero or Pliny's friend as his standard for proper behavior. To begin with, the prophet permitted the behavior. Cytheris certainly did not massage Cicero's feet; just her attendance was enough to incite a moral, if somewhat posed, crisis. Jesus did not "demand his shoes" (*calceos poscunt*) when the woman entered, to use the Latin idiom of Pliny's letter meaning to depart from a banquet (*Ep.* 9.17.3). In fact, the account in Luke does not indicate when exactly the woman stopped massaging Jesus' feet. Her sins were forgiven, and she was dismissed at the end of the pericope (7:48, 50), but Jesus instructs the host and guests with a short parable and critiques the hospitality of the host before these summative acts. The scene would have been truly remarkable if the woman continued to touch and kiss the feet of the prophet while he addressed the Pharisee. The imperfect verbs κατεφίλει and ἤλειφεν (7:38) do imply repeated, on-going action. Instead of moral indignation at sexual impropriety, Jesus directs his criticism at the host for his failure to behave in a way similar to the sinful woman! Simon was behaving less appropriately than the woman was.

---

29. See Pliny, *Ep.* 9.17 and 3.3.5.

Other Examples of Sensual Dining in the Gospels

If the events at Simon's banquet were the only evidence to link Jesus to conventionally disreputable and sensuous behavior, that evidence might be easily dismissed as anomalous. There are, however, several other gatherings that raise questions about Jesus' behavior and attitude toward the expression of desire in convivial contexts. The sinful woman of Luke 7 is not the only woman who positions herself at Jesus' feet at dinner. In chapter 10 of the same gospel (vv. 38–42), the prophet is entertained at the house of Mary and Martha. Martha is described as Jesus' host; in fact, some early and important manuscripts specify that the home itself belongs to Martha, and the verb Luke chooses (ὑπεδέξατο) is the same he uses for the activity of the hosts Zacchaeus, the chief tax collector (19:6), and Jason of Thessalonica, who bails Paul out of jail in Acts 17.[30] If there were male members of the family present, they are not explicitly mentioned. Such interaction between unrelated men and women would be considered liberal if not improper.[31] Mary, moreover, sits at Jesus' feet and listens to his sermon. The conventional time for such a presentation would be after dinner, during a symposium, and Mary would be at the foot of Jesus' couch, just as the sinful woman of Luke 7. Such an arrangement would imply some close relationship between the two—familial, pedagogical, and/or sexual/romantic.[32] Mary, furthermore, fails to fulfill the traditional duties of a host at the meal thus stirring her sister's complaints (40). Even if the pericope is to be read as a metaphor for spiritual service, it is a metaphor whose ostensible meaning is based on dining. Although the vocabulary of this section—"receive," "sit by," "service," "serve," "stand by," and "portion"—need not refer to a meal or banquet, taken together these words strongly argue for such a context.

In a home near Tyre, a Syro-Phoenician woman also threw herself at Jesus' feet to beg for the health of her daughter, according to the Gospel of Mark (7:24–30).[33] The prophet's association with a Gentile woman might

---

30. ... ὑπεδέξατο αὐτὸν [εἰς τὸν οἶκον αὐτῆς] "... and she received him [into her own home] (10:38)." The expanded version is represented in many modern translations, and there are also variant readings for vv. 41 and 42.

31. Corley, *Private Women*, 59–66, 133–44.

32. The question of Mary's posture is a red herring. Whether she sits or reclines on the couch, the fact that she shares Jesus' couch implies a relationship between the two. See Roller, *Dining Posture*, 96–156.

33. The scene is a public one in Matt 15:21–28. The priority of Mark's version is generally accepted. See Focant, "Mc 7.24–31 par. Mt 15.21–29," 52–60.

easily raise concerns from a Jewish perspective; Mark describes her as Syro-Phoenician by ethnicity but also a Greek (26), and thus she was likely to know the sympotic and convivial practices of the Hellenistic culture. The scene is not clearly depicted as a banquet, but the woman's clever retort to Jesus' initial denial of her request fits best with the context of the dining room. Her use of the aphorism, "Even the dogs under the table eat from the crumbs of the children" (7:28), encourages the audience to imagine a convivial context, even if Jesus and his companions were not dining when the unwelcome female guest entered the house. If Jesus and his companions were reclining and dining above her, her complaint would have been even more poignant. She reacted with quick wit to the holy man's use of the derogatory metaphor "dog, puppy" (κυνάριον) by placing it in the metaphorical if not spatial context of the dining room.[34] She was doubly clever if she intended to refer to herself as a Cynic, either jokingly or earnestly, rather than a bitch, since Cynics might plant themselves on the floor at feasts and/or accept scraps, and, according to Gerald Downing, only a Cynic would accept the title κυνάριον without insult.[35] The women most-commonly credited with clever apophthegms at dinner in Graeco-Roman culture were prostitutes, however. The use of *chreiai* (clever sayings) was a common tactic of both courtesans and Cynics, at least according to literary portrayals, and a dialogue in book thirteen of Athenaeus sets the philosophers and prostitutes against each other in a battle of wits, as also noted by Cicero in his letter above.

To turn to non-canonical sources, we must consider saying 61 of the Gospel of Thomas. In that passage the woman Salome states that Jesus has "climbed onto (her) couch and eaten from (her) table as a stranger."[36] The context is clearly Hellenistic and likely sympotic. Although Jesus is now the guest on the floor, the audience is to envision him and Salome reclining on a couch and reaching out to dine from a table positioned at its end. The extant Coptic version is a translation of a Greek original, borrowing τράπεζα ("table") in accord with sympotic terminology and containing at least one other Graecism.[37] A man and woman sharing a couch at a meal would again imply a close association, especially with the

---

34. Dufton, "Syrophoenician Woman," 417 suggests the wordplay between the woman and Jesus.

35. Downing, "Woman from Syrophoenicia." For Cynics dining on the floor, see notably Diogenes Laertius 6.46 (Diogenes), and Lucian, *Symp.* 13–14.

36. The translation comes from Valantasis, *Gospel of Thomas*.

37. For a discussion of the original Greek, see Attridge, "Greek Equivalents," 30–32.

possible sexual connotation of the verb "to climb." If the original Greek verb was ἀναβαίνω, that verb allows a secondary meaning of "to mount" with reference of the male on the female. One does not usually assume a place upon a couch by climbing on to it, whatever the original Greek, unless first splayed upon the floor, and thus the statement implies issues about Jesus' own behavior in addition to any promiscuity on the part of Salome. She, however, implicitly argues against the sexual allusion by her statement, "I am your disciple," later in the logion and thus establishes herself in the same difficult social position as Mary in Luke 10 noted above. As a disciple, Salome may assume a place at the feet of her teacher with less risk of sexual association.

The Beloved Disciple in a Sympotic Setting

The final example will serve as a key to understanding this complex of significant sensuality. The depiction of the Last Supper in the Gospel of John differs in several respects from that of the synoptic gospels: it is only loosely connected to the festival of Passover and the seder (13:1); Jesus washes the feet of the disciples before the meal (13:4–10); Jesus makes several speeches during the course of the meal, recorded over four chapters of text (13–16); and his words not the meal itself are the focus of the text, in keeping with the subgenre of the philosophic symposium. Even if we do identify the meal in John as a seder, that ritual itself, whether solely in literary portrayal or in actual practice, seems to have been influenced by Graeco-Roman culture by the first century CE, as noted by Bahr, Stein, Noy and others.[38] Famously in both the Palestinian and Babylonian Talmud one finds: "On the eve of Passover, close to *minḥah*, one does not eat until it gets dark. And even a poor man in Israel does not eat until he reclines" (*m. Pesahim/b. Pesahim* 10:1).[39]

John also uses the scene to draw attention to the disciple ὅν ἠγάπα ὁ Ἰησοῦς (13:23), traditionally called "the Beloved Disciple," or, more literally, "the disciple whom Jesus loved" or even "with whom Jesus was in love," to emphasize the on-going aspect of the imperfect tense of the verb.[40]

38. Bahr, "Seder of Passover"; Stein, "Influence of Symposia Literature"; Noy, "The Sixth Hour."

39. The translation comes from Bahr, "Seder of Passover," 183, 185. See also Smith, *Symposium to Eucharist*, 133–72.

40. Much of the scholarship on the Beloved Disciple focuses on his role in the composition of the gospel; his identity is important to tracing the textual history. The

During the meal Jesus announces that one of the disciples will hand him over to the authorities. He subsequently identifies that individual, Judas, with a commensal gesture, presenting him with a bit of bread dipped in wine (13:26). The declaration disturbs the other disciples, and they direct questions to the Beloved Disciple who lies next to Jesus, (ἀνακείμενος ἐν τῷ κόλπῳ, 13:23), which would mean, "lying on/at his breast." A few verses later (13:25) and at the end of the gospel (21:20), the disciple is said to fall back ἐπὶ τὸ στῆθος "toward/on Jesus' chest" in order to speak with him. This individual, because of his intimate position, his epithet, and the sympotic context would be assumed to be Jesus' lover by any audience with minimal exposure to the Graeco-Roman symposium as either a social practice or a literary genre.[41]

For lovers of the same sex or different sexes, to recline next to each other at a banquet is well attested in Graeco-Roman literature and art.[42] As noted above, lovers were stock characters in the sympotic genre. The most famous example comes from Plato's *Symposium*, where one finds Alcibiades sharing a couch with his old love Socrates and his new interest Agathon, after the young politician stumbles into the party late and drunk (213b). Alcibiades also recounts his attempt to seduce Socrates at a previous private dinner where they shared a couch (217d). Other same-sex couples from sympotic literature would include Callias and Autolycus from Xenophon's *Symposium* (1.2; 1.8–11; 8.7–8, 37, 42), Pausanias and Agathon from the same work of Plato (193b), Diphilus and Zenon from Lucian's *Symposium* (26, 29), Solon and Aesop from Plutarch's *Symposium of the Seven Wisemen* (150a, 152c), and Silenus and Dionysus from the Emperor Julian's banquet of the Caesars (308c).[43] The context in John, just as that found in Luke 7 surrounding the sinful woman, would have contributed to the suspicion of a romantic relationship. The scene comes only one chapter after the Johannine reflection of Luke 7. In John's version, it is Mary, the sister of Lazarus who anoints Jesus' feet with perfumes and dries them with her hair, and subsequently Jesus himself strips down

---

historical identity of the individual has little bearing on our discussion.

41. A few commentators have suggested that the Beloved Disciple was the *eramenos* of Jesus but without supporting exegetical or critical framework. See Phipps, *Sexuality of Jesus*, 69–72; Martin, *Sex and the Single Savior*, 96, 99–100.

42. For artistic representations, see the groundbreaking work of Dover, *Greek Homosexuality*, 94, C42, R200, R283, R795, R797. Representations of heterosexual couples at banquets are also extant. See Dunbabin, *Roman Banquet*, 52–63, plates I–II.

43. Martin, *Symposion*, 113–16.

to a loin cloth and washes the feet of the disciples at the beginning of this last earthly banquet (13:4). The phrase ἐν τῷ κόλπῳ ("on/at his breast") is highly charged and multivalent. It may connote a sensual, romantic, or familial relationship but it can even convey a spiritual connotation, as in the special phrase "the breast of Abraham" (ὁ κόλπος Ἀβραάμ), found at Luke 16:22. There it signifies a special honor after death, perhaps in association with the celestial banquet. The usage in sexual or romantic contexts is frequent, since ὁ κόλπος may also imply either the vagina or cleavage of a woman. In Euripides' *Helen*, Zeus conceives his daughter ἐν κόλποις Λήδας "in the lap of Leda" (1145–46). Yet, at *Iliad* 6.136, Diomedes tells the tale of the baby Dionysus who fled under the ocean where Thetis received him in her lap/breast (κόλπῳ). In short the meaning of the phrase is often sexual but need not necessarily be so.

The same audience that knew well the conventions of the symposium would notice that the relationship between master and disciple is marked in an unusual way, however. If there was a physical relationship between Jesus and the Beloved Disciple, why did the author of John avoid the usual terms for such a relationship—*erastēs* (ἐραστής), "lover," and *erōmenos* (ἐρώμενος), "beloved"? These are terms that are sprinkled liberally throughout well-known works of the sympotic genre, notably in the speeches of Phaedrus and Pausanias in Plato's *Symposium* (178a–185e) and Socrates' speech toward the end of Xenophon's treatise of the same title (8). They derive from the Greek verb ἐράω which at its root indicates physical, sexual desire and may, of course, be used in reference to an attraction between two people of the same of or different sexes.[44] The names for the roles of the Beloved Disciple and Jesus in their relationship should strictly be *agapōmenos* and *agapastēs* respectively, since they would derive from the verb ἀγαπάω, famously important in New Testament theology, not ἐράω. The former of these is a regular, participial formation of the verb but the latter is curiously not extant, to my knowledge.[45] There is no indication that the bond between Jesus and the Beloved Disciple was expressed physically, beyond the closeness of the dining couch. There is not a direct statement in John of an unambiguous sexual act between them. The audience encounters many of the signs of the traditional physical desire of a sympotic setting without open sexual-

---

44. See Dover, *Greek Homosexuality*, 42–54, for a review of the vocabulary and its development.

45. ἀγαπητός, regularly used in the New Testament and translated as "beloved," is a verbal adjective in origin, and at its root implies obligation or necessity—"one who must be loved."

ity. Jesus furthermore uses ἀγαπάω with regard to the desire of the sinful women in Luke: "her sins, which are many, have been forgiven, because she loved (ἠγάπησεν) much" (7:47), and thus in that pericope we also find the external signs of sexuality but the emotion expressed in sum by a verb that eschews sexuality.

Philosophical and Theological Meanings

The gospel writers were not alone in struggling with the sexual elements in the sympotic paradigms. We have already noted the admonitions of Philo's treatise on the Therapeutae. The *erastēs/erōmenos* formulation, whose institutional framework practically ceased after the classical period in Greece, was a particular problem for later philosophical writers who rejected sexual expression in general, and all later authors who were distrustful of same-sex relations. In Plutarch's *Sympotic Questions* 8.2, for example, the conversants in fact pretend to be lovers as a joke (719a) when trying to a solve a thorny Platonic problem.[46] Note also the relationship between the Neopythagorean philosopher Apollonius of Tyana and his faithful disciple Damis. Philostratus' biography emphasizes Apollonius' celibacy and general asceticism, although Damis was called the *erastēs* of his teacher. That language mimics the Platonic proposition that the divine member of the pair should be the beloved and the human pursuer the lover.[47] From a Christian context, the second-/third-century bishop Methodius transforms the classic lovers of the symposium into Christ and the Church as bride and bridegroom (*Symp.* 2.7; 3.8–10; 6.4–5; 7.1, and elsewhere) or into a spiritual union of virgin and Christ (*Thecla's Hymn*). His *Symposium* (or *Treatise on Virginity*) is a panegyric on celibacy and thus the original, implied eroticism of the literary genre is highly diminished.[48] Instead of speeches in praise of love, the ten virgins—all women—honor celibacy and its attending benefits, including attainment of the Platonic heaven where the true forms reside (8.3).[49]

---

46. See Roskam, "Plutarch's 'Socratic Symposia,'" 67, for a discussion of this passage.

47. See Philostratus, *Vit. Apoll.* 1.13.3; 1.19.3.

48. See, however, König, *Saints and Symposiasts*, 51–76, who argues that Methodius has a more positive attitude toward physical desire than many of his contemporaries in the emerging church.

49. The notes in the edition of Bonwetsch provides an extensive, running list of allusions to Plato, *Symp.* as well as all other Platonic works.

There even seem to have been conflicting interpretations of the nature of the relationship between Jesus and the Beloved Disciple within the Johannine community itself. That gospel concludes with a brief debate about the status of ὃν ἠγάπα ὁ Ἰησοῦς:

> And Peter, seeing (the one whom Jesus loved), said to Jesus, "Lord, what about this man?" Jesus said to him, "If I wish him to remain until I come, what is it to you?" And so the story spread among the brothers that that disciple would not die. Yet Jesus did not say to him that he would not die, but "If I want him to remain until I come, [what is it to you?]" (John 21:21-23)

One assumes that the beloved of Jesus, even without physical expression between the two, would have a special claim to eternal life, or, at least, one understood by some to be the lover of Jesus would have naturally been granted such special status. The text makes clear that not all accepted the tradition related to his status and that differing understandings of the relationship between Jesus and that disciple arose. The textual history reflects these disputes, since the final chapter appears to be a later addition that responds to the death of a historical individual assumed to be the Beloved Disciple.[50]

Such a dissonance between a sexually charged environment and a lack of physical expression would correspond to that presented at many philosophic symposia, since most philosophic schools of classical antiquity believed the physical to be an impediment to the cultivation of the psychic or, at least, argued for a separation of the two. Yet Jesus' lack of sexual expression does seem to have more in common with the Platonic and Xenophonic ideas of love than a general disdain for the physical. We should not ignore the resolution of the flirtatious affair between Socrates and Alcibiades: the relationship was not physical in nature. Socrates rejected his student's advances, at least according to Plato (*Symp.* 213d, 217-219). Xenophon's Socrates also devalues physical expression, claiming the love (*eros*) of the soul is better than that of the body, for the former of these produces positive human associations and good deeds through *philia* (8.10-30). The unconsummated flirtation may be most thoroughly interpreted through Socrates' speech about love in Plato, where he proposes that physical desire is a means to a greater form of love, a non-sensual, psychic love (201d-212a). He reports a discussion

---

50. A large majority but not all commentators view the chapter as an addition, although the authorship is unknown.

with a mysterious Mantinean woman, Diotima, who explains the instrumental value of sexual desire. By noting the common nature of beauty in all physical bodies one desires, the lover discovers beauty as a more general concept and possibly even the divine form of beauty itself, "in which all beautiful (and thus good) things must participate (211e)."[51]

The instrumental value of the sensuous scenes in the gospels also seems evident. By surrounding Jesus with courtesans and lovers, foot washing and free-flowing hair, kisses and couch companions, the authors of these episodes incite an expectation of titillation, but Jesus, as either literary character or historical being, redirects this physical excitement to a metaphysical one. Jesus does not abuse the sinful woman to fulfill his physical desire but describes it as something other than *eros*; he forgives her sins and grants her peace (Luke 7:48, 50). Similarly, his love for the Beloved Disciple is not expressed sexually, as is the case with that of many Graeco-Roman deities, but as with Alcibiades and Socrates, that love is a potential means to greater revelations to follow. For Alcibiades, the relationship results in a "philosophic madness," leaving him "struck in heart or soul by the arguments of philosophy" (218a). For the Beloved Disciple, the love of Jesus is expressed in the crucifixion and resurrection, which directly follow that last symposium in John, and in a direct linguistic connection to the new commandment unveiled at that event: "that you love (ἀγαπᾶτε) each other, just as I have loved (ἠγάπησα) you" (13:34). The relationship between Jesus and the Beloved Disciple in essence inverts the structure described in Plato, where the divine, since it is beautiful and immortal, is the *erōmenos*. In John, the beloved is human, and Jesus is the divine figure who pursues him. The introduction of *agape* and associated vocabulary to the sensual context of the symposium also solves a cumbersome problem of language encountered in Plato and Xenophon. One no longer need distinguish between the two types of *eros*, the heavenly and the common (Plato, *Symp.* 180e, etc.; Xenophon, *Symp.* 8.9–10, and so forth). If we are correct and there is an instrumental value to the sexual or sensual expressed in the gospels, then a review of the concept of *agape* seems warranted. We cannot, however, take up that investigation here but leave it to theologians and philosophers.[52]

51. The bibliography on this topic is, of course, immense. See the Works Cited for further reading, including Dover, *Greek Homosexuality*, 153–70.

52. A foundational work on this topic is Nygren, *Agape and Eros*. For developments subsequent to Nygren, see Osborne, *Eros Unveiled*; and Grant, "For the Love of God: Agape."

Works Cited

Attridge, Harold W. "Greek Equivalents of Two Coptic Phrases: CG I, 1.65, 9-10 and CG II, 2.43.26." *Bulletin of the American Society of Papyrologists* 18 (1981) 27-32.
Bahr, Gordon J. "The Seder of Passover and the Eucharistic Words." *Novum Testamentum* 12 (1970) 181-202.
Blomberg, Craig L. *Contagious Holiness: Jesus' Meals with Sinners*. New Studies in Biblical Theology 19. Downers Grove, IL: InterVarsity, 2005.
Bonwetsch, G. N. *Methodius*. Die griechische christliche Schriftsteller 27. Leipzig: Hinrichs, 1917.
Charlesworth, James H. *The Beloved Disciple: Whose Witness Validates the Gospel of John?* Valley Forge, PA: Trinity, 1995.
Clarke, William M. "Jewish Table Manners in the *Cena Trimalchionis*." *Classical Journal* 87 (1992) 257-63.
Coakley, J. F. "The Anointing at Bethany and the Priority of John." *Journal of Biblical Literature* 107 (1988) 241-56.
Corley, Kathleen E. *Private Women, Public Meals: Social Conflict in the Synoptic Tradition*. Peabody, MA: Hendrickson, 1993.
Cosgrove, Charles H. "A Woman's Unbound Hair in the Greco-Roman World, with Special Reference to the Story of the 'Sinful Woman' in Luke 7:36-50." *Journal of Biblical Literature* 124 (2005) 675-92.
D'Arms, John H. "Slaves at Roman *Convivia*." In *Dining in a Classical Context*, edited by William J. Slater, 171-83. Ann Arbor: University of Michigan Press, 1991.
Davidson, James N. *Courtesans & Fishcakes: The Consuming Passions of Classical Athens*. New York: St. Martin's, 1997.
Delobel, J. "L'onction par la pécheresse." *Ephemerides theologicae lovanienses* 42 (1966) 415-75.
Derrett, J. Duncan M. *New Resolutions of Old Conundrums: Fresh Insight into Luke's Gospel*. Shipston-on-Stour, UK: Drinkwater, 1986.
Dixon, Suzanne. *Reading Roman Women: Sources, Genres, and Real Life*. London: Duckworth, 2001.
Dover, K. J. *Greek Homosexuality*. Cambridge: Harvard University Press, 1989.
Downing, F. Gerald. "The Woman from Syrophoenicia, and Her Doggedness: Mark 7:24-31 (Matthew 15:21-28)." In *Women in the Biblical Tradition*, edited by George J. Brooke, 129-49. Studies in Women and Religion 31. Lewiston, NY: Mellen, 1992.
Dufton, Francis. "The Syrophoenician Woman and Her Dogs." *Expository Times* 100 (1989) 417.
Dunbabin, Katherine. *The Roman Banquet: Images of Conviviality*. Cambridge: Cambridge University Press, 2003.
———. "The Waiting Servant in Later Roman Art." *American Journal of Philology* 124 (2003) 443-68.
Fear, A. T. "The Dancing Girls of Cadiz." *Greece & Rome* 38 (1991) 75-79.
Focant, Camille. "Mc 7.24-31 par. Mt 15.21-29: critique des sources et/ou étude narrative." In *The Synoptic Gospels: Source Criticism and the New Literary Criticism*, edited by Camille. Focant, 39-75. Bibliotheca Ephemeridum theologicarum Lovaniensium 110. Leuven: Peeters, 1993.
Gallo, S. "'Peccatrix in civitate' (Lc 7, 36-50)." *Verbum Domini* 27 (1949) 84-93.
Grant, Colin. "For the Love of God: Agape." *Journal of Religious Ethics* 24 (1996) 3-21.

Henderson, Jeffrey. "Satire Writes 'Woman': *Gendersong*." *Proceedings of the Cambridge Philological Society* 25 (1989) 50–80.

Keuls, Eva C. *The Reign of the Phallus*. New York: Harper & Row, 1985.

Klinghardt, Matthias. *Gemeinschaftsmahl und Mahlgemeinschaft: Soziologie und Liturgie frühchristlicher Mahlfeiern.* Texte und Arbeiten zum neutestamentliche Zeitalter 13. Tübingen: Francke, 1996.

König, Jason. *Saints and Symposiasts: The Literature of Food and the Symposium in Greco-Roman and Early Christian Literature*. Greek Culture in the Roman World. Cambridge: Cambridge University, 2012.

LaGrange, M.-J. *Evangile selon Saint Luc*. Études bibliques. Paris: Coffre, 1948.

Martin, Dale B. *Sex and the Single Savior: Gender and Sexuality in Biblical Interpretation*. Louisville: Westminster John Knox, 2006.

Martin, Josef. *Symposion: Die Geschichte einer literarischen Form*. Studien zur Geschichte und Kultur des Altertums 17,1/2. Paderborn: Schöningh, 1931.

Niehoff, Maren R. "The Symposium of Philo's Therapeutae: Displaying Jewish Identity in an Increasingly Roman World." *Greece, Roman, and Byzantine Studies* 50 (2010) 95–116.

Noy, David. "The Sixth Hour Is the Mealtime for Scholars: Jewish Meals in the Roman World." In *Meals in a Social Context: Aspects of the Communal Meal in the Hellenistic and Roman World*, edited by Inge Nielsen and Hanne Sigismund Nielsen, 134–44. Aarhus Studies in Mediterranean Antiquity 1. Aarhus: Aarhus University Press, 1998.

Nygren, Anders. *Agape and Eros*. 2 vols. Translated by Philip S. Watson. Chicago: University of Chicago Press, 1953.

Osborne, Catherine. *Eros Unveiled: Plato and the God of Love*. Oxford: Clarendon, 1994.

Phipps, William E. *The Sexuality of Jesus*. Cleveland: Pilgrim, 1996.

Richlin, Amy. "Invective against Women in Roman Satire." *Arethusa* 17 (1984) 67–80.

Roller, Matthew B. *Dining Posture in Ancient Rome: Bodies, Values, and Status*. Princeton: Princeton University Press, 2006.

Roskam, G. "Plutarch's 'Socratic Symposia': The *Symposia* of Plato and Xenophon as Literary Models in the *Quaestiones Convivales*." *Athenaeum* 98 (2010) 45–70.

Smith, Dennis E. *From Symposium to Eucharist: The Banquet in the Early Christian World*. Minneapolis: Fortress, 1993.

Starr, Chester G. "An Evening with the Flute Girls." *Parole del passato* 33 (1978) 401–10.

Steele, E. Springs. "Luke 11:37–54—a Modified Hellenistic Symposium?" *Journal of Biblical Literature* 103 (1984) 379–94.

Stein, S. "The Influence of Symposia Literature on the Literary Form of the Pesaḥ Haggadah," *Journal of Jewish Studies* 8 (1957) 13–44.

Taussig, Hal. *In the Beginning was the Meal: Social Experimentation and Early Christian Identity*. Minneapolis: Fortress, 2009.

Taylor, Joan E. *Jewish Women Philosophers of First-Century Alexandria: Philo's "Therapeutae" Reconsidered*. Oxford: Oxford University Press, 2003.

Taylor, Joan E., and Philip R. Davies. "The So-Called Therapeutae of *De Vita Contemplativa*." *Harvard Theological Review* 91 (1998) 3–24.

Thomas, John C. *Footwashing in John 13 and the Johannine Community*. Journal for the Study of the New Testament: Supplement Series 61. Sheffield: Sheffield Academic, 1991.

Valantasis, Richard. *The Gospel of Thomas*. New Testament Readings. London: Routledge, 1997.

15

Gluttony and Drunkenness as Jewish and Christian Virtues

From the Comic Heracles to the Christ of the Gospels

COURTNEY J. P. FRIESEN

Many philosophical moralists and religious pietists have pondered and debated the place of alcohol and food in the life of the virtuous and enlightened individual. In ancient Mediterranean cultures, numerous stances were adopted, ranging from absolute abstinence to ritual drunkenness, from feasting to fasting, with diverse justifications to offer. This study explores the role of eating and drinking in Jewish and Christian constructions of virtue, particularly strategies for excusing, condoning, or even valorizing gluttony and drunkenness in legendary heroes.[1] The analysis converges around two of antiquity's most famous and popular heroes, both divine men who acquired a reputation for excessive eating and drinking: Heracles and Christ. The comparison of these two

1. This essay represents an abbreviated and revised version of the paper of the same title submitted for the 2017 Paul J. Achtemeier Award for New Testament Scholarship (Society of Biblical Literature). I am most grateful to the participants at the SBL session in Boston for their constructive suggestions, especially the moderator (Laurence Welborn), panelists (Albert Harrill and Jennifer Knust), and Melissa Sellew who, as always, offered warm encouragement and probing insights. A closely related presentation was also delivered at the Manfred Lautenschläger Colloquium hosted by the University of Chicago Divinity School—I thank my "Lautenschläger cohort" and also Michael Cover and Margaret Mitchell for their thoughtful advice, and finally my colleague Arum Park for kindly reading this in its earliest draft.

heroes foregrounds the study's second and interrelated line of inquiry, that is, to revisit from a fresh angle possible influences from the cults and mythologies of Heracles on Judaism and Christianity. As early as Justin Martyr (*1 Apol.* 21; *Dial.* 69), interpreters have been attentive to commonalities between Christ and Heracles: both were born of a human and divine parent; acquired universal kingdoms; underwent suffering and death in obedience to their divine fathers; descended into Hades to overcome mortality; and finally ascended into heaven.[2] Yet, no one, to my knowledge, has considered (alleged) gluttony and drunkenness as a common feature of their heroic biographies. This oversight is surprising given that Heracles' drinking problem and prolific appetite will have been well known to anyone familiar with Greek comedy;[3] and Jesus' reputation as a "glutton and a winebibber" was proverbial already within the earliest gospel sources and has a strong claim to historical authenticity (Luke 7:34 = Matt 11:19).[4]

Evidence of literary influences from Heracles legends on the New Testament gospels are notoriously inconclusive, and no such hypothesis will be advanced here.[5] The most one can say with confidence is that the

---

2. Within modern scholarship on Christ and Heracles, see, e.g., Pfister, "Heracles und Christus"; Rose, "Herakles and the Gospels"; Toynbee, *Study of History,* 6:465–86; Knox, "'Divine Hero'"; Simon, *Hercule et le Christianisme*; Malherbe, "Heracles"; Aune, "Heracles and Christ." Another biblical hero commonly compared with Heracles is Samson; see Eusebius, *Praep. ev.* 10.9.7; Augustine, *Civ.* 18.19.

3. New Testament scholarship in general has rarely explored the significance of comic drama; on Paul, however, see esp. Grant, "Early Christianity and Greek Comic Poetry," 157, 160; Welborn, *Paul, the Fool of Christ*; Cover, "Divine Comedy at Corinth." Albert Harrill demonstrates that characters in Luke and Acts cohere closely to stock comic types, such as Rhoda the "running slave" in Acts 12 and "the dishonest manager" in Jesus' parable (Luke 16) (Harrill, *Slaves in the New Testament*, 59–83).

4. Translations of all texts are mine throughout. The claim for the historical authenticity of this allegation does not establish anything about Jesus' actual behavior. This slogan was slander and as such likely distorted reality.

5. Pfister made a case for the gospels' dependence upon a Cynic-Stoic Heracles biography ("Heracles und Christus"). The detailed list of parallels compiled by Pfister has remained unconvincing, however, not least because many of them are superficial and belong more broadly to numerous Greco-Roman heroes. Already Rose ("Herakles and the Gospels") issued a decisive rebuttal, and more recent scholarship has been influenced by Toynbee's suggestion of "folk-memory" (*Study of History,* 6:465–86). That is, Toynbee argued for influence from Heracles legends on the gospels; but this resulted from various cultural mechanisms, such as cult and ritual. Toynbee's approach has been adopted by, e.g., Simon, *Hercule et le Christianisme*, 56–63; Malherbe, "Heracles," 661–63; Aune, "Heracles and Christ," 11–13.

gospels were first produced and read in communities where knowledge about Heracles as a cultural hero would have been ubiquitous and inevitable, and similarities in narrative presentation could have emerged naturally and would have been readily detectable by at least some readers. Yet, whereas direct literary connections between the gospels and Heracles are lacking, Philo of Alexandria, a contemporary Jewish intellectual, cites the hero's drunkenness as evidence of his virtuous character, reflecting at length on Euripides' satyr play the *Syleus* in his ethical treatise *That Every Good Person Is Free*. As such, Philo represents a cultural bridge between the biblically informed world of Hellenistic Judaism central to the formation of Christianity and traditional Greco-Roman divine men such as Heracles. His appropriation of the hero's excessive eating and drinking as a moral exemplum offers fresh insight into this study's two driving problems, that is, the place of gluttony and drunkenness in Jewish and Christian piety and the role of Heracles in shaping their religious ideals.

The analysis proceeds in three sections. First, I survey classical sources on the comic Heracles, noting especially his close association with banquets and symposia. The second section examines Philo as a participant in and critic of Greek and Roman culture, highlighting his religious attitudes toward drunkenness, on the one hand, and his treatment of Heracles, on the other. It is especially noteworthy that Philo construes the persistence of Heracles' comic persona even while temporarily in the status of a slave as evidence of the hero's virtuous character and possession of genuine freedom. In the third section, I take up Jesus' reputation for excessive eating and drinking in the gospels. As Philo does with Heracles, the gospel writers manage to turn what Jesus' critics took as a vice into evidence of higher spiritual virtue, in his case the inauguration of the messianic banquet.

Heracles between the Banquet and the Comic Stage

In the modern world, Heracles is best known for his feats of strength, especially his celebrated labors which already in antiquity developed into a canonical list of twelve.[6] These super-human achievements have a timeless quality that still today lend themselves to action movies and

---

6. The standard treatment of Heracles in antiquity remains Galinsky, *Herakles Theme*. See also Anderson, "Heracles and His Successors."

comic books.[7] For the ancients, however, Heracles was a complex and varied character. Though honored with cultic celebrations widely across the Greek and Roman world, he was ambiguously positioned between divine and human status. Subjected to the hostile whims of Hera and her relentless persecution, he was driven to madness so that he slaughtered his own wife and children (Euripides, *Herc. fur.*; Seneca, *Herc. fur.*). Consequently, he was relegated to servitude under Eurystheus. Nevertheless, he mastered his own fate, performing unparalleled feats of strength and ultimately securing his place among the immortals. He became not only a model of strength and courage, but also a paragon of virtue. The latter was articulated most influentially by the fifth-century BCE sophist Prodicus who composed an allegory of Heracles' choice between two paths, one leading to virtue, the other to vice (Xenophon, *Mem.* 2.1.21–34).[8] In this tradition, philosophers and orators deployed him as an exemplum. Isocrates implores Philip of Macedon to follow the example of his heroic ancestor, who, Isocrates claims, subjugated only barbarian nations, leaving Hellenes free to rule themselves (*Or.* 5.105–15). Similarly, Dio Chrysostom addressing the Emperor Trajan, notes how from youth Heracles chose *Basileia* over *Tyrannis*, and that the central thrust of his labors was to eradicate savage tyrants, rather than merely wild beasts. If Trajan modeled his own reign after Heracles, he likewise would prove to be a savior of humanity (*Or.* 1.51–84). For Epictetus, Heracles is an ideal sage who, because of his detachment from externals and complete obedience to God, purged the world of evils (*Diatr.* 2.16.44–45).[9]

Less commonly known among moderns, but also ubiquitous in ancient Greece was the comic Heracles, whose prolific capacities focalized on his baser appetites.[10] To be sure, Heracles' fondness for food and drink was not an invention of the comic stage; early on in literature and

---

7. Recent popular productions include the Walt Disney Pictures' 1997 *Hercules*; Flynn Picture Company's 2014 *Hercules* starring Dwayne Johnson; and a TV series *Hercules: The Legendary Journeys* (Renaissance Pictures), which ran from 1995 to 1999. Hercules is a regular character in Marvel Comics with diverse roles, ranging from the 1965 *Journey into Mystery Annual* to their current series *Gods of War*.

8. On Heracles in philosophical discourse, see Höistad, "Cynic Hero," 22–73; Galinsky, *Herakles Theme*, 101–25.

9. For additional philosophically informed reflections on Heracles, see Lucretius 5.22–54; Diodorus Siculus 4.8–39; Seneca, *De constantia* 2.1–3; Dio Chrysostom, *Or.* 8.26–36; Ps.-Lucian, *Cynicus* 13.

10. On the comic Heracles, see esp. Hošek, "Herakles auf der Bühne"; Galinsky, *Herakles Theme*, 81–100.

art he was closely associated with banquets and feasting.[11] This theme was already popular in the earliest surviving comedies: in Epicharmus' *Bousiris* (ca. 480 BCE), a speaker says of Heracles, "if you see him eating, you might die," then proceeds to describe the outlandish spectacle of the hero's consumption (frag. 18 K.-A.). By the time of Aristophanes, Heracles' comic persona had developed into a cliché, such that his chorus declare that it was he who "first dishonored and drove off [from the stage] those Heracleses that chew and crave" (*Pax* 741-42).[12] Aristophanes nevertheless later deploys this stereotypical Heracles to comic effect. In the *Birds*, when the hero is sent by Zeus along with Poseidon to negotiate peace with their avian rivals, he is quickly distracted from his mission with the promise of a feast. Poseidon chastises him: "you are vain and a glutton" (ἠλίθιος καὶ γάστρις εἶ, 1604).

As with comedy, Heracles was also a favorite character in satyr plays, and thus tragedians experimented with his persona in various directions.[13] Perhaps the best known instance is Euripides' *Alcestis*. As a tragedy produced in place of a satyr play, the hero represents aspects both of his comic character and of his more serious side. In keeping with his celebrated labors, at the conclusion of the play he ambushes Thanatos in order to retake Alcestis to the land of the living. This extraordinary performance only occurs, however, after, in ignorance of his host's state of mourning, he makes a boor of himself, eating and drinking "intemperately" (οὔτι σωφρόνως, 747-72, at 753).

The comic Heracles retained widespread popularity in much of the ancient Mediterranean.[14] In his *Alexandrian Oration*, Dio Chryso-

---

11. (Ps.-)Hesiod's *Marriage of Ceyx* (according to Zenobius 2.19) attributed to Heracles the well-known proverb, "of their own accord, noble men attend the feasts of noble men," describing the hero's habit of regularly visiting the home of Ceyx. For artistic representations, see the Eurytios Krater (Louvre E 635) (ca. 600 BCE), with Wolf, *Herakles beim Gelage*, 11-12, 51-53. More broadly, see also Carpenter, *Dionysian Imagery*, 111-18; Lissarrague, *Aesthetics of the Greek Banquet*, 91-93; Wolf, *Herakles beim Gelage*, 22-29.

12. On the implied target of Aristophanes' criticism, see Hošek, "Herakles auf der Bühne," 122. "Heracles tricked out of his dinner" (Ηρακλῆς τὸ δεῖπνον ἐξαπατώμενος, *Wasps* 60) was apparently proverbial. See also *Frogs* 503-48.

13. Galinsky, *Herakles Theme*, 82-84. For a comparison between Heracles in comedies and satyr plays, see Hošek, "Herakles auf der Bühne," 125-26. The *Syleus* of Euripides will be discussed further below.

14. At Rome, however, Heracles' heroic gravitas was favored, and his burlesque aspect and comic persona were largely absent; on this point, see Galinsky, *Herakles Theme*, 127-28.

stom criticizes his audience for their infatuations with base entertainments. Whereas they do not find it funny when comic playwrights bring drunken slaves on stage, "they think it hilarious when they see such a Heracles carried about and, as customary, dressed in saffron" (*Or.* 32.94). In book 10 of his *Learned Banqueters* devoted to the theme of gluttony, Athenaeus frames his discussion around the heading, "Heracles was a glutton (ἀδηφάγος)," a point made clear by "nearly all poets and prose writers" (10.411b). The proverbial excesses of the comic Heracles also lent themselves to various forms of polemic. For instance, Plutarch notes that Mark Antony, who apparently touted his Heraclean lineage, mimicked the hero's "vulgar" behaviors: "boasting, jesting, [with] visible drinking vessel, sitting next to the person eating and standing while eating at the soldiers' table" (*Antony* 4.2).[15] Whereas his elite critics regarded this as boorish, it earned him favor among the soldiers.[16] In a related vein, Christian writers would seize upon the disgraceful conduct of Heracles both to differentiate the morality of Jesus as a true divinity, and to denounce paganism more broadly. Origen observes, for example, in literature "much intemperance (ἀκολασία) of Heracles is recorded, and his womanly servitude to Omphale" (*Cels.* 3.22; see similarly Eusebius, *Theoph.* 3.61; Lactantius, *Inst.* 1.9).

The brief foregoing overview reveals the enduring popularity of Heracles in ancient art and literature, in philosophy and on stage. His varied instantiations enabled him to be both an ethical paradigm for philosophers and orators and a comic buffoon, controlled by his appetites and overcome by intemperance.

Philo of Alexandria, Drunkenness, and the Comic Heracles

As an educated Hellenistic Jew in Alexandria, Philo was fully immersed in Greek and Roman culture. Though best known for his engagement with philosophy and Jewish scripture, he was intimately acquainted with mythology, literature, and religion, and even claims to have attended the

15. On Antony's kinship with Heracles, see also Appian, *Bell. civ.* 3.16; and Anderson, "Heracles and His Successors," 42–44.

16. Antony's reputation for excessive drinking was widely known. Apparently, he had published a treatise on the subject of his own inebriation (see Pliny, *Nat.* 14.28.148). Elsewhere, his drunken behavior was associated with Dionysus: e.g., Cicero, *Phil.* 2.104; Athenaeus, *Deipn.* 4.148c.

GLUTTONY AND DRUNKENNESS AS JEWISH AND CHRISTIAN VIRTUES

theater (*Good Person* 141; *Drunkenness* 177).[17] And he has much to say about the twin themes of this study, namely, drunkenness and the heroic Heracles. The former takes up one-and-a-half treatises: first, in the latter part of *On Planting* (140–77), he engages with philosophical arguments, especially those of Stoics, opposed to drunkenness, arguing on the contrary that the true sage will maintain his virtue even while inebriated.[18] Then, in *On Drunkenness* Philo turns to biblical regulations regarding alcohol, observing that while it is forbidden for certain individuals, most notably Priests and Nazirites (Lev 10:9; Num 6:2–3),[19] these prohibitions are exceptional rather than universal, and their ultimate significance is allegorical rather than literal.[20]

As for Heracles, Philo discusses the hero explicitly in two treatises. In the *Embassy to Gaius*, he ridicules the theatrical pretences of Caligula who apparently adorned himself on occasion with a lion skin and club (*Embassy* 79; see also Athenaeus, *Deipn.* 4.148d; Josephus, *Ant.* 19.30). Such extravagant self-glorification was widely viewed as repugnant.[21]

---

17. At the same time, however, Philo is critical of spectacle entertainments involved in Greco-Roman games and festivals (*Agriculture* 35, 111–26). On Philo's theater attendance, see Bloch, "Von Szene zu Szene," 66–67, 70–72; Jay, "Problem of the Theater," 221–32. For his use of dramatic texts, Lincicum, "Preliminary Index"; Niehoff, *Philo on Jewish Identity*, 52–58; Koskenniemi, "Philo and Classical Drama"; Friesen, "Attending Euripides."

18. Philo cites a Stoic syllogism (*Plant.* 176) which is also quoted by Seneca and attributed to Zeno of Citium (*Ep.* 83.9 = *SVF* 1.229). See Richardson-Hay, "Drunk on False Argument," 35–39; Phillips, "Will the Wise Person Get Drunk?" 387–94. Opposition to drunkenness was a common ethical stance. For example, like Seneca, Pliny the Elder, in a book devoted to cataloging the varieties of wines, also warns his readers against the numerous harms of drunkenness (*Nat.* 14.28). In a very different context, the sage and divine-man Apollonius, according to Philostratus, although he often attended banquets and symposia (e.g., *Vit. Apoll.* 2.28; 3.27–28), refused wine, maintaining abstinence as part of his philosophical lifestyle (1.8; 2.7).

19. Indeed, as noted below, several contemporary Jewish communities practiced abstinence or highly limited alcohol consumption, including the Essenes, the Qumran community, and the Therapeutae described by Philo (*Contempl.* 84–89).

20. Note, e.g., Philo's discussion of "sober inebriation" in *Drunkenness* 148–52; see also *Contempl.* 84–89; *Creation* 71; *Alleg. Interp.* 3.82; *Flight* 166; *Rewards* 122; *Good Person* 13–14; *QG* 2.68; see Lewy, *Sobria ebrietas*, 3–41; also Mackie, "Passion of Eve," 158–60.

21. According to Philo, Gaius' imitation of certain deities and claims to divine honors corresponded closely with his endeavors in theatrical performance (see also Suetonius, *Cal.* 54.2; Dio 59.5.5). For relevant discussion, see Simpson, "Cult of Emperor Gaius"; Price, *Rituals and Power*, 68–69, 184; Barrett, *Caligula*, 140–53; Pollini, "'Insanity' of Caligula"; Gruen, "Caligula"; Niehoff, *Philo of Alexandria*, 53–65.

Moreover, Philo observes, the emperor's own administration fell far short of the legendary achievements of Heracles: "Have you also imitated Heracles in your own tireless labors and ceaseless acts of courage, having filled up both mainlands and islands with good law and justice and with abundance and fertility?" (90; see also 81).

In his treatise *That Every Good Person Is Free*, Philo evokes the stereotypical gluttony and drunkenness of the comic Heracles in his defense of the Stoic paradox that the good person is free even if enslaved.[22] His central argument is that there are two types of freedom, one of the soul, the other of the body; true freedom concerns the former, not the latter, and cannot be revoked even under physical slavery. It is secured ultimately by virtue, freedom from the passions, and submission to God alone as one's true master (17–20). This moral principle is illustrated by Philo with numerous exempla, and given the nature of the topic and the implied audience they are drawn from "Greek and barbarian" rather than biblical sources (62–160, at 73).[23] Philo quotes from 10 dramas, but none more extensively than the *Syleus*, from which he provides five excerpts (99–104; *TrGF* 5.687–91).[24]

In the context of Philo's treatise, the character of Heracles in the *Syleus* serves to establish his central thesis. The hero found himself in a temporary state of servitude because, in a scheme to destroy the murderous tyrant Syleus, Hermes had sold to the latter the disguised Heracles.[25] Repeatedly throughout the drama, however, Heracles' heroic nature cannot be contained. This is well illustrated in the first fragment:

> See, then, what kinds of things Heracles says in Euripides:
>
> Ignite and burn up my flesh, be filled with drinking my dark blood; for the stars will come down to earth, and the earth

---

22. On this treatise, see Petit, *Quod omnis*, 17–132; Niehoff, *Philo of Alexandria*, 81–84. For similar treatments of the same Stoic paradox, see Cicero, *Paradoxa Stoicorum* 5; and Epictetus, *Diatr.* 4.1.

23. While biblical exempla are lacking, the Essenes are given first place as ideals of virtue (*Good Person* 75–91); see Niehoff, *Philo of Alexandria*, 81–88. For an outline of the treatise and a list of the exempla, see Petit, *Quod omnis*, 29–34.

24. Philo issues programmatic statements on the value of poetry generally and of Euripides in particular for moral instruction; see *Good Person* 98, 116, 141–43. Cf. also Koskenniemi, "Philo and Greek Poets"; Hernández, "Philo and Greek Poetry"; Friesen, "Dying Like a Woman"; Friesen, "Virtue and Vice on Stage."

25. For discussion and reconstruction of the *Syleus*, see Sutton, *Greek Satyr Play*, 66–67; Pechstein, *Euripides Satyrographos*, 243–83. On Philo's application of this play in *Good Person* 99–104, see Koskenniemi, "Philo and Classical Drama," 139–41.

ascend to the sky before a flattering word from me meets you. (99; *TrGF* 5.687)[26]

Philo comments that a "flattering word" is "most befitting a slave" (δουλοπρεπέστατα, *Good Person* 99), and the hero declares his preference for death over that.[27] Indeed, even with Heracles' best efforts to disguise himself in the market so as to be purchased by Syleus, his heroic character shows through, as Hermes observes, "is he most base? Rather, quite the opposite, he is honorable and not humble in form," and an onlooker would readily perceive that he is "effective with a club" (*Good Person* 101; *TrGF* 5.688). Because of this, Hermes (or Syleus) doubts his fitness for slavery: "no one wishes to purchase masters for his house that are stronger than himself" (101; *TrGF* 5.689), and looking at Heracles' "form" (εἶδος), it appeared he "would rather give orders than take them" (101; *TrGF* 5.690).

For Philo, however, Heracles' refusal to flatter and inability to conceal his hulky appearance are penultimate; the culminating demonstration of his "slave-free nature" comes when, "having sacrificed the best of the bulls there to Zeus as a pretense, he was feasting, and having plundered much wine, he consumed it unmixed all at once after reclining very happily" (102). When he returns home, Syleus chastises his gluttonous slave; still, Heracles remains undeterred. In Philo's final fragment, the hero invites his "master" to a competition of drinking: "lie down, and let us drink; take the test at once to see whether in this you are stronger than I" (103; *TrGF* 5.691).[28] This culminating performance of comic heroism, expressed in the tenacity of his eating and drinking, establishes Heracles' status as master rather than slave, and, Philo adds, exposes the institution of slavery itself as a "joke" (γέλως) and "much folly" (φλυαρία πολλή, 104).[29]

26. This fragment had been quoted earlier in the treatise (*Good Person* 25), but without attribution of the source or identification of the speaker as Heracles. Philo was apparently fond of these four lines, quoting them twice elsewhere, albeit without mentioning Heracles or noting the context of the play (*Alleg. Interp.* 3.102: "the tragic expression in the face of suffering," τὸ τραγικὸν πρὸς τὴν ἀλγηδόνα; *Joseph* 78: "as the tragedian says," ὡς ὁ τραγικός φησιν). See also Koskenniemi, "Philo and Classical Drama," 143–44.

27. On flattery see also Epictetus, *Diatr.* 4.1.55.

28. Heracles challenging his foes to eating or drinking contests is attested elsewhere in his heroic biography; on Lepreus, e.g., see Athenaeus 10.411e–412b.

29. Philo omits the conclusion of the play in which Heracles diverts a river in order to flood Syleus' fields and ultimately kills him; on which, see Pechstein, *Euripides*

In sum, by contrast to later Christian writers who would take aim at Heracles for his moral outrages, not least his excessive eating and drinking, Philo deploys common conceptions of this hero as a moral paragon. Thus, for instance, he contrasts the Emperor Gaius' administration with Heracles whose labors destroyed threats to humanity and set up just laws for society. Yet, whereas such applications can be found in authors ranging from Prodicus (via Xenophon) to Isocrates and Dio Chrysostom, there is little precedent for Philo's use of the *Syleus*. In an apparently innovative move, he identifies the comic hero's habitually excessive eating and drinking known from comedy as decisive evidence of his genuinely free nature. This is consistent with Philo's treatment of intoxication elsewhere—that is, against some other moralists he argues that the sage may get drunk without compromising his virtue. Nevertheless, his choice of Heracles the buffoon as a model of freedom, and in particular his use of gluttony and drunkenness as demonstrations of rather than detractions from his virtuous character will undoubtedly have struck some of his readers as amusing.

From Wilderness to Messianic Appetite: The Gospels on John the Baptist and Jesus

Within the earliest gospel traditions, excessive eating and drinking posed a special problem in connection with Jesus as a divine hero. Like Heracles, Jesus had an especially strong association with feasting and banquets, making table-fellowship a central characteristic of his public ministry.[30] As with the comic hero, Jesus' critics viewed him as a "glutton and a winebibber" (φάγος καὶ οἰνοπότης, Luke 7:34 = Matt 11:19). Moreover, some disapproved that Jesus' disciples did not fast when others did (Mark 2:18–22 = Matt 9:14–17 = Luke 3:33–39). In the synoptic gospels, Jesus' approach to food and wine is set in contrast to John the Baptist, whose rigorous lifestyle was well known, and whose fame for piety and religious purity extended beyond the Christian community

---

Satyrographos, 252–54.

30. Scholars of the historical Jesus generally regard this as authentic; see Perrin, *Rediscovering the Teachings of Jesus*, 105–8, 119–21; Smith, *From Symposium to Eucharist*, 221–39. For the place of Greco-Roman banquets and symposia in the gospels more broadly, see Smith, *From Symposium to Eucharist*, 119–77; König, *Saints and Symposiasts*, 130–34; Sick, "Symposium of the 5,000."

(e.g., Josephus, *Ant.* 18.116–19).³¹ Mark notes that John's distinctive diet consisted of "locusts and wild honey" (ἀκρίδας καὶ μέλι ἄγριον, 1:6; also Matt 3:4). On the one hand, these foods would have been more accessible to him in his wilderness abode, but, on the other, due to their acceptance as alternatives to meat and wine, they represented the extent of John's fasting.³² John's rigorous approach to food and drink was not unique to him; as an endeavor of religious devotion and spiritual valor his fasting and abstinence from wine resembled both the piety of certain Jews—for example, the Essenes and Qumran community (Josephus, *J.W.* 2.133),³³ Philo's Therapeutae (*Contempl.* 84–89), Nazarites (Num 6:3–4), priests (Lev 10:9), and Rechabites (Jer 35)—and the ideals of some Greeks and Romans (e.g., *SVF* 1.229; Seneca, *Ep.* 83; Pliny, *Nat.* 14.28; Philostratus, *Vit. Apoll.* 1.8; 2.7).³⁴

Because of John's fame as a prophet and for strict piety, gospel writers were careful to establish the priority of Jesus. Indeed, that he was baptized by John (Mark 1:9; Matt 3:16; Luke 3:21) seems to have been an embarrassment to some early Christians.³⁵ This was dealt with in a variety of ways: Matthew has John demur (3:14–15); Mark stresses that John's baptism was merely "with water," which would be surpassed by a

---

31. For further discussion, see Friesen, "Getting Samuel Sober," 467–77.

32. A later rabbinic tractate from the Mishnah distinguishes locusts and fish from meat (*m. Hullin* 8:1). For fasts from meat and wine, see, e.g., *T. Jos.* 3:4–5; *T. Jud.* 15:4; *T. Reu.* 1:10; *m. Ta'anit* 4:7. Among the studies on John the Baptist in history and the synoptic gospels, see Scobie, *John the Baptist*; Tilly, *Johannes der Täufer*; Taylor, *Immerser*; Rothschild, *Baptist Traditions*.

33. At Qumran, for example, rather than "wine" (יין), communal meals consisted of "bread and *grape juice*" (הלחם והתירוש, 1QS 6.6), a drink of lesser or no alcoholic content; see Magness, *Archaeology of Qumran*, 114–15, 126; Smith, *From Symposium to Eucharist*, 152–58.

34. Jews sometimes avoided meat and wine on account of their connection with "pagan" religion (e.g., Dan 1:8–16; Rom 14:1–4); see esp. Böcher, "Ass Johannes der Täufer," esp. 91; Fraade, "Ascetical Aspects," 262–63. It has been proposed that John was in fact an Essene or a Nazarite. For the former, see Davies, "John the Baptist"; Betz, "Was John the Baptist an Essene?"; and for the latter, Berger, "Jesus als Nazoräer/Nasiräer," 326. The evidence for such identification, however, remains inconclusive; see Scobie, *John the Baptist*, 137–39; Taylor, *Immerser*, 15–48. As for the requirements for Nazirites, for example, there is no indication that John did not cut his hair or avoided corpses (cf. Num 6:5, 6). Moreover, his clothing consisting of camel's hair and leather belt (Mark 1:6 = Matt 3:4) would have connected him more broadly with biblical prophets; see Tilly, *Johannes der Täufer*, 37–38. For discussion of Nazirites in Second Temple Judaism, see Chepey, *Nazirites*.

35. For further discussion, see Taylor, *Immerser*, 261–77.

greater baptism "with the holy spirit" (Mark 1:8 = Matt 3:11 = Luke 3:16; also John 1:33; Acts 1:5; 11:16); the Gospel of John omits the baptism entirely (see 1:33); and in Q, John's prophetic ministry brought the era of biblical revelation to culmination and was to be supplanted by Jesus (Luke 16:16 = Matt 11:13; see also John 3:22–30).[36]

In view of this relationship between John and Jesus, the latter's laxer approach to food and drink required special explanation. This is treated in an important passage in Q (Luke 7:18–35 = Matt 11:2–19) where John sends messengers from prison to inquire of Jesus whether he was in fact "the one who is to come." Jesus responds with reference to his deeds—the sick are healed, the dead are raised, the gospel is preached to the poor—and praises John as the greatest among prophets (Luke 7:22–28 = Matt 11:4–11). He then turns to the matter of food and drink, which he addresses by comparing "this generation" to children in the market saying, "we played the flute for you, and you did not dance, we mourned, and you did not weep" (Luke 7:32 = Matt 11:17). The distinction between mourning and celebration is precisely what differentiates Jesus from John: "John the Baptist has come neither eating bread nor drinking wine, and you say, 'he has a demon.' The son of man has come eating and drinking, and you say, 'look: a man who is a glutton and a winebibber, a friend of tax-collectors and sinners'" (Luke 7:33–34 = Matt 11:17–18).[37]

A similar response is given by Jesus in Mark when asked why his disciples do not fast: "The groomsmen cannot fast when the groom is with them, can they? [. . .] But the days will come when the groom will be taken away from them, and then they will fast on that day" (Mark 2:19–20 = Matt 9:15 = Luke 5:34–35). In this instance, the contrast between feasting and fasting is set within an eschatological framework of the messianic banquet, a theme to which Jesus returns as he approaches his death: "truly I say to you that I shall no longer drink from the fruit of the vine (ἐκ τοῦ γενήματος τῆς ἀμπέλου) until that day when I should drink it new in the kingdom of God" (Mark 14:25 = Matt 26:29 = Luke 22:18). Jesus partially fulfils his prediction in his final moments: "and

36. In addition, the *Gospel of the Hebrews* has Jesus deny his need to be baptized for forgiveness (Jerome, *Pelag.* 3.2); and according to Ignatius of Antioch, Jesus' baptism was for the purification of the water rather than for his own (*Eph.* 18.2).

37. On these verses, see Kee, "Jesus: A Glutton and a Drunkard"; Phillips, "Will the Wise Person Get Drunk?"; Cotter, "Parable of the Children." The Matthean version of John's restricted diet is shorter: "neither eating nor drinking" (μήτε ἐσθίων μήτε πίνων, Matt 11:18). Luke's "bread" (ἄρτον) and "wine" (οἶνον) are likely secondary additions; for this argument, see Böcher, "Ass Johannes der Täufer."

they began to give him wine mixed with myrrh (ἐσμυρνισμένον οἶνον), but he did not take it" (Mark 15:23).[38] Precisely why Jesus would shift to abstinence from wine in the face of death remains unclear, although it is broadly analogous with a report that a sizable number of Jews pledged themselves no longer to eat meat or drink wine due to the temple's destruction in 70 CE (*b. Bava Batra* 60b). The significance of his expectation to drink again in the coming kingdom is more apparent, as it reflects a common anticipation that wine would figure prominently in the future messianic banquet (e.g., Isa 25:6; 55:1-2; 1QSa 2:20-21).[39]

Alongside the foregoing treatments of feasting and drinking, Luke's special source offers further explanation for John's abstinence. Its origin is situated within John's birth narrative, where the angel declares to his father Zechariah, "wine and strong drink (οἶνον καὶ σίκερα) he shall never drink, and he shall be filled with the holy spirit while still in his mother's womb" (1:15). This injunction calls to mind several biblical sources, such as the Nazirite vow (Num 6:3) and the rule for ministering priests (Lev 10:9).[40] In the context of the miraculous conception of a prophetic child by a barren woman, however, clearly Samson and Samuel are relevant, both of whom, like John, were associated with abstinence (see LXX Judg 13:4, 7, 14; LXX 1 Sam 1:11). In particular, Samuel's birth narrative is especially influential throughout Luke 1 and 2 where there are numerous literary allusions to 1 Samuel 1-2.[41] As Raymond Brown contends, "the Samuel background is drawn upon by Luke for the whole infancy narrative and not merely the JBap portion."[42] The correlation between Samuel and John establishes abstinence from wine not as a superior mode of piety *per se* (over against Jesus), but as a marker of the latter's prophetic

---

38. In Matt 27:34, however, Jesus does taste the wine first before refusing it. This verse is absent from Luke. Subsequently, a bystander offers Jesus vinegar (ὄξος), but the synoptic gospels do not indicate whether or not he drinks it (Mark 15:36; Matt 27:48; Luke 23:36). By contrast, in John 19:28-29, Jesus declares his thirst and receives the vinegar, which is said to fulfill scripture (i.e., LXX Ps 68:22).

39. On the Messianic Banquet, see Smith, *From Symposium to Eucharist*, 166-71.

40. François Bovon emphasizes the latter in view of John's priestly origin (*Luke*, 36).

41. E.g., Luke 1:48 / 1 Sam 1:11; Luke 1:46b-47 / 1 Sam 2:1; Luke 1:53 / 1 Sam 2:5, 7-8a; Luke 1:52 / 1 Sam 2:8b; Luke 1:80; 2:40, 52 / 1 Sam 2:21, 26; see also von Harnack, "Das Magnificat," 68, 71; Fitzmyer, *Luke (I-IX)*, 325-26; Brown, *Birth of the Messiah*, 273-74, 357-59; Tilly, *Johannes der Täufer*, 127-29, 132-36. Oddly, Bovon excludes Judg 13, asserting that "the account of Samson does not include the prohibition of alcohol"; and he fails to note LXX 1 Sam 1:11 (*Luke*, 36).

42. Brown, *Birth of the Messiah*, at 451.

ministry akin to that of the former.[43] For the author of Luke and Acts, Samuel concluded the era of the judges (Acts 13:20) and was also the first of the prophets who all "announced these days" (κατήγγειλαν τὰς ἡμέρας ταύτας, Acts 3:24). Indeed, by modeling John after Samuel, Luke further subordinates him to Jesus; for just as Samuel had anointed Israel's first king, so now John would anoint God's new and final king.

In addition to revealing his distinctive prophetic standing, John's abstinence from wine highlights a thematic juxtaposition in Luke and Acts between prophetic inspiration and drunkenness. As the angel emphasizes, rather than drinking wine, "he will be filled with the holy spirit" (πνεύματος ἁγίου πλησθήσεται, Luke 1:15). A similar apposition between wine and inspired speech occurs at the Pentecost when the apostles were "all filled with the holy spirit" (ἐπλήσθησαν πάντες πνεύματος ἁγίου, Acts 2:4) and spoke in other tongues, prompting some observers to supposed that "they were filled with sweet wine" (γλεύκους μεμεστωμένοι εἰσίν, Acts 2:13).[44] Peter retorts that they were not inebriated but that this was the fulfillment of Joel's prophecy: "I shall pour out from my spirit upon all flesh" (ἐκχεῶ ἀπὸ τοῦ πνεύματός μου ἐπὶ πᾶσαν σάρκα, Act 2:17, quoting LXX Joel 3:1). Thus, as with the angel's declaration regarding John in Luke 1:15, filling with wine functions as a negative foil for filling with the spirit and prophecy (cf. Eph 5:18).

In sum, the gospel writers were faced with a (most likely authentic) tradition of criticism against Jesus for his easy-going approach to feasting and drinking and at the same time John the Baptist's fame for rigorous asceticism. Rather than omitting or rewriting this aspect of Jesus' lifestyle, they resolved it in part by valorizing Jesus' table-fellowship as a sign that the kingdom of God was at hand. His inclusive and celebratory way of life was depicted as an anticipation of the final messianic banquet. By contrast, John the Baptist's rejection of wine was relativized; while appropriate to his prophetic calling, it was subordinated to the higher

---

43. See similarly Tilly, *Johannes der Täufer*, 125-26. Regarding Samuel's abstinence from wine (LXX 1 Sam 1:11), Josephus understood this together with his uncut hair as evidence for his role a prophet (*Ant.* 5.344-47). Elsewhere, these were understood explicitly in connection with the Nazirite vow: e.g., 4QSam^a 1:22; Ben Sirach 46:13. Luke gives no indication that John was a Nazirite; elsewhere, when he refers to such a vow he employs εὐχή explicitly (Acts 18:18; 21:23). On these, see Neusner, "Vow-Taking"; Chepey, *Nazirites*, 159-74.

44. Whereas in the Gospel of Luke, the only individuals who are said to be "filled with the holy spirit" are John, his mother Elizabeth (1:41), and father Zechariah (1:67), in Acts, this phenomenon is more broadly attested (Acts 2:4; 4:8, 31; 9:17; 13:9).

kingdom ethic of Jesus. Indeed, as established by Luke, John's abstinence was modeled on Samuel, the prophet who inaugurated the new age by anointing God's appointed king in Israel.[45]

Conclusion

Both Heracles and Christ—two of the most revered divine heroes in antiquity—share in common a reputation for their regular participation in feasting and wine-drinking. On the comic stage, Heracles became a stock character whose heroism expressed itself in prolific consumption and inebriation. In the gospels, Jesus was criticized as a "glutton and a winebibber," especially compared with the rigorous asceticism of John the Baptist. Such behaviors were subjected to opprobrium; indeed, numerous moralists—Greek, Roman, Jewish, and Christian—warned against the dangers of these excesses and advocated for moderation and even complete abstinence. Nevertheless, for Heracles and Jesus indulgences in food and wine had the potential to be turned into virtues rather than vices. For the former, Philo of Alexandria finds the consistency in the character of the comic hero in Euripides' *Syleus* as conclusive proof of his genuine freedom of soul. Even in his disguised status as a slave, he cannot resist the allures of his master's meat and wine, in which he partakes abundantly while the latter is out in his fields. For Jesus, the celebratory aspect of his public life was taken in the gospels as a foretaste of the messianic banquet to come. While John abstained from meat and wine and regularly fasted with his disciples, this was a characteristic of mourning and of the prior prophetic age initiated, according to Luke, by Samuel. With Jesus, a new messianic kingdom was at hand wherein wine signified festive abundance. The (alleged) gluttony and drunkenness of Heracles and Jesus represents a common element in their respective heroic biographies that has hitherto been overlooked by scholars. The aim of this study has been to bring this hero of the comic stage more fully into conversation with his counterpart in the gospels.

---

45. Although it is beyond the scope of the present discussion, the Gospel of John also addresses Jesus' relationship with wine. In 2:1–11, he miraculously produces wine for the wedding at Cana, and later identifies himself as the "true vine" (15:1) as a metaphorical explanation of his mystical connection to his disciples.

Works Cited

Anderson, Andrew Runni. "Heracles and His Successors: A Study of a Heroic Ideal and the Recurrence of a Heroic Type." *Harvard Studies in Classical Philology* 39 (1928) 7–58.

Aune, David E. "Heracles and Christ: Heracles Imagery in the Christology of Early Christianity." In *Greeks, Romans, and Christians: Essays in Honor of Abraham J. Malherbe*, edited by David L. Balch et al., 3–19. Minneapolis: Fortress, 1990.

Barrett, Anthony A. *Caligula: The Corruption of Power*. London: Batsford, 1989.

Berger, Klaus. "Jesus als Nazoräer/Nasiräer." *Novum Testamentum* 34 (1996) 323–35.

Betz, Otto. "Was John the Baptist an Essene?" *Bible Review* (December 1990) 18–25.

Bloch, René. "Von Szene zu Szene: Das jüdische Theater in der Antike." In *Juden in ihrer Umwelt: Akkulturation des Judentums in Antike und Mittelalter*, edited by Matthias Konradt and Rainer Christoph Schwinges, 57–86. Basel: Schwabe, 2009.

Böcher, Otto. "Ass Johannes der Täufer kein Brot (Luk. vii. 33)?" *New Testament Studies* 18 (1971) 90–92.

Bovon, François. *Luke 1: A Commentary on the Gospel of Luke 1:1—9:50*. Translated by Christine M. Thomas. Hermeneia. Minneapolis: Fortress, 2002.

Brown, Raymond E. *The Birth of the Messiah: A Commentary on the Infancy Narratives in the Gospels of Matthew and Luke*. Anchor Bible Reference Library. London: Chapman, 1993.

Carpenter, Thomas H. *Dionysian Imagery in Archaic Greek Art: Its Development in Black-Figure Painting*. Oxford Monographs on Classical Archaeology. Oxford: Clarendon, 1986.

Chepey, Stuart. *Nazirites in Late Second Temple Judaism: A Survey of Ancient Jewish Writings, the New Testament, Archaeological Evidence, and Other Writings from Late Antiquity*. Ancient Judaism and Christianity 60. Leiden: Brill, 2005.

Cotter, Wendy J. "The Parable of the Children in the Market-Place, Q (Lk) 7:31–35: An Examination of the Parable's Image and Significance." *Novum Testamentum* 29 (1987) 289–304.

Cover, Michael. "The Divine Comedy at Corinth: Paul, Menander, and the Rhetoric of Resurrection." *New Testament Studies* 64 (2018) 234–50.

Davies, Stevan L. "John the Baptist and the Essene Kashruth." *New Testament Studies* 29 (1983) 569–71.

Fitzmyer, Joseph A. *The Gospel according to Luke (I–IX): Introduction, Translation, and Notes*. Anchor Bible 28. Garden City, NY: Doubleday, 1979.

Fraade, Steven D. "Ascetical Aspects of Ancient Judaism." In *Jewish Spirituality: From the Bible through the Middle Ages*, edited by Arthur Green, 253–88. World Spirituality: An Encyclopedic History of the Religious Quest 13. London: Routledge & Kegan Paul, 1986.

Friesen, Courtney J. P. "Attending Euripides: Philo of Alexandria's Dramatic Appropriations." In *Euripides-Rezeption in Kaiserzeit und Spätantike—The Reception of Euripides in Imperial Era and Late Antiquity*, edited by Michael Schramm. Millennium Studies. Berlin: de Gruyter, forthcoming.

———. "Dying Like a Woman: Euripides' Polyxena as Exemplum between Philo and Clement of Alexandria." *Greek, Roman, and Byzantine Studies* 56 (2016) 623–45.

———. "Getting Samuel Sober: The 'Plus' of LXX 1 Sam 1:11 and Its Religious Afterlife in Philo and the Gospel of Luke." *Journal of Theological Studies* 67 (2016) 453–78.

———. "Virtue and Vice on Stage: Philo of Alexandria's Theatrical Ambivalences." In *Jews and Drama*, edited by Lutz Doering and Sandra Gambetti, 241–56. Journal of Ancient Judaism Supplements. Göttingen: Vandenhoeck & Ruprecht, 2017.

Galinsky, G. Karl. *The Herakles Theme: The Adaptations of the Hero in Literature from Homer to the Twentieth Century*. Oxford: Blackwell, 1972.

Grant, Robert M. "Early Christianity and Greek Comic Poetry." *Classical Philology* 60 (1965) 157–63.

Gruen, Erich S. "Caligula, the Imperial Cult, and Philo's *Legatio*." *Studia Philonica* 24 (2012) 135–47.

Harnack, Adolf von. "Das Magnificat der Elisabet (Luk. 1, 46–55) nebst einigen Bemerkungen zu Luk. 1 und 2." In *Studien zur Geschichte des Neuen Testaments und der alten Kirche I: Zur neutestamentlichen Textkritik*, 62–85. Arbeiten zur Kirchengeschichte 19. Berlin: de Gruyter, 1931.

Harrill, J. Albert. *Slaves in the New Testament: Literary, Social, and Moral Dimensions*. Minneapolis: Fortress, 2006.

Hernández, Pura Nieto. "Philo and Greek Poetry." *Studia Philonica* 26 (2014) 135–49.

Höistad, Ragnar. "Cynic Hero and Cynic King: Studies in the Cynic Conceptions of Man." PhD diss., University of Uppsala, 1948.

Hošek, Radislave. "Herakles auf der Bühne der alte attischen Komödie." In *GERAS: Studies Presented to George Thomson on the Occasion of his 60th Birthday*, edited by Ladislav Varcl and Ronald F. Willetts, 119–27. AUC Philosophica et historica 1, Graecolatina Prasgensia 2. Prague: Charles University, 1963.

Jay, Jeff. "The Problem of the Theater in Early Judaism." *Journal for the Study of Judaism* 44 (2013) 218–53.

Kee, Howard Clark. "Jesus: A Glutton and a Drunkard." *New Testament Studies* 42 (1996) 374–93.

Knox, Wilfred L. "The 'Divine Hero' Christology in the New Testament." *Harvard Theological Review* 41 (1948) 229–49.

König, Jason. *Saints and Symposiasts: The Literature of Food and the Symposium in Greco-Roman and Early Christian Culture*. Greek Culture in the Roman World. Cambridge: Cambridge University Press, 2012.

Koskenniemi, Erkki. "Philo and Classical Drama." In *Ancient Israel, Judaism, and Christianity in Contemporary Perspective: Essays in Memory of Karl-Johan Illman*, edited by Jacob Neusner et al., 137–51. Studies in Judaism. Lanham, MD: University Press of America, 2006.

———. "Philo and Greek Poets." *Journal for the Study of Judaism* 41 (2010) 301–22.

Lewy, Yochanan. *Sobria ebrietas: Untersuchungen zur Geschichte der antiken Mystik*. Beihefte zur Zeitschrift für die neutestamentliche Wissenschaft 9. Giessen: Töpelmann, 1929.

Lincicum, David. "A Preliminary Index to Philo's Non-Biblical Citations and Allusions." *Studia Philonica* 25 (2013) 139–67.

Lissarrague, François. *The Aesthetics of the Greek Banquet: Images of Wine and Ritual*. Translated by Andrew Szegedy-Maszak. Princeton: Princeton University Press, 1990.

Mackie, Scott D. "The Passion of Eve and the Ecstasy of Hannah: Sense Perception, Passion, Mysticism, and Misogyny in Philo of Alexandria, *De ebrietate* 143–52." *Journal of Biblical Literature* 133 (2014) 141–63.

Magness, Jodi. *The Archaeology of Qumran and the Dead Sea Scrolls*. Studies in the Dead Sea Scrolls and Related Literature. Grand Rapids: Eerdmans, 2002.

Malherbe, Abraham J. "Heracles." In *Light from the Gentiles: Hellenistic Philosophy and Early Christianity*, edited by Carl R. Holladay et al., 2:651–74. 2 vols. Leiden: Brill, 2014.

Neusner, Jacob. "Vow-Taking, the Nazirites, and the Law: Does James' Advice to Paul Accord with Halakah?" In *James the Just and Christian Origins*, edited by Bruce Chilton and Craig A. Evans, 59–82. Supplements to Novum Testamentum 98. Leiden: Brill, 1999.

Niehoff, Maren R. *Philo of Alexandria: An Intellectual Biography*. Anchor Yale Bible Reference Library. New Haven: Yale University Press, 2018.

———. *Philo on Jewish Identity and Culture*. Texts and Studies in Ancient Judaism 86. Tübingen: Mohr/Siebeck, 2001.

Pechstein, Nikolaus. *Euripides Satyrographos: Ein Kommentar zu den Euripideischen Satyrspielfragmenten*. Beiträge zur Altertumskunde 115. Stuttgart: Teubner, 1998.

Perrin, Norman. *Rediscovering the Teachings of Jesus*. New York: Harper & Row, 1967.

Petit, Madeleine. *Quod omnis probus liber sit: introduction, texte, traduction et notes*. Les oeuvres de Philon d'Alexandrie 28. Paris: Cerf, 1974.

Pfister, Friedrich. "Heracles und Christus." *Archiv für Religionswissenschaft* 34 (1937) 42–60.

Phillips, Thomas E. "Will the Wise Person Get Drunk? The Background of the Human Wisdom in Luke 7:35 and Matthew 11:19." *Journal of Biblical Literature* 127 (2008) 385–96.

Pollini, John. "The 'Insanity' of Caligula or the 'Insanity' of the Jews? Differences in Perception and Religious Beliefs." In *From Republic to Empire: Rhetoric, Religion, and Power in the Visual Culture of Ancient Rome*, 369–411. Oklahoma Series in Classical Culture 48. Norman: University of Oklahoma Press, 2012.

Price, Simon. *Rituals and Power: Roman Imperial Cult in Asia Minor*. Cambridge: Cambridge University Press, 1984.

Richardson-Hay, Christine. "Drunk on False Argument—Seneca's *Epistulae Morales*, Epistle 83." *Prudentia* 33 (2001) 12–40.

Rose, H. J. "Herakles and the Gospels." *Harvard Theological Review* 31 (1938) 113–42.

Rothschild, Clare K. *Baptist Traditions and Q*. Wissenschaftliche Untersuchungen zum Neuen Testament 190. Tübingen: Mohr/Siebeck, 2005.

Scobie, Charles H. H. *John the Baptist*. London: SCM, 1964.

Sick, David H. "The Symposium of the 5,000." *Journal of Theological Studies* 66 (2015) 1–27.

Simon, Marcel. *Hercule et le Christianisme*. Paris: Les belles lettres, 1955.

Simpson, C. J. "The Cult of Emperor Gaius." *Latomus* 40 (1981) 489–511.

Smith, Dennis E. *From Symposium to Eucharist: The Banquet in the Early Christian World*. Minneapolis: Fortress, 2003.

Sutton, Dana F. *The Greek Satyr Play*. Beiträge zur klassischen Philologie 90. Meisenheim: Hain, 1980.

Taylor, Joan E. *The Immerser: John the Baptist within Second Temple Judaism*. Studying the Historical Jesus. Grand Rapids: Eerdmans, 1997.

Tilly, Michael. *Johannes der Täufer und die Biographie der Propheten: Die synoptische Täuferüberlieferung und das jüdische Prophetenbild zur Zeit des Täufers*. Beiträge zur Wissenschaft vom Alten und Neuen Testament 137. Stuttgart: Kohlhammer, 1994.

Toynbee, Arnold J. *A Study of History*. Vol. 6. London: Oxford University Press, 1939.

Welborn, Larry L. *Paul, the Fool of Christ: A Study of 1 Corinthians 1–4 in the Comic-Philosophic Tradition*. Early Christianity in Context. Journal for the Study of the New Testament Supplement Series 293. London: T. & T. Clark, 2005.

Wolf, Simone Ruth. *Herakles beim Gelage: Eine motiv- und bedeutungsgeschichtliche Untersuchung des Bildes in der archaisch-frühklassischen Vasenmalerei*. Arbeiten zur Archäologie. Cologne: Böhlau, 1993.

16

The Drama of Apocalypse

From Tragic Hymns to the Hymns of Revelation

JUSTIN P. JEFFCOAT SCHEDTLER

In a midrash on the story of Ruth's conversion, Naomi reveals that becoming a daughter of Israel required certain sacrifices, one of which was never attending the theater: "My daughter, it is not the custom of the daughters of Israel to frequent theaters and circuses" (*Ruth Rab.* 2:22). In this particular midrash, Ruth's famous declaration, "Wherever you go, I shall go," is thought to signal her acceptance of this prohibition. The Talmud presents an even harsher view of the theater. In a tractate devoted to addressing the problems associated with living in a gentile environment, Jews are explicitly forbidden from attending the theater (*Avodah Zarah* 18a).

At the time of the composition of these texts, and for many centuries prior—including during the period of the composition of early Jewish and Christian texts such as the New Testament—theaters served as vibrant hubs for the expression of Roman sociopolitical-religious life. In cities across the Roman world, theaters served as popular gathering spaces for large crowds to experience the centuries-old spectacle of the dramatic arts. So why would the midrashim and Talmudic tractates so strictly forbid any kind of participation in the goings-on of the theater?

According to the rabbis, dramatic performances were not only replete with idolatry (sacrifices to the gods regularly accompanied dramatic performances and took place within the context of the dramatic action itself) and violence, but were also simply a waste of time. Inasmuch as shows in the theater might depict humans dressed up as gods, sacrificial rites, hymns of praise to the gods, gladiator battles, they were deemed (at least by these textual authorities) to be gateways into inappropriate pagan conduct. Moreover, with a few exceptions, any time spent in the theater might considered to be worthless because it was time that could have been used instead to study the Torah.

In *Theatrical Liberalism: Jews and Popular Entertainment in America* (2013), Andrea Most has outlined a host of other obstacles that may have prevented Jews from assimilating to the theater culture and producing distinctively Jewish theatrical traditions. Nevertheless, evidence confirms that Jews regularly attended theater—both as audience members and as performers. The clearest evidence that Jewish folks regularly attended the theater comes from Miletus, an important city in Asia Minor (western Turkey) where an inscription has been found in the fifth row of seats in the theater itself.

Place for the Jews and the God-fearers

It was not uncommon for seats in the theater to be reserved for groups of persons and/or particularly important persons (such as the emperor!) and indicated as such by inscriptions. Thus, while there is some dispute over whom exactly these seats were reserved for—that is, were are there *two* groups intended (Jews and God-fearers) or *one* group (Jews who are God-fearers)?—the inscription suggests that at least in this place there were some "Jews" who attended the theater regularly enough that seats (and really good seats at that!) were permanently reserved for them.[1] So much might be inferred in other locales as well. Aside from those who enjoyed reserved seats in the theater, we might conclude that Jews observed dramatic performances elsewhere. During the time of Augustus, as many as 43 days were reserved for dramatic performances—inside of theatrical venues and in *ad hoc* locations such as a temple—as part of larger Roman festivals that might also include chariot races, mimes, beast-fights, wrestling, boxing, and so forth. In light of the knowledge that all sorts of folks attended these festivals, from those who occupied the highest positions in imperial society to those much further down the social hierarchy, that

---

1. On this, see Rajak, "Jews and Christians as Groups," 258–59.

is, women, children, slaves, prostitutes, etc., it stands to reason that at least some Jews may have participated in these festivities and witnessed the dramatic performances thereof.

So, too, is there evidence that Jews performed in the theater. Josephus mentions a certain Alitirus who was an "actor of plays, beloved by Nero, but a Jew by birth" (*Life* 3.16), while the Roman poet Martial mocks a Jewish actor Menophilus for sexual lasciviousness on the stage (*Epig.* 7.82).[2] We know of one Jewish playwright from antiquity, Ezekiel, who wrote a tragedy sometime in the second century BCE concerning the biblical story of the exodus from Egypt, the *Exagōgē*. Only 269 lines of iambic trimeter remain from the original text from which scholars infer a number of things about the production, contents, and performance(s) of the play. In a similar vein, the so-called pseudonymous Greek poets were Jewish authors from around the second century BCE who borrowed known quotes from classical playwrights (Aeschylus, Sophocles, Euripides, et al.), and then composed additional lines of their own but attributed them to these poets anyway—hence their designation as *pseudepigraphy* (see, for example, Pseudo-Justin, *De monarchia*). At any rate, such texts confirm that Jewish authors were quite interested in, and familiar with, dramatic poets and poetry in the Greek and Roman traditions.

Thus, we observe that ancient Jewish views of the theater vacillate from aggressive resistance on one hand to eager participation on the other. In light of the popularity and prevalence of the theater in the Roman world, and the willingness of at least some Jews to participate in theatrical performances, it should come as little surprise that early Jewish and Christian texts reflect an awareness of various aspects of dramatic conventions. Scholars have long recognized the influence of Classical drama on biblical texts. For scholars from generations past who relied on Aristotle's (now out-of-vogue) guidance on the function of tragedy to engender a cathartic release of emotions in the audience, it was possible to find the "tragic" lurking just about everywhere, from Abraham's near slaughter of Isaac to the crucifixion and resurrection of Jesus.

Many have seen in biblical characters the same kinds of "tragic" traits one finds in the protagonists of classical tragedy—doubt, betrayal, misfortune, suffering, crisis, etc. Some even find in biblical texts the

2. Some have supposed that a Jewish sarcophagus (container for holding the remains of a deceased person) decorated with two dramatic masks contains the remains of an actress "Faustina." However, masks were popular sarcophagi decorations, and thus they do not necessarily indicate that Faustina was in fact an actress.

structural building blocks of classical tragedy: discernible scenes and/or acts, plot devices, stock characters, and so on. And while attempts to cast particular books of the Bible as proper *tragedies* or *comedies* by classical standards are often strained, it is most certainly the case that the world of the theater influenced biblical authors in their own textual exhibitions. Given the prevalence and popularity of the theater in the world at the time of the composition of many biblical texts, how could it not?

In what follows, I explore the hymns in Revelation, which have long been thought to evoke choral lyrics in Greek and Roman tragedy insofar as they "comment upon" the surrounding narrative. My own doctoral dissertation on Revelation's hymns, the groundwork for which was laid during a Masters level course on Greek hymns with Melissa Harl at the University of Minnesota, challenged this consensus and concluded instead that Revelation's hymns fail to display the formal or functional range and depth of classical dramatic choruses. In classical tragedy, the chorus functioned for the playwright as a kind of all-purpose character for staging various dramatic elements in the production, announcing character entrances, providing synopses of the past and present circumstances of the characters, foreshadowing dramatic events, and serving as a dialogue partner and/or audience for the protagonists' speech(es). At the same time, the chorus operated apart from the other characters and to a certain extent outside of the dramatic action by casting the dramatic action itself into a particular mythological, historical, philosophical, and/or theological light.[3] While Revelation's hymns simply do not evince most of these functions of the chorus, they do situate the surrounding dramatic activity into specific mythic-theological contexts, which happens to be precisely the function of choral *hymns* in tragedy. In this way, Revelation's hymns are most profitably considered not in terms of choral lyrics generally, but in terms of tragic *hymnic* lyrics in particular.

Hymnic Form and Function in Greek and Roman Tragedy

Hymns in Greek and Roman drama can be identified as they are in any other context, on the basis of the appearance of several formal elements: an invocation of the god(s), a summary of the god's attributes, exploits, and/or past assistance, and a petition for present or future help.[4] While

---

3. See Jeffcoat Schedtler, *Heavenly Chorus*, 196-261, 283-97.
4. For discussion of these elements, see Furley and Bremer, *Greek Hymns*, 1-40.

the presence and configuration of these formal elements vary, praise of the divine constitutes the essence of all ancient hymnic forms, as Plato first suggested when he contrasted praise of the gods (hymns) with praise of mortals (encomia) (*Resp.* 10.607a).

Dramatic hymns most often took the form of well-known hymnic types (or combinations thereof), for example, *paean, dithyramb, epinician ode*, etc. As such, a hymn occurring as part and parcel of a dramatic production was typically performed in a manner that reflected the contents, style, performance of the hymn in non-dramatic contexts, that is, according to appropriate dialectic and metrical tendencies, musical accompaniment, choreographic arrangement, and so forth. Very often sung by the chorus, or group of 12–15 singers who performed in the *orchestra*, the central, semicircular space in front of the theatrical stage, dramatic hymns were essential to Greek tragedy. From what little remains of tragedies in the Roman period (primarily those of Seneca), it appears that hymns continued to shape the genre. By looking at some individual hymns in their dramatic contexts—that is, in relationship to the surrounding speech and dialogue of the actors, to the overarching themes evident elsewhere in the drama, etc.—one is able to see precisely how hymns functioned to frame the surrounding dramatic activity within precise mythic-theological perspectives.

The hymn to Zeus that occurs during the *parodos* (the opening song and dance of the chorus in a Greek tragedy) of Aeschylus' *Agamemnon* provides a good starting point to explore the function of dramatic hymns vis-à-vis the surrounding dramatic activity. The *parodos* itself consists largely of a theological reflection on the suffering that Zeus has inflicted upon Greeks and Trojans alike on account of Paris' abduction of Helen: the events that led to the sacrifice of Iphigenia, an account of the sacrifice itself, and foregrounding of the tragic denouement of the play, Agamemnon's murder at the hands of his wife, Clytemnestra. The hymn to Zeus occurs in the midst of this account. The central themes of the hymn are twofold: the supreme divinity of Zeus (160–175), and the notion that Zeus confers wisdom upon mortals through suffering (176–183). Hymnic claims that Zeus "sets mortals on the road to understanding" (176–177) and that "wisdom comes through suffering . . . whether men want it or not" (178, 180), provide a mythotheological framework for understanding the suffering entailed in the Trojan War. In other words, the hymn makes clear that the misery described in the *parodos*, as well as the afflictions about to transpire in the play, are part and parcel of an ultimately benevolent mechanism by which Zeus confers wisdom upon mortals.

This example must suffice to illustrate a phenomenon that can be observed across classical tragedies, that is, the use of choral hymns to connect dramatic events of the protagonists with divine phenomena. As in the example above, this often takes the form of a hymn setting the dramatic events into a precise mythotheological context, diagnosing dramatic events in terms of the divine phenomena that led to them, or exploring their divine ramifications. The hymns in Senecan tragedy perform a similar function, though they do so in a way that is less conspicuous than in Greek tragedy. That is, Senecan hymns likewise function to situate the dramatic activity of the characters in mythotheological contexts, connecting the activities of the protagonists with those of the gods whose worlds were thought to be integrally connected.

The first *stasimon* (choral song between acts) of Seneca's *Phaedra* presents a straightforward example of this (274–357). Phaedra, against her marriage-vows and the laws of humankind, seeks an incestuous liaison with her stepson, Hippolytus. The introductory dialogue between Phaedra and her nurse reveals two opposing positions on the nature of Phaedra's forbidden desire. On one hand, Phaedra claims that she is overwhelmed by Cupid's power, one which she claims is strong enough to subjugate mortals and gods alike. On the other hand, the Nurse rejects such an idea as a fabrication of mortals to justify illicit love. The hymn to Cupid functions specifically to confirm Phaedra's claim. A description of Cupid's divine attributes and exploits buttresses Phaedra's claim: the god's power is universal and cannot be thwarted even by the gods. By recounting Cupid's conquests of Apollo, Jupiter, Diana, and Hercules, the hymn situates the dramatic debate over the nature of Phaedra's illicit yearnings into a precise mythotheological context: all are subject to such powers, including even the gods themselves.

The second ode in Seneca's *Oedipus*, a dithyramb, a hymn to Dionysus (Bacchus), provides another good, though slightly more complicated, example of Seneca's use of choral hymns to contextualize dramatic activity in a mythotheological context. At first glance, the hymn might appear out of place in the tragic scheme. The preceding dialogue is foreboding: the audience is well aware of the ominous circumstances in which Oedipus is placed, but of which he is totally unaware, which creates the dramatic tension. By recounting several well-known legends of Bacchus, the hymn betrays little trace of the portentous plot, and seems rather to take the audience for a moment *out* of the dramatic tension. A deeper look into an underlying theme evident in most of these tales, however, reveals specific ways in which Oedipus' circumstances and fate are connected to the god. At one level, each of the legends recounted in the hymn tells of some kind of *transformation*. The very first lines recount how Bacchus was raised as a girl (405–428) in order that he might be protected from the vindictive Hera, who was upset that Zeus would sire a boy (Bacchus) with a mortal woman. The hymn then moves to a description of the *maenads*, the female followers Dionysus who were famous for transforming into ecstatic creatures capable of monstrous deeds, including notoriously the dismembering king Pentheus (429–443). After a brief mention of Dionysus' nanny, Ino, who became mad (that is, was transformed from sanity to madness), the hymn moves to the story of Dionysus' kidnapping at the hands of Tyrrhenian pirates who were unaware of his divinity (449–466). Upon capture, Dionysus rescued himself by transforming into a lion, which caused the pirates to jump overboard where they were mercifully transformed into dolphins.

It is little coincidence that transformation is one of the primary themes in *Oedipus* as a whole. That is, the overarching plot in Seneca's *Oedipus* is the unfolding discovery that Oedipus, as the (previously unbeknownst) son of Laius, king of Thebes, and Jocasta, Oedipus' current wife, has fulfilled the prophecy of the Delphic oracle that he would kill his own father and marry his own mother. In this way, the tragedy is ultimately a story of the *transformations* of Oedipus, which occur on several levels. On one hand, he was transformed from the rightful heir to the kingdom of Thebes to the adopted son of Polybus, king of Corinth; on another level, against every effort to subvert it, Oedipus is transformed into the patricidal murderer and incestuous husband that the Fates had predestined for him. Thus, hymnic treatments of well-known exploits of Bacchus function within Seneca's *Oedipus* to frame the story of the transformation of Oedipus within a larger trajectory of mythic transformations. Further connections between Oedipus and the hymnic accounts of Bacchus can be drawn: all are situated generally within Theban history; allusions to Lycurgus' tale (433–434) conjure images of another tragic figure who, having rejected Bacchus, killed a blood relative which caused the land to become barren; references to the myths of Pentheus (who rejects Bacchus) and Agave (who is driven mad by Bacchus) situate Oedipus' fate within the tragic history of the house of Cadmus (626) which, as the hymn makes clear, was notorious for bloodshed between relatives. Whatever more might be said about the social-political-religious function(s) of the theme of transformation in *Oedipus*, or the connections between the plot of Oedipus and the larger trajectory of Bacchus myths, for the purpose of this paper it suffices to draw attention to the primary function of the choral hymn to situate the contents of the surrounding dramatic activity within this larger mythological frame. Having very briefly considered the function of dramatic hymns in classical tragedy, we turn now to Revelation's hymns.

Revelation's Hymns in Light of Tragic Hymnody

Revelation's hymns (4:8–11; 5:9–14; 7:9–12; 11:15–18; 12:10–12; 15:3–4; 16:5–7; 19:1–8) are not, as some scholars have incorrectly concluded, mere interludes that function simply to demarcate the surrounding narrative. Rather, they interact dynamically with the surrounding dramatic sequences and thus constitute an integral part of the narrative as a whole. More precisely, the hymns constitute carefully crafted *responses* to the narrated events, framing them in precise theological and Christological terms. To see the ways in which they do so, I survey each of the hymnic groupings in what follows.

The first set of antiphonal hymns (a hymn followed by hymnic response[s]) concludes the vivid description of the heavenly throne room in Revelation 4, at the center of which is the throne itself, the "one seated upon the throne," and the heavenly retinue: the 24 Elders seated on 24 thrones, four living creatures, the seven lamps which are the spirits of God, etc. With images that recall detailed depictions of God from the LXX and other early Jewish literature (for example, Isa 6; Ezek 1–3; Dan 7; *T. Levi* 5:1), the scene depicts the sovereign majesty of the one seated upon the throne. A sea of glass, a rainbow encircling the throne, and thunder and lightning provide context for the acts of obeisance offered by the four living creatures who offer unceasing praise to God:

> Holy, holy, holy, the Lord God the Almighty, who was and is and is to come. (Rev 4:8)

To this the twenty-four elders, casting their own crowns before the throne of God, respond:

You are worthy, our Lord and God, to receive glory and honor
and power, for you created all things, and by your will they existed and were created. (Rev 4:11)

If chapter 4 constitutes a graphic depiction of the eternal sovereignty of God, the antiphonal hymns provide an explicit theological framework for justifying it on the basis of God's creative power. With long histories in the LXX and other early Jewish literature, and drawing upon the traditional *Trisagion* ("Holy, holy, holy is the Lord of hosts..." [Isa 6:3; *1 Enoch* 39:12–12; *2 Enoch* 21:1; *1 Clem.* 34:6]), the terms used to characterize God, "holy," "Lord," and "Almighty," pronounce God's status as sovereign, while the end of the clause ("the one who was, is, and is to come") confirms God's eternal nature. The hymn then confirms that it is appropriate to accord to God ("You are worthy to receive") three prerogatives ("glory, honor, and power"), each of which connote the superior status of God as divine sovereign, on the basis of the fact that God has "created all things." Thus, the hymn sets the graphic depiction of God as eternal sovereign in the beginning of the chapter into a precise theological context: it is forever justified on the basis of God's creation of the world.

The hymns in chapter 5 function similarly insofar as they provide a christological framework for justifying Jesus' investiture as God's chosen vicegerent. The hymns conclude the chapter in which Jesus is introduced as a "Lamb looking as if he had been slain" (5:6), and identified as the "Lion of the tribe of Judah" and the "Root of David" (5:5). The central activity in the chapter consists of the Lamb taking a "scroll with writing on both sides and sealed with seven seals" (5:1) from the one seated on the throne (5:7). Whatever exactly the scroll is supposed to represent, its significance lies in the fact that the opening of its seals unleashes the destructive power of God upon God's enemies. For example, the opening of the first seal corresponds with the unleashing of the rider on the white horse who comes "conquering and to conquer" (6:1-2), while the opening of the second seal corresponds with the coming of the rider on the red horse with a great sword, who permits people to slaughter one another (6:2), and so on. Thus, transfer of the scroll to the Lamb ultimately represents the notion that the Lamb has been granted the power and authority of God to act uniquely on God's behalf, that is to be God's vicegerent. The hymns that follow this scene provide justification for this action:

> You are worthy to take the scroll and to open its seals; because you were slaughtered and you redeemed for God with your blood [people] from every tribe, tongue, people and nation; and you made them to be a kingdom and priests for our God and they will rule upon the earth. (Rev 5:9–10)

Following this sing the "voice of many angels," the living creatures, and the elders:

> Worthy is the Lamb who was slain to receive power, wealth, wisdom, might, honor, glory, and blessing. (Rev 5:12)

Finally, the entire heavenly retinue concludes:

> To the one seated upon the throne, and to the Lamb, be blessing and honor and glory and strength forever and ever. (Rev 5:13)

In language that recalls the hymns to the one seated upon the throne in chapter 4 ("You are worthy ..."), the Christological hymn in chapter 5 proclaims that Jesus the "Lamb" is indeed "worthy" to receive the power of God ("to take the scroll and open its seals") precisely because he was crucified ("because you were slaughtered"). Moreover, the crucifixion "redeemed" people of every "tribe, tongue, people, and nation." Redemption was a technical transaction in antiquity whereby a person paid a price in order to achieve some improved status as a result. So, for example, a slave might purchase his own freedom, or someone might purchase it on his behalf. The notion that Jesus' own death purchased (that is, *redeemed*) people for God, for example, freedom from living "cursed under the law," is well attested in the New Testament; though here the resulting improved status is something quite different: the redeemed people will "rule upon the earth" as "a kingdom and priests" for God. The notion that God's people would receive some kind of political power in the eschatological age—most often as a reversal of the current misfortunes of those to whom the claim is being made—is a recurring theme in apocalyptic literature.

The hymn concludes with the claim that Jesus is legitimately accorded the prerogatives of someone of high-standing: power, wealth, wisdom, etc. Insofar as some of these prerogatives ("glory," "honor," and "power") are precisely those associated with God in chapter 4 and elsewhere in Revelation, it stands to reason that the hymnic acclamation represents a high view of Jesus' status relative to God, if not a claim that Jesus himself *shares* in the status of divinity. The notion that Jesus is granted such a standing as God's chosen vicegerent recalls several instances in the

Hebrew Bible whereby God's chosen king likewise receives divine prerogatives. For example, Daniel proclaims to King Nebuchadnezzar, "You, O king, the king of kings, to whom the God of heaven has given the rule, the kingdom, the power, the honor, and the glory ..." (Dan 2:37). The notion that Jesus shares in divinity is further suggested by the concluding clause in which God and the Lamb are hymned *together* and accorded further prerogatives: "blessing," "honor," "glory," and "strength."

Thus, insofar as chapter 5 introduces the character of the Lamb and depicts his acquisition of the power of God via the scroll, the hymns provide a Christological framework in which to contextualize this act. Because the Lamb has been slaughtered, and because his blood has redeemed people for God, he has rightfully been appointed as God's chosen vicegerent and now duly receives divine prerogatives as such.

A critically important context in which to view the theological and Christological claims advanced in Revelation's introductory hymns is the Roman Imperial context in which Revelation was written. Any claim for the sovereignty of God and/or the Lamb must be understood within a broader socio-political context wherein sovereignty in the Roman world was thought to be concentrated in the person of the emperor. Any claim that God and/or the Lamb were worthy of divine prerogatives, those which were otherwise understood to reside in the emperor, constituted an implicit rejection of, and thus a subversive attack upon, competing imperial claims. In this way, the hymnic acclamations resonate with attacks on the Roman imperial apparatus elsewhere in Revelation which, as Schüssler Fiorenza has noted, are among the most widely accepted tenets in Revelation scholarship.[5]

After the judgments of God have been enacted by means of the opening of six of the seven seals of the scroll (Rev 6), and the 144,000 have been sealed (7:1-8), we are introduced to a "great multitude" before the throne of God and the Lamb, which have "come out of the great tribulation." In Jewish apocalyptic and early Christian literature, a time of "great tribulation" (for example, "day of tribulation") had come to denote a fixed period of intense suffering during an eschatological period. Inasmuch as Revelation itself depicts a kind of eschatological crisis, the "great multitude" appears to represent a group of those who have died in this crisis—perhaps as martyrs. It is precisely this group who sing the first hymn:

5. Schüssler Fiorenza, *Book of Revelation*, 181-203.

> Salvation belongs to our God, who sits on the throne, and to the Lamb. (Rev 7:10)

The crux of the hymn consists of the "salvation" that is said to be the prerogative of God and the Lamb. A common term in ancient Mediterranean literature, it most often denotes an act of rescue from a perilous situation, such as a battle, shipwreck, illness, and so forth by means of a particular agent, for example, a favorable wind, a good doctor, a beneficent king, etc. In the LXX, the term regularly denotes God's deliverance of a person or persons from conflict—sometimes an eschatological crisis. The same is true in the New Testament, where the agent of salvation is sometimes identified as Jesus. Thus, this hymn provides further information as to the circumstances of the depiction of the "great multitude" in chapter 7: those having been killed in the great tribulation have in fact been delivered from the crisis. The hymn then presumably functions to comfort those hearing it: despite the apparent external threats described throughout Revelation, the present circumstances of those already killed should assuage the fears of anyone still suffering in the crisis on earth.

The short hymn of the Great Multitude is immediately followed by an antiphonal hymn of the heavenly retinue:

> Amen! Praise and glory and wisdom and thanks and honor and power and strength be to our God for ever and ever. Amen! (Rev 7:12)

The conclusion of the hymn takes a similar doxological form to previous hymns, while similar prerogatives are offered to God as elsewhere. Though it is not explicit as in past hymns, the justification for these prerogatives can be inferred from the previous hymn in which God granted "salvation" to those having been killed in the eschatological crisis in Revelation. Thus, the hymns in chapter 7 function as do those in chapters 4 and 5 to situate the preceding narrative into a precise theological context: God has in fact delivered those suffering under the persecution narrated in the text to a place of eternal, heavenly reward seated before God and the Lamb. As we will see below, the dimensions of this reward come into further relief as the narrative unfolds.

Following this, the seven trumpets are sounded, which unleashes further destruction upon the earth. After two intermediate scenes—the Angel with the Little Scroll (10:1–11) and the Two Witnesses (11:1–14)—the seventh trumpet is sounded, which culminates in an antiphonal hymn sung by "loud voices in heaven":

> The kingdom of the world has become
> the kingdom of our Lord and of his Messiah,
> and he will reign for ever and ever. (Rev 11:15)

Interpretation of the hymn hangs on an understanding of the "kingdom of the world," a notion that appears elsewhere in the New Testament to signal that which is in opposition to God (for example, the lands visible from the mountain that are said to be under the control of Satan in Matt 4:8). In Revelation, the "kingdom of the world" is likely to consist of those peoples and lands under the control of Satan and Satan's overlords—for example, the Dragon (12:3-9) and the beasts (13:1-18). To say that the "kingdom of the world" has become the "kingdom of our Lord and of his Messiah" signals that God and the Lamb have assumed control over these lands and peoples. In other words, the hymn proclaims that Satan and his mythic vicegerents (which in some cases represent earthly realities, for example, agents of the Roman imperial apparatus) have been forever deposed by God and the Lamb.

The responsive antiphonal hymn of the twenty-four elders provides further depth on this proclamation:

> We give you thanks, Lord God Almighty, who are and who were,
> for you have taken your great power and begun to reign.
> The nations raged, but your wrath has come,
> and the time for judging the dead, for rewarding your servants,
> the prophets and saints and all who fear your name, both small and great,
> and for destroying those who destroy the earth. (Rev 11:17-18)

With epithets that reaffirm God's eternal sovereignty, and with language that evokes investiture scenes in the Hebrew Bible (for example, 1 Sam 5:10; 2 Kgs 9:6, 13; Ps 46:9; 47:8; 92:1; 96:1; 98:1), God's assumption of power over Satan's dominion is reiterated. The conclusion of the hymn constitutes an excursus on the process by which this has occurred. The claim that the "nations" (which can be identified as God's adversaries on the basis of its use elsewhere in the text—11:2, 9; 16:19; 17:15; 18:3, 23; 19:51; 20:3, 8) have "raged" is a characterization of the actions of the enemies of God as they have been depicted in Revelation, for example, throwing those of the church of Smyrna into prison (2:10), the murder of the "witnesses" (2:13; 11:3-10), the slaughter of the faithful (6:9-11; 13:7), etc. Such a characterization conforms with the notion of "enraged nations" battling with God in eschatological conflict elsewhere in apocalyptic literature (for example, *4 Ezra* 13:30-39; *Jub.* 23:23-31; *1 Enoch* 55:5-6; 99:4; *Sib. Or.* 3:660-668). God's response entails "wrath" and "judging of the dead," which constitutes on one hand "rewards" for God's people (the "prophets," "saints," and "all who fear [God's] name") and on the other hand destruction for those who "destroy the earth." Insofar as the "wrath" of God is used elsewhere in Revelation and in the Hebrew Bible as a metonym for the destruction of God's adversaries (cf. the destruction unleashed by the "bowls of wrath" [15:1—16:21; cf. 14:10, 19; 19:15]), it can be understood here as a hymnic affirmation of such actions. Likewise, the "rewards" offered to God's people, though not identified explicitly here, can be surmised as those rewards detailed elsewhere in the text, for example, salvation from the eschatological conflict, being made a "kingdom and priests" (1:6), a place on the throne (3:21), etc. Thus, the hymns in chapter 11 follow the established pattern of providing a theological context with which to frame the surrounding narrative events. The hymns proclaim that the sounding of the trumpets that unleashes eschatological destruction on the enemies of God constitutes the very act by which God wrests power of the world from Satan and his agents, thereby establishing God's own eternal, sovereign rule. The hymn further proclaims that this act has consequences for the whole world insofar as it entails an eschatological judgment: a reward for the servants of God and destruction for all those who stand in opposition to God.

The very next chapter consists of an isolated narrative in which a pregnant "woman clothed with the sun" is threatened by a "great dragon" who seeks to "devour her child" (12:1-4). Following the script of a well-known ancient Mediterranean combat myth, the baby and the mother are saved by an unknown intermediary, while the dragon is left to battle in heaven against the angelic forces of God. The dragon, now identified as "the Devil and Satan, the deceiver of the whole earth," is then thrown from heaven unto earth along with his angelic retinue. The hymn that follows this narrative provides a new theological and Christological frame with which to understand the ancient myth:

> Now has come the salvation and power and kingdom of our God and the authority of His Messiah. Because the accuser of our brothers has been thrown, the one who was accusing them before our God day and night; they conquered him by the blood of the Lamb and by the word of their testimony, for they did not love their soul to the point of death. Rejoice, therefore, heavens and those who dwell in them; but woe to the earth and the sea,

for the Devil has come down to you with great wrath, because
he knows that his time is short. (Rev 12:10-12)

If in the narrative in chapter 12 the ancient "combat myth" has been invested with language and characters drawn from the author's (and presumably audiences') own purview (for example, the infant child under duress is clearly Jesus insofar as he is identified as the one snatched up to the throne of God and who will "rule all nations with a rod of iron"), the hymn situates the myth more specifically within the context of the imagined eschatological battle described throughout Revelation. At one level, the hymn reveals that the initiation of God's sovereign rule entails a successful cosmic battle with the ultimate adversary of God and God's people, Satan. Insofar as chapter 13 reveals that Satan confers authority to the earthly adversaries of God's people—the Beast from the Land and the Beast from the Sea—the expulsion of Satan from heaven thus foreshadows the ultimate defeat of Satan and his minions. Moreover, the explicit identification of Satan as "the accuser of our brothers" goes further to link the present suffering of the community of followers of the Lamb ("brothers" is a well-attested term to denote religious compatriots in Jewish and Christian texts) with the machinations of Satan in heaven. More than this, however, those who have died in the eschatological conflict are said to be partly responsible, along with the "blood of the Lamb" (Jesus' death on the cross) for Satan's expulsion from heaven! This is a remarkable claim, one that may have its roots in martyrological texts in which the martyrs themselves are imagined to be responsible for the ultimate demise of those persecuting them. Stories in 4 Maccabees (6:10; 7:4; 9:6; 11:20; 16:14; 17:15) and the *Martyrdom of Perpetua* (10:13-14) detail how the virtues of patient suffering in the face of death constitute a victory over physical pain, anxiety, fear, and even the Devil responsible for them. Thus, the hymn proclaims the efficacy of the deaths of the martyrs in Revelation's eschatological conflict in helping to instantiate God's cosmic reign, a clear call to those actually hearing or reading Revelation that the deaths of their friends and family—or even their own eventual deaths—are not in vain. The final line of the hymn reminds them that while those already having died and in heaven are saved, those on earth remain under the temporary control of Satan.

In the following chapters, we are introduced to Satan's earthly entourage, the Beast from the Sea (13:1-10) and the Beast from the Land (13:11-18), which are widely imagined to represent various aspects of the Roman Imperial apparatus. Their association with Satan underscores the author of Revelation's belief that these entities are wholly corrupt and in complete opposition to God and the Lamb, a belief that manifests insofar as the beasts are imagined to utter blasphemies against God (13:5–6), to make war on God's people (13:7, 15), and to deceive the whole world (13:14). If chapter 13 introduces us to these grotesque caricatures of Roman Imperial authority, chapter 14 provides the author's view of the consequences for those who participate in Imperial systems, and the benefits conferred upon those who resist them. On one hand is a vision of those who have been marked with the names of the Lamb and the Father (14:1), who represent the antithesis of those who have received the "mark of the beast" (13:16), and who, "blameless and undefiled" stand in heaven singing hymns of praise. On the other hand are visions of angels forecasting the demise of "Babylon" (read: Rome) and describing in agonizing detail the calamities that befall those who "worship the beast." Following these narrative sequences is a hymn sung by those "who had conquered the beast":

> Great and marvelous are your works, Lord God Almighty; righteous and true are your ways, O King of the Nations. Lord, who will not fear and glorify your name? For you alone are just, and all nations will come and worship before you, for your righteous judgments have been revealed. (Rev 15:3)

The hymn frames the accomplishments of the sovereign God to eliminate all oppositional forces, including especially here the "beast" (who represents Roman imperial authority), and to reward those who have remained steadfast to God and the Lamb even to the point of death, as "great and marvelous works" and "righteous and true ways." The use of these particular terms functions to situate such deeds within a much larger trajectory of history of God's actions as described in the Hebrew Bible, wherein these terms regularly denote the salvific work of God vis-à-vis God's people. The identification of this hymn as a "Song of Moses" (15:3) links more specifically these events described in Revelation to those heralded by Moses following the Exodus from Egypt in Deut 32:5–43: escape from the Pharaoh, trials in the desert, arrival in the promised land, punishment for turning away from God, etc. The message is the same in both hymns: God ultimately vindicates God's people. The rhetorical question "who will not fear and glorify your name?" signals that the expanding reign of God described in Revelation is such that *all* will soon reverence and worship God. This notion is made explicit in the subsequent antiphon, "... all nations will come and worship before you." Critically, the unspoken assumption here is that these same nations will *stop* coming before and worshipping those who would claim sovereign authority instead of God, for example, the Roman emperor. The hymn concludes with additional claims that God alone is "just," while God's revealed judgments are "righteous," which denote God's capacity to act in a way that is appropriate given the circumstances. Given the extent to which the Roman imperial apparatus is portrayed as utterly deplorable and beyond redemption, it is no surprise that its complete destruction is lauded as a justifiable act in the hymn. And so the hymn in chapter 15 conforms to those elsewhere in Revelation insofar as it casts the preceding narrative events into a precise theological framework: the punishment of God's enemies and rewards to God's people as graphically depicted in chapter 14—and elsewhere in Revelation—is linked to a long history of similar acts of God in the Hebrew Bible and praised as such.

The penultimate hymns occur in the midst of the pouring of the seven "bowls of wrath" which, like the opening of the seals and the sounding of the trumpets, coincide with various acts of destruction unleashed upon the earth (16:1–21). After the third bowl is poured, an angel sings:

> You are righteous, the Just One, who is and was, for you have judged these things; because they shed the blood of saints and prophets, you have given them blood to drink. They deserve it! (Rev 16:5–6)

Following this, the heavenly altar responds:

> Yes, O Lord God, the Almighty, your judgments are true and just! (Rev 16:7)

With acclamations that continue to affirm the eternal sovereignty of God, the hymn lauds the destruction of God's enemies as represented by the pouring of the bowls of wrath. By characterizing these acts as "judgments," the hymn proclaims that God is ultimately responsible for them, while the next clause provides an explanation for it: "because they shed the blood of saints and prophets." The indefinite "they" certainly refers to those responsible for the deaths of the "saints and prophets," terms which can be found elsewhere in Revelation to denote members of the communities to whom Revelation was written. Thus, the objects of God's wrath are precisely those Roman imperial entities presented throughout

Revelation as responsible for making war upon God's people. So much is clear from the results of the pouring of the first bowl, which caused sores to come upon those who had the "mark of the beast" (16:2), which again refers to those who participate in Roman imperial systems, as well as the pouring of the fifth bowl whose target is the "throne of the beast" itself (16:10–11). On the basis of the notion *lex talionis*, the idea that punishment for a crime should be equal to the crime committed, God metes out a just and deserving penalty. Those responsible for the deaths of those in the community of saints shall meet the very same fate. In this way, the hymns perform double-duty: they both frame the graphic depictions of destruction upon the earth in the surrounding narrative in terms of God's righteous judgment of the enemies of God, and then connect this to the present suffering (perceived or otherwise) of the communities of believers at the hands of these enemies. As such, the hymn is a proclamation of God's justice that functions both within the narrative to make sense of the destruction and also outside of the narrative as a means of assuaging those hearing the proclamation.

Following the pouring of the seven bowls, the text introduces the character of the "great harlot" who rides the beast with seven heads and ten horns (17:1–18). Clearly recalling the beast(s) from earlier chapters, the depiction of the harlot upon the beast again symbolically represents, though in slightly different terms than in previous chapters, the malevolent power of Roman imperial power, who is imagined to "fornicate" with the kings of the earth (17:2) and to be "drunk with the blood of the saints and the blood of the witnesses to Jesus" (17:6). With the name "Babylon" written upon her forehead, she is clearly associated with Rome itself, as the name had become a cipher for Rome amongst early Jewish and Christian apocalyptic authors, an association which is made even clearer later in the text when she is identified as "the great city that rules over the kings of the earth" (17:18). Her introduction sets the stage for chapter 18, in which her total annihilation is depicted and followed by the lamentations of those who suffer as a result: kings (18:9–10), merchants (18:11–17), and sailors (18:18–20). The laments of those who mourn the destruction of "Babylon" provide the narrative context for the hymnic adulations of those in chapter 19 who celebrate its demise. The voice of a great multitude sings:

> Hallelujah! Salvation, glory and power belong to our God. For his judgments are true and righteous: He has judged the Great Harlot who destroyed the inhabitants of the earth with her

fornication, and he has avenged the blood of his servants shed by her. Hallelujah! The smoke goes up from her forever and forever. (Rev 19:1–3)

To this the 24 elders and four living creatures respond:

Amen. Hallelujah! (Rev 19:4)

Next, a voice from the throne proclaims:

Praise our God, all you God's servants
And all who fear God, small and great. (Rev 19:5)

The hymn concludes with the voice "like the sound of many waters and like the sound of many thunder-peals crying out":

Hallelujah! For the Lord our God reigns. Let us rejoice and exult and give God the glory, for the marriage of the Lamb has come, and his bride has made herself ready; To her it has been granted to be clothed with fine linen, bright and pure. (Rev 19:6–8)

With acclamations confirming the sovereignty of God and in language recalling the previous hymn in which the "true and righteous judgments" (that is, the destruction of the enemies of God) are lauded, this hymn likewise confirms that the judgment of the Great Harlot, the destruction of Rome itself depicted in chapter 18, is worthy of praise. Moreover, the hymn affirms that the destruction of Rome is part and parcel of the process of "avenging" the blood of the innocent who were slaughtered by her, a fate presaged by the hymn in chapter 16. Finally, the image of the ashes of the decimated city smoking "forever and ever" recalls the ruined city of Edom, likewise a representation of a nation opposed to God, prophesied by the prophet Isaiah (Isa 34:1–10), and signals an eternal victory to those whose present suffering is only temporary. After the living creatures and elders affirm this praise with cries of "Amen!" and "Hallelujah!"—a voice from the throne signals that those who persevere who can do nothing other than to praise God.

If the hymns to this point look backwards to the prior destruction of Rome, the conclusion of the hymn looks forward to the denouement of the Apocalypse: the final defeat of God's enemies culminating in God's rule upon the earth (19:1—22:5). Beginning with the well-known "rider on the white horse," who leads a heavenly army to defeat the "beast" and his armies (19:11–21), the symbolic destruction of Rome is again envisaged, as is the annihilation of the forces lending authority to Rome, the Dragon (Satan) itself (20:1-3, 7-10). Coinciding with the destruction of these enemies of God is a final judgment: heavenly rewards for those who have remained faithful to God throughout the eschatological crisis and eternal punishment for those who sided with the Beast (20:4-6, 11-15). All this is followed by the advent of the New Jerusalem descending from heaven to replace the "first earth" which had "passed away" (21:1-27). The final antiphonal hymn affirms that the beginning of God's reign corresponds with the descent of the heavenly Jerusalem: "The Lord God reigns!" With the Lamb depicted as the "bridegroom" (19:9) and the eschatological city of Jerusalem envisioned as the "bride," the final consummation of the reign of God is imagined in nuptial terms. Drawing on prophetic traditions in the Hebrew Bible in which the (faithful) people of God are imagined to be wedded to God (for example, Hos 2:14-20; Isa 54:1-6; Ezek 16:8-14), the hymn envisions a city (and here the "city" functions metonymically for the inhabitants of it) who has remained faithful to God and the Lamb, as connoted by the "bright and pure" linens with which they are adorned. Thus, the judgment of the inhabitants of the world as depicted in the final chapters of Revelation is given a precise theological framework in the hymns: God will dwell eternally only with those mortals who have not participated in Roman imperial activities. They shall be wedded to the Lamb while all others will suffer eternal punishment.

Revelation as Drama?

Having now established that the Apocalypse utilizes heavenly hymns to set into precise mythotheological terms the surrounding narrative activity, and that this function mirrors that of hymns in ancient drama, how shall we conceptualize the relationship between them? Many scholars who recognize such resonances between ancient drama and Revelation go so far as to claim that the text is itself a kind of drama. Such attempts, though they helpfully point us in the direction of the theater as one conceptual world from which the author(s) of Revelation was drawing, are ultimately unconvincing. The apocalypse is *not* a drama in any technical sense or by just about any reasonable generic standard. Yet, as our study has shown, the world of drama is most certainly brought to bear on the visions of John of Patmos.

Claude Lévi-Strauss provides a methodological path forward. His notion of the *bricoleur*, the crafty tradesman who makes use of a variety of otherwise unrelated raw materials in order to fashion some new craft, supplies a model for thinking about the way myth-makers utilize a variety of heterogeneous conceptual resources to create new myths:

> [The *bricoleur*] interrogates all the heterogeneous objects of which his treasury is composed to discover what each of them could 'signify' and so contribute to the definition of a set which has yet to materialize but which will ultimately differ from the instrumental set only in the internal disposition of its parts. A particular cube of oak could be a wedge to make up for the inadequate length of a plank of pine or it could be a pedestal ... but the possibilities always remain limited by the particular history of each piece and by those of its features which are already determined by the use for which it was originally intended or the modifications it has undergone for other purposes. The elements which the 'bricoleur' collects and uses are 'pre-constrained' like the constitutive units of myth, the possible combinations of which are restricted by the fact that they are drawn from the language where they already possess a sense which sets a limit on their freedom of manoeuvre.[6]

Like the *bricoleur* and the myth-maker, the author(s) of Revelation had at their disposal an "implicit inventory" of culturally available conceptual resources with which to compose the Apocalypse. It is already generally agreed that the text is invested with language, imagery, structure, etc., from all sorts of conceptual realms: the temple, the synagogue service, imperial procession, emperor worship, letter-writing, drama, prophetic modes of imagining the heavenly throne, etc. In the case of the hymns, we see a similar blending of language, imagery, and functionality. On one hand, the author presents a scene of the heavenly retinue surrounding the throne of God and praising God (and the Lamb) in terms drawn quite clearly from prophetic traditions in the Hebrew Bible. On the other hand, while the author has fashioned the hymns within this conceptual framework he invested them with functionality drawn from the world of classical drama. In so doing, the author has—consciously or unconsciously—blended language, imagery, and functionality from heterogeneous conceptual realms.

---

6. Lévi-Strauss, *Savage Mind*, 18–19.

The author(s) of Revelation drew from the conceptual realm of the theater in the presentation of the heavenly hymns to God and the Lamb simply because they were conceptually *available* for the task. In other words, there existed a predetermined hymnic functionality available to the author(s) from the world of Greek and Roman drama that the author(s) imported into their own presentation. As Lévi-Strauss argues, this is the primary tendency of the myth-maker. The recognition of this mode of imagination allows us to appreciate the extent to which the author draws upon the conventions of particular genres while obviating the need to try to fit the text into the straightjacket of any particular genre (for example, drama). It also provides a profitable way to think about the many other ways in which the author(s) of Revelation blended language, imagery, myth, and so forth, from multiple conceptual realms.

Works Cited

Furley, William D., and Jan Maarten Bremer. *Greek Hymns: Selected Cult Songs from the Archaic to the Hellenistic Period*. Vol. 1, *Texts in Translation*. Studien und Texte zu Antike und Christentum 9. Tübingen: Mohr/Siebeck, 2001.

Jeffcoat Schedtler, Justin. *A Heavenly Chorus: The Dramatic Function of Revelation's Hymns*. Wissenschaftliche Untersuchungen zum Neuen Testament 2/381. Tübingen: Mohr/Siebeck, 2014.

Lévi-Strauss, Claude. *The Savage Mind*. Chicago: University of Chicago Press, 1966.

Most, Andrea. *Theatrical Liberalism: Jews and Popular Entertainment in America*. New York: New York University Press, 2013.

Rajak, Tessa. "Jews and Christians as Groups in the Pagan World." In *"To See Ourselves as Others See Us": Christians, Jews, "Others" in Late Antiquity*, edited by Jacob Neusner and Ernest S. Frerichs, 247–62. Scholars Press Studies in the Humanities. Chico, CA: Scholars, 1985.

Schüssler Fiorenza, Elisabeth. *The Book of Revelation: Justice and Judgment*. 2nd ed. Minneapolis: Augsburg Fortress, 1988.

17

Divine Chemistry

*Nymphs, Sacrament, and Substance
in the Greco-Roman World*

RABUN TAYLOR

Why is there a category of deities called nymphs? On the face of it, this question may seem presumptuous. A simple bibliography search will quickly reveal that academic interest in the character and qualities of Greek and Roman nymphs has soared in recent years. My own winding path to this topic can be traced back a quarter century to Melissa Harl's graduate seminar on the Asclepius cult, in which I was confronted for the first time with serious questions about the intersection of the material and the spiritual. A surge of interest in the culture of water, baths, and bathing accounts partly for the more recent phenomenon, provoked further by Jennifer Larson's panoramic monograph on Greek nymphs. Some scholars have sought to understand the nymphs by drawing variously from literary and religious studies, art history, anthropology, and cognitive science. Others have given careful attention to the archaeology and geographic scope of nymph worship. Progress has been made.[1]

1. Larson, *Greek Nymphs*; Lhôte-Birot, "Les nymphes en Gaule"; Gasperini, *Usus veneratioque fontium*; Sineux, "Asklépios"; Dvorjetski, *Leisure*; Giacobello et al., eds., *Ninfe*; Maggi, "Santuari delle sorgenti"; Pache, *Moment's Ornament*; Andreu Pintado, "Aspectos sociales"; Calderone, *Cultura e religione*; De Cesare, "Le 'Nymphai' e

Yet the question persists: Why does the word νύμφη, "nymph" (when referring to a minor female deity, not to a bride), even exist, and what significance did this categorical distinction have to ancient Greeks and Romans? Most gods, whether generalist or specialist, were simply presented as themselves—they needed no further taxonomy. Nymphs, however, constitute a subcategory of deities. In this respect they are not unique in classical culture—one thinks of Muses, Furies, Sirens, satyrs, tritons, and so forth—but for the most part, those other specialized classes of beings, though they roamed promiscuously through the landscape of myth, were actually *worshiped* sparsely, or not at all. I leave aside ancestral deities and the spirits of the dead; these are a fundamentally different category, having once been living persons. Nymphs, by contrast, were full-blooded deities enjoying widespread devotion. Yet while many had names, a majority seem to have answered to no more specific appellation than "Nymph" or "the Nymphs," taking satisfaction in that classification alone, often with a generic toponym added. What does it mean to be a category within a category—deities who are also nymphs—and what's more, to be identified principally by that category, rather than as individuals, as if it were enough to be known and cherished as equids, albinos, or shoemakers?

What seems to justify the taxonomic approach is their categorical relationship to geography.[2] Nymphs are place spirits. They embody a *topos* more than a personality or a concept; and though most of them inhabit unique places, it is not this fact alone, but the fact that they are *defined by and affixed to* their proprietary geographic feature, that causes them to be regarded as a class. Moreover, to borrow a term from urban design, they are placemakers: their defining presence and cultural resonance enrich and enliven a physical space, inviting people to approach and experience it, thereby enriching it further. Greek cities (*poleis*), especially of the diaspora, exploited these advantages. Many *poleis* chose water deities as their most salient signifiers, representing their local eponymous river gods or nymphs (the latter often elaborately syncretized) on coinage.[3]

Leaving aside their conventional literary roles as agents or victims of sexual adventures, which had little to do with their popularity in cult

---

l'acqua"; Petraccia and Tramunto, "Il termalismo curativo"; Bassani et al., eds., *Aquae salutiferae*; Fabiano, "La nympholepsie"; Anibaletto et al., eds., *Cura, preghiera e benessere*; Wagman, *Cave of the Nymphs*.

2. Fabiano, "La nympholepsie," 171–72.

3. Picard, "Les nymphes"; Salamone, "La categoria iconica."

practice, nymphs have almost no meaning or function independent of their defining topographical adjunct. Indeed, some nymphs (hamadryads, oak spirits) were so bound to their defining feature that they died with it. Originally, dryads haunted oak forests, oreads mountains, naiads fresh water. Nereids populated the seas (though Arethusa famously became a freshwater spring). Other, less well-developed categories of geographically defined beings also appeared in the Archaic and Classical periods—for example, river gods, who in art (though less often in literature) generally took the form of Acheloös, the fish-tailed man or man-headed bull—himself the father of nymphs.[4] By the Roman imperial period, the Greek nymphs' internal distinctions had blurred, but their categorical significance remained intact: whatever their status in myth and literature, in actual cult practice nymphs were attached almost exclusively to fresh, running water, usually springs.

More to the point, they were personifications of water's role in helping or harming humans. It has even been argued recently that the word νύμφη to mean "nymph" is etymologically distinct from the same word meaning "bride," and is an assimilated form of the older λύμφη, meaning "water."[5] Indeed nymphs embodied not just a source, but the distinctive substance and behavior of its waters—for it was those qualities, coalescing with their divine will and the will of any additional gods overseeing the place, that mattered most to worshipers. The benefits they bestowed on a pilgrim could be oriented either inward (healing, fertility) or outward (fulfilling curses, delivering oracular responses).

Extraordinary Devotion: Nympholepsy

Living, flowing water is a particularly potent natural asset to have in one's divine portfolio, not only because of its primacy in *sustaining life* but also because of the many cultural functions that it has acquired as a consequence of that fact. Two of these subsidiary roles, broadly defined, will occupy our attention in this study: water as a conduit to occult knowledge (*divinatory power*) and water as a means to health and fertility (*therapeutic power*). In theory, every terrestrial source of water—well, spring, river, pond, lake—harbored this triad of potentialities, therein endowing the resident or tutelary deities with uncommon authority. It

4. On Acheloös and his prototypes see Molinari and Sisci, ΠΟΤΑΜΙΚΟΝ.
5. Hyllested, "L'esprit des eaux."

should be no surprise, then, that in one important respect nymphs possessed a capacity generally reserved for gods with more developed cults, such as Apollo, Demeter and Kore, Dionysus, and Asclepius: the power of mystic possession.

Called nympholepsy, literally "seizure by nymphs," it was a kind of divine rapture resembling poetic ecstasy. Actual instances of the phenomenon are rare in the historical record, but its persistence as a matter of interest in literature and folklore bears witness to its cultural resonance. In the Greek intellectual tradition, as W. R. Connor has shown, the nympholept was seized not by an irrational frenzy, as ecstatic states are often mistakenly characterized, but by a state of heightened awareness, sharpened intellect, and eloquence.[6] In essence, he was possessed as much by the Muses as by the nymphs—a perfectly understandable synthesis, given the close kinship that the one group had with the other. The condition is most famously characterized by Socrates in Plato's *Phaedrus*, who claims repeatedly to have been overcome by the clarity and fluency of the Nymphs (author's translation)—

> SOCRATES: Besides, under the plane tree runs the loveliest spring of exceedingly cold water; our feet bear witness to that. And to judge from the *korai* and statues, the place seems to be a sanctuary of certain nymphs and Acheloös (230b)...
>
> PHAEDRUS: Some unaccustomed fluency (εὔροια) has altogether taken hold of (εἴληφεν) you, Socrates.
>
> SOCRATES: Hush, then, and hear me out. This place seems divine to me, so if periodically I should wax nympholeptic as I speak (ἐὰν ἄρα πολλάκις νυμφόληπτος προϊόντος τοῦ λόγου γένωμαι), don't be surprised. Even now I'm not far from intoning dithyrambs. (238 c–d)...
>
> SOCRATES: Surely you noticed, my friend, that I'm already voicing epic verses, and no longer dithyrambs, even as I critique these matters? Don't you know that at the hands of the nymphs, before whom you cleverly threw me, I will surely be possessed (σαφῶς ἐνθουσιάσω)? (241e)

Nympholepsy in practice—as opposed to a literary topos—is documented in perhaps four instances. Recent scholarship has scrutinized

---

6. Connor, "Seized by the Nymphs." On nympholepsy, see also Borgeaud, *Cult of Pan*, 88–116; Larson, *Greek Nymphs*, 11–20; Pache, *Moment's Ornament*; Fabiano, "La nympholepsie."

these cases in considerable detail,[7] and so I will discuss them only briefly. A certain Theran named Archedamos looked after a sacred cave of Pan and the nymphs on a spur of Mount Hymettos near Vari in Attica around 450–400 BCE. Carved into the cave's walls, inscriptions—some evidently by Archedamos himself and others by later devotees—refer to him as νυμφόληπτος, and to his prodigious housekeeping, undertaken according to "the insights (φραδαῖσι) of the nymphs" (*IG* 12 788); for he shaped and even sculpted his rocky domain into a shrine and tended its gardens. His hermit-like existence bespeaks a permanent, formalized, even cultic attachment to the place and its resident deities—resident, it would seem, because a spring once emerged within the cave. A similar arrangement is evident near Pharsalos at the cave-shrine of a certain Pantalkes, who lived in the fifth century BCE. This man too tended his sacred grotto and garden, and again his devotion was recorded in inscriptions—in this case celebrating Pan, Hermes, Apollo, Heracles, Chiron, Asclepius, and Hygieia, but especially the nymphs. It is they who "walk upon these grounds," who "made Pantalkes a worthy man and overseer," and who granted him "a gracious living for all his days."[8] Many pious pilgrims sought out Archedamos' cave, as its votive deposits demonstrate; Pantalkes seems to have had a cult following too. Other historical examples of likely nympholepts are known at Kafizin on Cyprus[9] and Mt. Cithaeron near Plataea. At the latter site, Plutarch says, the natives of old were possessed by the Sphragitic nymphs, whose cave was on one of the mountain's spurs; thus they were called νυμφόληπτοι (*Arist.* 11). By virtue of their relationship with the nymphs, the Cithaeronians seem to have enjoyed a reputation for divination; Plutarch specifically observes that an oracle had once dwelt in the cave (ἄντρον . . . ἐν ᾧ καὶ μαντεῖον ἦν πρότερον).

Indeed, some kind of prophecy probably played a role in most or all of these instances of nympholepsy, otherwise it is hard to understand why nympholepts would have gained a following at all. In one semi-historical case, the connection was explicit: a famous Boeotian diviner named Bakis, who forecast many events in the Persian Wars (Herodotus 8.20, 77, 96; 9.43), acquired his power by nympholepsy, according to Pausanias (κατάσχετον ἄνδρα ἐκ νυμφῶν, 10.12.11). As Connor observes,

---

7. In addition to citations in the previous note, see Jim, "Seized by the Nymph?"; Schörner and Goette, *Pan-Grotte*.

8. Pache, *Moment's Ornament*, 52–55; Wagman, *Cave of the Nymphs*, and bibliographies.

9. Mitford, *Nymphaeum of Kafizin*; Jim, "Seized by the Nymph?"

nymphs represented springs, and springs famously brought inspiration and vision. In the metaphorical reaches of high literature, such advantages might have been strictly poetic or philosophic, but in Greek devotional life oracular responses were meant to provide practical solutions to real-life problems, even when delivered in verse. Archedamos, the cave-keeper of Vari, seems to have been in direct communication with his patron goddesses, for either he or his followers claimed in an inscription that he had perfected the cavern "with the φραδαῖσι (knowledge, or insights) of the nymphs." And Onesagoras, the evidently nympholeptic protagonist of the third-century-BCE inscriptions at Kafizin, seems to have described himself using the unique word μανζιαρχῆσας, that is, ex-mantiarch, or chief diviner.[10] The reading of this word is not entirely secure, so it would be incautious to speculate further. But the notion that this man had presided over a *society* of seers, perhaps all devoted to his patron nymph, is intriguing.

Were Nymphs Fearsome?

Intense religious experiences are never without risk, and few gods of the Greco-Roman world were entirely benign. It is fair to ask, then, whether our goddesses of the countryside were prone to malice as well as grace.[11] Studies of nympholepsy unfailingly interject the sad tale of Hylas (Theocritus 13; Apollonius, *Argonautica* 1.1207–72) and the more ambiguous one of Hermaphroditus (Ovid, *Metam.* 4.274–388), rare examples in myth of nymphs actively seizing or abducting an innocent youth. Callimachus' epigram 22 laconically invokes a certain Astakides, a goatherd of Crete, snatched from his hillside by a nymph. But in truth, these episodes tell us almost nothing useful, even as metaphors, about the phenomenon of nympholepsy or the worship of nymphs. Nor do they capture the essence of nymphs categorically any more than, say, the peculiar case of the Nereid Arethusa tunneling under the sea and emerging as a freshwater spring. Roger Caillois marveled at the schizophrenic nature of nymphs, who oscillated in his view between identities as exuberant, health-giving benefactors and "midday demons," malicious, sexually rapacious spirits of the sea and countryside who took nympholepts as victims and sub-

---

10. Mitford, *The Nymphaeum of Kafizin*, 194 no. 258; Connor, "Seized by the Nymphs," 164; Jim, "Seized by the Nymph?" n63.

11. Schirripa, "La ninfa cattiva."

jected them to their enervating heat.[12] Yet many aspects of his argument can be challenged.

There is little evidence that people worried much about the maleficence of nymphs, whether or not they sought possession by them. To the contrary: as deities of healing and wellness, the whole cohort of them might even merit distinction alongside Asclepius and Hygieia as outstandingly benign gods when compared to the common run of prejudiced, volatile, and overprivileged rogues ensconced in the Greek and Roman pantheon. Doubtless the nymphs could let you down in one way or another, if you did not propitiate them in the customary manner. It is also true that a residue of the dire, fay-like nymphs of myth persist in a few inscriptions of the Roman period commemorating children who died too soon, but the influence of Greek literary conceit in these epitaphs is obvious and heavy-handed.[13] On the whole, outside of a handful of literary narratives, nymphs seem neither vindictive nor even capable of dreadful deeds.

To be sure, ecstatic trances were apt to induce states of abject terror. But this condition should not be confused with conventional dread of a vindictive god improperly propitiated; it is more abstract and disembodied than that. A mental rapture had its harrowing moments, but these attendant fears likely emerged from vertiginous dislocations of self and identity. Further, if the trance was successfully induced, such fears would properly yield to the ineffable clarity, sometimes even euphoria, of full possession. Nymphs are the natural consorts of Pan in ancient Greek folklore, and the related phenomenon of Panolepsy is presented as a violent and frightening kind of mental rapture befitting the god of Panic fear.[14] Pan's typological proximity probably played a role in common perceptions of nympholepsy. Commenting on Theocritus' telling of the tale of Hylas, the handsome youth of myth abducted by nymphs, a scholiast observes that their characterization as "dreadful goddesses" (δειναὶ θεαί,13.44) is apt, "because of the fear that seizes those who meet them; this fear causes nympholepsy." Emphatically, for the possessed this kind of terror was *natural and unavoidable*. It had nothing to do with appeasing or displeasing the gods, or with the gods' temperament at all.

---

12. Caillois, "Les démons de midi"; Caillois, "Les démons de midi (suite)"; Caillois, "Les démons de midi (suite et fin)."

13. Borgeaud, *Cult of Pan*, 105–6; Larson, *Greek Nymphs*, 70.

14. Borgeaud, *Cult of Pan*, 88–116.

In short, within the framework of actual human interaction with nymphs, as opposed to a literary construct, they seem to be reduced to agents of a psychic condition. Varro even implies that the term νυμφόληπτος had evolved in Greek to refer to persons who achieve ecstatic states in general, and its Latin equivalent too:

> In Pacuvius: "Mind-bent, as if lymphatic (*flexanima, tamquam lymphata*), or stirred by the mysteries of Bacchus." *Lymphatic* is derived from *lympha* (liquid), which is from *nympha* ... In Greece, those of displaced mind (*commota mente*) whom they call νυμφολήπτους, our people have called lymphatics (*De lingua latina* 7.87).

Later, Festus tinges Varro's gloss with a heavier dose of affect, but narrows the scope of the phenomenon: "Tradition has it that anyone who sees an apparition (*species*) in a spring—that is, the image of a nymph—will be seized by unending madness (*furendi non finem*). These are what the Greeks call nympholepts. The Latins call them lymphatics" (120M, s.v. *lymphae*). In both cases, the emphasis is decidedly on the fear or psychic dislocation instilled in a *process*—indeed, in a process that Varro even insists, by contextualizing it within the cult of Bacchus, was not confined to a cult of nymphs but constituted a universal experience among those who undergo possession. Festus, however, may proceed from a minor misunderstanding, first by implying that nympholepsy is a condition, not a state (i.e., it is chronic) and also by confining it to a visual process, specifically the vision of a nymph in a spring. As we shall see, he is not necessarily wrong in this second characterization, only too limiting. Holy madness could be induced by any number of means, ordinary or abstruse. And as regards water, many modes of contact with it, as long as it was properly sanctified or enshrined, could induce the desired state.

Ordinary Devotion

None of this is to suggest that holy madness or clairvoyance were necessary or even common adjuncts to the worship of nymphs. The tendency to associate nymphs with nympholepsy in classical literature simply confirms the proposition that the most concentrated, extreme manifestations of a construct leave the strongest residue in cultural memory. As Larson has exhaustively demonstrated, most sites associated with nymphs in the Greek world offer no evidence of mantic activity, and one that did—at

Illyrian Apollonia—was celebrated not for any known water feature, but for a perpetual flame issuing from the bituminous depths (Cassius Dio 41.45). What I wish to stress is that because nymphs were attached to revered locales and especially to a single element—water—that was habitually exploited for either therapeutic or divinatory properties, they enjoyed an unusual capacity for inducing profound emotional states simply through their worshipers' experience of the place. This kind of experience leaves no trace in the archaeological record, and it is likely to go unremarked in literature or inscriptions. Nymphs' placemaking potency suggests that human devotion toward them, especially if exercised through the medium of water, habitually carried intimations of divine possession, even if these were merely figurative. That is, it was possible to enjoy the nymphs' presence and favor through an ordinary ritual act of drinking, immersion, or washing, whether or not it involved intense experiences such as healing rituals or altered mental states. I will suggest below that such processes were akin to a sacrament.

In terms of religious devotion—which might be taken categorically as a function of concentration and immediacy rather than of diffusion, distance, and broad scope—the waters from below, not from the sky, took priority. Springs, the most sacred of waters, emerged from the depths. Given the nature of the underworld through which water notionally cycled, we should therefore not be surprised that it sometimes carried the potential to do harm. The nymphs invoked in lead curse tablets found at the recently discovered spring sanctuary of Anna Perenna along the Via Flaminia at Rome seem to have played a mediating or activating role alongside other paraphernalia of sorcery;[15] another example of such an invocation is known from the sulfur springs of Pergine Valdaro.[16] Either way, there is nothing to suggest that the waters themselves were insalubrious; quite the opposite! Their potential for mediating curses was simply an extension of their health-giving properties. These resident nymphs, just as in the overwhelmingly more numerous cases on record of benign assistance, were invoked because they could bring aid to those seeking it, not because they were noted for a baleful or malevolent spirit.

In truth, there is little evidence that ordinary persons understood nymphs in the rarefied manner of a Socrates or even shamanic nympholepts. Nor did they waste much time appealing to the deities of reputedly

---

15. Piranomonte, "Religion and Magic."
16. Petraccia and Tramunto, "Il termalismo curativo," 176, 188 no. 34.

bad waters, to the extent that such gods even existed. It is instructive, for example, that the people of Halikarnassos, whose spring of Salmakis was widely reputed to be insalubrious and enfeebling, celebrated both the spring and its dubious nymph with full-throated praise.[17] In fact, dedicatory inscriptions to nymphs found at sanctuaries or on votive objects are almost uniformly celebratory. They do not dwell on death or the underworld, nor do they attribute to the resident deities any special psychotropic properties. The default mode of the devotional discourse is virtually identical to that of their companion gods such as Pan, Apollo, Hermes, Acheloös, Heracles, and Asclepius. But these latter gods, even if they act alongside the nymphs, cannot be understood to act in precisely the same way. With the possible exception of Acheloös, they are highly mobile, and thus deeply invested in narrative.

To be sure, *named* nymphs may have had a story; if they were Nereids of the sea, where it was possible to range widely without quitting one's element, they might even have possessed the semblance of a literary persona, like Thetis, Galatea, or (before she turned into a spring) Arethusa. But in the realm of religious devotion, where real people consulted deities for practical purposes through the mediation of drinking or immersion, prayers, inscriptions, and votive objects, most nymphs seem to have remained nondescript and generic, either little more than a name or completely anonymous. Territorial by definition, they characteristically stayed put; they were geographically fixed and their potential for narrative was limited. (Poets breathed life into nymphs by bringing the stories to *them*—usually by means of intruding strangers or importuning gods.) And while healing deities with more complex narratives often demanded elaborate, mediated mystery rituals or altered states of mind, sometimes realized within the highly structured context of patient incubation, nymphs seem to have been amenable to simpler and more direct forms of invitation.

The fact that most nymphs who were objects of devotion occupied prized springs and mineral baths suggests that the basic process of activation was straightforward: their salutary, restorative, or curative properties were absorbed bodily, along with the water's chemical elements, through drinking or immersion accompanied by prayer. Such processes were probably attended by a general sense of sanctity and well-being—not

---

17. Sourvinou-Inwood, "Hermaphroditos and Salmakis."

full-fledged nympholepsy, by any standard, but a simple and universal exercise of religious experience.

Common Characteristics of Nymphs

Thus we may confidently envision two tracks of connectivity between humans and nymphs: 1) the road less taken, more angular but more glamorous, to full *possession* by them; 2) the wider, straighter road to *communion* with them by pilgrimage to their sanctuaries, experiences of the place, and contact with its waters. Especially to grasp the shrouded cultural influence of the second path, we might inquire what specific properties of freshwater nymphs encouraged or enabled such communion. Specifically as objects of devotion and petition, they are characterized by six salient traits:

1. Generic anonymity. Nymphs can have names and stories, but most do not. A group of nymphs may also be named as a group, but when they are, they are rarely further distinguished by individual names. Examples of this type are the Deliades on Delos, the Appiades in Rome and the Nitrodes from the island of Ischia. Usually these names are geographical or otherwise classificatory; that is, they refer to something apart from the deities themselves, but to which they are inseparably anchored. The Nitrodes' name, for example, refers to the beneficent alkalinity of their therapeutic waters (*aquae salsae, vel quae nitri habeant qualitatem,* Caelius Aurelianus, *De morbis chronicis* 5.77).[18]

2. Liminality. Nymphs never belong to society, even a society of gods. The countryside and the sea, where no social structures or polities may be found, are thus their favored domains. Even in myth, if a nymph enters a social relationship such as marriage, she does so against her will, or like Egeria, "consort" of Numa, in an indeterminate manner that provokes confusion or skepticism.[19] It is intriguing too that our paradigmatic nympholepts were liminal figures. As anthropologists have often observed, those who are given to holy madness dwell on the fringes of society, but not in utter isolation;

---

18. On the Nitrodes and their dedicatory reliefs see Adamo Muscettola, "Gli exvoto delle ninfe."

19. Larson, *Greek Nymphs*, 71–73. Egeria: Lambardi, "Le nozze ninfali."

they play important social roles on behalf of those who beseech them. The career nympholepts of Vari and Pharsalos seem to fit this profile rather well, even to the extent that they resemble shamans.[20] We have already seen how Socrates, who was not exactly a shaman but who certainly cut a liminal figure in Athenian society, ascribed his own states of special mental clarity to nympholepsy.

3. Femininity. This is not the place to elaborate on water and gender; on this topic, Muthmann's monumental *Mutter und Quelle* (1975) remains an essential, though ultimately frustrating, reference. Nymphs are uniformly female, but water deities in general are not. In cult they almost exclusively adhere to springs, and that association with water emanating from its source—and from Mother Earth—suggests to most interpreters the essence of maternity. However, the purest manifestation of springs in Roman cult, Fons, is male; and rivers too tend to be masculine, like the words that represent them (*flumen*, ποταμός). When a river obviously emanates from a single, copious source, the masculine identity and nomenclature may extend to the source too, as in the case of the Clitumnus discussed below. Could it be that nymphs, like so many allegorical gods, acquired their gender etymologically—i.e., simply because the word representing them, νύμφη, which may originally have meant "water," is feminine? (*Fons*, after all, is masculine.) The abundant material culture surrounding nymph worship—art and votive objects in particular—is slanted toward female devotees, confirming that from the Archaic to the Hellenistic period, at least, the nymphs were deemed especially attentive to girls and women.[21] But their appeal to the distaff side of society, reinforcing their femininity, may derive from an early confusion with the other meaning of the word νύμφη, "bride," which may be etymologically distinct. In song and story nymphs are alluring and promiscuous, and in the visual arts they unfailingly follow the archetype of Aphrodite or other young, nubile goddesses. Concomitantly nympholepts are always male, and thereby fulfill the metaphorical coupling with these "water-brides."[22]

---

20. Connor, "Seized by the Nymphs," 174–79.

21. Larson, *Greek Nymphs*, 100–120; De Cesare, "Le 'Nymphai' e l'acqua."

22. On the sexual dimension of nymphs and their tendency to interact in myth with males, see Larson, *Greek Nymphs*, 87–90.

4. Geographic fixity. Nymphs are inseparably attached to the feature from which they gain their identity; the term *hamadryad*, for example, "together with oaks," specifies the bond between a particular class of nymph and her sacred tree by adding the strong but inessential prefix ἁμα-. Likewise, freshwater nymphs are also physically bound to the hydrological features they represent. Occasionally, if a nymph is famous, more than one place may serve as her haunt; Egeria, for example, was worshiped both at the sanctuary of Diana Nemorensis by Lake Nemi and at the Camenae outside Rome (Vergil, *Aeneid* 7.761–64; Ovid, *Fasti* 3.259–76; Strabo 5.240; Livy 1.21.3; Martial 10.35.13–14). Similarly, Acheloös seems to have taken on characteristics of a general god of rivers, as his widespread cult presence (even alongside the Ilissos River in the *Phaedrus*) suggest. But the great majority of nymphs invoked around the Greek and Roman world adhered to one spot or a cluster of loci within a small area.

5. Plurality. The less attached such places are to stories and personalities, the more likely their resident nymphs were several, rather than one. Their divisibility and interchangeability—you might even call it their transparency, since they have few personality traits to flesh them out—is like water itself. On votive reliefs it is often their multiplicity (usually three) and identical appearance, along with the presence of a dominant god beside them, that identifies them. Pluralities of female deities are a commonplace in Greek tradition; the Graces, Hours, Fates, Furies, and Muses all come immediately to mind, and the kinship among these groups has been often noted.[23] Less intelligible is the reason for their multiplicity, but in the case of squads of undifferentiated minor divinities such as nymphs, often invoked alongside a greater and more mobile god like Apollo or Pan, their numbers may have provided a welcome sense of mass, redundancy, and attentiveness to the petitioner.

6. Therapeutic agency. In the Greek world, nymphs played a pronounced role in overseeing fertility, childbirth, childcare, and child development; thus, like many liminal figures of unusual potency, they were seen to reinforce social norms and structures.[24] In the Roman period their beneficial roles varied significantly by region, but from what we can glimpse of religious praxis through dedicatory inscriptions

23. Ibid., 7–8, 259–64, and bibliography.
24. Ibid., 5, 85–86.

and reliefs, health and therapy dominated their portfolio of real-life duties. Overwhelmingly, these inscriptions identify nymphs in the context of living water, especially springs. Either explicitly or implicitly, they convey a *pro salute* message: springs are for maintaining or restoring physical wellbeing, and their resident nymphs either have sovereign control over that function, or if they do not, assist in expediting human communication with a greater god who does. Venerated as common pastoral companions of Apollo in the Greek period,[25] nymphs kept this relationship in Roman times, but in such a manner as to emphasize Apollo's healing role.[26]

If all these characteristics could themselves be characterized in a single word, it would be *immediacy*—that is, the availability of the nymphs' assistance through a minimum of cultural mediating structures such as priesthoods, state cults, a calendar, and elaborate ritual. Nymphs dwelt apart from society, but ironically that fact made them more directly accessible because they stood free of burdensome social norms, customs, and barriers. They were available for invocation directly within their defining landscape, not off in some remote Olympian retreat.[27] As females, they took a nurturing role in helping their devotees, whether the matter related to healing, marriage, child-rearing, or fertility. As groups, they strengthened the force of their assistance and lent a sense of community to their efforts.

Sacrament

True, one had to travel to the nymphs, not vice versa, and that required time and effort. But such is the nature of therapeutic cults, especially the majority of them associated with springs.[28] It could not have been oth-

---

25. Ibid., 96–97

26. For example, at Ischia and Vicarello; see Adamo Muscettola, "Gli ex-voto delle ninfe"; Falkenstein-Wirth, *Quellheiligtum*. Particularly in Roman times, thermal waters were often associated with Apollo, nymphs, or both; for their prevalence among dedications at therapeutic thermal spas in Roman Italy, see Buonopane and Petraccia, "Termalismo e divinità."

27. Larson, *Greek Nymphs*, 65. Gaifman, "Visualized Rituals," however, notes that some Attic ex-voto reliefs show Pan, Hermes, or both playing a mediatory or protective role between the nymphs and specifically male dedicants. In effect, they play the role of a male guardian in Athenian society.

28. Arnaldi, "La valenza 'salutare'"; Petraccia and Tramunto, "Il termalismo

erwise when the benefits inhered in the waters themselves. Invocation of nymphs seems to presuppose what I call (rightly or wrongly) a sacrament—the deities' transmission of their divine grace by material means. Devotees partook of the nymphs' grace through contact with and consumption of their elemental form, water. Indeed, their instrumental nature is evident in the fact that their Latin name on inscriptions is often *Lympha* rather than *Nympha*, binding their identity directly to their liquid element. And let us recall that Latin speakers, according to Varro and Festus, called nympholepts *lymphatici*.

Sometimes the very chemical quality that makes the water therapeutic confers identity to the water's nymphs. I have mentioned the Nitrodes of Ischia, named for the alkaline properties of the local waters. Another inscription commemorating them has been found near Rome, referring apparently to a completely different spring.[29] In this case, then, rather like Mefitis (the goddess of foul, sulfurous vapors and waters), the identity is tied immutably to the nature of the substance.

Nymphs, then, could be perceived in antiquity as agents in achieving a particular bodily state. Sometimes in the context of divination, or in the unusually circumscribed environs of a nympholept's cave, that process of agency may also have been accompanied by an altered state of mind. But for the great majority of pilgrims who left behind ex-votos or inscriptions to the nymphs and their companion gods, we may conclude that the corporeal benefits, or even the promise of it, were enough. So when we think of freshwater nymphs, perhaps we ought to acknowledge that outside the limited domain of their literary presence, their capacity for signification is minimal. As objects of interest to ordinary persons, they are best understood as embodiments of their defining element, water, and as agents in the acquisition and transmission of water's sacramental character. We might interpret the phenomenon as a manifestation, in Alfred Gell's terms, of *distributed personhood*, the imprint of the goddesses' agency "distributed in the milieu, beyond the body-boundary." Perhaps the water can be interpreted as exuviae—physical traces—of the bodily prototype, but a more satisfactory interpretation is that it is an animated medium, a "social agent," which can express the nymphs' subjectivity or intentionality.[30]

---

curative"; Buonopane and Petraccia, "Termalismo e divinità."

29. Luschi, "Un rilievo della collezione Carpi."

30. Gell, *Art and Agency*, 103–4, 108, 121–26.

Water and Aura

If we understand a sacrament to be a physical or ritual manifestation of divine grace, how might the sacrament mediated by nymphs be understood? Most often, their grace or goodwill seems to have been transmitted either as an act of oracular vaticination or of healing or fertility. Further, it was often achieved with the agency of a more potent god, commonly Apollo or Pan. But it took no canonical ritual form: to say the least, these were not the seven sacraments of Catholicism! Every sanctuary had its own protocol, because every site was acknowledged to have unique properties characteristic of its history, geography, and salient natural features, among which water usually played the most critical part. Each sacrament belonged to its own site. The water's inherent properties played an essential role in the ritual, but not an exclusive one; otherwise we would be discussing nothing more than a medical regimen. The essential *additional* ingredient that the resident gods could guarantee, if properly invited, was their own presence. This could be direct and invasive, as in a possession, or conveyed as an expression of will—sometimes ill will, perhaps, but usually (one hoped) a more benevolent impulse. The resulting divine chemistry created a sort of reaction by activating the extraordinary properties of the local waters. Only by joining presence to substance could the magic happen. Aelius Aristides, who as a devotee of Asclepius qualifies as a connoisseur on matters of divine presence, characterized this chemistry as something similar to the divine justice that issued from the law courts of the Areopagus in Athens:

> Should someone seek the paragon [of justice], he need look no further than the Areopagus. But just as all mantic waters and vapors exercise a direct force (αὐτόθεν ἰσχύει) among those possessed by a god (ἐν τοῖς θεοφορουμένοις), so does this place seem to emanate (ἀνιέναι) an understanding of justice that is clear and as close as possible to that among the gods. (*Or.* 1 [*Panathenaic*] 46 [171d])

In effect, Aristides acknowledges the dyadic chemistry of inspiration: on the one hand, the emanation of some special, and geographically fixed, substance (water, gas, the local spirit of the law courts). On the other, he recognizes the need of the gods' presence—in this case, either by possession (of an oracle) or by divine approval (of the Athenian way of justice). As a rule, divine presence was as provisional and transitory as the will of any god.

Like objects of special reverence or attention, substances—and specifically water—can have something akin to aura—a field of influence that inheres in unique things of powerful devotion. Aura may attend a condition that David Freedberg terms presence or inherence, a powerful manifestation of a prototype through an object, which thereby acquires a kind of personhood.[31] Freedberg and Walter Benjamin before him were thinking most fundamentally about artworks, but there is no reason why either aura or presence should be confined to objects, let alone fashioned ones; natural substances too can retain or channel a prototype. Presence *itself* could be regarded as a transferrable substance; consider the "contact relics" in early Christian Rome, like the *brandea*, cloths whose task was to transmit to the pilgrim the *praesentia* of a saint by contact with the shrine. Sacred water, then, should be understood not simply as a numinous thing—after all, nearly everything of significance had its attendant god—but also as a material which, like the relics of a martyr, has a palpable, proximate effect on the bodies or minds of those who encounter it. Thereby it effects an encounter: it heals or it hurts, strengthens or weakens—but in some sense it always transforms by contact. Plutarch conjectures how water served to mediate and assist the most sacred of "potencies," prophecy:

> But that which foretells the future, like a tablet without writing, is both irrational and indeterminate in itself, but receptive of impressions and presentiments through what may be done to it, and inconsequently grasps at the future when it is farthest withdrawn from the present. Its withdrawal is brought about by a temperament and disposition of the body as it is subjected to a change which we call inspiration (ἐνθουσιασμόν). Often the body of itself alone attains this disposition. Moreover the earth sends forth for men streams of many other potencies (δυνάμεων), some of them producing derangement, diseases, or deaths; others helpful, benignant, and beneficial, as is plain from the experience of persons who have come upon them. But the prophetic current and breath is most divine and holy (θειότατόν ἐστι καὶ ὁσιώτατον), whether it issue by itself through the air or come in the company of running waters; for when it is instilled into the body, it creates in souls an unaccustomed and unusual temperament, the peculiarity of which it is hard to describe with exactness, but analogy offers many comparisons. (Plut. *Def. orac.* 40 [470–71], trans. Babbitt)

31. Freedberg, *Power of Images*; Maniura and Shepherd, eds., *Presence*.

To be sure, Plutarch is not characterizing water according to its full range of mantic possibilities, which would also incorporate properties of sight and sound, or even the inhalation of its essences. Here he refers only to bodily consumption and a consequent state of prophetic inspiration, which could be taken as the purest form of divine chemistry.

Drinking from sanctuary springs, or ablution or immersion in their waters, would have been an almost reflexive ritual act not just for professional seers, but for the great mass of pilgrims too, if only to partake of the deity in a sacramental, quasi-eucharistic sense. Unfortunately, such simple, unmediated action leaves no trace in the archaeological record and is rarely attested in literature or inscriptions. Pausanias and Strabo do mention healing by immersion at a few sanctuaries of nymphs, notably at Samicon in Elis (Pausanias 5.5.11; 6.22.7; Strabo 8.3.19). Similar cures were surely widespread, perhaps normative, at therapeutic springs; but significant details about the use of sacred waters for ritual purposes other than purification emerge more often when the host sanctuary is famous, and usually when some notable form of professional mediation is involved. Few sanctuaries dedicated to nymphs alone ranked among these, but their companion gods, particularly Asclepius and Apollo, score very high in this regard.

Almost by definition, sanctuaries of Asclepius were founded around springs; the same could be said for curative or oracular sanctuaries of Apollo.[32] The famous oracle at Claros drank the sequestered and notoriously toxic "mantic" water (μαντικόν ... τὸ ὕδωρ; *fontis arcani aqua*: Iamblichus, *Myst.* 3.11 [124], Tacitus, *Annals* 2.54) before issuing pronouncements.[33] At Didyma, the oracle received Apollo's inspiration by various means, for example by breathing vapors from the sacred spring in the adyton or by dipping her feet and skirt into it (Iamblichus, *Myst.* 3.11 [127]).[34] Even at Delphi, where the hypnotic *pneuma* of ethylene gas, rather than the famous local waters, dominated the mantic experience in the classical and Hellenistic periods, water evidently defined the ritual architecture of the earlier Archaic temple: a carefully constructed channel passed from a springhouse embedded in the platform through the

---

32. Cole, "Uses of Water"; Sineux, "Asklépios."

33. Ustinova, *Caves and the Ancient Greek Mind*, 109–12; Johnston, *Ancient Greek Divination*, 76–78, and citations. Recent investigations by Jonathan Flood of the site's groundwater indicate alarmingly high levels of toxic metals and metalloids such as arsenic, antimony, and lead; see Flood, "Groundwater."

34. Johnston, *Ancient Greek Divination*, 85–88.

foundations and probably straight into the adyton. At least by the Roman period, the sanctuary of Zeus at Dodona, whose oracle demonstrated no special affinity for water in earlier times, nonetheless seems to have acquired a spring by the sheer force of association.[35]

Water played equally important roles at second-tier pilgrimage sites. The *katabasis* ordeal undertaken by visitors to the sanctuary of Trophonius at Lebadeia involved drinking the water from two springs, named Lethe and the Mnemosyne. These names, not only suggestive of the underworld, also bespeak the kind of altered states of consciousness delivered on cue—forgetting and remembering—that characterize a quest for healing or oracular revelation.[36] Excavations of the Temple of Apollo Pythaeus at Rhodes revealed a hydraulic system connecting the adyton to a well, undoubtedly for oracular responses.[37] The Sibyl's cave at Lilybaeum harbored a spring that was deemed curative. The spring at the Amphiareion of Oropus, where the nymphs were worshiped alongside other gods and heroes, played some role in mantic healing; however, Pausanias says nothing about the process of curative "divination" (μάντευμα), observing only that coins were tossed in as thank-offerings (1.34.4). The Acherusian Cave dedicated to Pan and the Nymphs at Heracleia Pontica and the sanctuary of Apollo Ptoios in Boeotia both preserve circumstantial evidence suggesting that the resident oracle consulted, or drank directly from, a sacred spring, enshrined in a grotto.[38] Pausanias (7.21.13) reticently observes that at the sanctuary of Apollo Thryxeus in Lycia, seekers gazing into a spring there would find what they wished—an oblique reference, we must conclude, to a visually activated hallucinatory ritual akin to those at healing sites. The same author mentions a derelict Apollonian sanctuary at Hysiai, which according to the native Boeotians delivered prophecies to those who drank from it (9.2.1).

Where a more interpretive rather than hallucinatory kind of divination prevailed, professional hydromancy could be practiced. This was principally visual, but even the sound of the spring at Dodona was interpreted by an oracle, according to Servius (commenting on Vergil, *Aen.* 3.466). T. J. Dunbabin hypothesized that an artificial pool between the sanctuaries of Hera Limenia and Hera Akraia at Perachora, from which

---

35. Ibid., 65–66, 71–72, 98–99.

36. Ibid., 95–98; Ustinova, *Caves and the Ancient Greek Mind*, 90–96, and bibliographies.

37. Segre, "L'oracolo d'Apollo."

38. On these sites see Ustinova, *Caves and the Ancient Greek Mind*, and citations.

a mass of votive *phialai* was recovered, was the μαντεῖον Strabo attributes to the latter site (380); he speculated further that its heavy use could be attributed to Corinthians embarking on their westward travels, who would naturally have wanted to secure an auspicious sign before setting sail.[39] But there seem to have been hybrid modes of interpretation that oscillated between interpretation and mania: at the sanctuary of Demeter and Kore at Patrai, in Pausanias' day, an oracle divined the future of sick pilgrims by means of a mirror lowered down to the surface of a sacred spring by the temple. The mirror provided a binary response: on its surface, the petitioner appeared either alive or dead (Pausanias 7.21.11–12). In one sense, the resident goddesses' response seems like the simplest form of cleromancy, the drawing of a lot answering a yes–no question. But the mirror required a *vision* of the patient, and indeed of the patient in the *future*. Catoptromancy, divination by mirrors, was a pronouncedly hallucinatory form of soothsaying, and so we must imagine that this ritual involved a concentrated mental journey in order to summon such a vision.

Enclosure and Concentration

For all their variability, these cases share one characteristic: physical confinement of the water source. The cave sites go without saying. Other sanctuaries presented the sacred water in a well. At Patrai, the spring occupied a depression delimited by a wall; at Claros, a well in a secluded underground chamber. Like the holy water in a Catholic font, sacred water in Greek and Roman experience carried meaning and potency only in limited and comprehensible amounts. In effect, its auratic power varied inversely with its volume: what is precious is rare. In rituals of healing or divination there is a pronounced need to *confine* and *control* water, along with access to it—be it the Castalian Spring at Delphi, or the divinatory wells at Claros and Hysiai, or the small libation bowls at Perachora. The need to hold, concentrate, and distill—to seize one tiny patch of the fabric dividing worlds, and wring it—seems to be a universal requirement for oracular divination. Inspiration, ἐνθουσιασμός, nympholepsy: the hand of

---

39. Dunbabin, "Oracle of Hera." He postulates that the *phialai* themselves were the principal tools of this divination by means of lecanomancy, that is, the practice of reading patterns of oil on the surface of water in a bowl.

a god seizes the soul through a small window, an aperture approached and opened only with due care and reverence.

Let us momentarily consider this seizure or enclosure in distinctly Greek metaphorical guise. In myth, a powerful and memorable method of transmitting occult knowledge from the watery realm, where all things are known, to the human domain, where knowledge is sorely limited but eagerly sought, takes the form of a wrestling match—or, to be precise, a seizure and pacification. A hero on the quest for essential knowledge must seek out one of the curious class of liminal and infinitely mutable gods who shuttle between the two worlds: Glaucus, Proteus, and Nereus.[40] All are water deities of an antisocial sort, jealously guarding their knowledge from prying interlocutors. All must be seized at their resting-places in an enclosure at the edge of the sea. There the hero leaps upon his quarry unawares and holds on for dear life. In each case, the startled sea god struggles against the hero's grip, cycling furiously through a myriad of forms, both animate and inanimate. Finally the exhausted god gives in and divulges the information his adversary seeks. Along with the related story of Peleus wrestling Thetis (Ovid, *Metam.* 11.221-65), these tales frame the action within a multiplicity of nesting enclosures as if to emphasize the challenges of perforating the tight and layered chambers of knowledge: a firm embrace within a grotto, which in turn typically lies within a harbor or bay. As I have asserted elsewhere, the infinitude of these strange, endlessly shape-shifting beings is like the infinitely changeable repertory of water itself. But it is the hero's firm *containment* of the god as he cycles furiously through forms that gives results:

> The truth-seeker's struggle with a mutable monster is a beautifully apt metaphor. The acquisition of truth, after all, is a kind of containment of an unruly foe—the realm of a thousand possibilities, each taking a different form. The seeker wrestles equally with all possible outcomes, of which only one outcome, the authentic one, must be singled out.[41]

Translated into the usage of real-life ritual and devotion at shrines and sanctuaries, the concentrated *capturing* and *enshrinement* of water took an architectonic turn, usually in the form of a grotto, a basin, or a vessel. Obviously the qualities of vastness are important in religious experience, but principally as indices of the grandeur of godhead and

---

40. Forbes Irving, *Metamorphosis in Greek Myths*, 171-94.
41. Taylor, "River Raptures," 31.

corresponding human inadequacy: they comport with divinity alone, exceeding any useful human capacity to comprehend them. In a vaguely pantheistic sense, sky, rain, rivers, or sea were understood to be the province of gods with power over human lives and destiny, but their vastness and variability merely diluted and depersonalized them. Too large a physical scale overwhelmed the possibility of human-divine reciprocity. Accessibility thus came through concentrated channels and contrived portals plumbed or breached by individual will. Not unlike other religious architecture and apparatus, these were reservoirs of intensification, meant to effect and to elucidate arranged encounters between the human and the divine.

Typically in Greco-Roman myth, the sacredness of water is characterized by the shelter of caverns containing it, or in undersea galleries. Here mortals encounter the aura among gods and nereids. *Enchantment* by water—that is, the full appreciation of its aura—attends the *enchamberment* of water. And the most elemental architectural manifestation of such religious transactions is the cave sheltering a collecting pool. The forced intimacy of the enclosure invites a powerful concentration. Cognitively speaking, this cloistering of the transformative element is akin to the mental vortex, the widely documented perception in various states of altered consciousness that one is descending into a cave-like space, even as one achieves a heightened state of awareness, infinitude, or supreme unity.[42]

We can appreciate the importance of divisibility, limited size, and close proximity in rendering a place or a thing functionally sacred and thus capable of providing the thing sought (usually, in the case of water gods, specific knowledge, health, or fertility). Dividing up the earth notionally was easy because its variable parts perdured, were visibly distinct, and by all appearances were fixed in space both relatively and absolutely. The sky had, at least, a relative logic: its seven heavenly bodies followed independent but comprehensibly cyclical tracks against a predictably rotating and otherwise fixed backdrop of stars arranged into constellations. It could also be partitioned radially according to the points of the compass, as in the rites of celestial augury. But how to carve up water, and notionally isolate its parts? Something so amorphous, so much less differentiable, so locked in perpetual, churning motion, was more challenging; as Iamblicus says of this difficulty, "the sacred (θεῖον) has not permeated

---

42. Ustinova, *Caves and the Ancient Greek Mind*, 13–52.

those things that partake of it in such an extensive and partitioned manner" (οὕτω διαστατῶς καὶ μεριστῶς, *Myst.* 3.11 [124–25]). By necessity its binary qualities of sacred and nonsacred were differentiated by means of permanent, rigid enclosures or markers through which or by which the water could freely flow. Consequently, that sacredness *did not inhere in the substance*, but instead was *transmitted to it* by the place it occupied, if only briefly—and thus by the distinctive properties of that place, whether physical, chemical, or numinous. If, by virtue of its great extension, a nearly infinite substance lacked aura, sacredness, or presence, it had to be presented in a more *thing-like* form to acquire such properties. The liquid tincture of the nymphs or other freshwater gods was strong at the places of their abode, but quickly dissipated with distance. Thus the mold into which it was poured was instrumental in activating its divine chemistry.

Clitumnus

As a demonstration of this principle of temporary transmission and containment, consider the celebrated open spring at the sanctuary of Clitumnus, described in a letter of Pliny.

> There rises a little hill, densely wooded with old cypresses. From beneath it emerges a spring, forced out by several unequal veins, which, forcing its way out, opens out into a broad-bosomed pool, so pure and glassy that you can count the votive coins (*stipes*) and shining pebbles within. From there it is driven not by any slope but by its own abundance and mass, as it were; a spring up to that point, now an ample river beyond, it accommodates even boats ... The water is as cold as snow, and just as pure. An ancient and venerable temple lies nearby. There stands Clitumnus, clothed in the *toga praetexta*. Oracular verses (*sortes*) indicate the god is present, and even inclined to divination. Several shrines, and as many gods, are scattered about. The name of each invites veneration, but some are attached to springs as well. For in addition to the main source, which is a parent, as it were, to the others, lesser sources stand apart from the headwaters; but they all merge with the river, which is crossed by a bridge. This is the boundary of sacred and profane (*terminus sacri profanique*). Upstream only boating is permitted; downstream, swimming. (*Ep.* 8.8.1–6)

This sanctuary had considerable religious infrastructure: a temple, a *temenos*, a cult statue, multiple shrines, and presumably an attendant priesthood to look after the place and control its oracular protocols. Significantly, it also had *sortes*: lots, perhaps inscribed tablets, used in the process of divination.[43] Inscriptions celebrated the god and his spring: "you will read many of the inscriptions on the columns and on the walls on which the spring and that god are praised" (*leges multa multorum omnibus columnis omnibus parietibus inscripta, quibus fons ille deusque celebratur*, 8.8.7). Their dominant attribute being celebration, these would not have been the oracular tablets themselves; most of them were probably the quasi-formulaic *votum solvit libens merito* ("willingly s/he fulfilled his/her vow, and rightly so") dedications characteristic of healing cults, which record the devotee's fulfillment of a vow to the god, often in the form of a thank-offering for therapeutic favors bestowed.

The springs feeding the Clitumnus River were numinous and sacred. No person was permitted to defile the sanctuary by swimming in it. Like a modern display fountain, the pool glistened with coins tossed in by visitors. As such it was a votive repository, an inviolable sanctuary of token gifts to the resident gods. What is striking—and perfectly practical too—is the manner by which sacredness was transmitted. Welling up in an open pool, as it does today, this spring had no sheltering enclosure in antiquity. Lacking any architecture to arrest and delimit the water, the source had to acquire its intensified, auratic status by other spatial means. Thus a *temenos* was laid out, its border downstream defined by a bridge. Water flowed naturally and perpetually across this boundary, destined to regress from *sacra* to *profana*. What flowed through this bowl was sacred, but it was the bowl itself that made it so. Moreover, if a small part of the *aqua sacra* was captured for the purpose of interpreting the lots—which seems likely, given that this sanctuary was devoted to local water gods—it would certainly have been sanctified further by some means, its twice-intensified aura nested in protective layers like the Old Men of the Sea napping in their grottos set within encircling bays. What is precious is rare.

Of the resident deities, only Clitumnus himself is characterized unambiguously. What of the others? Pliny's laconic phrase, "to each its own cult for its own name" (*Sua cuique veneratio suum nomen*), seems to emphasize their uniqueness and obscurity (did their cults comprise

43. On lots, cleromancy, and sortition, see Buchholz, "Identifying the Oracular 'Sortes.'"

nothing more than their names?), but the following phrase, "for some, moreover there were springs" (*quibusdam vero etiam fontes*), intimates that several of these gods were one-offs associated exclusively with subsidiary springs—in other words, nymphs. Their subordination to Clitumnus followed the well-established pattern in which nymphs operated in the train of a greater god, usually male.

Breaching the wall between worlds, spring water was deemed a substance particularly suited to divination. So it stands to reason that at spring sanctuaries where divination was practiced, the results were not achieved by the drawing of lots (*sortes*) alone, but required some manner of interpretation of cues drawn from the water itself. At sites of particular importance, the process may have required the interpreter to enter a state of *mania*, a divine trance, or achieve some similar state of inspiration by ingestion, aspersion, or immersion. To acquire the proper auratic character, the water required enchamberment or definition of some kind—whether to concentrate its power, or in the case of interpretation, to limit and control the kind of visual water play that could be subjected to close inspection.

Liminality, Nymphs, and Nymphaea

Sacred water, it seems, could be reduced to two spatiotemporal properties. On the one hand, it was *limited*; about this I have said enough already. On the other hand, it was *liminal*, confined to the edges of things. This physical edginess seems to have been transmitted to the characters of terrestrial water gods in general—not just nymphs, but the Old Men of the Sea and river gods too. They shun society, for to yield to social or political norms would dilute their distinctive potency.

Because sacredness does not easily encompass entire rivers or oceans, it must be concentrated at strategic, sheltered, and ritually delimited points of extremity—usually at the sources of springs, in eddying pools, or in caves at the edges of open bodies of water—both of them permeable interfaces between the worlds of the living and the dead, or of mortals and the gods. When needed for ritual ablutions, water was characteristically placed in a small basin (such as a *perirrhanterion*) near an entrance or a point of passage, or else it was simply contained temporarily in a bowl (for example, a *phiale*). When water assisted in divination, it was captured in a border zone between the underworld and the realm above. Only there, at the boundary, could the window into the all-knowing earth be unclouded. When a curse tablet was deposited in a spring, the dedicator understood that the spring was a portal of communication with the nether world, and that its resident deities could serve as agents in delivering or even fulfilling the malediction. Should a person develop a special compatibility with nymphs or other gods of spring sanctuaries, then he or she was impelled into a *social* liminality attached to sacred water too; this is the underlying state of nympholepts like Archedamos at Vari, or such resident oracles as practiced their craft at the source of the Clitumnus—or, for that matter, at the great oracular and healing sanctuaries of Apollo and Asclepius.

Like the nymphs themselves, the quintessence of "locally sourced" deities, the two properties of limitation and liminality are imprinted on the visual and spatial culture of the Greek and Roman landscape. Nymphaea—named appropriately after abodes of the nymphs—cradle water in simulation of sacred springs. They are typically concave for occult as well as overt reasons. The obvious reason is that they simulate the natural form of the grotto, the ideal spring source. The deeper reasons are embedded in the half-remembered symbolism of old-time religion and ritual. The grotto-like enclosure, with embracing wings, is meant to connote the intimacy that attends aura and the seclusion that engenders oracular visions. A nymphaeum, no matter how artificial or monumental, is designed to nourish and cherish its precious cargo, to arrest the flow of its chattering bounty, which it delivers from secret sources within and behind, before letting it flow on its way, again to cycle through the earth, sea, and sky. But containing water is as tricky and as ephemeral as taking a Nereid to wife. Both in time will return to their wild and natural state. In this respect, nymphs best reflect the substance that gave them meaning and assured them an important and long-enduring role in Greek and Roman religious practice.

Works Cited

Adamo Muscettola, Stefania. "Gli ex-voto delle ninfe di Ischia: la parabola di una cultura marginale." *Rivista dell'Istituto Nazionale d'Archeologia e Storia dell'Arte* 3 (2002) 37–61.

Andreu Pintado, Javier. "Aspectos sociales del culto a las aguas en Hispania: las dedicaciones a las Nymphae." In *L'eau: usages, risques et répresentation dans le sud-ouest de la Gaule et le nord de la péninsule ibérique, de la fin de l'âge du fer à l'antiquité tardive (IIe s. a.C.—VIe s. p.C.)*, edited by J.-P. Bost, 333-47. Saldvie / Hors série; Aquitania. Supplément. Pessac: Fédération Aquitania, 2012.

Anibaletto, Matteo, et al., eds. *Cura, preghiera e benessere: le stazioni curative termominerali nell'Italia romana*. Antenor quaderni 31. Padova: Padova University Press, 2014.

Arnaldi, Adelina. "La valenza 'salutare' del culto delle *'nymphae'* nell'Italia romana." In *Usus veneratioque fontium: atti del convegno internazionale di studio su "Fruizione e culto delle acque salutari in Italia," Roma-Viterbo 29-31 ottobre 1993*, edited by Lidio Gasperini, 55-83. Tivoli: Tipigraf, 2006.

Babbitt, Frank Cole, trans. *Moralia*, vol. 5, by Plutarch. LCL 306. Cambridge: Harvard University Press, 1936.

Bassani, Maddalena, et al., eds. *Aquae salutiferae: il termalismo tra antico e contemporaneo. Atti del convegno internazionale (Montegrotto Terme, 6-8 settermbre 2012)*. Antenor Quaderni 29. Padova: Padova University Press, 2013.

Borgeaud, Philippe. *The Cult of Pan in Ancient Greece*. Translated by Kathleen Atlass and James Redfield. Chicago: University of Chicago Press, 1988.

Buchholz, Laura. "Identifying the Oracular 'Sortes' of Italy." In *Studies in Ancient Oracles and Divination*, edited by Mika Kajava, 111-44. Rome: Institutum Romanum Finlandiae, 2013.

Buonopane, Alfredo, and Maria Federica Petraccia. "Termalismo e divinità." In *Cura, preghiera e benessere: le stazioni curative termominerali nell'Italia romana*, edited by Matteo Anibaletto et al., 217-45. Antenor quaderni 31. Padova: Padova University Press, 2014.

Caillois, Roger. "Les démons de midi." *Revue de l'histoire des religions* 115 (1937) 142-73.

———. "Les démons de midi (suite)." *Revue de l'histoire des religions* 116 (1937) 54-83.

———. "Les démons de midi (suite et fin)." *Revue de l'histoire des religions* 116 (1937) 143-86.

Calderone, Anna, ed. *Cultura e religione delle acque: atti del convegno interdisciplinare "Qui fresca l'acqua mormora ...," Messina, 29-30 marzo 2011*. Archaeologica 167. Rome: Giorgio Bretschneider, 2012.

Cole, Susan G. "The Uses of Water in Greek Sanctuaries." In *Early Greek Cult Practice: Proceedings of the Fifth International Symposium at the Swedish Institute at Athens, 26-29 June 1986*, edited by Robin Hägg et al., 161-65. Skrifter / utgivna av Svenska institutet i Athen 38. Göteborg: Aström, 1988.

Connor, W. R. "Seized by the Nymphs: Nympholepsy and Symbolic Expression in Classical Greece." *Classical Antiquity* 7 (1988) 155-89.

De Cesare, Monica. "Le 'Nymphai' e l'acqua in Sicilia: l'imagerie vascolare." In *Cultura e religione delle acque: atti del convegno interdisciplinare "Qui fresca l'acqua mormora ...," Messina, 29-30 marzo 2011*, edited by Anna Calderone, 141-68. Archaeologica 167. Rome: Giorgio Bretschneider, 2012.

Dunbabin T. J. "The Oracle of Hera Akraia at Perachora." *Annual of the British School at Athens* 46 (1951) 61-71.

Dvorjetski, Estée. *Leisure, Pleasure, and Healing: Spa Culture and Medicine in Ancient Eastern Mediterranean*. Supplements to the Journal for the Study of Judaism 116. Leiden: Brill, 2007.

Fabiano, Doralice. "La nympholepsie entre possession et paysage." In *Perception et construction du divin dans l'antiquité*, edited by Philippe Borgeaud and Doralice Fabiano, 165–95. Recherches et rencontres 31. Geneva: Droz, 2013.
Falkenstein-Wirth, Vera von. *Das Quellheiligtum von Vicarello (Aquae Apollinares): Ein Kultort von der Bronzezeit bis zum Ende des Kaiserreichs*. Darmstadt: Zabern, 2011.
Flood, Jonathan M. "Groundwater Geochemistry and Water Ritual at the Temples of Apollo at Delphi, Didyma, and Claros." Paper presented at the Annual Meeting of the Geological Society of America, Baltimore, MD, November 2015. https://gsa.confex.com/gsa/2015AM/webprogram/Paper267583.html/.
Forbes Irving, P. M. C. *Metamorphosis in Greek Myths*. Oxford: Clarendon, 1990.
Freedberg, David. *The Power of Images: Studies in the History and Theory of Response*. Chicago: University of Chicago Press, 1989.
Gaifman, Milette. "Visualized Rituals and Dedicatory Inscriptions on Votive Offerings to the Nymphs." *Opuscula* 1 (2008) 85–103.
Gasperini, Lidio, ed. *Usus veneratioque fontium: atti del convegno internazionale di studio su "Fruizione e culto delle acque salutari in Italia," Roma–Viterbo 29–31 ottobre 1993*. Tivoli: Tipigraf, 2006.
Gell, Alfred. *Art and Agency: An Anthropological Theory*. Oxford: Clarendon, 1998.
Giacobello, Federica, et al., eds. *Ninfe nel mito e nella città dalla Grecia a Roma*. Parabordi 71. Milan: Viennepierre, 2009.
Hyllested, Adam. "L'esprit des eaux: grec νύμφη, sanskrit *Rámbhā*, lituanien *Laumê*, et quelques autres formes semblant apparentées." In *Per aspera ad asteriscos: studia indogermanica in honorem Jens Elmegård Rasmussen*, edited by Adam Hyllested, 219–33. Innsbrucker Beiträge zur Sprachwissenschaft 112. Innsbruck: Institut für Sprachen und Literaturen der Universität Innsbruck, 2004.
Jim, Theodora Suk Fon. "Seized by the Nymph? Onesagoras the 'Dekatephoros' in the Nymphaeum at Kafizin in Cyprus." *Kernos* 25 (2012) 9–26.
Johnston, Sarah Iles. *Ancient Greek Divination*. Chichester: Wiley-Blackwell, 2008.
Lambardi, Noemi. "Le nozze ninfali di Numa." *Prometheus* 14 (1988) 247–52.
Larson, Jennifer. *Greek Nymphs: Myth, Cult, Lore*. Oxford: Oxford University Press, 2001.
Lhôte-Birot, Marie-Chantal. "Les nymphes en Gaule Narbonnaise et dans les trois Gaules." *Latomus* 63 (2004) 58–69.
Luschi, Licia. "Un rilievo della collezione Carpi e le Ninfe Nitrodi a Roma." *Bollettino d'arte* 108 (1999) 57–70.
Maggi, Stefano. "Santuari delle sorgenti in Gallia Narbonese: dal culto epicorico al culto imperiale." In *Società indigene e cultura greco-romana: atti del convegno internazionale, Trento, 7–8 giugno 2007*, edited by Elvira Migliario et al., 185–98. Monografie / Centro ricerche e documentazione sull'antichità classica 33. Rome: "L'Erma" di Bretschneider, 2010.
Maniura, Robert, and Rupert Shepherd, eds. *Presence: The Inherence of the Prototype within Images and Other Objects*. Histories of Vision. Aldershot: Ashgate, 2006.
Mitford, Terence Bruce. *The Nymphaeum of Kafizin: The Inscribed Pottery*. Kadmos: Supplement 2. Berlin: de Gruyter, 1980.
Molinari, Nicholas, and Nicola Sisci. ΠΟΤΑΜΙΚΟΝ: *Sinews of Acheloios; A Comprehensive Catalog of the Bronze Coinage of the Man-Faced Bull, with Essays on Origin and Identity*. Archaeopress Archaeology. Oxford: Archaeopress, 2016.

Muthmann, Friedrich. *Mutter und Quelle: Studien zur Quellverehrung im Altertum und im Mittelalter*. Basel: Archäologischer Verlag, 1975.
Pache, Corinne Ondine. *A Moment's Ornament: The Poetics of Nympholepsy in Ancient Greece*. Oxford: Oxford University Press, 2011.
Petraccia, Maria Federica, and Maria Tramunto. "Il termalismo curativo dei testi epigrafici: il caso delle Ninfe / Linfe." In *Aquae salutiferae: il termalismo tra antico e contemporaneo*, edited by Maddalena Bassani, 175–91. Antenor Quaderni 29. Padova: Padova University Press, 2013.
Picard, Olivier. "Les nymphes, images de l'eau sur les monnaies des cites grecques." In *L'eau en Méditerranée de l'antiquité au moyen âge: actes du 22e colloque de la Villa Kérylos à Beaulieu-sur-Mer les 7 & 8 octobre 2011*, edited by Jacques Jouanna et al., 55–73. Cahiers de la Villa Kérylos 23. Paris: Boccard, 2012.
Piranomonte, Marina. "Religion and Magic at Rome: The Fountain of Anna Perenna." In *Magical Practice in the Latin West: Papers from the International Conference Held at the University of Zaragoza, 30 Sept.–1 Oct. 2005*, edited by Richard L. Gordon, 191–213. Religion in the Graeco-Roman World 168. Leiden: Brill, 2010.
Salamone, Grazia. "La categoria iconica delle ninfe eponime." In *Polis, urbs, civitas: moneta e identità; atti del convegno di studio del Lexicon Iconographicum Numismaticae (Milano, 25 ottobre 2012)*, edited by Lucia Travaini and Giampiera Arrigoni, 9–41. Moneta 6. Rome: Quasar, 2013.
Schirripa, Paola. "La ninfa cattiva." In *Ninfe nel mito e nella città dalla Grecia a Roma*, edited by Federica Giacobello et al., 71–98. Parabordi 71. Milan: Viennepierre, 2009.
Schörner, Günther, and Hans Rupprecht Goette. *Die Pan-Grotte von Vari*. Schriften zur historischen Landeskunde Griechenlands 1. Mainz: Zabern, 2004.
Segre, Mario. "L'oracolo d'Apollo Pythaeus a Rodi." *Parola del passato* 4 (1949) 72–82.
Sineux, Pierre. "Asklépios, les nymphes et Achéloos: réflexions sur une association cultuelle." *Kentron* 22 (2006) 177–98.
Sourvinou-Inwood, C. "Hermaphroditos and Salmakis: The Voice of Halikarnassos." In *The Salmakis Inscription and Hellenistic Halikarnassos*, edited by Signe Isager and Poul Pedersen, 59–84. Odense: University Press of Southern Denmark, 2004.
Taylor, Rabun. "River Raptures: Containment and Control of Water in Greek and Roman Constructions of Identity." In *The Nature and Function of Water, Baths, Bathing, and Hygiene from Antiquity through the Renaissance*, edited by Cynthia Kosso and Anne Scott, 21-42. Technology and Change in History 11. Leiden: Brill, 2009.
Ustinova, Yulia. *Caves and the Ancient Greek Mind: Descending Underground in the Search for Ultimate Truth*. Oxford: Oxford University Press, 2009.
Wagman, Robert S. *The Cave of the Nymphs at Pharsalus: Studies on a Thessalian Country Shrine*. Brill Studies in Greek and Roman Epigraphy 6. Leiden: Brill, 2016.

Subject Index

Acts of the Apostles, 49–50, 54, 65, 67–68, 70, 72–93, 103, 111, 203–11, 228, 233, 256
Adam, 17, 28, 118–19, 125–26, 136, 138, 147–48
Aphrodite, 24–25, 28, 32, 116–17, 205, 226, 295
Apollo, 27, 204, 205, 267, 287–88, 293, 296–97, 299, 301–3, 309
Aristophanes, 117–18, 247
Asclepius, xviii, 284, 287–88, 290, 293, 299, 301, 309
Athanasius, 82n17, 157–64
Athenaeus, 227, 229n21, n22, 234, 248
Augustus, 24–32, 263

Bacchus. *See* Dionysus
banquet(s). *See* meals
baptism, 5–14, 30, 33, 65–66, 76, 78–81, 119–20, 135, 138, 142–43, 149, 161, 164, 253–54

cena, xix, 222–24, 227, 230
Cicero, 221–23, 232, 234
comedy, xix, 68, 227, 244–52, 247, 252, 257
Corinth, xviii, 89–92, 97–114, 268

Delphi, 89–90, 268, 301, 303
Dio Chrysostom, 107, 110–12, 204n2, 246–48, 252

Dionysus, 25, 30, 116, 229, 236–37, 248n16, 267–69, 287, 291
disciple(s), 4–14, 18, 33, 49, 60, 64–65, 69–70, 86, 107, 110, 115, 139–43, 145–49, 159, 214–18, 222, 235–40, 252, 254, 257
drunkenness, 32, 81–82, 236, 243–57, 279

Epictetus, 107, 226, 246
Eucharist, 5, 10–14, 149, 301
Euripides, 204, 237, 245–47, 250, 257, 264
Eve, 17, 28, 118–19, 125–26, 135, 138

female, 25, 45–48, 50, 78–79, 101, 116–18, 120–22, 124–26, 128–28, 131, 160, 228, 231, 234–35, 268, 285, 295–97
feminine. *See* female
feminism, 38, 48n35 122, 127, 130, 150
First Corinthians, 67, 77, 89–92, 97–114, 218

Gaius Caligula, 21, 127, 249, 252
Galilee, 9, 22, 40, 86, 216
gender, xi, xviii, xx, 38, 45, 47–48, 52–53, 115–31, 225, 228, 295
Genesis, 17, 67, 69, 77, 118–19, 121, 138–41, 147, 149, 154, 218

Gentile(s), 7–13, 21, 30–31, 49–52,
    75, 81–82, 86, 149, 181–82,
    186, 189, 198, 233, 262
glossolalia. *See* tongues
gnosis. *See* Gnosticism
Gnosticism, xviii–xix, 97–112,
    133–51, 154

Heracles, xix, 243–52, 257, 267, 288,
    293
Hermaphroditus, 115–18, 120–21,
    289
Hermes, 116–17, 250–51, 288, 293
Homer, xviii, 69, 203–10, 223, 229

Irenaeus, 138–46, 149–50

Jerusalem, 16, 18–19, 21, 30–31,
    33–34, 37, 40, 62–63, 74–75,
    82–86, 92, 205, 281
Jew(s). *See* Judaism
John the Baptist, 61–62, 77–81, 157,
    216, 252–57
John, Gospel of, 49n37, 61, 63,
    68, 77–78, 137, 141, 147,
    149, 222, 224, 235–40, 254,
    257n45
Judaism, xviii–xix, 9–13, 17, 21–23,
    27, 30, 37, 48–50, 52, 74–75,
    77, 82–84, 87, 102–105,
    118–19, 121, 124–28, 138–
    45, 149, 175–86, 189–99,
    207–10, 223–24, 226, 231,
    234, 243–45, 248–49, 253,
    255, 257, 262–64, 269–70,
    272, 276, 279

Koester, Helmut, xi, xvi, 31–33, 42,
    101n8, 133n2

Livy, 25, 205, 209–10, 296
Luke, Gospel of, xviii–xix, 3–4, 14,
    18–20, 22, 36–54, 57–70,
    73, 75–81, 83–86, 92, 147,
    203–10, 218, 222, 224–33,
    235–38, 240, 244, 252–57
LXX. *See* Septuagint

male, 25, 37, 46–48, 50, 101,
    115–31, 148, 160, 215,
    225, 228–28, 231–35, 295,
    297n27, 308
Mark Antony, 67n17, 221–22, 248
Mark, Gospel of, xvi, xviii, 3–14,
    16–34, 49n37, 58, 61–63,
    65, 69–70, 72, 78–81, 204,
    212–19, 233–34, 252–55
Mars, 24–26, 28, 30–32
Martyrdom of Polycarp, xix, 189–99
martyrdom, 6, 9, 11, 193–94, 197,
    272, 276, 300
Mary, 115, 121, 128–31, 143, 233,
    235–36
Mary, mother of Jesus, 57, 61–66,
    135
masculine. *See* male
Matthew, Gospel of, 3–5, 18, 31,
    47n37, 61–63, 65–66, 70,
    78–81, 147, 218, 252–54
meal(s), 6, 9–13, 61, 214–19, 223–
    37, 252–57
monasticism, xix, 72, 139, 153–70

Nag Hammadi, xviii, 135–36, 139,
    150, 153–54, 168–70
Nero, 16, 27, 29–30, 32, 107, 264
nymph(s), xix, 116, 284–309

Ovid, 28, 116, 227–28, 289, 296, 304

parable(s), xvii, 19–20, 37, 59–60,
    62, 68, 70, 222, 232, 244n3
patriarchy, 28, 38, 46–50, 52, 123,
    125, 128, 130–31
Paul, ix–xi, xviii, 33, 67–68, 70, 73,
    77, 86, 89–92, 97–112, 130,
    141, 149, 206–7, 209, 212,
    218, 228, 233
Pentecost, xviii, 72–92, 256
Peter, 18, 61, 65, 67, 81, 86, 121,
    129–30, 147–48, 206, 218–
    19, 239, 256
Pharisee(s), 4, 12, 63, 66, 139,
    214–15, 217, 222, 224–25,
    227, 231–32

SUBJECT INDEX

Philo of Alexandria, 108, 118–19, 125–29, 195, 231, 238, 245, 248–53, 257
Philostratus, 107–9, 111, 204n2, 238, 249n18
Pilate, 21, 31, 37, 63, 65
Plato, 108, 117–31, 138–41, 143–44, 223, 225, 229–31, 236–40, 266, 287
Pliny the Elder, 25–27, 116, 232, 249n18, 306–7
Plutarch, 24–25, 28, 30, 32, 67–68, 107, 204n2, 229–30, 236, 238, 248, 288, 300–1
prophecy, 4, 16, 19–21, 27, 31, 33–34, 49, 61, 63, 66–67, 76–78, 80–81, 89–91, 99–102, 105, 110, 130, 178, 185, 225, 232–33, 253–57, 268, 274–75, 278, 280–82, 288, 300–2
prophet(s). *See* prophecy

Q, 3n3, 72, 78–81, 254

Revelation, xix, 22, 29, 32–33, 149, 262–83
Roman Empire. *See* Rome
Romans, Epistle to the, ix, 67, 102
Rome, 16–34, 53, 74–75, 121, 131, 168–70, 189, 206, 209–10, 212, 247n14, 262–64, 272, 274, 277–81, 292, 294, 298
Romulus, 23–26, 28, 32, 205

Sabbath, xviii, 8, 11, 13, 36–38, 40–45, 47–50, 52–53, 191, 213, 231
Second Sophistic, 104n11, 106–12, 203–4
Secret Gospel of Mark, 3–5, 133
Seneca, 246, 249n18, 266–68
Septuagint, xix, 66, 75, 77, 79, 88, 90–91, 101–3, 149, 175–86, 209, 269–70, 273

Socrates, 122, 223, 236–37, 239–40, 287, 292, 295
spirit(s), xviii, 9–10, 20, 22, 26–27, 30, 37, 44, 47, 67, 74–81, 84–87, 89–92, 97–101, 111–12, 115, 119, 121, 124, 126, 128–30, 135, 141, 147–48, 158, 204, 207, 209, 213, 233, 237–38, 245, 253–56, 259, 284–86, 289, 292, 299
symposium, xix, 216–17, 222–24, 227, 229–33, 235–40, 245, 249n18, 252n30
synagogue(s), 37, 40–46, 48–50, 52–54, 75, 101n8, 191n12, 196–98, 212–13, 216, 219, 282
temple(s), 16, 18–23, 25–26, 28–34, 63, 76–77, 81–84, 107, 127, 191n10, 213, 255, 263, 282, 301–3, 306–7
theater(s), xix, 109–10, 112, 195n36, 248–49, 262–66, 281, 283
Thomas, Gospel of, xvii–xviii, 115–31, 133, 224, 234
tongues, 74, 76–77, 81–82, 84, 89–91, 99–100, 256
tragedy, 247, 251n26, 262–83

Venus. *See* Aphrodite
Vergil, 26–27, 204, 207, 210, 296

wine, 74, 155, 161, 222, 231, 236, 244, 249n18, 251–57

Xenophon, 223, 225, 229–31, 237, 239–40, 246, 252

Zeus, 21–22, 25, 29, 117, 179, 237, 247, 251, 266–68

315